International Perspectives on Education Reform
Gita Steiner-Khamsi, Editor

South–South Cooperation in Education and Development
*Linda Chisholm and
Gita Steiner-Khamsi, Eds.*

Comparative and International Education: Issues for Teachers
*Karen Mundy, Kathy Bickmore, Ruth Hayhoe,
Meggan Madden, and Katherine Madjidi, Eds.*

SOUTH–SOUTH COOPERATION IN EDUCATION AND DEVELOPMENT

Edited by

Linda Chisholm

Gita Steiner-Khamsi

Teachers College
Columbia University
New York and London

HSRC Press
Cape Town, South Africa

Published simultaneously by Teachers College Press, 1234 Amsterdam Avenue, New York, NY 10027, and HSRC Press, Private Bag X9182, Cape Town, South Africa, 8000.

Distributed in Africa by Blue Weaver
Tel: +27 (0) 21 701 4477
Fax: +27 (0) 21 701 7302
www.oneworldbooks.com

Copyright © 2009 by Teachers College, Columbia University

All rights reserved. No part of this publication may be reproduced or transmitted in any form or by any means, electronic or mechanical, including photocopy, or any information storage and retrieval system, without permission from the publisher.

Library of Congress Cataloging-in-Publication Data

South–South cooperation in education and development / edited by Linda Chisholm, Gita Steiner-Khamsi.
    p. cm. — (International perspectives on education reform)
  Includes bibliographical references and index.
  ISBN 978-0-8077-4921-0 (pbk. : alk. paper) 1. Education—Developing countries—International cooperation. 2. Education assistance—Developing countries. 3. Economic development—Developing countries—International cooperation. I. Chisholm, Linda. II. Steiner-Khamsi, Gita.
  LC2605.S68 2009
  370.9172'4—dc22
                                                                              2008033533

Teachers College Press ISBN: 978-0-8077-4921-0 (paperback)
HSRC Press ISBN: 978-0-7969-2251-9 (paperback)

Printed on acid-free paper
Manufactured in the United States of America

16 15 14 13 12 11 10 09   8 7 6 5 4 3 2 1

Dedication

Hubert O. Quist was a professor of educational foundations at the University of Cape Coast, Ghana, as well as a close colleague and a former advisee during his doctoral studies at Teachers College, Columbia University, New York. Hubert intended to contribute a chapter in which he would have analyzed an early case of South–South transfer: the dissemination of the British colonial policy of Adapted Education within the African continent between the 1920s and 1950s. He was unable to complete this research project. His untimely death left a big void in our professional lives as well as in this book. It is to him that we dedicate this book.

Contents

1. Introduction: Rhetoric, Realities, and Reasons   1
   Linda Chisholm

   PART I: CONCEPTUALIZING THE SOUTH AND SOUTH–SOUTH COOPERATION

2. Imperial Connections, Entangled Peripheries:
   Cadiz and the Latin American Monitorial Schools   17
   Marcelo Caruso

3. South–South Cooperation:
   Past and Present Conceptualization and Practice   39
   Michelle Morais de Sá e Silva

   PART II: MODALITIES OF TRANSFER AND COOPERATION

4. Japan's Official Development Assistance Strategies and
   UN Conceptualizations of South–South Cooperation   63
   Yoko Mochizuki

5. Transnational Corporations as Propellers of
   Educational Transfer in the Middle East   87
   Zahra Bhanji

6. The New Regionalism in African Education:
   Limits and Possibilities   103
   Leon Tikly and Hillary Dachi

7. **Foreign Aid to Education:**
   Managing Global Transfers and Exchanges 123
   Joel Samoff

8. **The Strategic Triad: Form and Content in**
   Brazil's Triangular Cooperation Practices 157
   Adriana Abdenur

   PART III: CONTRADICTIONS, COMPLEXITIES, AND AMBIGUITIES

9. **Reclaiming the Empire: Turkish Education Initiatives**
   in Central Asia and Azerbaijan 173
   Iveta Silova

10. **BRAC Goes Global** 192
    Colette Chabbott

11. **African Students in China: Past and Present** 210
    Sandra Gillespie

12. **India and South Africa: Diaspora and Transfer** 226
    Crain Soudien

13. **Conclusion: A Way Out from the Dependency Trap**
    in Educational Development? 241
    Gita Steiner-Khamsi

References 259

About the Editors and the Contributors 285

Index 291

ONE

Introduction

Rhetoric, Realities, and Reasons

Linda Chisholm

This book emerged from a collaborative effort to understand why South–South cooperation has suddenly entered the talk of major international donors in educational development. When we started the project, South–South cooperation had just started to become a new slogan. But it was also clear that Northern agencies and donors were playing an increasingly powerful role in determining global and national educational agendas and were themselves engaged in promoting South–South transfer and cooperation. How did these two issues square up, and what does South–South cooperation mean in this context? Although we, as coeditors of this book, firmly believe in the value of institutional and individual cooperation across borders and boundaries, we were skeptical about the contemporary uses of the term and wanted to explore a more critical approach than that found in much of the development literature.

We approached the topic from different angles. One of us is based in South Africa, and has had an abiding interest in relationships of educational inequality within and between nations, and how these have changed over time, both generally and in particular contexts, such as southern and eastern Africa. From this perspective, South–South cooperation can be seen as a form of collective organization to undertake activities that will improve countries' unequal position on a global scale. But it is likely to reflect inequalities within and between countries at the same time that it promotes overcoming inequalities. The other is based in the United States and has been intrigued for years about the proliferation of "traveling reforms," that is, educational reforms that are uncritically transferred or transplanted from one continent to another. Fueling into globalization research in education, the study of transnational policy transfer has lent itself to investigating the reasons, actors, and consequences of reforms that, in most cases, travel from the North to the South. From the angle of policy borrowing and lending research, South–South cooperation can be seen as a logical consequence of North–South transfer. Unraveling the links between this body of literature and new uses of the concept is vital. Approaching the topic of this book from two distinct but related research interests, we solicited analyses on South–South collaboration from renowned researchers or experienced practitioners in development work, situated in different parts of the world.

The contributors to this book have focused their analyses of South–South cooperation in education on the role of bilateral and multilateral development agencies, such as the World Bank, UNESCO, and UNDP; regions such as Africa, Latin America, and the Middle East; and individual countries such as Brazil, China, India, Japan, Jordan, Turkey, and South Africa. They examine institutional histories, rationales, varieties, and impacts of South–South collaboration. They critically investigate the occurrence, types, and content areas of South–South transfer, and also identify areas in which such a transfer among equals has occurred and is most unlikely to occur. These include triangular partnerships, bilateral agreements, and regional initiatives to ensure, for example, "best practice" transfers. Such cooperation is often facilitated through technical assistance by consultants, regional meetings and joint planning among policy-makers, and educational exchanges. Professionals in multilateral agencies, governments, transnational corporations, and nongovernmental organizations (NGOs) might also promote cooperation around "solutions" to problems of access of quality in education that include elite or low-cost models of schooling. Another popular "solution" that is seen as easily transferable to developing countries is that of information and communication (ICT) technologies.

The authors give special attention to the history and rhetoric of South–South transfer and cooperation initiatives. They demonstrate that the formulation of South–South transfer assumes a centrality of a North–South axis that is belied by complex and unequal geopolitical international and national histories and contexts. They provide challenging critical accounts of South–South cooperation, but none of them eschews it as a goal—collectively, they ultimately argue for contextually situated and theoretically informed engagement with the issues raised by the concept and practices of South–South cooperation. This book is offered as an attempt to grapple with the concept and its practices in a manner that promotes understanding of the disconnected and unequal connections between people, nation-states, and contexts, and supports efforts to improve them.

This introduction provides an overview of the thematic concerns of the chapters. They are organized into three parts: conceptualizations of the South and South–South cooperation; modalities of transfer and cooperation; and contradictions, complexities, and ambiguities that emerge in the process. Finally, it considers the implications of the different positions taken by the authors for research and the politics of South–South transfer and cooperation. Although all the chapters in the book traverse a similar set of conceptual questions, they analyze a diverse range of countries and contexts and they differ in how their authors understand the South, South–South transfer, and South–South cooperation. Some authors concentrate specifically on either processes of transfer or on cooperation; several use both concepts either interchangeably to signify relationships across time and space or situate them within particular theoretical traditions. All probe and question the deeper, hidden, and constructed meanings and realities of transfer and cooperation. This introduction intends to tease these out.

CONCEPTUALIZING THE SOUTH AND SOUTH–SOUTH COOPERATION

What defines a country as belonging to the South, North, East, or West? Three points can be made. First, it is important to note that belonging to the South is not defined by being located in the Southern Hemisphere. Mexico and Mongolia are both in the Northern Hemispehere but are considered Southern. Australia and New Zealand are both in the Southern Hemisphere but one would be hard-pressed to describe these countries as belonging to the South. The same difficulties are shared by the notion of the West. Considered in relation to "the West," a second point about the definition of "the South" emerges. "The West" has more often stood for a country's political orientations and affiliations than its geographical location. The terms *South* and *Southern* have similarly carried social and political meanings that are unrelated to countries' actual geographical position. Third, South is a concept seldom used without reference to the North, invoked as its opposite. As such, it is a relational concept that invariably refers to a relationship of inequality. Indeed, the notions of North and South have become a proxy or metaphor for rich and poor, developed and underdeveloped, First and Third World, givers and recipients of aid. But such definitions can also oversimplify relationships between and within countries that are defined along these geographical axes.

Relationships between regions or countries referred to as Northern, Southern, Eastern, and Western are best located within, and have most frequently been understood in terms of, the theoretical frameworks of modernization or dependency theory, political economy or postcolonialism. Here, the key issues in recent decades have centered on globalization, the state and civil society, the "newness" and specificity of globalization in its current forms, and the resilience and autonomy of the state and civil society relative to new forms of global governance and unfettered market forces. More specifically, questions have been raised about the relationship between globalization and the Southern state: on the one hand, the latter's limited room for maneuver and weakness in terms of capabilities to assert an independent, "developmentalist" path in the face of new global agendas, and on the other, the extraordinary diversity, heterogeneity, and conflict not only between Southern states but also within them (see, for example, Jomo & Fine, 2006; Saul, 2003; Williams, 2006, 2007). Inequality and diversity within as well as between nations suggest that every Southern state may have its own North and South, that an East may exist within a West and a South within a North. Within this context, a renewed call for South–South cooperation has emerged.

Recognition that the idea of South–South cooperation is nothing new and that it is socially constructed lies at the heart of the majority of chapters in the book. It is also at the core of the approach developed in Chapters 2 and 3 in Part I. These chapters deal with the history of South–South transfer and cooperation. The treatment of history in each differs, however. For Caruso, South–South cooperation, conceptualized as a "real" event or "a shared cultural horizon" through which exchange is facilitated, has occurred over time, even though social actors in history might not have defined their activities in this way. His main concern is with the "center/periphery" proxies for North and South. His account of the spread of the idea of the monitorial school system through the agency of the *Sociedades Económicas* in the early 19th century from Cadiz, a city on the Spanish south coast, to colonies in the North of the Spanish periphery, demonstrates just how constructed the notions of "center" and "periphery" are. Caruso seeks to understand the "enacting moment" of such processes. By this, he means the actual mobilization of resources and concretization of plans to realize a specific educational model or idea in practice.

By contrast with Caruso, who examines a process of cooperation that entails transfer of a model, Chapter 3 by de Sá e Silva is interested in the history of the self-consciously defined movement and idea of South–South cooperation. She defines *South–South cooperation* as "any cooperative initiative between two or more developing countries." Like Caruso, she does not see this as a new idea, but one "with a past and a present." While recognizing the idea of the South as a discursive construct, she traces the history of the South–South cooperation movement to the post–World War II period, and sees it as having gone through three main phases. The first lasted from 1949 to 1979, the second through the 1980s and 1990s, and the third began in the last decade or so.

Whereas Caruso decenters the idea of Northern center and Southern periphery within a world-systems perspective, de Sá e Silva highlights the diversity, difference, and inequality within the South at the same time as she constructs a history of a movement toward unity and cooperation across social, political, and economic divisions.

MODALITIES OF TRANSFER AND COOPERATION

A variety of agents and social actors have promoted South–South transfer and cooperation, which has also taken different forms in the post–World War II period. Bilateral and multilateral agencies, transnational corporations, national governments, and NGOs have all facilitated transfer and cooperation through international development aid, regional and triangular initiatives, and staff exchanges. Their reasons, motivations, and outcomes have varied over time, as have roles, responses to, and reception of different forms of cooperation and transfer. Chapters 4–8 in Part II reflect on the dynamics and modalities of transfer and cooperation introduced by such social actors. They show that within the South there are inequalities and differences, both along the vertical North/South axis and the horizontal South/South axis, that have an impact on who transfers, mediates, and exports what, how, and to whom.

Yoko Mochizuki in Chapter 4 provides a magisterial overview of how Japan's post–World War II focus on infrastructural development gradually shifted to South–South cooperation. By the 1990s, Japan was the largest donor country in the world. Japan significantly influenced the approach taken by United Nations Development Program (UNDP), but also increasingly aligned its own priorities with the basic education and Education For All (EFA)–related goals and targets of international development cooperation. The stronger focus of the United Nations Education, Science and Cultural Organization (UNESCO) on South–South cooperation is in no small part due, Mochizuki suggests, to the appointment of Koichiro Matsuura as director-general of UNESCO in 1999. Along with Japanese influence had come a new approach to South–South cooperation that focuses on bringing together partners in the North to promote Southern solidarity for the purposes of development. Africa–Asia relations have enjoyed particular prominence. But Japan's agenda in committing to African development through international development cooperation, for example, Mochizuki argues, forms "part of Japan's ongoing efforts to expand its [economic, political, and diplomatic] power on the international scene."

Transnational corporations, the subject of Zahra Bhanji's Chapter 5, are equally significant players. Her study of the Jordan Education Initiative shows how transnational corporations combine with bilateral donors, governments, and foundations to promote educational reform through information and communication technologies (ICTs). In effect, these initiatives, she argues, "integrate the poor in developing countries as a market within the core business strategies of the firm." Like Caruso's "shared cultural horizon," these social actors are bound together as an "epistemic community" by a common set of normative beliefs about the capacity of ICTs to overcome the digital divide. And like international development agencies, they combine a number of players through the goal of educational development. The specific agenda of the Jordanian government remains subordinate, however, to that of the transnational corporation.

But how do those constituted as the South respond to and act in this context of powerful global social actors and agendas, and how much room for maneuver is there? Chapter 6, coauthored by Leon Tikly and Hillary Dachi, examines what they call the "new regionalism" in Africa to explore these issues more closely. Their chapter underlines the "weakness" of the Southern state in the context of globalization. South–South cooperation is, in effect, "the way in which African governments, donors, and NGOs manage the globalization process." The new regionalism is essentially "a top-down affair controlled by national governments." Its education initiatives are all substantially donor-supported, and demonstrate the role of the region in mediating global policy agendas. Regionalism is not, they argue, a new phenomenon in the African context, and they divide the period in much the same way as de Sá e Silva divides South–South cooperation in general. There are three phases: the first lasting from 1945 to the 1980s, the second beginning with the onset of structural adjustment programs in the 1980s, and the third inaugurated in 1989 at the end of the Cold War. Each phase sees a different set of actors and initiatives, and so there are both differences and continuities between older and newer forms of regionalism, with newer and more recent forms showing strong resonances with the idea of the European Union. But—and this is important—economic goals have, over time, been consistently prioritized over sociopolitical ones, elites have consistently dominated regional structures and processes, and these also remain consistently undemocratic in their character. As Mochizuki scrutinizes Japan's motivations, Tikly and Dachi question South Africa's role in regional structures. Their work suggests that there are different possibilities for the role of the nation-state in international and regional structures: on the one hand, as relatively supine and passive, and on the other, as actively pursuing an agenda through these structures that have more to do with national ambitions in the international terrain than with altruism.

Despite their somewhat pessimistic view of the role of regionalism, Tikly and Dachi use the notion of "mediation" rather than "transfer" of global agendas. In Chapter 7, Samoff uses the concept of "transfer and exchanges" not to denote the direct transmission of ideas, but instead a material good managed by foreign aid: "Foreign aid," he says, can be understood "as a tool or set of tools for managing international transfers and exchanges." In many contexts where South–South transfer and exchange are facilitated by donor aid, cooperation is constrained by inequalities in wealth and power between donor and recipient that are manifested in the aid relationship. Neither "transfer" nor "aid," Samoff argues, is necessarily a negative phenomenon or activity. What renders them problematic is the inequality at the heart of the relationship. Concepts such as "partnership" and "ownership" simply serve to "obscure the structured roles that perpetuate inequalities" insofar as they do not acknowledge the inequalities inherent in the relationship. Far from challenging such relationships, African states seem to acquiesce in them. They are also, by extension, embedded in activities that purport to be initiated by the South but are only made possible by Northern aid.

In the light of such apparently intractable inequalities and relationships, Adriana Abdenur's Chapter 8 on triangular cooperation proposes that, as "a new form of cooperation that builds alliances across developed and developing countries," triangular cooperation "represents a departure from the autarkic rhetoric of leftist developing states in earlier decades" and "a new compromise." It commonly comprises a form of cooperation between two countries to provide assistance to a third. Triangular cooperation is exemplified in the India–Brazil–South Africa (IBSA) and Brazil–Russia–India–China–South Africa (BRICS) partnerships. Abdenur takes Brazil as her case study. She suggests that, rather than taking official justifications for South–South cooperation at face value, triangular cooperation should be seen as constituting "a specific tactic for national self-promotion with a broader strategy of foreign relations." The novelty of this modality of transfer and cooperation is the pragmatism of the relationships both between North and South and within the South itself.

As such, there is much in common between the roles and motivations of individual countries involved in international development cooperation, the new regionalism, and triangular partnerships. From the analyses provided by Mochizuki (on Japan), Tikly and Dachi (on regionalism and the role of South Africa in Africa-wide and regional structures), and Abdenur (on Brazil), it seems clear that the promotion and achievement of broader regional and international, diplomatic, and political goals on an international platform are key components of motivations for involvement and participation by nation-states in global institutions and agendas. But the analyses also reveal differential contributions to this global agenda, with Japan firmly incorporated within a Northern network, regardless of its discursive construction as Eastern, having helped to shape the South–South cooperation agenda, and African states, by contrast, for example, appearing to achieve much less. This is an area that clearly needs much more research.

CONTRADICTIONS, COMPLEXITIES, AND AMBIGUITIES

Among the common forms of educational exchange and cooperation across national borders is the introduction of special models of schooling, staff, and student exchange. As Chapters 9–12 in Part III make clear, intra-Southern contradictions, complexities, and ambiguities abound in such exchanges.

In Chapters 9 and 10, Iveta Silova and Colette Chabbott, respectively, overturn the idea of the South as passive recipient of aid in their accounts of the Turkish Fetullah Gülen movement and the Bangladesh Rural Advancement Committee (BRAC). Chabbott uses BRAC, arguably the largest NGO in the world, to provide an example of a modality of transfer and cooperation in which a Southern actor provides and finances a model of low-cost schooling that it also attempts to share with other low-income countries. The schools of the Turkish Islamic reform movement of Fetullah Gülen that Silova discusses provide an example of a private school model combining religious and secular goals established in Central Asia and Azerbaijan within the context of a broader "Turkish" model of secular democracy based on the market and modern education. Unlike the BRAC schools, the Fetullah Gülen schools are more popular abroad than at home, and they develop a curricular emphasis on imparting "the tools of science and religion" that may or may not share something with the adaptations that the BRAC model has undergone in Afghanistan. In the low-cost BRAC model, the provision of classrooms and teachers to ensure access is key. In the private-school, Fetullah Gülen model, values and attitudes are central.

Chabbott's account of the BRAC initiatives uses the concept of "transfer" as "export" of an idea and a model. In Sierra Leone and southern Sudan, BRAC worked in close cooperation with the United Nations Children's Fund (UNICEF) to establish the model, but its efforts were ultimately more successful in Afghanistan than in African contexts, testimony to the irreducible intransigence of local contextual differences in enabling transport of models. The chapter implicitly questions assumptions about similarities across impoverished contexts (the South) through its account of African responses to the Bangladeshi model. Profound differences manifest themselves in efforts to cooperate and share, confounding the "enacting moment" of transfer and challenging the universality of context so often assumed in the literature extolling the virtues of South–South cooperation.

In tracking the differential reception of the model, there are strong synergies between Chabbott's chapter and the one by Caruso, dealing with the reception more than a century earlier of the monitorial school system. There, the model of export was the monitorial school. Here, the model is the BRAC school. Each is a low-cost model for managing the provision of schools, classrooms, and teachers to poor children. Although the idea in each historical and geographical context found popular reception among elites—in the 19th century, the *Sociedades Económicas*, and in the 20th the NGO-agency network of alliances—their "importation" or "concretization" was, in practice, limited across time and space, whether it was the monitorial school system or the BRAC model. For Caruso, this was because colonial elites had priorities other than setting up schools for the poor, despite their enthusiasm for the idea. For Chabbott, the necessary condition of "individuals with vision and stamina" to drive the idea suggests similar drawbacks and constraints on the spread of the BRAC model in the contemporary period.

The success and popularity of the Fetullah Gülen movement schools, assessed by their reception in Central Asia and Azerbaijan, paradoxically has much to do with "the shared goals of the Gülen community, Turkish state, and Central Asian governments": On the one hand, they fill the vacuum left by the collapse of the Soviet Union and reduce Russian influence; on the other, they adroitly position themselves as providing quality education in a context where state schools are seen as failing.

"Shared cultural horizons," "shared goals," and "epistemic communities" across borders and continents thus appear, as Caruso argues in Chapter 2, to be critical preconditions for the processes of transfer and cooperation; they do not necessarily and invariably, however, result in the direct translation of an "exact copy" of a model from one context to another. Models are not only promoted for different reasons, but are also differentially received and enacted. Contrasting strongly with the idea of "multiple internationalities" (see Chapter 2) manifest among the social actors and movements discussed in the chapters above is the idea of a conflict between national and local cultural scripts suggested in the chapters by Gillespie and Soudien, which deal with the experience of student and academic exchanges between Africa and China and Africa and India.

China's role in South–South cooperation is explored in Chapters 3, 4, and 11. In Chapter 3, de Sá e Silva highlights the centrality of Mao's Three Worlds Theory to early notions of South–South cooperation. In Chapter 4, Mochizuki is concerned with China's recent "prime mover" role. In Chapter 11, Gillespie examines the experience of African students in Chinese universities since the 1960s when such exchanges were first organized. She shows that students experience forms of extreme segregation and racism that call into question the high-flown commitments to South–South cooperation. The everyday realities of xenophobia and racial hostility stand in marked contrast to the noble goals and ideals espoused on the international stage, whatever the purpose, goal, and rationale. This chapter opens a Pandora's box of questions about South–South cooperation. It reveals that South–South relations need to grapple with the very same issues that North–South relations have to confront: inequalities of power, wealth, and racism. It also suggests, as Mochizuki proposes, that Chinese motivations, as much as others', may be based on "profit-driven" and political/diplomatic rather than altruistic imperatives.

India's growing role in South–South cooperation is addressed in this book by Chabbott's Chapter 10 (on BRAC) and Soudien's Chapter 12, which examines the South–South relationship between India and South Africa. Cultural exchanges have not only occurred across the Indian Ocean, between Africa and India, for several centuries; there are also large Indian diasporic minorities in many African countries, including South Africa. Reflecting on two academic exchanges initiated between scholars in India and South Africa, Soudien argues that South–South cooperation works as a global imaginary, but that the local always asserts itself, "imperceptibly, on the terrain of the interrelationship." Like Samoff, Soudien holds that sociologies and inequalities in each local context "configure[d] the basic architecture and substance of the transfer process." In recounting the experience of racism by Africans during an exchange visit to India, he argues that South–South relationships can themselves reinscribe old colonial relationships between countries as the local asserts itself. Like Gillespie, he is concerned with the racism experienced by Africans in unfamiliar contexts, but explains this as mobilization of old apartheid and colonial histories that are present within both societies. And, as in Caruso's story, local conditions have the upper hand.

The chapters in Part III contradict the notions of the South as the passive victim of unbridled Northern rapacity, that transfer occurs principally across North–South coordinates, according to plan, and that South–South cooperation is a process without contradiction, complexity, and ambiguity. They show that South–South cooperation may be based on "shared cultural horizons" and "multiple internationalities," but that it is as fraught with inequalities and differences within and between countries as North–South relationships are troubled by them. But what, then, are the implications suggested by these chapters for further work in this area?

IMPLICATIONS

The authors in this book dislodge the salience of North–South conceptualizations by privileging the agency and movement of people and ideas within and across regions and realms structured by political and economic relationships of considerable complexity. They critically examine the current institutionalized expression of Northern power, showing how dependence is re-created at multiple levels through such agencies even as they promote the idea of South–South cooperation. And they explore and question the nature of the initiatives and agency of local actors and institutions in attempting to overcome such dependence.

If we acknowledge the social constructedness of the notion of South–South cooperation and the constraints on real relationships of equality along whichever geographic coordinates we operate, as the authors in this book encourage us to do, what possibilities remain for activity in this terrain? How useful, ultimately, are the concepts for research and action?

None of the authors in the book suggests that the idea of transfer and cooperation be rejected *tout court.* All call for a more nuanced, historical, and theoretically informed approach to inform research and practice. Critical as de Sá e Silva is of notions of Southern homogeneity and unity, she has a firm belief in the "real potential of South–South cooperation and South–South transfer." Abdenur also believes that, despite triangular cooperation being a national tactic for self-promotion, it is a new and innovative form of cooperation that offers pragmatic solutions. Less optimistic is Mochizuki, who suggests that in the new scramble for Africa and the resultant competition between traditional and emergent donors, "regionalism can be a mechanism both for promoting economic interests as well as a potential buffer and protection against unmitigated exploitation." Tikly and Dachi doubt that regional structures actually behave as buffers, but they believe that they are important in promoting greater connectedness between African countries, and can improve the quality of North–South engagements. They specify, however, that a requirement of the latter is greater support for and involvement of grassroots movements and local expertise in such engagements. Samoff argues that responsibility needs to be taken on both sides if structurally unequal relationships intrinsic to the aid process and relationship are to be turned into real partnerships: Donors need to enable more equality and African social actors need to be more assertive. Soudien posits a more radical disruption of the metropole–satellite dependency relationships through intensive self-consciousness and interrogation of "what happens in knowledge transfer processes." He urges the reader to examine these processes closely "for what they tell us about new postcolonial relations of domination and subordination." "We need to be aware," he says, "of how privilege is reconstituted at new levels" and start asking how those involved in these processes can begin to deconstruct their positions from inside those situations. Soudien's line of argumentation suggests that a more thorough and critical engagement with the nature of South–South transfer and cooperation is necessary and opens a range of new questions for research.

The authors draw from several interpretive frameworks that are tied to political economy, world-systems theory, globalization studies, and borrowing/lending research. They use a variety of methods of inquiry, from single case-study approaches to social network analysis. Overall, they suggest that the term *South–South* is often used too indiscriminately. In many cases, it is a misnomer, given that the dissemination of reform ideas and packages in education reflects at closer examination, more often than not, a North–South–South or, in some cases, a South–North–South transfer. This is sharply highlighted in Gita Steiner-Khamsi's concluding chapter, which argues, on the one hand, that the new logic of donor aid stimulates internal reform and South–South cooperation by remote control through benchmarking and standard-setting processes, and on the basis of contradictory information. On the other hand, it also shows how irrelevant and unenforceable these tools of strategic planning are in the majority of local contexts. She draws on research conducted in Mongolia to show that "while government officials are quick to discover the political and economic gains that come with speaking the universal language of educational reform," "there is no great cause for concern that [schools] are coerced into externally imposed reforms," given their disregard for decisions made between government and donors. Into the picture she also brings "a new class of unruly donors" who fund what, where, and whom they like, with little interest in global aid agendas.

Steiner-Khamsi concludes the book with the observation that South–South cooperation can be seen as a vehicle to accelerate the accomplishment of development targets established by the North through standardized aid. She would probably concur with Said (1983) that recognition of the dialectic of power underlying modern societies is critical for any analysis, including that of the term *South–South cooperation*. Its contemporary uses, it could be argued, belie continuities of power and inequality between nations. Her chapter is a salutary reminder of the disciplinary uses to which terms such as *South–South cooperation*, which carry a certain positive ca-chet and different meanings in some contexts, are being propelled by global agencies. But it also speaks critically of a certain "unruliness" both at the center and at the periphery.

In this "unruliness" lies both a metaphorical threat and possibility. The issues are simultaneously economic, political, and symbolic. Although the floating meaning and contextualized use of the term *South–South cooperation* ultimately suggests that intellectual responses to its uses and engagement in its practices should be situation-specific and context-dependent, the certainty of continuing interconnection and recognition of the unruliness of the relationships of power and inequality at the heart of this interconnection provides the basis for the development of new perspectives on the subject.

PART ONE

Conceptualizing the South and South–South Cooperation

TWO

Imperial Connections, Entangled Peripheries

Cadiz and the Latin American Monitorial Schools

Marcelo Caruso

PERIPHERIES AS CONSTRUCTIONS AND THE HISTORIC DYNAMICS OF TRANSFER

The South is not only a point on the compass. It has also become a word with polyvalent meanings ranging from "poverty" and "social exclusion" to "paradise" and "adventure." The South often depicts those regions known as "the periphery" in world-systems analysis. Processes of South–South transfer, therefore, mainly display relations between two or more peripheries. In Northern academia, the concepts and language of "periphery" have largely been coined by the analytical frame set forth by Immanuel Wallerstein, who associated the divide between center and periphery with the emergence of a worldwide network of relationships related to the birth, expansion, and consolidation of the capitalist economy. From the 16th century on, this capitalist world system began to emerge, with a series of regions located in the North, West, and in Europe as its center. As a part of this process, other countries and even whole continents underwent a deep transformation of their own center–periphery relations and became subordinated to Northern core countries. Between industrial centers and peripheral food and manpower suppliers—the latter relevant in the age of slavery—Wallerstein (1974, 2004) also identified a semi-periphery comprising those countries with a certain industrial development and a relatively consistent market.

The overreliance of world-systems analysis on the market as its main focus has been repeatedly criticized from different perspectives (Arnove, 1980; Bergesen, 1984; Skocpol, 1993). Nonetheless, one of the greatest achievements of this approach has been its anticipation of themes and dynamics pertaining to later theories of globalization. One major point of critique against world-systems analysis remains its crude realistic assumptions. Certainly, the market-based analysis led to this reduction and is still popular with economists and so-called realist sociologists. The problem of educational transfer, however, encompasses realistic as well as symbolic and cultural dimensions, if we accept for a moment this divide in social and policy analysis. This chapter addresses the issue of constructed centers and peripheries against the background of a particular educational transfer: the export and import of the monitorial system of education, also known as the Bell-Lancaster System, a system of schooling in which abler children were used to teach and control other children, from the periphery of the Spanish peninsula to the periphery of the moribund Spanish empire in the second and third decades of the 19th century. I intend to show that this process of transfer could be characterized as a South–South transfer by taking into account the cultural constructions of center and periphery of that time.[1]

The last point is extremely important because social actors are always embedded in particular constellations of internationality. By internationality, I am not referring to the real extent of international development (e.g., the formal political structure of the Spanish empire), but rather to the distinctive constructions of internationality produced in different settings at different times (e.g., which regions of this empire were considered to be central or peripheral) (Schriewer, 1994). Changing constructions of the "world" emerged, spread, and contracted over time, having their own construction of center and periphery. What kind of centrality constructed the Mexican Revolution in the field of education in the 1920s, when actors as disparate as John Dewey and Arab nationalists in Iraq looked to the Mexican village school reforms of this decade for inspiration (Bashkin, 2006; Dewey, 1929)? What kind of new culturally constructed centrality was implied in the work of Paulo Freire as applied to the literacy campaigns in Guinea-Bissau or in countries searching for an African socialism, where cultural authority was transferred from the core industrialized countries and even from the communist countries to South America (Mehnert, 1980)? Which constellation of reasons, traditions, and designs of transformation determined the preferences of the actors in each case? The construction of such horizons for the analysis of processes of transfer is of utmost importance because they build relevant preconditions of transfer. Actors delimit the space within which selections are performed, giving preference to certain regions, so constituting changing centers, peripheries, and, possibly, in the long run, multiple internationalities.[2] The historical analysis of a concrete process of educational transfer delivered in this article, the introduction of the monitorial system of education through different regions of the Spanish empire, addresses these questions by considering a situation of crisis and disintegration, of emerging centers and new peripheries.

WORLDS IN MOTION: THE GLOBAL SPREAD OF THE BELL-LANCASTER SYSTEM AND ITS INTRODUCTION IN SPAIN

The fate of the monitorial system of education in the early decades of the 19th century could be labeled as the first process of global diffusion of an educational model for elementary schooling (Schriewer & Caruso, 2005). The system of teaching conceived and practiced separately by the Reverend Andrew Bell (1753–1832) in the English enclave of Madras, southern India, and by the teacher Joseph Lancaster (1778–1838) in London shared a common feature, which induced contemporary observers to treat both methods of instruction as equivalent. Both built systematically on the help of the better and older pupils in order to manage schools with up to 400 and 500 students, supervised by only one adult teacher (Bell, 1797; Lancaster, 1803). The name, the Bell-Lancaster Method, or the Bell-Lancaster System, expresses this commonality regardless of the bitter struggles in England over the authorship of the system of teaching and the controversial issue of religious education. Both Bell and Lancaster were supported respectively by the Anglican Church and by English religious dissenters, and these supporters created their own organizations—the National Society for the Education of the Poor in the Principles of the Established Church and the British and Foreign School Society—with the purpose of diffusing the new system of teaching (Binns, 1908; Burgess & Welsby, 1961). The dynamics of competition within England were astonishing, but the international activities of the British and Foreign School Society outdid apparently all known efforts for the diffusion of a specific model of schooling ("The Foreign Work," 1906/1909).

It is not surprising that the monitorial system of schooling, as it was called due to the name given to the helpers (monitors), expanded into five continents in only a few years.[3] The promise of saving money by reducing the number of paid teachers, as well as the celebrated "industrial" rationality of all devices of this system of teaching, attracted the attention of elites around the world, preoccupied as they were by the lack of schooling for (and disciplining of) the poor but, at the same time, unwilling to finance an expensive system of popular education (Hogan, 1989; Kaestle, 1973). The missionary efforts of both English organizations, the zeal of religious missionaries around the world, and the particular political situation at the beginning of the century, when European armies occupied Paris after Napoleon and Latin American independence fighters were exiled to London and Paris, gave an additional impetus for diffusion. Between 1815 and 1830, this model of teaching played a major role in the new market of innovations in the field of mass schooling (Hopman, 1990). In the monitorial system of teaching, students were enlisted as assistant teachers, or monitors, to teach classes. Monitors that supervised an entire class (at the time consisting of hundreds of students) instead of instructing small groups of students were referred to as "general monitors." Figure 2.1. presents a general monitor (standing on a chair) who under the command of a teacher (right corner) controlled the work of the other monitors.

Needless to say, the Bell-Lancaster-System experienced numerous transformations and adaptations as it spread. It was also further developed and applied, mainly in England and France. In addition, the enthusiastic adoption of the model of monitorial schooling in France in the years 1814 and 1815 overcame religious boundaries through the establishment of a Protestant system of teaching in a Catholic country.[4] All over Europe, monitorial and Lancasterian schools, as they were often called, mushroomed. Educated audiences praised the rationality of the model and the consistent order displayed by images included in the manuals of the system of teaching. And a number of civic associations for the promotion of education on the basis of the Bell-Lancaster-System were brought into being.[5]

Figure 2.1. A General Monitor Controlling the Entire Class

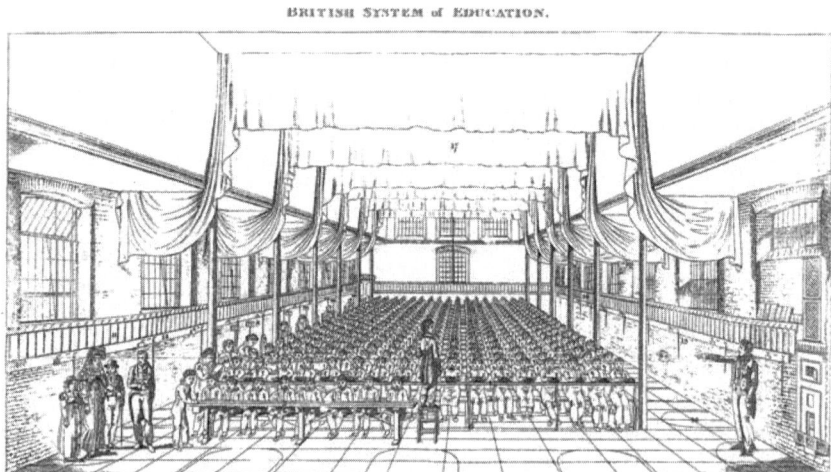

Source: British and Foreign School Society, 1834, plate 2.

This expansion of the Bell-Lancaster-System became a matter of general interest, and many governments in Europe initiated educational missions with the purpose of scrutinizing the famous model schools in London and Paris. Figure 2.2 provides an illustration of a reading lesson in the Central School of the British and Foreign School Society. It shows how classes were divided into small groups and assigned to students who acted as teaching monitors.

This was also the path chosen by the Spanish elites for the import of the Bell-Lancaster System to their country. A group of high-ranking nobles, all holding key positions in the military and in the royal administration, sent a captain of Irish descent, Juan Kearney, to both cities in 1816 and 1817.[6] After his training in these model schools, this informal group of nobles decided to organize a model school at their own cost under Kearney's direction. At a time of acute financial crisis (Fontana, 2002), this initiative found a benefactor in the king, Ferdinand VII, who visited the school after its opening in January 1818 and declared its usefulness for all of Spain in September 1819. He also transferred the supervision of all monitorial schools to a new *Junta Protectora y Directora de la Enseñanza Mutua* (Commission for the protection and direction of the mutual/monitorial teaching; hereafter, *Junta Protectora*), institutionalizing the group of nobles involved in the educational mission to London and Paris.[7]

The model of further diffusion of the Bell-Lancaster-System sketched by the *Junta Protectora* and the Crown was a centralized one. All initiatives for the establishment of Bell-Lancaster schools had to be approved by the

Figure 2.2. A Teaching Monitor and His Reading Group

Source: Manuale del sistema di Bell e Lancaster, 1819, plate 3.

Junta Protectora in Madrid, which presided over a centralized system of supervision of all monitorial schools. The first school in Madrid, directed by Kearney, became the central institution for the training of teachers in the new system.[8] In this scheme, the Crown continued the policy of centralized modernization in the field of elementary schooling, which had become prevalent in two waves of elementary school reform since the second half of the 18th century. After the expulsion of the Jesuits from all Spanish territories in 1767, the Crown had protected a group of reformist teachers and pedagogues in Madrid, who spread their organizational and didactical innovations to the Spanish periphery with the financial and organizational support of the central government. A movement to thoroughly modernize Spanish elementary schools started in San Ildefonso during the 1780s and 1790s and spread throughout Spain. The movement, however, was short-lived, and it focused only on the teaching of reading and arithmetic (instead of the sole prevalence of writing and penmanship) and the organization of schooling (not the old individual method). The second attempt to centralize school modernization was the failed experiment to introduce Pestalozzian pedagogy in the years 1805–1808. Although the model school in Madrid, sponsored by the leading minister of the Crown, had been fairly successful and the government had designed a centralized model for its diffusion from Madrid to other Spanish cities, its surprising closure on the eve of the French invasion truncated this drive.[9]

Faced with the promise and possibility of monitorial schooling, Ferdinand VII and his advisors envisioned a similarly strictly centralized scheme for the spread of the new system of teaching. In spite of all these promising plans, however, Spanish society had become more complex and more dynamic as a corollary of liberal mobilization and politicization in the years 1808–1813. The break with the old regime symbolized by the famous liberal constitutional charter of Cadiz (1812) represented a kind of alternative social and political order, which also aimed at establishing rational and centralized policies, now under parliamentary control. The first plans for the centralization of control over the spread of monitorial schools conceived in Madrid faced the challenge of competing forces. And these forces of change were particularly strong in the Spanish periphery.

BECOMING PERIPHERAL AND REMAINING CENTRAL: BOURGEOIS CIVIL SOCIETY IN CADIZ OR THE CONDITIONS OF LENDING (1717–1820)

Centers and peripheries in Spain were in the process of deep transformation at the beginning of the 19th century, which affected not only the inner order of the metropolis, but also the whole structure of the empire. The decadence of the once-powerful Spanish empire has fascinated scholars interested in processes of political, military, and economic stagnation. The mighty impulse in the organization of a transatlantic empire favored by the modernization of the Castilian state apparatus, the cultural cohesion of the country due to the early codification of the Castilian language, and the religious vitality following both Renaissance scholarship and the challenge of Lutheranism had rapidly dissolved during the 17th century (Kamen, 1985; Nalle, 1989; Pérez, 2001), although the most visible symptom of this crisis, the loss of the colonies, did not begin until the first decades of the 19th century. In fact, the efforts of the new Bourbon dynasty in the 18th century to create a more rational and centralized state administration may have delayed the processes of colonial disintegration of this enormous and heterogeneous empire—by conceding restricted free trade and by challenging old corrupt local elites both in Spain and in the colonies. A new dynamism emerged in the Spanish periphery, along the coasts far from Madrid. The Basque metal industry and the first textile industries in Catalonia, together with a few booming harbor cities, were good examples of this new drive. However, these enclaves of modernization did not impede the dramatic chain of political and structural changes unleashed by the Napoleonic invasion of 1808.[10]

These changes encompassed both the inner political order of the mainland and the status of the colonies. In Spain, reformist and enlightened forces took over the duties of government in the absence of the arrested king and elaborated a constitution based both on the principles of popular sovereignty and parliamentary monarchy. French occupation in 1808 hindered the general and consistent enforcement of the constitution, but, at the same time, the mere interruption of dynastic continuity caused by the invasion produced considerable turmoil abroad. In Caracas, Santiago de Chile, Buenos Aires, and even in the loyal Mexican colonies, local elites took over government, a move that led to the independence of many colonies by 1820. Old colonial strongholds such as Mexico City and Lima were initially untouched by this wave of "insurrection." But by 1825, Spain had kept only Cuba and Puerto Rico. Older colonies, such as Guatemala, Panama, and some Colombian cities in the Atlantic coast, leaned toward loyalty to Spain and sought independence only after Spanish military defeats.[11]

Within such a convulsive setting, the harbor city of Cadiz (Andalusia) became something of a point of reference in this emerging and unstable liberal Atlantic.[12] Cadiz had bridged two different zones of the "Atlantic world" during early modern times. Its proximity to the northern coast of Africa had led to the presence of a considerable black community, an exception in peninsular Spain (Domínguez Ortiz, 1986; Ringrose, 1996).

Thanks to the slave trade, Cadiz had connected the "black" and the "Northern" Atlantic, an entanglement of trade routes between Africa, Europe, and North and South America. Territorial redesign under the Bourbons in the 18th century included the transfer of the *Casa de contratación* (House of Trade) in 1726 from Seville to Cadiz, which, in theory, controlled all Spanish exploration and colonization overseas. This key office of royal administration unleashed a noticeable growth of urban and commercial structures. The quasi-monopoly of trade with America between 1717 and 1778 transformed Cadiz into a thriving city that displaced Seville as the most dynamic town in Andalusia. With the introduction of free trade between Spanish and Spanish-American cities in 1778, a period of economic decadence commenced, whose results would become generally visible during the second third of the 19th century. In 1818, Cadiz, at least within the Spanish empire, was economically moribund, its centrality peripheralized.

At the same time, other contemporary political and cultural processes paved the way for another kind of centrality for Cadiz. A significant community of foreigners, including several French and English families, had for decades been receptive toward modern proposals of social and political organization (García Fernández, 2005; Maxwell, 1999; Ringrose, 1996). The Crown and the Spanish Inquisition had persecuted freemasonry in the second half of the 18th century, as the cosmopolitism of the city had been a recurrent source of disquiet (Ferrer Benimeli, 1986). The local bourgeoisie's lack of political power, in spite of its flourishing economic position during the eighteenth century, changed to certain degree as a result of the political processes unleashed by the French invasion of 1808. Before 1813, the cultural and political ferment among the local bourgeoisie, regardless of Cadiz's noticeable gentrification, coalesced with a broader liberal mobilization of the whole country. The adoption of the first European liberal constitution in Cadiz in 1812, a contingent fact made possible only by the Napoleonic invasion of Spain, now symbolized the strong position of an active and ambitious bourgeois elite in the city. After 1812, Cadiz remained a liberal stronghold and strongly supported the insurrection led by Major Rafael del Riego in 1820, which reintroduced the Spanish constitution.[13]

On the eve of independence in Latin America, Cadiz played a central role as a hub for enlightened and liberal ideas. American deputies from Mexico to Buenos Aires stayed in Cadiz for some time during the constitutional assembly. Cadiz became central to the politics of the time, both in Spain and in the American colonies, although the loss of almost all colonies in South and Central America by 1825 diminished the economic role of the city (Bustos Rodríguez, 2005; Ringrose, 1996). Altogether, despite becoming noticeably peripheral at the economic level, Cadiz advanced to a new kind of centrality for some years, a centrality related to liberal models of government and to processes of political modernization. Cadiz became both a symbol and a concrete point of reference for this new liberal Atlantic.

In this changing setting, the establishment of a local economic society in 1814, the *Sociedad económica de amigos del país de Cádiz*, became a cornerstone of bourgeois life in the city. A large number of *sociedades económicas*, mostly supported by the central government, had been founded in big Spanish towns and cities from the middle of the 18th century. Almost 100 of them existed in 1808 (Calderón España, 2001; Sarraillh, 1957). At first sight, the establishment of such societies seems to have been a part of a broader European movement toward a bourgeois civil society. A closer look at their membership and activities displays not only a world of progress and utility, but also a culture of ancient forms of sociability, a traditional approach to social issues, and a tendency to perceive this membership as a practice of cultural distinction in an enlightened setting. Very few of these societies became promising laboratories for reform projects and new ideas during the 18th century.[14] Interestingly enough, the most dynamic cities of the Spanish periphery, such as Bilbao, Barcelona, and Cadiz, did not have economic societies, whereas smaller cities—in the region of Cadiz, for instance—did. Only in 1814 did citizens of Cadiz found their own *Sociedad económica*, following an exhortation issued by the last Parliament of 1813.

The foundation of this *Sociedad económica* as an act of Parliament marked a clear tendency for the Cadiz associates that contrasted with other, similar societies in the country. The *Sociedad económica* in Cadiz was indeed more bourgeois than its sisters and reflected a more modern approach to sociability. I found information on 42 of the members of the committee for education of the *Sociedad* between 1817 and 1835. Whereas members of the "old" elites, such as priests, government officials, and high-ranking military personnel, are certainly present, a good number of teachers and merchants collaborated with the committee. Scattered information about political affiliation is also available, and shows that 13 members were certainly liberal and only five were clearly conservative or absolutist. There are some indications suggesting that the bulk of the remaining members tended toward a liberal disposition (Jiménez Gámez, 1991).

It is not surprising that the committee for education within the *Sociedad económica* came to know the monitorial system of education relatively early on in its history. Already in 1817, the members of the committee decided to establish a model school of the Bell-Lancaster-System type at the expense of the *Sociedad* (Jiménez Gámez, 1991, 1992). The *Sociedad económica* developed its own path of "import" of monitorial schooling, thanks to its own networks in Paris and London (Jiménez Gámez, 1991, p. 198).[15] The committee's correspondence does not display a significant exchange with the efforts simultaneously being made in Madrid.[16] The committee invested a good deal of time in deciding which manual should be used as a guide for the establishment and management of the school. In the end, a French manual was chosen, probably because the Bell and Lancasterian techniques were combined with Catholic religious teachings (Real Sociedad Económica de Amigos del País de Cádiz, 1818).

The model monitorial school in Cadiz, mainly a free school for the urban poor, opened in July 1818, a few months later than the model school in Madrid. Press and other printed reports and accounts show an impressive popularity of the new establishment.[17] The *Sociedad económica* offered a complete program for the introduction of monitorial schooling on a large scale. Its own model school stood under the superintendence of the committee of education, which possessed its own manual, a teacher training program, and even specific school regulations, a real novelty for the city.[18] The *Sociedad económica* expanded its offer of schooling by founding a pay school for the middle classes of the city. The school faced many difficulties before its closure in 1821. A separate school for women was opened in 1827.[19] The male and female free schools became model schools for the city, and they were respectively integrated into the emerging local system of primary schools in 1838 and 1843 (Jiménez Gámez, 1991).

The consistent work of the *Sociedad económica* helped to consolidate the excellent reputation of the monitorial system of education in Spain. It is not surprising that in Cadiz the Bell-Lancaster-System was seen as an attractive technique for teaching other school subjects pertaining to higher learning (*Nuevo método para aprender el inglés*, 1834; Sánchez de Madrid, 1823) and that the *Sociedad* initiated a lasting work that led to a development of variations of monitorial schooling in the city that survived until the last third of the 19th century (Espigado Tocino, 1996).[20] In terms of educational transfer, it is now possible to appreciate the extent to which the *Sociedad* ignited a purposive lending process, and how its consistent approach was honored in other contexts. In terms of constructed centralities and peripheries, I will now analyze the impact of the structural and political transformations on the ascendancy of the *Sociedad* in the diffusion of the monitorial system in Latin America. Did the activities of the *Sociedad* slow down in Cadiz because the city was starting to become economically marginalzied? Or did the short-lived, but noticeable, political ascendancy of the city and its relationship networks, as an equivalent to the lost economic centrality, prevail?

ENACTING TRANSFER: IMPACT OF THE IMPULSE FROM CADIZ (1818–1825)

The success story of the first monitorial school in Cadiz was by no means unique. Other Spanish *Sociedades económicas* managed to establish similar schools of mutual instruction, or they took these ideas into serious consideration. Simultaneous with the establishment of the school in Cadiz, the local *Sociedad económica* of the small town of Baeza (Andalusia), which had its own university until 1807, organized its own school, inspired along the lines of the Bell-Lancaster-System.[21] Two years later, the monitorial school in Seville, also supported by the local *Sociedad económica*, attracted some public attention on account of local Catholic hostility toward it (Corts Giner & Calderón España, 1995/96; del Marmol, 1821; Fernández Bulete, 2001). Nonetheless, only in the case of Cadiz did I find a purposive attempt to propagandize its own efforts and to recommend the monitorial school model to other institutions. Local elites in Cadiz were able to challenge the centrality of Madrid in the process of diffusion of these schools in Spain, and also in the colonies.

First of all, Cadiz became a proper center for the further propagation of the monitorial system within Spain. The royal decree issued on October 6, 1819, indicated the emergence of a second pole, after Madrid, for the diffusion of the method with its own manual, model school, and supporters. This was just one month after Ferdinand VII resolved to give the *Junta protectora* extensive competencies for the centralized regulation and superintendence of all monitorial schools in the country. The new decree extended the right to establish monitorial schools to all *Sociedades económicas* in the Spanish mainland (Junta Protectora y Directora de la Enseñanza Mutua, 1820, pp. VIII–X). With the exception of the female monitorial school in Madrid, patronized by the ladies' committee of the local *Sociedad económica*, the already functioning monitorial school in Cadiz was probably the only one in existence at that time. Cadiz now offered not only a coherent but also a legitimate "reform package" to all those wanting to establish monitorial schools.

An assessment of the respective manuals and the model schools in Madrid and Cadiz shows that they construct a kind of centrality of lending in two ways. Although I can offer only scattered evidence of these processes due to the loss of crucial archive materials, it is likely that the manual published in Cadiz was more widely circulated and available than the manual from Madrid. The committee for education of the *Sociedad* in Cadiz sent information and manuals of the method to at least 25 similar societies in Spain and Central America. This constitutes the most extensively recorded attempt to circulate this school model via institutional channels during these years (Jiménez Gámez, 1991). I have no evidence of similar efforts by the group in Madrid. The archives of other *sociedades económicas* show almost no significant connections to the *Junta Protectora* or to the model school led by Kearney in Madrid. Concerning the training of teachers in both model schools, the picture of a constructed centrality of Cadiz is even more pronounced, although the royal decree from 1819 had defined the school in Madrid as a normal school for the entire kingdom. This applied first of all to other teachers of the city of Cadiz and its surroundings.[22] In addition, teachers from all of Andalusia went to Cadiz, and not to Madrid, in order to be trained in the management of monitorial schools (del Marmol, 1821). Teachers from the northern cities of Zamora and Zaragoza also chose Cadiz for their training, although the journey to Madrid could have been cheaper and shorter (Corts Giner & Calderón España, 1995/96). In this process, the centrality of Cadiz in the diffusion of new models of teaching was a part of a general crisis of central authority during the late absolutist era. Not only did the lack of money in Madrid frustrate many ambitious plans, but the end of the political restoration in 1820 also unleashed a dynamic that led to the emergence of local and regional centers in the diffusion of monitorial schooling. In Catalonia and the Basque provinces, teachers and societies established many monitorial schools without any noteworthy connections to Madrid. The dismantling of the centralized model of diffusion envisioned by the Crown was consistent in the liberal period until 1823, and Cadiz managed to consolidate its position in these years as a supra-regional center for the diffusion of monitorial schooling (Caruso, 2007b).

The associates in Cadiz not only bore in mind the other Spanish *sociedades*. They also repeatedly sent information, as well as issues of their manual of monitorial teaching, to other social actors in Latin America. This was a distinctive feature of the activities of the *Sociedad económica* in Cadiz compared with all the other associations involved in the spread of monitorial schooling in Spain. Perhaps following a pattern of relationships instituted by trading and commercial networks, news about the school in Cadiz, including successful public examinations, had already been sent to the municipal council of Guatemala City in January 1819. News related to the schools in Cadiz was also sent to Havana. These contacts with Cuba were the most lasting, surviving until at least 1833. Finally, the committee of education in Cadiz received requests to supply teachers with school materials, manuals, and hints for the establishment of such schools in Mexico (Jiménez Gámez, 1991). Although the links between these actors located at the ends of the Atlantic world were not so robust and frequent, their strategic position in the spread of monitorial schooling in Latin

America cannot be underestimated. Eugenia Roldán Vera and Thomas Schupp showed, in a pioneering quantitative analysis of the network of "early adopters" engaged in the rapid introduction of the monitorial system of education in Latin America, that the few connections to Cadiz within this network were of the utmost importance for the almost simultaneous introduction of this system of teaching in really disparate contexts. Roldán Vera and Schupp (2005) demonstrated "the efficiency of this society in conveying its message and influencing other parts of the network through a relatively small number of direct connections" (p. 82). In this sense, they conclude that the *Sociedad económica* in Cadiz played a central role in the spread of the model. I want briefly to assess the fate of these contacts by focusing on their respective contexts of import.

Guatemala

The news of the school in Cadiz and the manual of the system caused a stir in Guatemala City from 1819 on. Many issues of the manual are mentioned in the Guatemalan sources. One inspired the teacher Mariano Córdova to present a plan for the establishment of such a school to the local authorities in April 1819. At the same time, the local authorities also noticed the two decrees regulating the diffusion of the Bell-Lancaster-System issued by the king in Madrid (Somoza Guevara, 1959). The fact that the *Sociedad* in Cadiz sent the manual and other school materials to the town council of Guatemala and not to the local *Sociedad* (established in 1794) suggests that the Guatemalan Society was either unsuccessful beyond its local boundaries or inoperative. The positive reception of the news from Cadiz was by no means surprising, as there were existing antecedents in the field of educational transfer. In 1796, the newly established Academy of Noble Arts in Guatemala had copied the regulations of a similar school in Cadiz (Jones Shafer, 1958). The ascendancy of Cadiz as a center delivering models of modernization was unbroken and the enlightened elites of Guatemala still perceived this Spanish harbor as an attractive laboratory for social experimentation.

Despite the unreserved support shown by Guatemalan elites, concretization of these plans was limited. Municipal authorities ordered some experiments based on the new model of schooling in the local free schools, but financial difficulties proved stronger. In 1824, during a discussion of a general plan for a comprehensive reform of local schools, officials invoked input from Cadiz (Lira González, 1970), although the new model school in Mexico City (established in 1822) also attracted some attention.[23] The promise of monitorial schooling remained popular among the elites, although the agent of the British and Foreign School

Society in the region—the future secretary of the organization, Henry Dunn—was pessimistic:

> The most strenuous exertions have been made to introduce the Lancasterian system . . . , but hitherto unsuccessfully. Congress has publicly expressed its determination to establish it, commissioners have been appointed and reports made, but from some cause or other no active steps have been taken to forward the object. (Dunn, 1828, p. 104)[24]

It was not until 1830 that the first Bell-Lancaster school opened in Guatemala City. It was one of the most successful monitorial schools among those established in the 1830s (Williford, 1967).

Cuba

Whereas the connections to Cadiz were crucial in Guatemala, the situation in Havana was very different. Havana had advanced in the last decades of the 18th century to become one of the more dynamic centers for the production of sugar, an economic activity entirely in the hands of *criollo* elites. The advent of a sugar-based economy dramatically altered power relations among the elites, placing Spanish merchants in control of the monopolistically organized tobacco trade. Cuban elites achieved remarkable cultural and economic autonomy within the Spanish empire. They were keen on technical progress and new social techniques for the management of an economy that was heavily reliant on slavery. The privileged and relatively autonomous position of these elites, together with the anxiety provoked by the possibility of slave rebellion, partly explains the limited interest of local elites in independence from Spain. Under these conditions, it is not really surprising that Cubans knew about the existence and success of monitorial schooling even before the news in Spain attracted widespread interest (Moreno Fraginals, 2002). In August 1814, the daily *La cena* reported on the new system of elementary schooling and called for its general introduction among the "laboring classes," a term clearly excluding the enslaved population and only related to the white or "mixed" poor (Huerta Martínez, 1992, p. 388).

The *Sociedad económica* in Havana (established in 1792) also showed enormous interest in the model. In 1815, a year before the court in Madrid first considered supporting the system, associates became active in the issue (Corts Giner & Calderón España, 1995/96). With the establishment of a committee for education within the *Sociedad*, the interest raised by the new system of teaching found a more supportive environment. In its first meeting, held on August 2, 1816, its members discussed the necessity of introducing the model of monitorial teaching into local elementary schools and prepared translations related to the new system. Nonetheless, the efforts of the committee were dedicated to the fostering of "chairs" for political economy, chemistry, and physics (Cartaya Cotta, 2005) and to the establishment of a school of painting in 1817 (Lightfoot, 2002), rather than to the establishment of a monitorial school in the city. Maybe these priorities and the chronic financial shortages of the *Sociedad* were responsible for the lack of implementation of the ambitious plans for Havana and its surroundings as they were developed in 1817.[25]

I do not have conclusive evidence about the subsequent course of events. Intensive archival work still has to be done. However, the plans for the establishment of the first monitorial school on the island of Cuba were put into practice only after news came from Cadiz, possibly together with news of the Crown's approval of the system of teaching in Madrid. In January 1820, the first Lancasterian school opened its doors in Cuba (Huerta Martínez, 1992). It apparently trained some teachers in the management of the system of teaching,[26] although it did not survive the wave of political repression after the restoration in 1823 (de la Sagra, 1826). Members of the *Sociedad económica* saw the backlash against monitorial schooling after 1823 as responsible for the "lack of system" in elementary Cuban schools.[27] Like their fellows in Cadiz and other cities, they strongly supported the renaissance of monitorial schools following the liberalization of political life in 1832–1833.[28] During these years, Cuban liberals— not only from Havana, but also from Santiago de Cuba—maintained fluent connections with Cadiz, asking for manuals and school materials. On the whole, Cadiz did not play the same crucial role for the Cuban public as it did in Guatemala, but the impulse from Cadiz probably accelerated the concretization of plans.

Puerto Rico

A side effect of this "enacting" impact of the Cadiz school in Cuba was its further spread on the isle of Puerto Rico. Cuban elites maintained close links with Puerto Rico. Here, there were old political bonds, as Puerto Rico only became autonomous from Havana in 1811. The arrival of monitorial teaching in Puerto Rico, unlike the early Cuban interest, was part of a wave of liberal activism after 1820. The governor, the municipality of San Juan, and the local *Sociedad económica* looked attentively at developments in Cuba. It was the only place where they could find a trained teacher to establish a new school (Cuesta Mendoza, 1946). The local *Sociedad económica* was responsible for the organization and support of the monitorial school, but in close cooperation with the municipal authorities. The *Sociedad* helped the city council pay the costs of the schools for at least 2 years (*Junta general de la sociedad económica*, 1821; *Junta general de la sociedad económica*, 1824). Even during the second absolutist period, between 1823 and 1833, the system of monitorial schooling, which had decayed for political reasons in the metropolis, continued to attract some attention (*Junta general de la sociedad económica*, 1825).

Mexico

In the case of Mexico City, connections with Cadiz are multiple and significant, although it is difficult to assess their importance in any detail. Not only did issues of the manual from Cadiz circulate in Mexico City, probably leading to the early establishment of two private monitorial schools in 1819, but personal connections also played a major role. There was the case of the physician Manuel Codorniú y Ferreras (1788–1857), who, after having participated in Spanish politics on the side of the moderate liberals, particularly in Seville, lived in Santa Maria near Cadiz and accompanied the last Spanish official government to Mexico (Gil Novales, 1991). Codorniú, also a very active freemason, was a founding member of the famous *Compañía Lancasteriana* in Mexico City in 1822, a driving institutional force in the modernization of school policies after Mexican independence. The networks of another founding member of the *Compañía Lancasteriana* in Mexico City, Jacobo de Villaurrutia (1757–1833), reinforce the picture of well-connected members of the elite throughout Central America, Mexico, and the Caribbean. He had not only been an influential and high-ranking official in Guatemala City, where he had helped to establish the local *Sociedad económica* (Chandler, 1976), but he was also close friends with Alejandro Ramírez (1777–1821). Ramírez was a delegate of the Crown in Cuba, strongly supported the Cuban *Sociedad económica*, and translated writings on monitorial schooling himself (Jones Shafer, 1958).

Other Places in the South

Countless informal, unrecorded connections may also have played a significant role in the spread of the Bell-Lancaster-System to Latin America. Links between Buenos Aires and Cadiz, for instance, are apparent due to the reprint of the manual from Cadiz in Buenos Aires in 1823 under government auspices. The choice of the manual, probably made by the leading minister of the Province of Buenos Aires, Bernardino Rivadavia (1780–1845), was by no means compelling, particularly because Rivadavia and many other local policy-makers knew other manuals from the English and French systems (Roldán Vera & Trentin, 2006).[29] Also, the fact that the local *Sociedad económica* in the city of Manila (Philippines) published a manual of the system of mutual instruction with a similar title to the one used in Cadiz suggests connections between the two. I do not have evidence of a concrete connection in this last case, but consistent relations related to the improvement of the economy had existed between the two societies since the 18th century (Alzona, 1932).

COMPARING TRANSFER PROCESSES FROM MADRID AND CADIZ (1820–1835)

Again, a comparison with the impact of the work of diffusion organized in Madrid may be instructive in order to assess the specific role of the *Sociedad económica* in Cadiz in the adoption of the system in Guatemala, Cuba, Puerto Rico, Mexico, and other places. After the reestablishment of the *"constitución de Cádiz"* in 1820, Ferdinand VII governed only in collaboration with the liberal-dominated Parliament, which consistently supported all legal initiatives for the general introduction of the monitorial system in Spain and its colonies. Issued in Madrid, the royal decree of April 31, 1820, had ordered the creation of a model school in Mexico City, which was required to become a normal school for teacher training for all Spanish colonies in Central America and the Caribbean, and even for the Philippines. Probably because of the enormous distances, a further decree was issued on December 31, 1820, ordering the establishment of a separate normal school in Havana. It was to be attended by teachers coming from Santiago de Cuba, Puerto Rico, Santo Domingo, and Caracas (Corts Giner & Calderón España, 1995/96). Needless to say, neither the Mexican nor the Cuban school was implemented, and only in Guatemala, where local authorities showed some interest in sending teachers to Mexico City, did the project of these schools coming from the center attract the attention of the elites (Somoza Guevara, 1959). Direct transfer of a proposal from Madrid was evident only in the case of the Cuban town of Matanzas (*Plan y reglamento*, 1835).

Although the monitorial system of education came from England or France and many of its outstanding supporters knew the French and English schools directly, the paths of diffusion in the northern parts of Latin America often went through Cadiz. In all cases, the operations of transfer included an enacting moment. The movement of ideas through the Atlantic did not necessarily culminate in a more or less adequate copy of the model school in Cadiz. But it was effectual in the sense of the existence of coherent encouragement for the establishment of such schools. Sometimes, the news from Cadiz transported the first recorded information of the existence of the Bell-Lancaster-System (Guatemala); sometimes, the arrival of news from Cadiz seems to have accelerated "retarded" plans (Havana); and sometimes a combination of information and personal commitment rendered possible the establishment of associations for the promotion of monitorial schools (Mexico City). Other developments, as in Puerto Rico, but also in Puebla (Mexico), may have expanded the wave of this impact. On the whole, transfer is related here to mobilization of resources and to concretization of plans. In this sense, I speak of "enacting transfer." These enacting connections superseded, in many cases, the references to England and France, and inspired more activities than the celebration of schools situated in culturally unreachable settings such as London and Paris. Cadiz championed the centers of monitorial schooling, but not in the field of conveying messages that were also transported directly from these centers to the Latin American young republics, but rather in the field of animating and accelerating concrete actions. The political centrality of Cadiz, in spite of all present symptoms of economic decay and marginalization, played a crucial role in activating actors and, in so doing, in transferring the new model of schooling.

EXPLAINING ENACTING TRANSFER: ISOMORPHISM AND COLLECTIVE IDENTITIES IN THE CONSTRUCTION OF CENTERS AND PERIPHERIES

The processes of educational transfer sketched in this chapter did not lead to homogeneous outcomes. Processes of transfer were embedded in their respective contexts, where local conditions had the upper hand. Mexico City saw the early establishment of an influential society for the promotion of the method (*Sociedad Lancasteriana*), and a model for numerous societies founded in the Mexican federal states; the society promoted a consistent introduction of the monitorial system of education. By contrast, the fate of the monitorial system in Guatemala remained closely associated with the unstable political situation of the country without the anchor of a civil society. In the case of Cuba, although some Lancasterian schools were established in the main towns, the plans for the establishment of a Normal School for the island did not succeed, and in the middle of the century, local school policies leaned toward the anti-monitorial Catholic Church.

The isomorphism of actors engaged in these scenes of transfer contrasts with the variety of outcomes. All of them were members of elite groups, which had been marked by enlightened rational administration and a culture of commerce. They also associated often for purposes of economic, social, and educational betterment, as in the *Sociedades económicas*. The unreservedly positive reception of the model of mutual teaching, which encompassed a positive view of competition among pupils to attain the positions of monitors, concretely demonstrates a shared cultural horizon across the Atlantic, only disrupted in these years by the issue of political independence. On the side of almost all receivers related to Cadiz—Buenos Aires being an exception—social actors lived in regions of the moribund Spanish empire, and were certainly not the most ardent champions of independence. Central America and Mexico belonged to those regions that achieved independence only after military intervention, while Cuba, Puerto Rico, and the Philippines remained Spanish colonies until takeover by the United States in 1899. This geographical focus of the influence of Cadiz forms the core regions of a postulated common Hispanic-American identity that included early liberal projects of political reform, a perspective strongly advanced by scholars working on Mexico. Only under these conditions were the agents of lending and receiving able to construct the centrality of Cadiz as a point of reference in educational modernization. Cadiz became a symbol for political and educational reform models implemented in similar and well-known settings.

The enacting transfer of the monitorial system of education from Cadiz to Latin America was a particular process of South–South transfer insofar as a political periphery town outdid the central government in Madrid in conveying its message. Within the moribund Spanish empire, there had been many configurations of centers and peripheries (Daniels, 2002). In the time of the emergence of an early liberal Atlantic, where ideas, drafts of constitutions, and revamped representations of republicanism circulated widely, the construction of Cadiz as a center for educational transfer was indeed closely related to the politics of the time and to a phase of broad politicization and mobilization among the elites.

Both Cadiz and the Latin American colonies referred to here are located in the Northern Hemisphere. But they constituted the margins of a decaying imperial power, which was still a frame of cultural reference, at least among the elites. Processes of peripheral enacting transfer, here referred to as "South–South," are the result of a twofold construction. First, the lender pole has to be constructed as a kind of center, as a place associated with acceptable cultural authority and ascendancy. Second, receivers and lenders have to perceive one another as somewhat compatible or similar in order to facilitate transfer. This perceived or constructed isomorphism—in this case, still embedded in a Hispanic-American identity—is oftentimes used to justify why ideas and models should be transferred from one context to another. In any case, "Southern" actors construct their "North" as a point of cultural reference and orientation. Arab nationalists in Iraq did it in the interwar period (postrevolutionary Mexico), and *guerrilleros* also did it in Guinea-Bissau in the 1970s (Brazil). But in the first case, real and perceived differences hindered effective transfer, whereas the community of language, the vocabulary of liberation and revolution, and perhaps also the ethnic compatibilities between some Brazilian areas and West Africa may have facilitated actual transfer. The latter also occurred in the case of the associates in Cadiz and their contacts overseas: They not only constructed their centrality, but perceived commonalities also may have played a major role in the success of the Cadiz associates. Due to their own "peripheral" situation, social actors in processes of educational transfer in the "periphery" are certainly not only attracted by models coming from the "North." Practices and models stemming from settings perceived as similar and compatible may have been a more promising source of inspiration for educational modernization than the distant drafts coming from Paris, London, or even Madrid.

NOTES

1. Thanks to Jürgen Schriewer for suggesting the approach to the work of the *Sociedad económica* in Cadiz taken below. Archival and bibliographical research was made possible through the support of the German agency for research, *Deutsche Forschungsgemeinschaft*, for the project on *National Education and Universal Method: Dynamics of Global Diffusion and Culture-Specific Forms of Adoption of the Bell-Lancaster-Method in the 19th Century*, coordinated by Jürgen Schriewer and myself at Humboldt University in Berlin.

2. This term points to the different constructions of "world" in concrete settings, particularly relevant for the case of educational knowledge during the 20th century (see Schriewer, 2004).

3. On the decisive role of this device, see Caruso (2004).

4. For France, see the detailed work by Tronchot (1972).

5. For accounts from France, Italy, and Portugal, see David (1967), Previti (1985), and Veríssimo (2006).

6. See *First Register of Student Teachers at Borough Road, 1804–1821* (British and Foreign School Society, 1817, p. 21). Spanish and English sources give different time data for Kearney's training.

7. On the establishment of the normal school in Madrid, see Junta Protectora y Directora de la Enseñanza Mutua (1820, p. LXIII). A detailed report on Kearney's school, which replaces partly the archival materials lost from the Archives in Alcalá de Henares, is that written by Ramon Chiamoni for the Economic Society in Madrid. His report is available in the Archivo de la Real Sociedad Económica Matritense de Amigos del País (ARSEAP) in Madrid, dated July 18, 1818, section 262/12. The royal decree approving, recommending, and protecting the Bell-

Lancaster-System was issued on September 10, 1819. See the complete text in Gaceta (1819).

8. More information on the regulations for the *Junta Protectora* was found in the Archivo Histórico Nacional (AHN) in Madrid, Consejos 3597/5, fol. 31–32. The regulation is entitled "*Reglamento que para su gobierno interior y relaciones exteriores propone a S. M. la Junta Protectora del metodo de la Enseñanza mutual.*"

9. On the emergence of a centralized policy of pedagogical modernization between 1770 and 1810, see Caruso (2007a, Chapter 2).

10. For a general view of Spanish society in the 18th century, see Domínguez Ortiz (1986; Chapters 8–15). For the economic aspects of the beginning of a new kind of commercial and industrial dynamic, see Lluch (1973) and Ringrose (1996).

11. For a comprehensive analysis of this process, see Lynch (1994). On the uneven support to independence projects in Colombia, where some older regions remained loyal to Spain, see Sosa Abella (2006).

12. On the concept and history of the Atlantic as a specific space of transcontinental connections, see Bailyn (2005).

13. See Gil Novales (1980, pp. 1–4). Political radicalization continued in the years 1820–1823 (see Gil Novales, 1975, pp. 401–418; Butrón Prida, 2001). Cadiz in these years symbolized the European liberal resistance against late absolutism (Candido, 2001).

14. Some of these societies never worked, and their members did not pay their subscriptions so that many projects on charity, education, and promotion of industry were not carried out (see Ruiz Carnal, 2002, p. 61; Arias de Saavedra Alías, 1987, p. 157). On the membership of the economic society in Santiago de Compostela, see Torres Santomé (1979, p. 23).

15. The society collected some works on the monitorial system of teaching. See "*Inventario de los impresos que custodia en su achivo la comision de Educacion,*" available at the Archivo Municipal de Cádiz (AMC, caja 3419, exp. 14). One of the mentioned manuals in this list is probably an American one. This fact shows the extended commercial networks of the membership (British and Foreign School Society, 1817).

16. See the letter from José Joaquín de Mora to the *Sociedad económica*, April 1, 1817 (AMC, caja 3419, exp. 1).

17. See *Crónica* (1818, 1819). See also *Gaceta* (1818, pp. 1123–1125). A complete report on the first public examinations has also been published, see *Exercicios de Enseñanza Mutua* (1818).

18. See *Reglamento para el gobierno interior de la escuela de enseñanza mutua establecida en el Callejon del Tinte por la Real Sociedad Económica Gaditana de Amigos del País*, August 16, 1819 (AMC, caja 3419, exp. 8).

19. See the school reports of the teacher of the female school from 1830 (AMC, caja 1437, exp. 18).

20. See also the report of the local school inspector from 1864: "*Escuelas públicas: Resultado de las visitas practicadas por una Comision de la Junta Provincial, con otra de la local y vecinos*" (AMC, caja 2028, exp. 18). For a critique against the monitorial system of education raised only in the second half of the century, see Benot (1857).

21. *Escuela de primera enseñanza establecida en Baeza bajo la proteccion de la Real Sociedad Economica de Amigos del Pais* (AMC, caja 3419, exp. 7; see also Gaceta, 1820).

22. See the letter from José Mediavilla González to the *Sociedad económica*, June 13, 1821 (AMC, caja 3419, exp. 2). See also *Prospecto al público*, an appendix to the letter from José María Brander to the committee of education of the *Sociedad económica*, December 30, 1819 (AMC, caja 3422, exp. 20).

23. See *La Revue américaine* (1826).

24. Efforts seem to have been repeatedly initiated (see Thompson, 1829, p. 294).

25. See *Informe de una comisión de la sección de educación sobre el método lancasteriano para la Habana*, and *Plan de enseñanza que ha formado la referida comisión*, both printed in Real Sociedad Económica de Amigos del Pais de la Habana (1818, pp. 339–360; 409–412).

26. Petition of Juan Claudio Díaz submitted to the government of Cuba, November 22, 1837 (Archivo Histórico Nacional, Madrid, Ultramar 7, exp. 13, documento 2). Díaz describes his training in monitorial techniques in 1821.

27. See *La Cartera Cubana* (1839).

28. See *Revista Bimestre Cubana* (1832) and del Monte (1838).

29. Our argument varies slightly from Roldán Vera's and Trentin's, who assess the connection between Buenos Aires and Cadiz, invoking the work of José María de Mora. We found a very weak relationship between the Cadiz-born Mora and the *Sociedad económica* in Cadiz. At the same time, Rivadavia seems to have had family members living in Cadiz, where he died.

ARCHIVAL SOURCES

AHN: Archivo Histórico Nacional. Madrid.
AMC: Archivo Municipal de Cádiz. Cadiz.
ARSEAP: Archivo de la Real Sociedad Económica Matritense de Amigos del Pais. Madrid.
BFSS: Archives of the British and Foreign School Society. London.

THREE

South–South Cooperation

Past and Present Conceptualization and Practice

Michelle Morais de Sá e Silva

> It is increasingly fashionable these days to talk about South–South Cooperation. Is this another passing fad or is it a new trend, mirroring long-term realities? Is this just a by-product of the current disillusionment with the North? Is it merely a romantic notion, based on an "idealized" South that does not exist? Or is there far more to it? (ul Haq, 1980, p. 139)

When this chapter was being drafted,[1] something very similar to the above was written for its introduction. However, in revising the literature, it was found that Mahbub ul Haq had already written along those lines in 1980. The contemporary character of ul Haq's words reinforces one of the arguments advanced by this chapter: South–South cooperation is not a brand-new practice or trend. It is internationally more fashionable in current years, but its origins date back at least to the Cold War. During that period in history, Paulo Freire himself assisted a number of countries in Africa, China attempted to lead an autonomous Third World bloc (Steiner-Khamsi, 2006), and a battalion of Cuban teachers was sent to the newly independent socialist countries in Portuguese-speaking Africa. The latter were not sent to fight the capitalist forces on the battlefield, but rather to fight illiteracy in the classroom.

This chapter defines *South–South cooperation* as any cooperative initiative between two or more developing countries; it may be carried out by governmental institutions, nongovernmental organizations, universities, independent professionals, scholars, and researchers. Considering this, the chapter proposes that South–South cooperation has evolved through three different phases. The first phase, which comprises the period from 1949 (with Harry Truman's speech on the underdeveloped regions of the world) to 1979, coincided with most of the Cold War. It was fueled by strong political motivations and practiced by autonomous militants or officially provided by socialist countries. However, during that time, the most prominent aspect of South–South cooperation was its conceptualization as a means for developing countries' self-reliance and political strengthening. The second phase, which extended from 1980 to 1998, could be called the phase of demobilization, as a result of the debt crisis and structural adjustment that dominated the agenda of most developing countries. Finally, the third and current phase began in 1999, when the World Bank created the Global Development Network (GDN). In this phase, South–South cooperation has been internationally revamped, this time being valued not only by developing countries but also by international agencies[2] (IAs), especially knowledge banks.[3] Also, the meaning of South–South cooperation has been expanded and new flavors added to it. Under the auspices of international agencies, it has been significantly conceptualized as a means for "best-practice" transfer, to the extent that the expressions "South–South cooperation" and "South–South transfer" can be now used interchangeably.

But if South–South cooperation has existed since at least the "making" of the Third World (Escobar, 1995), why has it gained "international fame" only now? Why is it only now being promoted by international agencies and portrayed as an innovative development practice? This chapter will argue that those questions can best be answered through the concept of "externalization to world situations" (Schriewer & Martinez, 2004) and visualizing South–South cooperation as part of the practice of international agencies, particularly of "knowledge banks" (Jones, 2004; see also Steiner-Khamsi, 2007). Once the past and present of South–South cooperation have been exposed, the chapter will move on to examine some of the myths that have been built around it.

Overall, this chapter intends to bring together different conceptual frameworks that have addressed South–South cooperation and transfer from their own disciplinary perspectives. Mainly, it will utilize theoretical concepts from the field of comparative and international education, specifically the "borrowing and lending literature." Situated within current debates on globalization's impact on education, scholars who have contributed to building the borrowing and lending literature have asked new questions concerning educational transfer in a context of globalization. "Why did transfer occur? How was the transfer implemented? Who were the agents of transfer?" (Steiner-Khamsi, as cited in Rappleye, 2006, p. 227). This chapter intends to join their efforts by addressing questions such as "How has South–South cooperation been conceptualized and practiced throughout time?" and "Why is it only now recieveing such international publicity?"

Additionally, the chapter will bring in references and concepts from works on policy transfer, both those applied to education and to other fields. It benefits from perspectives in the fields of development studies and international relations, from which the term *cooperation* has been "borrowed." Bits and pieces from each of those research areas, rooted in different interdisciplinary traditions, can add meaning and clarity to the overall South–South cooperation picture. After all, "comparative and international education is certainly a diverse, multidisciplinary and ever-changing field to which contributions from many disciplinary perspectives have long been welcome" (Crossley & Watson, 2003, p. 20).

SOUTH–SOUTH COOPERATION'S THREE HISTORICAL PHASES

This chapter emerged from a puzzling feeling (or an "itchy nose," as Brazilian professor Carlos Pio usually calls it) about why South–South cooperation is now everywhere. Be it in the framework of international cooperation, development studies, policy transfer, or, in education, borrowing and lending, the fact is that it has attracted considerable attention from both scholars and practitioners. Such astonishment led to further investigation, which revealed that South–South cooperation is not a novelty of the present time. By looking back at its historical development, one can identify it as a practice of nongovernmental activists and intellectuals, governments and international agencies, taking different forms and being undertaken for different reasons at different times. One of the most common rationales for South–South cooperation is to strengthen poorer countries, identified as being predominantly in the South, against those that are stronger and richer, commonly identified as being in the North. Although there are significant weaknesses in this conceptualization, as will be shown, the chapter departs from the assumption that there is value in such cooperation when conceptualized as strengthening international solidarity against inequality and social injustice. The main focus of the chapter, however, is on the different forms and modalities of South–South cooperation over time.

Phase 1: Self-reliance and Political Strengthening (1949–1979)

South–South cooperation has probably existed since the very first independence movements in colonized nations. However, it was only in the 1940s that it acquired an institutionalized character. This was part of a revamping of international cooperation by governments in general, as a reflection of an overall attitude of rejection of conflict and cooperative predisposition to maintain peace in the aftermath of World War II. In the words of Edwards (1999), "the trauma of war and economic devastation did create the conditions in which the spirit of Wilsonian internationalism could find the political support it required. The stage was set for the birth of international cooperation" (p. 32).

As far as the cooperation between newly independent countries was concerned, there were three main driving forces for its consolidation in the postwar period: the intensification of independence/decolonization movements, the Cold War, and the emergence of the developing world as an entity derived from the idea of "underdevelopment," as first highlighted by President Truman's 1949 inaugural speech. Hence, "the making of the Third World" (Escobar, 1995) in Washington, D.C., in 1949 marked the beginning of a historical period when South–South cooperation could institutionally exist because the South, the Third World, or developing countries[4] were believed to exist and to form a homogeneous group.

According to a recent United Nations Educational, Scientific, and Cultural Organization (UNESCO) document, "SSC [South–South Cooperation] has its origins in the liberation and anti-colonial movements after the Second World War" (2006b, p. 2). Additionally, the Cold War and Truman's conceptualization of underdevelopment symbolically gave unity to those countries that shared a colonial past and were, at the time, taking the first steps toward industrialization. They constituted what was viewed as a single bloc over which the two superpowers desired to establish their influence. The creation of a Third World identity and the image of an in-between bloc created the conditions for the establishment of an alliance between countries that were—and still are—quite heterogeneous in their cultural, economic, social, and political aspects. Some found it preferable not to take sides in the Cold War dispute and formed the Non-Aligned Movement (NAM). In 1955, those countries that had adhered to the Non-Aligned Movement met for the first time at the Bandung Conference, excluding the participation of the Soviet Union, the United States, and Western Europe (Edwards, 1999). Additionally, in the framework of the United Nations Conference on Trade and Development (UNCTAD), the G-77 was formed and met for the first time in Algiers in 1967 (Nyerere, 1980). It was meant to be a group of developing countries that would vote together on issues discussed at the conference, especially in terms of ensuring that priority would be given to development issues and negotiating better conditions of trade for developing countries.

In that phase, South–South cooperation was conceptualized as a strategic form of international cooperation that could serve two purposes. First, if practiced in the form of economic cooperation, the enhancement of trade among developing countries could allow them to be less dependent on the developed world, so that they could achieve "collective self-reliance" (Amin, 1980). South–South cooperation was presented as an alternative to the traditional path of development that was tied to unequal terms of exchange with the North. From a dependency theory perspective, economic South–South cooperation could help release developing countries from the exploitative relations that Northern countries had forged since the colonial era. As these were the times when dependency theory was on the rise in the scholarly world, advocacy for South–South cooperation was not only practiced and promoted by developing countries' political leaders and diplomats, but also by scholars such as Mahbub ul Haq, Raul Prebish, and Samir Amin.

Second, when practiced in the framework of international negotiations, South–South cooperation was expected to allow for developing countries' political strengthening, enhancing their power to defend common interests and to push for a "New International Economic Order" (NIEO). As an increasing number of countries became independent during the 1950s, 1960s, and 1970s, the Third World outnumbered the First and Second worlds, which consequently gave them a clear advantage in multilateral negotiations where the rule of "one country, one vote" prevailed. This sort of collective action was, in many instances, spearheaded by political personalities such as Jawaharlal Nehru, prime minister of India at the time (Madeley, 2003), and Julius Nyerere, the first president of Tanzania. Nyerere once said that South–South initiatives such as the G-77 were the "Trade Union of the Poor" (Nyerere, 1980, p. 7). Mao Tsetung also attempted to bring developing countries together under his leadership. He formulated his Three-World Theory, in which he envisioned "China in the center of the South from where the anti-imperialist struggles against the richer nations was to be orchestrated" (Steiner-Khamsi, 2006, pp. 11–12).

In the social area, first-phase South–South cooperation initiatives were of limited scope, being either practiced by autonomous professionals or provided by socialist countries, especially Cuba. In the adult literacy field, Paulo Freire, the renowned Brazilian education thinker, helped newly independent Portuguese-speaking countries in Africa develop their national adult literacy policies. At the time, most of those countries had illiteracy rates beyond 70%, reaching up to 90% in the very postindependence years. Freire was urged by the governments of those countries to help them design policies that could cope with their educational needs. In his book *A África Ensinando a Gente* ("Africa Teaching Us"), Freire gives an account of his experience in Angola, Guinea-Bissau, and São Tomé and Principe

(Freire & Guimarães, 2003). He puts special emphasis on the issue of language diversity, which apparently was a major challenge for him. His educational philosophy places people's daily lives and problems at center stage, with a view to enabling them to reach autonomy and escape oppression. Therefore, for him, it was substantially challenging to assist in the design of national literacy programs that, for political reasons, were to be taught in Portuguese and not in the several spoken local languages. At the time, Freire was in exile and, therefore, this was not a sort of official South–South cooperation provided by the government of Brazil.

Actually, during that first phase, the precursor of today's government-to-government South–South cooperation in the social field was the Cuban case. Along with troops, Cuba sent abroad doctors and teachers, especially to those countries that aligned themselves with the socialist bloc, such as Angola and Mozambique. Its South–South cooperation strategy was marked by the "export" of large contingents of health and educational professionals, who were to be service providers in beneficiary countries. Although it can be stated that the kind of South–South cooperation in which Cuba has engaged has somehow evolved throughout the years (as indicated below), its "export of professionals" aspect has been maintained, being channeled to Cuba's main political allies. An article in *The Economist* recently pointed out that "about one in three of Cuba's doctors is working abroad at any given time" (2007, p. 35).

The United Nations General Assembly gave some support to South–South cooperation by establishing internal institutional arrangements and initiatives on the issue, such as the organization of the Conference on Technical Cooperation among Developing Countries, held in Buenos Aires in 1978.[5] The conference resulted in the Buenos Aires Plan of Action, whose implementation was to be monitored by the United Nations Development Program (UNDP), specifically by its Special Unit for Technical Cooperation among Developing Countries (TCDC).

To some extent, this was a vibrant phase for South–South cooperation, as different actors either practiced it or advocated for it. Scholars, especially dependency theorists, defended South–South cooperation as an exit strategy for the exploitative relations with the North. The governments of numerous developing countries practiced South–South cooperation in international negotiations with the aim to draw increased political power from it. Cuba did the same by sending doctors and teachers to countries that were fighting to establish socialist regimes. Individual professionals and intellectuals, like Paulo Freire, gave their own contributions to making South–South cooperation happen. All of this ended up having some repercussions within international agencies, but still at a very modest level.

At the end of the day, despite all the political mobilization around the idea of South–South cooperation during this first phase, little was accomplished in terms of producing the desired New International Economic Order. In the Cold War context, the room for maneuver and change was constrained by superpower interests. As indicated below, the following years represented a standstill for South–South cooperation.

Phase 2: Demobilization (1980–1998)

> The two decades that followed the Buenos Aires Conference were very difficult for most developing countries. Rampant inflation combined with a major recession in the big developed countries closed off expectations that the 1970s boom in energy prices could spread to other commodity exports of developing countries. . . . The 1990s brought little relief. (United Nations Development Programme, 2004, p. 8)

Years of large-scale borrowing of petrodollars left developing countries with a significant foreign debt. On the one hand, such borrowing had allowed for the "economic miracle" in a number of developing countries during the 1970s, especially in Latin America. However, in 1980, the United States decided to increase interest rates by as much as 20% in order to curb inflation. This increase trickled down to developing countries' loans (Stiglitz, 2006), making debt service the curse of those countries' economies. The economic hardships that followed the debt crisis initiated a more inward-looking phase. Consequently, a second phase emerged in the history of South–South cooperation, being marked by a fair amount of demobilization. As expressed by the UNDP in the above quote, most developing countries were absorbed in the 1980s with their own problems at home: unbearable indebtedness, sky-high inflation rates, and economic recession. Most Latin American countries were also deeply involved in re-democratizing their political systems, after two decades of military dictatorships.

Subsequently, during most of the 1990s, those countries were also busy with their internal affairs. This time, they were doing the homework assigned by the International Monetary Fund and the World Bank, according to the principles of the "Washington Consensus" (Williamson, 1993). The underlying assumption of structural adjustment programs was that developing countries actually needed less regulation and state intervention. Therefore, the idea of different states engaging in the generation of a New International Economic Order made no sense *vis-à-vis* the preached argument that the market was the one to tell what kind of economic order was to prevail.

The collapse of the Soviet Union was an important variable in this process. It changed the geopolitical order and the dynamics of international relations, extinguishing the value of an in-between, neutral bloc of countries. Besides, it became, for many, the concrete example of the failure of state-controlled economies and Marxist-oriented politics, both having been previously inspirations for South–South cooperation.

The institutions created back in the first phase—the Non-Aligned Movement, the G-77, and the Special Unit for TCDC—continued operating and following up on what had been decided in Buenos Aires in 1978 and in other South–South meetings. However, they no longer counted on the political mobilization of governments of the South, nor on the advocacy of specialists who defended the view that South–South trade was the way forward. All kinds of actors and advocates were, thus, demobilized. After all, the rationale was all about integrating world markets according to national comparative advantages and looking attractive to foreign investment. This was later the main propelling force for the replacement of the General Agreement of Tariffs and Trade (GATT) by the World Trade Organization (WTO) in 1995.

The phase of demobilization was also a transition phase. It marked the transition from a world characterized by the Cold War, Keynesian economics, and import substitution policies in the Third World to "another world" that came to be unipolar, neoliberal, and recognizably globalized. On the one hand, being this in-between space between the first and the third phases in the historical development of South–South cooperation, the demobilization phase was some sort of standby. However, it was at the same time the phase that engendered the forces that allowed the third phase to come about. After all, the "lost decade" of the 1980s and "the decade of conferences" (the 1990s) were actually also about political and economic change.

Phase 3: "Best-Practice" Transfer (1999–)

The unlimited belief in the "magic" of free markets and deregulation started to experience a drawback as the new century began. The adoption of structural adjustment programs in a number of countries of the South resulted more often than not in weakened systems of social security and social protection. In other words, widespread unemployment, poverty, and low-quality educational and health systems arose. This scenario had various political consequences, and all of them contributed to the strong international reemergence of South–South cooperation.

Once again, developing countries started mobilizing around the South–South cooperation agenda, as they perceived the need to bargain together at the WTO Ministerial Meetings. If they were to reverse the double standards in trade liberalization and advance issues such as the breaking of patents for HIV/AIDS treatment, they would need to organize against the powerful countries of the North, which were defending the interests of pharmaceutical industries. The first remarkable occasion when developing countries resumed drawing political power from South–South cooperation was at the WTO meeting in Cancun in 2003. They formed what was initially the G-20, then the G-23, and subsequently the G-X, as the number of countries that adhered to the group continued to grow. According to Madeley (2003), "developing countries sense that their cohesion will give them a new power to bargain for a better deal from world trade."

The revamping of South–South cooperation in this new century is also intimately linked to the fact that, since 2003, the election of left-wing presidents and prime ministers has flourished in the South. The trend has been most notable in Latin America, with the elections of Lula da Silva in Brazil and Nestor Kirchner in Argentina in 2003; Tabaré Vásquez in Uruguay and Manmohan Singh in India in 2004; and Evo Morales in Bolivia, Michelle Bachelet in Chile, and Alan García in Peru in 2006. These leaders were added to the group of leftist leaders who were already in power, such as Hugo Chávez in Venezuela, Fidel Castro in Cuba, and social-democrat Thabo Mbeki in South Africa. As these leaders took office, South–South solidarity became part of their governments' foreign policy agendas and, in some cases, South–South cooperation became an official strategic path, such as exemplified by the establishment of the India–Brazil–South Africa (IBSA) Trilateral Ministerial Forum (ICTSD, 2004).

On the one hand, this signaled the "renaissance" of South–South cooperation as it was conceptualized during the Cold War: a platform for the political strengthening of the developing world. On the other hand, this phase had something to add. For the reasons listed below, the concept of South–South cooperation was expanded and increasingly entailed notions of policy transfer—specifically, the transfer of "best-practice" policies and programs.

First, it became clear that structural adjustment programs had achieved poor results, at a high cost for people's standards of living. Those results, added to a mistrust of globalization processes, led to the organization of alternative development and counterglobalization movements in a number of countries, as well as across countries. Since the first years of the new century, those movements have manifested their capacity to gather considerable numbers of militants in international forums such as the European Social Forum and the World Social Forum. The "new social movements," as Morrow and Torres (2003) call them, have also demonstrated their mobilization capacity every time there is a G-8 meeting or a WTO Ministerial Meeting, the one in Seattle in 1999 being probably the most emblematic.

Combined with and also supported by this international mobilization around the idea that "another world is possible," strong criticisms emerged of the work developed by IAs (international agencies), highlighting their ineffectiveness in producing positive change in the South by means of development projects. As expressed by Sithembiso Nyoni from Zimbabwe, "No country in the world has ever developed itself through projects" (as cited in Edwards, 1999, p. 70).

Part of the efforts made by international agencies to improve their performance came in the form of support to "best-practices." Large-scale social programs came to be devised by developing countries as an attempt to clean up the mess left by structural adjustment. Programs that met IAs' criteria of good management were believed to be successful and, consequently, were given the label of a "best-practice." As Steiner-Khamsi (2004a) points out, "the design of best practices evokes associations with principles of efficiency, calculability, predictability, control" (p. 206). In 1999, the World Bank created the Global Development Network, which was intended to foster the transfer of "best-practice" programs between developing countries. This marked the chronological beginning of the current phase in the history of South–South cooperation, in which IAs, especially knowledge banks such as the World Bank, promote South-South cooperation as a means for "best-practice" transfer.

For instance, in the case of Brazil, some examples of "best-practice" social programs include the conditional cash transfer program *Bolsa Escola*, which has received strong support from the World Bank, the Inter-American Development Bank, UNESCO, and the UNDP; the national program against HIV/AIDS, which has been internationally praised by the WHO, UNESCO, and the World Bank; and the Solidarity in Literacy Program, which received innumerous international literacy awards from UNESCO (Morais, 2005).

The realization that some developing countries had been able to design good strategies to meet their social needs while other countries had failed to do so, especially the least developed ones, created the ideal conditions for international agencies to start operating as brokers of best-practice programs and to promote policy transfer in the South under the denomination of South–South cooperation. According to the definition provided by Dolowitz and Marsh (1996), *policy transfer* means "a process in which knowledge about policies, administrative arrangements, institutions, etc. in one time and/or place is used in the development of policies, administrative arrangements and institutions in another time and/or place" (p. 344).

Past and Present Conceptualization and Practice 49

Policy transfer can be seen as a response to critics who have blamed international cooperation projects for not being people-centered and being disconnected from people's realities. Thus, South–South cooperation could be the way forward, as cooperating countries are believed to have more similar realities and tend to develop more horizontal relations. Additionally, the assumption that South–South cooperation tends to be neutral and free from imperialistic motives brings political approval to it. At the end of the day, it is an appealing and "politically correct" modality of international development cooperation.

As IAs were not very successful in promoting the change they had pledged to achieve in some countries, they looked for programs that had worked somewhere else in the South. By means of "externalization to world situations" (Schriewer & Martinez, 2004, p. 31), they were likely to be more successful in persuading governments that internationally set goals were achievable and that proposed projects could finally yield the envisioned results, as they had already done so in developing country X. Thus, South–South cooperation provided the necessary "supplementary meaning" (Schriewer & Martinez, 2004, p. 32). In this case, however, externalization was not to world situations in general, but specifically to developing countries that were bearers of success stories and were to become reference societies.

Recent statements made in the framework of the United Nations exemplify this idea of promoting South–South cooperation as a means for experience sharing and "best-practice" transfer:

> South–South cooperation is traditionally viewed as encompassing technical cooperation among developing countries, with a focus on sharing of experiences or exchanges in capacity-building and technical assistance, and economic cooperation among developing countries, covering financial, investment, trade and technology flows. (UN, 2004, p. 1)

> Amid the perils and promise of globalization, South–South cooperation enables developing countries to share their experiences and successes with others. In particular, it provides a platform to cooperate on issues of concern to developing countries, from the struggle to eliminate extreme poverty to halting the spread of HIV/AIDS. (Annan, K., cited in UN, 2006)

> SSC [South–South cooperation] is a process whereby two or more developing countries pursue their individual or collective development through cooperative exchanges of knowledge, skills, resources and technical know-how. Linked by socioeconomic and political commonalities, the countries of the South have important lessons to share. (UNESCO, 2006b, p. 2)

Objectively, South–South cooperation recently became an integral part of the program strategies of international agencies such as UNESCO,

UNDP, the Food and Agriculture Organization (FAO), and Japan International Cooperation Agency (JICA), as comprehensively explained by Yoko Mochizuki in this book. UNESCO has adopted South–South cooperation as one of the strategic elements for the fulfillment of the UN Literacy Decade and the Education for All (EFA) goals. In June 2005, the UNESCO Institute for Education (UIE)[6] organized the conference entitled *South–South Policy Dialogue on Quality Education for Adults and Young People*. The meeting consisted of the presentation of "four outstanding national programmes on education for adults and young people" to representatives of 12 developing countries, so as to allow for an exchange of experiences and possibly the transfer of some of the elements of those success stories. In fact, UNESCO has adopted South–South cooperation as a tool within its overall EFA program and strategy. For instance, the 2007 EFA Global Monitoring Report states that, in promoting Education for All:

> The global leadership roles for UNESCO include . . . promoting South–South cooperation, particularly through the E-9 countries, in the areas of teaching and learning best practices, innovative financing and innovations in information and communications technology; and through exploring potential donor support for this cooperation. (UNESCO, 2006c, p. 101)

UNDP, in turn, renamed its long-existing unit for Technical Cooperation among Developing Countries (TCDC) the Special Unit for South–South Cooperation. The replacement of the expression "technical cooperation among developing countries" by "South–South cooperation" is further evidence of the additional meaning that the latter came to incorporate during this current third phase. The Food and Agriculture Organization (FAO) has also made use of South–South cooperation as a flagship for "best-practice" transfer among developing countries. Its Special Program for Food Security features "collaboration between developing countries through the exchange of successful technologies and technical experts. To date, 38 agreements have been signed—the most recent in July 2006, between Sierra Leone and China" (FAO, 2007). To some extent, South–South cooperation is no longer a flag hoisted only by developing countries. It is increasingly owned—and some critics would say hijacked—by international agencies.

In this third and current phase, traditional actors and advocates continue to give their support to the promotion of South–South cooperation. The governments of developing countries have officially made South–South cooperation agreements and have negotiated together in international forums. Cuba continues to send teachers, doctors, policies, and programs to its political allies. Different social movements have defended

South–South cooperation in the World Social Forum and in other instances. International and national NGOs have made use of South–South cooperation in their work. The differentiating characteristic of this phase, though, is that the "cause" of South–South cooperation has gone beyond the agenda of traditional actors. The epidemiological model, already used by the Borrowing and Lending literature in comparative education (Steiner-Khamsi & Stolpe, 2006), can bear some explanatory power in this situation. As in an epidemic, one could say that South–South cooperation has now reached the "burnout point": It went global and is no longer rooted in the political mobilization of the South. It is not an exclusive feature of specific countries (such as Brazil and Cuba), leaders (Nyerere, Nehru, Mao), scholars (Amin, Ul Haq), or organizations (G-77, Non-Aligned Movement). It is increasingly owned by international agencies and, in fact, has been adopted as a cooperation tool even by the North, by means of triangulation schemes. Japan is by far in the avant-garde of this movement.

THE INTERNATIONAL EDUCATION AGENDA

In a framework where development is no longer solely related to economic growth but is seen to encompass the enhancement of citizens' well-being, freedom, and empowerment, education is at the center of development strategies, and consequently is a target for South–South cooperation endeavors. South–South cooperation in education arose especially after an international agenda was defined at the World Conference on Education for All (Jomtien in 1990) and international targets were established in the form of the EFA goals (in Dakar in 2000). The determination of benchmarks in a framework of belief in positivist policy-making made room for the praising of "best-practices" in education. Crossley and Watson argue that more positivist assumptions continue to shape much social and educational policy and the mainstream of educational research and international development assistance (Crossley & Watson, 2003). Overall, they even state that "the World Conference on Education for All held in Jomtien, in 1990, marked what many saw as a new beginning in international development cooperation" (p. 94).

Recent EFA documents embody an overall trust in South–South cooperation (UNESCO, 2006a, p. 14). The group of E-9 countries[7] has been one of the main avenues through which UNESCO has attempted to promote South–South cooperation for EFA. E-9 countries have not only been recognized as crucial places for the promotion of universal quality education; they have also demonstrated internal capacity to design efficient EFA programs. They are, therefore, seen as important "reference societies" for other developing countries and, by means of South–South cooperation, their nationally engineered programs can be spread to other places counting on UNESCO's facilitation. According to UNESCO's *Note on South–South Cooperation*, "the E-9 Initiative has considerable potential to further develop South–South links, not only among E-9 countries, but also with other developing countries, and UNESCO should provide an umbrella under which South–South collaboration can thrive" (UNESCO, 2006b, p. 3).

At least in education, the expansion of the concept of South–South cooperation to entail policy transfer has not been limited to IAs from the North. Bilateral cooperation initiatives led by countries such as Cuba and Brazil have also involved some policy transfer. In the Cuban case, besides the "export" of teachers, South–South cooperation has also involved the transfer of social programs such as *Yo, Si Puedo* (YSP), the Cuban adult literacy program. According to Lindt, Aksornkool, and Heisohn (2006),

> YSP has been introduced in a total of 15 countries, most of them in the Latin American region, i.e., Argentina, Bolivia, Dominican Republic, Ecuador, El Salvador, Guinea Bissau, Haiti, Honduras, Mexico, Mozambique, New Zealand, Nicaragua, Paraguay, Peru and Venezuela. (p. 13)

Additionally, South–South cooperation in the form of South–South transfer has also been practiced by nongovernmental organizations (NGOs), such as the Bangladeshi BRAC and the Brazilian AlfaSol. The reasons why NGOs have engaged in South–South transfer are likely to be multidimensional and at the same time specific to each case, but there is no doubt that they have joined international agencies and some developing countries in building the current good reputation of South–South cooperation in education.

WHAT HAS CHANGED?

Bearing in mind this historical path that South–South cooperation has followed in the past 50 years or so, one might reasonably ask: What has changed along the way? One of the most evident and fundamental changes has been indicated above: The concept of South–South cooperation has been expanded, making it, in many cases, equivalent to the transfer of "best-practices" from one developing country to another. This is, however, intertwined with other equally significant changes that have occurred since 1949.

First, one can readily identify that the principal advocates of South–South cooperation are no longer the same. Whereas in the first phase the governments of developing countries were major advocates, supported by scholars linked to dependency theory and subaltern studies, currently South–South cooperation has, to some extent, escaped the "hands of the South." IAs (especially knowledge banks) have enthusiastically included South–South cooperation in their own agendas. On the one hand, this expanded advocacy network gives status and financial support to South–South cooperation initiatives. On the other hand, it entails practicing South–South cooperation according to the same fixed, standardized procedures used for North–South cooperation, which have failed multiple times.

As advocates expanded, so did the political motivations behind South–South cooperation. The original quest for Third World autonomy and increased international power is still part of the discourse, but now the rush for meeting all the countless development benchmarks has diverted attention to South–South cooperation's potential to spread "best-practices" worldwide and help achieve the innumerable goals and targets by 2015.

Finally, one of the most interesting changes that has occurred along South–South cooperation's trajectory relates to the "membership" of the North and of the South. Even though those categories have always been inadequate, their boundaries have become increasingly blurred. For instance, where should China be placed? Is it part of the "global South" or of the "global North?" What about East Asian countries and their "East Asian miracle"? And Islamic countries? Are they the new South in terms of constituting a "subversive" group of countries that refuse to conform to the dominating geopolitical order? Clearly, as the categories "North" and "South" are discursive constructs, they have not been able to keep track of the increased differentiation and inequalities among countries.

Another question that is equally worth asking is: For how long will South–South cooperation keep its prominent position in the development cooperation agenda and specifically in the international education field? As argued in the following section, this will depend on whether some myths around South–South cooperation will be deconstructed, whether expectations will be commensurate with the results it can actually yield, and whether it will not be framed and constrained by North–South cooperation.

DECONSTRUCTING SOME MYTHS

> The notions of underdevelopment and Third World were the discursive products of the post–World War II climate. These concepts did not exist before 1945.... Even after the demise of the Second, the notions of First and Third Worlds (and North and South) continue to articulate a regime of geopolitical representation. (Escobar, 1995, p. 31)

The above statement by Arturo Escobar points to one of the most fundamental critiques that can be directed to South–South cooperation: the recognition that the South is a geopolitical entity that has been socially constructed. Placing countries with diverse histories, cultural features, political systems, and social configurations naively under the same label can conceal more than reveal. According to ul Haq (1980), "The weakness of most proposals for South–South cooperation has been that they have tended to build grand designs of an aggregated, mythical South" (p. 141). For Meneses (2004), the idea of "one South" is brought by the modernization discourse and reinforced by international agencies, which "prefer to think of developing countries as a universe that is 'traditional,' uniform, and homogenized by poverty and by the numerous problems that are well identified by specialists from the North"[8] (p. 731).

This is not to say that developing countries have no reasons to cooperate among themselves. Quite the opposite: there are strategic political reasons why they can benefit from bargaining together in international forums. Additionally, experience-sharing can be fruitful if there is awareness about the limits of policy transfer. Instead of turning a blind eye to diversity, the recognition of each developing country's specific features can be turned into "capital," strengthening the "South" as a group of countries that have as many cultural riches as social problems. Therefore, the problem is not so much with the terminology (*South, developing countries, periphery*), but rather with the assumption that the label implies homogeneity.

The need to recognize diversity is intimately related to the need to recognize power disparities in the South. Bilateral relations between two developing countries are not horizontal, for the simple reason that power issues always arise in the relationship between any two countries. Additionally, vertical relations are likely to be even more pronounced if South–South cooperation comprises the transfer of a policy model from one country to another. "When knowledge is power" (Haas, 1991), the traditional teacher–student relationship occurs, one country being expected to teach its policy model and the other country to properly learn the lesson. In fact, the recognition and acceptance of the existence of power relations between countries of the South can make South–South cooperation more realistic, can call attention to some crucial issues when carrying out South–South transfer, and, equally important, can prevent future frustration or even accusations that it may be just another form of imperialism, this time imposed by the semi-periphery.

Besides homogeneity and horizontality, there is a third myth about South–South cooperation, which is recurrently expressed in statements such as the following:

> In certain policy areas, developing countries have much to learn from each other's experiences because of the sharing of similar structural conditions (global economic challenges, colonial legacies, failed institutions, declining social-economic contexts, etc.) and similar problems. (Lana & Evans, 2004, p. 191)

The above quote is representative of how South–South cooperation, in its current global meaning of South–South transfer, has been seen and justified. To convince those who find it unreasonable that developing countries may have anything to gain from cooperating among themselves and should better cooperate with the North, the argument has been that those countries have similar internal conditions and are plagued with similar problems; therefore, they should have lessons to share when it comes to policy-making. For instance, UNESCO's recent EFA Global Action Plan has reinforced this idea by stating that "cooperation among developing countries of the South has the particular advantage of sharing experience across contexts which face similar challenges, opportunities or constraints" (UNESCO, 2006a, p. 15). However, this assumption is flawed. Indeed, problems can be similar in terms of how they have been named: poverty, illiteracy, hunger, child labor, HIV/AIDS. However, the way those problems play into people's everyday lives and the way different social structures interplay with them results in different conditions or "policy environments" (Bryant & Kappaz, 2005). In other words, the elements that are conducive to or that constrain policy change and reform are, in many instances, context-specific. In each country, policy elites are subject to the influence of different lobby groups, count on different bureaucratic apparatuses to make change effective, and have different personal backgrounds, training, and ideologies (Grindle & Thomas, 1991).

Bearing in mind that South–South cooperation is currently conceptualized as South–South transfer in a context where the above three myths prevail, there is a significant risk that transfer may be carried out as the delivery of a closed package from one country to another (Morais, 2005). Hence, time, efforts, and resources should be allocated to make sure that transferred policies, programs, and projects are, as much as possible, tailor-made for the "recipient" country.

Furthermore, as South–South cooperation has gone global, it has become apparent that funding is a crucial issue. Triangulation, meaning the intermediation or facilitation of South–South cooperation by a Northern country, has been proposed as the solution for the funding handicap. However, it should be clear that triangulation does not only bring funding with it. It also implies inculcating to South–South cooperation the working culture of bilateral donor agencies, with their mostly results-oriented logic and managerial orientation. As a consequence, South–South cooperation would no longer represent a possibility for experimenting with alternative forms of development cooperation and would perpetuate "business as usual." In other words, taking South–South cooperation to scale without carrying out the needed changes in how most international cooperation projects operate brings the risk of further frustration in the future. On the other hand, because the lack of funding is a real problem, a viable solution could be the design of special and more flexible rules for triangulation schemes, in which developing countries are given more autonomy in carrying out their intercooperation projects, but at the same time are held accountable for the responsible use of funding.

Despite all of the above, this chapter will not make the case for equalizing South–South and North–South cooperation. Although the "North" and the "South" are discursive categories, there are reasons to believe that South–South cooperation does have special features. First, since the least developed countries have received less than a third of the Official Development Assistance provided by the North (Sogge, 2002), South–South cooperation can correct this distortion by establishing cooperative efforts between mid-development and poor countries.

At the same time, South–South cooperation may offer to multilateral agencies not only the possibility of transferring "best-practices" to the least developed countries, but may also help them adjust and redefine their relationship with mid-development member-states. Countries such as South Africa, India, China, Brazil, Mexico, Argentina, South Korea, and so on are daunting cases for multilateral organizations, because they face significant social challenges, but already have a pool of national experts to devise needed social policies.

Furthermore, South–South cooperation may have special features that are not of a technical nature. They may be subtle and may actually be related to policy-makers' perceptions and the level of mutual trust among those involved in the cooperation process. Jervis (1976), when arguing that cognitive factors influence foreign-policy decisions, relates perceptions to "decision-makers' beliefs about the world and their images of others" (p. 28). In the case of South–South cooperation, perceptions are not only important at the decision-maker level, but also at the level of all cooperation workers implementing a South–South cooperation initiative: lower-rank government officials, NGO workers, consultants, teachers, administrative personnel, and so forth.

In a hypothetical situation in which developing countries A and B are cooperating, the dynamics of their cooperation may be affected by the perceptions that cooperation workers in country A have about country B, and vice versa. In fact, this holds for any kind of cooperation, but the special feature of the South–South modality is that perceptions tend to be positive and there are fewer impediments for achieving mutual trust—not because social, economic, and political problems are the same, but possibly because working cultures are not as disparate as in the North–South case. Shared working cultures bring greater understanding among cooperation workers, reducing the likelihood of "cultural shocks" and smoothing the way cooperation is carried out. Government officials or consultants from developing country A working in developing country B will be less upset about having to deal with reduced Internet connectivity, energy shortages, unpaved roads, reduced working hours, and, very important, a different timing. This argument is certainly to be further developed. The dynamics of daily cooperation work should be looked at with greater attention by researchers, for cooperation or development workers play a core role and their perceptions and attitudes can have a crucial impact on the results of their projects.

In thinking about South–South cooperation practice, another set of questions remains for further investigation: Is South–South cooperation[9] less embedded in development discourse and, consequently, more creative in terms finding solutions designed to developing countries' social needs? Is it less imprisoned in mainstream development techniques and models? If that is the case, when triangulation occurs, is that freedom from closed formats and models lost?

CONCLUSION

This chapter examines the past and present of South–South cooperation, assessing some of the myths associated with it but also pointing to the real potential that it bears for development cooperation. Considering that South–South cooperation has come to be internationally celebrated, integrating the programs and strategies of international agencies and the foreign-policy agendas of a number of countries of the South, the chapter has attempted to meet the need for better understanding this modality of international cooperation.

In this framework, a historical overview was presented, mostly identifying how the concept and practice of South–South cooperation evolved in different phases throughout time. In the current phase, it keeps the traditional meanings of political strengthening and self-reliance, but also has come to mean South–South transfer. This additional meaning has been specially adopted by IAs, which have identified that South–South cooperation offers an opportunity to enhance the performance of their development projects and to reach the envisioned reforms in member-states, especially in the least developed countries. In this sense, the concept of "externalization" has been particularly useful in better understanding this process.

Added to that, the chapter argues that there is a need to be critical and reflective about current South–South cooperation, particularly when it comes to the myths of homogeneity, common problems, and similar contexts. On the other hand, it is argued that South–South cooperation does have peculiarities that can make of it an innovative form of development cooperation. Those peculiarities include greater attention to least developing countries; the redefinition of how multilateral agencies, specifically, relate to mid-development member-states; and increased mutual understanding and positive perceptions among cooperation workers.

Therefore, the chapter is a combination of pragmatic and critical analyses with a belief in the real potential of South–South cooperation and South–South transfer. About 30 years ago, ul Haq (1980) affirmed that "premises based upon wishful thinking will not long survive" (p. 139). Again, this chapter's thoughts and arguments go along the same lines. However, the major difference is that now South–South cooperation is in a new phase, one in which it counts on large-scale international support and can take advantage of the momentum to spell out what it can really offer to make international development cooperation more effective in yielding good reforms in the South.

NOTES

1. This chapter was written while the author was under the sponsorship of the Brazilian Ministry of Education (CAPES/MEC), Fulbright, and Teachers College's Partners for International Education.

2. The term *international agencies* (IAs) will be used throughout the text to encompass both multilateral and bilateral aid/cooperation agencies.

3. The concept of a knowledge bank emerged in 1996 at the World Bank's Board of Governors meeting (Jones, 2004; see also Steiner-Khamsi, 2007).

4. The geopolitical categories "developing countries," "Third World," and "South" will be used interchangeably throughout the text.

5. Note that those initiatives were not entitled "South–South cooperation" at that time, because such terminology was only created after "the South" and "the North" came to replace denominations such as First, Second, and Third World with the end of the Cold War.

6. This was recently renamed the UNESCO Institute for Lifelong Learning (UIL).

7. The expression *E-9 countries* emerged from the launching of the E-9 Initiative, which, in 1993, gathered the nine high-population developing countries

to promote EFA. Since those countries represent more than half of the world population, any progress they make in education has considerable impact on the aggregate worldwide progress toward EFA. The E-9 countries are Bangladesh, Brazil, China, Egypt, India, Indonesia, Mexico, Nigeria, and Pakistan.

    8. Quote translated from Portuguese to English by this chapter's author.

    9. When carried out by the South for the South, rather than via the North.

PART TWO

Modalities of Transfer and Cooperation

FOUR

Japan's Official Development Assistance Strategies and UN Conceptualizations of South–South Cooperation

Yoko Mochizuki

Madam Minister,
Excellencies,
Ladies and gentlemen,
    First, I would like to thank you, Madam Minister, for your kind invitation to this symposium of Global Transmission of "East Asian Development Approach." On behalf of UNDP, which, as you all know, has the development of Africa in its heart and as its core mandate, I am extremely grateful to Japan for its strong commitment to the assistance for our own efforts, both through your high level of contribution to UNDP and through your tireless efforts in bilateral economic cooperation. . . .
    UNDP has been promoting South–South cooperation with a strong support from Japan in the form of Technical Cooperation among Developing Countries (TCDC). . . . [T]he South–South cooperation has a number of advantages to complement North–South cooperation such as strong ownership of developing countries, sharing of appropriate level of technologies, best practices accumulated by developing countries, employment of Southern experts and strengthening of self-reliance in the South. Yet, it has limitations and constraints, including the weakness of institutional capacity to provide technical cooperation, limited resources and technology available. In this regard, great potential exists through Triangular South–South Cooperation. We are now promoting, facilitating and implementing such triangular type of cooperation involving Japan, Asian developing countries and African countries. (Diabre, Associate Administrator of UNDP, 2002)[1]

    The new emphasis on "South–South cooperation (SSC)" by the United Nations (UN), especially the United Nations Development Programme

(UNDP), cannot be adequately understood without taking into consideration substantial financial support provided by the Japanese government to the UNDP Special Unit for South–South Cooperation (SU/SSC)—formerly the Special Unit for Technical Cooperation among Developing Countries (SU/TCDC) and renamed in 2003—and changes in Japan's official development assistance (ODA) strategies. ODA has become the most important means for Japan to achieve its foreign policy ever since the country renounced war as a means of settling international disputes after World War II (Ishikawa, 2006). In 1954, Japan joined the Colombo Plan for Co-operative Economic and Social Development in Asia and Pacific and began providing technical assistance as a donor. Japan thus started engaging in technical cooperation while the country itself was a recipient of aid, humanitarian and otherwise, after the defeat in World War II. Counter-intuitively, it was not until 1990 that Japan finished repaying its World Bank loans. This chapter shows how development cooperation was used by Japan during the Cold War as a strategy to deepen its relationships with its Asian neighbors, and how SSC is now being used by Japan—through the UNDP SU/SSC—as a strategy to transfer "lessons learned" by recipient countries of Japanese aid to African countries, with which Japan largely lacks close historical, political, economic, and cultural ties. By looking at UNDP SU/SSC's and UNESCO's frameworks for promoting SSC today, the chapter will also explore implications of the UN's new emphasis on SSC, especially on triangular SSC in which traditional donors from the "North" offer "financial, technological and other supportive resources behind programmes conceived, designed and managed by countries of the South" (UNDP & UNFPA, 2004a, paragraph 4) and on "prime movers" of SSC—"advanced developing countries" from the South such as China, Thailand, Malaysia, and IBSA (India, Brazil, South Africa).

HALF A CENTURY OF JAPAN'S OFFICIAL DEVELOPMENT ASSISTANCE

From Technical Cooperation among Developing Countries to North–South Cooperation

On August 15, 1945, World War II ended and Japan came under the occupation of the Allied forces, led by the United States. Japan was under Allied occupation from 1945 through 1952, and in 1954, when Japan joined the Colombo Plan, it was still reconstructing the nation as a recipient of a substantial amount of assistance from overseas. Just around the time when Japan's technical cooperation in the form of trainees and dispatching experts began, Japan's financial assistance also began in 1954 in the form of providing reparations and "quasi-reparations" such as grant aid to Asian countries.[2] In 1958, Japan began full-scale economic cooperation by extending the first yen loan to India, independently of postwar reparations.

As MOFA (Ministry of Foreign Affairs, 2005) states in its brochure celebrating the 50th anniversary of Japan's ODA, "Japan's reparations and extension of yen loans in the 1950s and 1960s had the objectives of expanding export markets for Japan and securing imports of important raw materials, and there were high expectations of a beneficial effect from these actions for the Japanese economy." Indeed, Japan's aid practices in Asia played an important role in the country's rapid economic development in the 1960s, and it was not until 1972 that Japan introduced "untied" yen loans.[3] By the early 1970s, Japan's enormous trade surplus came under severe attack, not only from recipients of Japanese aid but also from the developed world. It was partly in response to Southeast Asia's criticism of Japan's export-oriented ODA that Japan embarked upon education cooperation in the 1970s (Kamibeppu, 2002).

Japanese "Hardware" Education Aid Until Jomtien

Until the World Conference on Education for All held in Jomtien in 1990, Japan's ODA in the field of education focused mainly on higher education, technical and vocational education, and vocational training, and it was mostly concentrated in Asia (Kuroda & Yokozeki, 2005, p. 10; Kamibeppu, 2002).[4] Kuroda and Yokozeki (2005) list three interlinked reasons for Japan's emphasis on higher education and vocational training that did not fall in line with the international aid community's focus on basic education such as primary education, general secondary education, and non-formal education (p. 10). First, according to Kuroda and Yokozeki (2005), basic education did not fit in with Japan's overall aid policy to support economic infrastructure development. Second, there was a general consensus among the Japanese people that basic education (in the narrow sense as primary and general secondary schooling) was the foundation of nation-building, and thus, Japanese policy-makers perceived it as a field "unfit" for external assistance. Third, closely related to the second point, because imperialist Japan imposed Japanese language and a Japanese education system upon its colonies and occupied areas before and during World War II, Japanese policy-makers deliberately avoided administering aid to basic education, reflecting upon the "mistakes of the past."

Significantly, since Japanese aid—technical and economic cooperation—began in tandem with postwar reparations to compensate for Japan's past aggression in Asia, Japanese officials—especially the Ministry of Foreign Affairs (MOFA) officials—were extremely careful not to be seen as an "intrusive donor" (Kamibeppu, 2002, p. 62; see also King & McGrath, 2004). Associating foreign assistance in primary and general secondary education with the donor country's (neo)colonial ambitions, Japan focused mainly on "hardware" assistance, such as construction of school facilities and supply of equipment throughout the 1970s and 1980s, carefully avoiding intervening in the "software" aspect of primary and secondary schooling of other countries. The notable exception was the Japan Overseas Cooperation Volunteers (JOCV) program, which dispatched many teachers to elementary and secondary schools all over the developing world.[5]

Japan's focus on "hardware" education assistance can also be attributed to Japan's Ministry of Education's failure to become a central player in Japanese ODA in the field of education. Monbusho or the Ministry of Education (currently Ministry of Education, Culture, Sports, Science, and Technology, Japan: MEXT) was excluded from the creation process of the Japan International Cooperation Agency (JICA), which was set up in 1974 to manage Japan's bilateral technical cooperation programs (Kamibeppu, 2002). JICA's education aid was shaped in the absence of influence from the Ministry of Education; JICA initially did not have an education unit, and the education sector was not even included in the Social Development Cooperation Department, which was a "blanket unit" created to "accommodate leftover minor sectors" (Kamibeppu, 2002, p. 73) that did not come under the jurisdiction of powerful ministries such as MOFA; the Ministry of Agriculture, Forestry, and Fishery (MAFF); and the Ministry of International Trade and Industry (MITI; currently Ministry of Economy, Trade, and Industry: METI). Kamibeppu (2002) argues that Japanese education aid accommodated differing interests of different ministries (*excluding* the Ministry of Education), namely, the interests of MAFF, MITI, and the Ministry of Health and Welfare in technical and vocational education (agricultural, engineering, and medical education, respectively), the interest of the Ministry of Labor in vocational training, and MITI's and the Ministry of Construction's interests in school construction and the associated equipment supply.

Japan's ODA Charter and the New Phase of Japan's Education Aid

As a result of consecutive medium-term "ODA Budget Doubling Plans" covering the years from 1978 to 1991, Japan's ODA disbursement reached $9.0 billion in 1989, which allowed Japan to surpass the United States ($7.7 billion in 1989) and become the largest bilateral donor for the first time in history (Kamibeppu, 2002, p. 57).[6] As Japan rose to the status of the largest donor country and maintained that status throughout the 1990s, major economic, geopolitical, and technological changes led the international development assistance community to review its aid policies. The end of the Cold War, the breakdown of the Soviet Union, and China's partial shift to a market economy marked the end of the dichotomous world of "East–West" divide, while the "North–South" divide was blurred by economic development in some parts of Southeast Asia, Latin America, and the Middle East.

In June 1992, Japan introduced the ODA Charter to formulate its ODA policies from medium- and long-term perspectives. The ODA Charter stated four basic philosophies of Japan's ODA, which were based on Japan's unique position as a country that had experienced being both a recipient *and* a donor of aid. One of the four philosophies was that Japan would attach central importance to the support of self-help efforts of developing countries toward economic takeoff.[7] The charter explicitly stated that Japan would provide all aid according to the principles of the UN Charter. Along with collaboration with UN organizations, the charter also emphasized utilization of knowledge and skills of developing countries as one of the criteria for the effective implementation of its ODA programs. In the Fifth Medium-Term Target of ODA adopted in 1993 and the Medium-Term Policy on ODA released in 1999, Japan shifted the focus of its education aid from the "hardware" aspect of assistance, such as construction of school facilities, to "human resources development" (*hitozukuri*), especially basic education. The 1999 Medium-Term Policy on ODA also stated that Japan would focus on the "quality," rather than quantity, of aid activities in the promotion of its ODA, and emphasized the importance of developing countries' ownership and their partnership with donor countries. At the G-8 Kananaskis Summit in 2002, Japan announced the "Basic Education for Growth Initiative (BEGIN)," expressing its commitment to supporting developing countries' efforts to improve the quality of their basic education. In the MOFA website, BEGIN is introduced on the "African Diplomatic Corps" page, under the heading "Solidarity between Japan and Africa—Concrete Actions."[8] BEGIN, therefore, marked a dramatic shift from Japan's traditional education aid practices, not only in the sense of being a departure from infrastructural focus but also in terms of geographic focus.

Japan's Commitment to African Development and the New Emphasis on South–South Cooperation

A dramatic shift of focus from higher education and technical and vocational education in Asia to basic education in Africa was an integral part of Japan's new ODA strategies, aimed at enabling Japan to play a more central role in international development cooperation. In October 1993, the Japanese government took the initiative to host the first Tokyo International Conference on African Development (TICAD), which emphasized, together with TICAD II in 1998 and TICAD III in 2003, "lessons from the Asian development that African policy-makers could adapt to their own contexts" (UNDP SU/SSC, 2003, p. 2). As an international conference on African development co-organized by the Japanese government, the UN, UNDP, the Global Coalition for Africa (GCA), and the World Bank, TICAD exemplifies Japan's commitment to supporting Africa, home to 34 least developed countries (LDCs) and 300 million of the world's poorest people, offering a platform for high-level policy dialogue between African governments and their development partners. TICAD III in 2003 confirmed the importance of "South–South Cooperation" and "human security"—the two concepts that the Japanese government is trying to mainstream in the work of the UN.

On August 29, 2003, Japan's ODA Charter was revised for the first time in 11 years. The new ODA Charter came to refer to SSC explicitly as Japan's ODA strategy, stating: "Japan will actively promote South–South Cooperation in partnership with more advanced developing countries in Asia and other regions" (JICA, n.d.). The 1999 Medium-Term Policy and the 2003 revision of the charter were in line with the direction of Japan's ODA policy, approved by the Cabinet in 1997, to decrease Japan's budget for ODA by 30% over 7 years, starting in 1997. Following the "bubble burst" in 1991, Japan suffered from prolonged economic stagnation, which made it difficult to justify a continuing increase in the volume of ODA. Despite economic difficulties and public criticism against the ODA program at home, Japan's ODA continued to grow in volume until 1997, and it was not until 2001 that Japan slipped from the position of the world's largest donor.[9] Japan's Medium-Term Policy on ODA, released in February 2005, again emphasized SSC as its important ODA strategy. JICA's Mid-Term Plan (covering the period from October 2003 to March 2007) also came to use the language of SSC: "JICA shall enhance its support for South–South Cooperation, which promotes Capacity Development in developing countries effectively and also leads to an increase in aid resources as well as promotion of intraregional cooperation" (JICA, n.d., p. 2).

While Japan's ODA policy after 1992 served to bring Japanese development assistance more in line with the Education for All (EFA) agenda and the Millennium Development Goals (MDGs), the new direction of Japan's ODA after 1997 until 2004 also corresponded to the general declining trend of ODA from the OECD's Development Assistance Committee (DAC) members that had begun in the mid-1990s (for the United States and Germany, it began immediately after the end of the Cold War). For better or for worse, Japan's ODA policy since 1992 has served to align Japanese aid more closely with international development assistance trends. At the same time, as evidenced by Japan's efforts to promote SSC and "human security" as important concepts that complement traditional North–South cooperation and conventional state security, Japan has also tried to characterize its ODA program as an innovative and commendable one that can serve as a model for other major Northern donors.[10] The Japanese ODA Charter adopted in 1992 and revised in 2003 was more than a deliberate move to demonstrate Japan's commitment to the internationally agreed-upon development goals; it was intended to demonstrate that Japan was entitled and ready to assume a leading role in the international community—to be more specific, to assume a permanent seat on the UN Security Council.

For several years, UN Secretary-General Kofi Annan and others had argued that the structure of the Security Council—currently consisting of the United States, Russia, China, the United Kingdom, and France as permanent members, and 10 rotating nonpermanent members—is outdated and should be made more representative of the 191 UN member-states today. MOFA (2005) prepared an eight-page brochure called *Reform of the UN Security Council: Why Japan Should Become a Permanent Member* to support Japan's bid to expand the UN Security Council in 2005, the 60th anniversary of the UN, but Japan's joint bid with Germany, Brazil, and India was, in the end, unsuccessful.[11] In this brochure that characterized the year 2005 as "a historic opportunity for a 'time of renewal' of the UN" (MOFA, 2005, p. 3), Japan is presented as a qualified candidate for permanent membership on the following four grounds: 1) Japan's role in the maintenance of international peace and security (pp. 4–5); 2) Japan's contribution to the financing of the UN (p. 5); 3) Japan's contribution to world development (p. 6); and 4) Japan's efforts for human security (p. 7). All of these four justifications highlighted Japan's generous financial contribution to the UN—to the UN peacekeeping operations; to the UN regular budgets, funds, programs, and specialized agencies; and to achieving MDGs through its ODA.

It is noteworthy that, in July 2005, in his "Message to Africa toward the G-8 Summit" at Gleneagles, Scotland, Japanese Prime Minister Jun'ichiro Koizumi pledged that Japan would increase its ODA volume by US$10 billion in aggregate above the 2004 net disbursement level by the end of 2009, and double its bilateral ODA volume to Africa by 2007 (to US$1.6 billion per annum on the basis of 2003 net ODA disbursement to Africa) (DATA, 2006, p. 72; UNDP Newsroom, 2006). This pledge was a symbolic act that not only demonstrated Japan's commitment to African development in front of G-8 leaders but also allowed Japan to pose as a generous benefactor to Africa. In addition to showing to the world that Japan is poised to assume a leading role in addressing international issues, Japan also has an immediate interest in developing allies in Africa—the largest regional group in the UN, with 53 member-states—in order to mobilize the 128 votes (two-thirds of the total member states) required for adoption of its proposal to expand Security Council membership. Seen in this light, Japan's commitment to African development and its emphasis on SSC constitute an integral part of Japan's ongoing efforts to expand its power on the international scene—not only economic but also political and diplomatic, if not military (although some suspect that Japan has ambition for rearmament).[12]

SOUTH–SOUTH COOPERATION IN THE UNITED NATIONS SYSTEM

In 1972, the UN General Assembly (UNGA) created a Working Group on Technical Cooperation among Developing Countries (TCDC). Two years later, in the same year that JICA was established to manage Japan's bilateral technical cooperation programs, UNGA created a Special Unit attached to the Office of the Administrator of UNDP to promote TCDC. When UNGA called for the Buenos Aires Conference on TCDC in 1976, the Special Unit was the focal point of the preparatory process. The Buenos Aires Plan of Action (BAPA) was signed by 138 governments in September 1978, and was endorsed by UNGA in December of the same year. After the Buenos Aires Conference, the Special Unit for TCDC was strengthened to deal with follow-up actions, and it was renamed the Special Unit for South–South Cooperation (SSC) in 2003. Also in 2003, UNGA declared December 19 as the UN Day for SSC (resolution 58/220). In September 2004, the UNDP Executive Board decided to make SSC a cross-cutting element in all its practice areas (UNGA, 2005, paragraph 70).

UNDP–Japan Partnership

Although the largest portion of Japanese ODA exists in the form of bilateral aid, Japan has also valued development assistance through multilateral development organizations. As is evident in the opening quotation to this chapter, there are close links between Japan's emphasis on SSC and UNDP's promotion of SSC. The UNDP Tokyo office's website is highly revealing of Japan's strategy to use the multilateral framework of UNDP to mainstream SSC within the UN and enhance the legitimacy of Japan's

ODA. Japan has worked with UNDP to capitalize on UNDP's unswerving legitimacy as the largest multilateral grant development assistance organization in the world. To borrow the words of the Tokyo office of the UNDP, UNDP's "comparative advantages and unique roles" include:

> 1) [its] global development network, 2) neutrality as the UN family, 3) the organization's coordination role in the UN system, 4) its comprehensive capacity combined with multi-sectoral approach and ability to deliver policy advice, [and] 5) its highly specialized skills and solid accomplishments in the development field (UNDP Tokyo, n.d.).

In the section entitled "UNDP and Japan's ODA," UNDP Tokyo (n.d.) states that Japan and UNDP share "similar development priorities," which led UNDP to establish "a particularly close partnership with Japan."

Japan has been one of the largest contributors to UNDP's core and non-core financial resources in recent years. In 2005, Japan was the fifth-largest contributor to UNDP core resources, with $82.4 million contribution, after the Netherlands, Norway, the United States, and Sweden (UNDP Newsroom, 2006). In 2000 and 2001, Japan was the largest contributor to UNDP core funding, and Japan's contribution of US$100 million accounted for 15.8% of UNDP's total core income in 2000 (UNDP Tokyo, n.d.). Ever since the creation of the South–South Cooperation Trust Fund under the Japanese Human Resources Development Fund (JHRDF) in 1996, Japan provided the UNDP with funds totaling US$28.4 million up to 2003. Contributions from the Japanese government and JICA account for 86.7% of the total of US$33.05 million of non-core resources contributed and mobilized for SSC between 1997 and 2003. In addition, in line with its renewed commitment to African development expressed at the 2005 G-8 Summit, Japan's trust-fund and cost-sharing contributions to UNDP projects in Africa increased more than sixfold, from approximately US$4 million in 2004 to US$25.6 million in 2005, and the government of Japan disbursed US$23.4 million to Africa through the UNDP in the first quarter of 2006 (UNDP Newsroom, 2006). Table 4.1. shows the breakdown of annual contributions for the SSC Trust Fund between 1996 and 2003. Whereas Japan continues to make substantial contributions as cost-sharing (approximately US$1.77 million in 2005 and 2006), it is noteworthy that China became the first developing country to contribute to the SSC Trust Fund in 2000, and its contribution has been gradually increasing to reach US$700,000 in 2006.[13] As will become clear in the pages that follow, in addition to Japan's financial contribution to UNDP SU/SSC, China's agenda to promote South–South trade and investment using the language of SSC holds a key to understanding the UN's new emphasis on SSC.

Table 4.1. Contribution of Non-Core Resources to South–South Cooperation (1996–2003) (in thousands of U.S. dollars)

Resources	Contributors	1996	1997	1998	1999	2000	2001	2002	2003	Total
SOUTH–SOUTH COOPERATION TRUST FUND (SSTF)	China					150	250	400	600	1,400
	Korea		200	100	100	100	50	50		600
	Ireland			37		27				64
	Ford Foundation					100				100
Subtotal			200	137	100	377	300	450	600	2,164
COST SHARING	Japan	2,000	2,000	5,015	6,000	5,267	4,500	150	3,500	28,432
PARALLEL FINANCING	JICA				98	109				207
	Rockefeller Foundation						50	67	40	157
	IDRC							400		400
	CIDA							320		320
	ITU								1,200	1,200
	Cameroon								170	170
Subtotal		0	0	0	98	109	50	787	1410	2454
Grand Total		2,000	2,200	5,152	6,198	5,753	4,850	1,387	5,510	33,050

Source: http://tcdc.undp.org/trustfund.asp

The New UNDP Framework of South–South Cooperation

> . . . a number of developing countries have become the world fastest growing economies, ready to scale up their assistance to LDCs [Least Developed Countries] especially in Africa, landlocked countries and Small Island Developing States. . . . South–South cooperation is indeed beginning to redefine the geography of trade, finance, investment, technology transfer and the entire development cooperation landscape.
>
> Madam Chairperson, supporting SSC and the work of the G-77 in this regard, is UNDP's long-term corporate policy. It is the very *"raison d'être"* of my Unit's existence, as the UN system-wide coordinator of SSC. (Zhou, director of UNDP SU/SSC, 2005)[14]

For over 20 years between its creation and the mid-1990s, UNDP SU/TCDC (currently SU/SSC) focused largely on promotional and supportive activities to popularize the concept of TCDC and bring TCDC partners together, rather than on operational ones. In 1992, in the same year that Japan introduced the ODA Charter, the UN Economic and Social Council (ECOSOC) invited all of its parties to give "first consideration to the use of the modality of technical cooperation among developing countries." In 1995, *New Directions for TCDC* was approved by the ninth session of the High-Level Committee on TCDC, and was subsequently endorsed by the UNDP Executive Board, ECOSOC, and the UNGA at its 50th session (resolution 50/119).[15] The *New Directions* strategy paved the way for a full-fledged UN scheme to promote SSC, recommending a closer operational integration between TCDC and Economic Cooperation among Developing Countries (ECDC), the identification of "pivotal countries" to serve as catalysts for implementing TCDC, and the promotion of "triangular cooperation" arrangements, under which traditional donors from the North fund TCDC. The *New Directions* report formed the basis of the First TCDC Cooperation Framework (1997–1999), which was followed by the Second Cooperation Framework (2001–2003) and the Third Cooperation Framework (2005–2007).[16] The Second and Third Cooperation Frameworks focused on activities that would support developing countries in dealing with challenges and opportunities of the global economic integration. In 2003, the Thirteenth High-Level Committee expressed the need to include ECDC on the SU/TCDC agenda (HLC/TCDC 13/2), and SU/TCDC was given a new name—SU/SSC.

ECDC refers mainly to SSC in trade, investment, and finance. Since the first United Nations Conference on Trade and Development (UNCTAD) in 1964, trade has been the main cause of tensions between the "North" and the "South." One of the major outcomes of the 1964 UNCTAD was the formation of the Group of 77 (G-77), an alliance of 77 developing countries for the purpose of pursuing common economic interests. While the number of countries joining the G-77 increased to more than 130, the original name of G-77 has been kept to this date. Although not a formal member of the G-77, since the end of the Cold War, China has become a supporter of the group's positions and has maintained close relations with the group. The association between the G-77 and China dates back to the preparatory meeting for the 1992 UN Conference on Environment and Development held in March 1991, when a position paper in the name of G-77 and China was jointly put forward for the first time. Since then, the level of China's participation in the G-77 activities has deepened, and cooperation between the G-77 and China has expanded.[17] The G-77 and China convened the First South Summit in Havana, Cuba, in 2000; the

High-Level Conference on SSC in Marrakech, Morocco, in 2003; and the Second South Summit in Doha, Qatar, in 2005, which resulted in the adoption of the Havana Programme of Action (G-77, 2000), the Marrakech Declaration (G-77, 2003a) and Framework of Implementation of SSC (G-77, 2003b), and the Doha Plan of Action (G-77, 2005), respectively. The current phase of SSC focuses upon empowering countries of the South to become effective partners with all other relevant actors in attaining the internationally agreed-upon goals such as MDGs and the targets set by the G-77 and China in the Havana and Doha Plans of Action. The appointment of former Chinese official Yiping Zhou, who is quoted at the beginning of this section, as the director of UNDP SU/SSC in 2003 may be interpreted as symbolic of the Special Unit's new emphasis on ECDC.[18]

ECDC has long been understood as conceptually distinct from TCDC in that ECDC aims at promoting development based on solidarity among countries of the South, rather than relying on development assistance from the North. With the end of the Cold War and the successful integration of the two Asian giants—China (the largest developing nation) and India (a country that has historically served as a leader of the developing world)—into the world economy, however, the emphasis of ECDC is changing from promoting South–South solidarity in the context of the North–South divide to facilitating the integration of the most vulnerable groups of developing countries—least developed countries (LDCs), landlocked developing countries (LLDCs), and small island developing states (SIDS)—into the global system, vis-à-vis promoting South–South trade and investment. How African countries, particularly LDCs, can enhance productive and trading capacities and attract foreign direct investment (FDI) from advanced developing countries in Asia has become one of the most important agendas of SSC. In short, the new UNDP framework on SSC aims at promoting the further integration of countries in the South to the global market. The 2003 Report of the UN Secretary-General on SSC focuses in particular on ECDC aspects of SSC and concludes that the concept of SSC is "having a positive impact on global, regional and national policies and actions relating to trade, investment, monetary and financial arrangements and on human development in general in the developing world" (UN General Assembly, 2003, paragraph 69).[19]

The current UNDP framework to promote SSC, the Third Cooperation Framework (UNDP & UNFPA, 2004b, DP/CF/SSC/3), covering the years from 2005 to 2007, has three programmatic components: 1) policy support to global efforts to enhance SSC (via strategic research and analysis, knowledge sharing, and support to policy dialogue), 2) backstopping country SSC initiatives undertaken by individual or multiple "prime mover" countries, and 3) mainstreaming SSC within UNDP (see Table 4.2.).

Table 4.2. Programmatic Components of UNDP's Third Cooperation Framework for SSC (2005–2007)

Three Major Components	Subtitles used in the Framework to describe elements constituting three major components
1. Policy support to global efforts to enhance SSC (paragraphs 25–28)	Strategic research and analysis (paragraph 26) Knowledge sharing (paragraph 27) Support to policy dialogue (paragraph 28)
2. Backstopping country initiatives to scale up SSC (paragraphs 29–42)	Promoting trade and investment (paragraphs 31–32) Promoting high-quality enterprise development (paragraphs 33–35) Mobilizing the resources of the global South (paragraphs 36–37) • Facilitating remittances and diversifying application (37) • Skill development through émigré expertise and capacities (38) South–South solutions to combat HIV/AIDS (paragraphs 39–40) Food Security (paragraph 41)
3. Mainstreaming SSC in the work of UNDP (paragraphs 43–45)	N/A

Source: UNDP & UNFPA, 2004b

The concept of "prime movers" is presented as an evolution of the concept of "pivotal countries" that was first introduced in the *New Direction* strategy in 1995. In November 2003, China hosted the High-Level Meeting of Pivotal Countries for South–South and Triangular Cooperation in Hangzhou (see Table 4.3. for the list of pivotal countries). This meeting stressed the special needs of LDCs and discussed several initiatives to help LDCs derive benefit from the enhanced capacity of the South in the fields of trade, investment, and capacity development. Among the pivotal countries, UNDP identified China, India, Malaysia, Thailand, South Africa, and Brazil as "prime mover" countries that are willing to take the lead (UNDP & UNFPA, 2004a, DP/2004/26).

Although fighting HIV/AIDS and ensuring food safety are highlighted as important areas in which "prime movers" are undertaking or will undertake SSC initiatives (UNDP & UNFPA, 2004b, paragraph 39–41), ECDC

Table 4.3. Comparison of UNESCO's E-9 Countries and UNDP's Pivotal Countries for South–South Cooperation

Region	UNESCO's E-9 Countries	UNDP's 26 "Pivotal Countries" for SSC	
Asia and the Pacific	Bangladesh **China** **India** **Indonesia** **Pakistan**	**China*** **India*** **Indonesia** Malaysia* **Pakistan**	Republic of Korea Singapore Thailand*
Africa	**Nigeria**	Ghana Mauritius **Nigeria**	Senegal South Africa*
Latin America and the Caribbean	**Brazil** **Mexico**	Argentina **Brazil*** Chile Colombia Costa Rica	Cuba **Mexico** Peru Trinidad and Tobago
Arab states and Europe	**Egypt**	**Egypt** Malta	Tunisia Turkey

Sources: UNESCO, 2006a; JICA, 2006; UNDP SU/SSC, 2003

Note: Countries included in both UNESCO's E-9 countries and UNDP's pivotal countries for SSC are in boldface. Among "pivotal countries," those that are reported to have expressed their wish to serve as "prime movers" in DP/2004/26 are marked with asterisks (*). UNDP SU/SSC (2003) also lists Cyprus, Poland, and Venezuela as "pivotal countries," making the total number of such countries 29, but I included only 26 in the table, based on JICA's (2006) data.

initiatives have a bigger presence than TCDC initiatives in the Third Cooperation Framework. Today, UNDP SU/SSC's "flagship" programs include initiatives to promote Asia–Africa economic linkages. One example is the China–Africa Business Council (CABC), a joint initiative launched in 2005 among UNDP, the Chinese government, and the China Guangcai Program, a nongovernmental organization that was established in 1994 by Chinese entrepreneurs to promote private-sector investment in poverty-stricken regions of the country.[20] With strong support from the governments of

Malaysia and Singapore, UNDP Malaysia has also promoted Asia–Africa business cooperation through various activities, including the Asia–Africa Business Forum, which "seeks to encourage the formation of direct commercial joint ventures between businesses in the two regions" (UNDP & UNFPA, 2004b, DP/CF/SSC/3, paragraph 33). The 1999 Asia–Africa Business Forum was opened by Prime Minister Mahathir Mohamad of Malaysia and supported through a triangular arrangement with the Japan Human Resources Fund.

In addition to promoting South–South trade and investment, UNDP SU/SSC calls for mobilizing the resources of the "global South"—"expatriate communities from the South resident in industrialized countries of the North" (UNDP & UNFPA, 2004b, paragraph 33). The mobilization strategy is devised in terms of facilitating the transfer of financial resources (remittances) and human resources (expertise and capacities in modern technological skills) from émigré communities to developing countries. Characterizing "better utilization of the resources of the global south as part of an extended form of South–South cooperation" (UNDP & UNFPA, 2004b, paragraph 36), UNDP SU/SSC is promoting a one-way transfer of money and other resources from the "global South" (remitting populations) to developing countries in the name of SSC, albeit with an eventual goal of enabling the poor South to become effective partners in achieving development. This "extended form of SSC" makes a huge departure from the more "traditional" forms of SSC that involve bidirectional exchanges of knowledge, skills, and technical know-how.

With the goal of broadening the SSC landscape, UNDP has incorporated new initiatives to facilitate South–South trade, investment, and monetary and financial arrangements into its framework to promote SSC in recent years. Many of these ECDC initiatives are predicated on the idea that accelerating Asian trade and investment in Africa holds bright promise for Africa's development. As the title of the recent World Bank book *Africa's Silk Road: China and India's New Economic Frontier* (Broadman, 2006) indicates, both India's and China's newfound interest in trade and investment with Africa is interpreted by major international development organizations as representing an important opportunity for Africa's integration into the global economy. The meaning of SSC is changing from cooperation among uniformly poor developing countries to cooperation between the rich South (including both "prime mover" countries and the "global South") and the poor South. As pointed out in the 2003 Marrakech Declaration on SSC and repeated in the UNDP's Third Cooperation Framework for SSC, what makes "beneficial exchanges" among developing countries is not so much affinity and solidarity among them but "the emergence of a differentiation in capacities and performances among countries of the

South" (UNDP & UNFPA 2004b, paragraph 9). It is precisely the vast and growing disparities within the South that gave the necessary political impetus for mainstreaming ECDC in the work of UNDP and reconceptualizing South–South trade, investment, commerce, and financial and monetary cooperation as indispensable parts of SSC.

UNESCO's Response: Mainstreaming South–South Cooperation into the EFA Movement

> SSC is a process whereby two or more developing countries pursue their individual or collective development through cooperative exchanges of knowledge, skills, resources and technical know-how. Linked by socioeconomic and political commonalities, the countries of the South have important lessons to share. SSC is built on the principles of fraternity, equality and solidarity. It is a multidimensional process, which can be bilateral or multilateral in scope and subregional, regional or interregional in character. SSC is an important complement to traditional North–South development cooperation. It constitutes a solidarity mechanism among developing countries in order to achieve common goals. (UNESCO, June 2006c, paragraph 3)

It is quite recently that UNESCO has begun to use the language of SSC explicitly. With its emphasis on "fraternity, equality, and solidarity" among developing countries, the UNESCO discourse on SSC has quite a different tone from that of the mainstream UNDP discourse on SSC. Given the history of controversy surrounding UNESCO and the critique of UNESCO as a platform for East–South alliances (communist and Third World countries) to attack the North/West, it is plausible that UNESCO consciously avoided using the language of SSC until the G-77 and China, in the 2005 Doha Plan of Action, urged UNESCO to develop and implement programs for SSC in science and technology and education. It is also plausible that UNESCO belatedly decided to use the concept of SSC simply because SSC became too mainstreamed to be ignored by UNESCO. In fact, UNESCO's (2006c) official document manifests a shallow understanding of the history of TCDC and ECDC, misrepresenting ECDC as "economic cooperation and development" (paragraph 6). Whether based on deliberate considerations or merely in response to the new "buzzword" in development cooperation, between January and August 2006, at least four official documents on SSC came out of UNESCO (UNESCO, 2006a, 2006b, 2006c, 2006d). In August 2006, the Executive Board of UNESCO (2006d) requested the EFA convening agencies (UNESCO, UNDP, UNFPA, UNICEF, and the World Bank) to "take specific measures to strengthen and link existing network of South–South Cooperation in EFA" by mid-2007 (p. 18, paragraph 56).

Pressures for UNESCO to address SSC explicitly came not only from the outside of the organization but also from the inside. Japan's Ministry of Education (MEXT), largely excluded from the provision of Japanese bilateral education aid through JICA, has been engaged in education aid through the multilateral framework of UNESCO, mainly focusing on basic education in Asia. After the formulation of Japan's ODA Charter in 1992, however, there does not seem to have been any move on the part of MEXT to push UNESCO to use the language of SSC. This may be attributed to the MEXT's traditional unwillingness to use aid to promote Japan's national interests from a trade or a foreign policy perspective. Describing how MEXT was excluded from the JICA creation process, Kamibeppu (2002) observed that MEXT officials "disliked the economic cooperation-focused and profit-driven nature" (p. 80) of MOFA- and JICA-based ODA. It was the appointment of Koichiro Matsuura, a MOFA official who had served as Japan's ambassador to France (1994–1999), as the director-general of UNESCO on November 12, 1999, that finally broke UNESCO's silence on SSC.[21] Nine months after becoming the head of UNESCO, at the E-9 Ministerial Review Meeting in Beijing in August 2000, Matsuura pointed out that "the E-9 initiative provides a chance to engage in genuine SSC" (UNESCO, 2006c, paragraph 11). The E-9 Initiative was launched in New Delhi, India, in 1993, on the occasion of the EFA Summit of the Nine High-Population Countries—Bangladesh, Brazil, China, Egypt, India, Indonesia, Mexico, Nigeria, and Pakistan—to provide their citizens with basic education as a human right and as a means to curb population growth. In view of the fact that those nine countries represent more than half of the world's population, the E-9 group established itself as a political lobby to achieve EFA. Three years after his first call for SSC, at the E-9 Ministerial Review Meeting in Cairo in December 2003, Director-General Matsuura again pointed out the potential of the E-9 initiative to serve as a mechanism for SSC.

Five months after the Second South Summit in Doha, the High-Level Group Meeting on EFA was held in Beijing in November 2005. In belated response to Director-General Matsuura's calls for SSC, and rather quickly responding to the G-77 and China's recommendation for UNESCO to develop and implement SSC programs, the High-Level Group Meeting on EFA requested "UNESCO and the other EFA partners to encourage and support South–South cooperation, mutual learning and exchange at the regional level, including strengthening the E-9 network and other groupings as platforms for doing so" (as quoted in UNESCO, 2006c, paragraph 12). As shown in Table 4.3., with the exception of Bangladesh, the E-9 countries are also "pivotal countries" in the UNDP's SSC framework. Given the overlap of E-9 countries and "pivotal countries," it is no surprise that

UNESCO proposed to "use the E-9 mechanism to facilitate SSC and to give new tasks to the E-9 Secretariat in UNESCO's Education Sector which will handle both E-9 matters and SSC, including the responsibility to coordinate and administer the proposed SSC programme/fund" (UNESCO, 2006a, paragraph 11).

In addition to making substantial financial contribution to the SSC Trust Fund (see Table 4.1.) and undertaking SSC initiatives as a "prime mover" country in close collaboration with UNDP, China is embarking on SSC in education. At the High-Level Group Meeting on EFA in Beijing in 2005, China launched initiatives "to donate US$1 million to education research and training projects in Africa, to expand the enrolment of students from developing countries in Chinese universities, and to increase financial support to countries stricken by national disasters" (UNESCO, 2006c, paragraph 12). UNESCO (2006c) commended these initiatives as setting a "powerful example of SSC" (paragraph 12). Since UNESCO subscribes to the conventional notion of SSC, which emphasizes "fraternity, equality, and solidarity," the UNESCO framework to promote SSC may well serve to underplay China's far-from-altruistic motives to engage in SSC—SSC in education as well as South–South trade and investment. The postwar history of Japanese ODA clearly demonstrates that education cooperation is no less affected by broader political and economic interests of the donor than economic and technical cooperation is. Whereas the history of Japan as an aggressor made Japanese officials very careful in administering education aid to Asian countries to avoid being accused of being an "intrusive donor," China has no need to be cautious in providing aid to African countries, especially with the endorsement from UNESCO. Although it is too early to evaluate UNESCO's SSC framework, UNESCO's seemingly opportunistic embrace of the concept of SSC might have significant ramifications for international educational cooperation in the future.

CONCLUSION

The Asian nations thus far have exercised ownership to achieve development, now becoming donors of aid rather than recipients. At the end of the day, ownership, or taking initiative yourself to forge development is crucial. For the developing countries to exercise ownership in social and economic progress, human resource development is an indispensable prerequisite. . . . Japan would like to support the South–South, or Asia-to-Africa Cooperation, to share with our African friends, the experience and wisdom of the Asian countries in achieving this economic growth amidst the globalization of the world economy. (Mizuno, Parliamentary Secretary for Foreign Affairs of Japan, 2002)

Since many of the recipient countries of Japanese aid had achieved "development" by the time Japan rose to the position of the largest donor country, Japan needed a new aid scheme that would allow it to achieve its broader goals in foreign relations, including attaining UN Security Council permanent membership. In its efforts to articulate Official Development Assistance (ODA) policies, Japan came to characterize itself as perfectly positioned to promote South–South Cooperation (SSC) as a form of development assistance it had once practiced and as an effective means to transfer "lessons learned" by recipients of Japanese aid to African countries. SSC became a new scheme that came to be highlighted in Japan's ODA Charter, adopted in 1992 and revised in 2003.

Historically, support to South–South exchanges by the UN system dates back to the 1970s, following the adoption of the Buenos Aires Plan of Action at the United Nations Conference on Technical Cooperation among Developing Countries (TCDC). The new emphasis on SSC by UNDP, however, cannot be adequately understood without taking into consideration substantial financial support provided by the Japanese government to the UNDP SU/SSC—formerly SU/TCDC—and emerging donors' interest in South–South trade and investment. Since 1997, the work of UNDP SU/SSC has been programmed within a cooperation framework that takes into account major economic, geopolitical, and technological changes that are reshaping the world. Precisely because there is broad international consensus on the renewed importance of SSC as a form of development cooperation, mainstreaming SSC through the multilateral framework of the UN has become Japan's strategy to legitimize its aid. The UNDP and UNESCO frameworks to promote SSC—however it is conceptualized—seem to have emerged at least partly in response to the Japanese government's agenda to use the language of SSC to defuse the international community's skepticism about Japan's contribution to international development cooperation.[22]

Engagement in SSC has always contributed to advancing the Japanese government's goal of establishing itself as a "first-class" developed country in the international community. Whereas SSC was first used to refer to cooperation between Japan and its Asian neighbors or cooperation between Asian recipient countries of Japanese aid, the same term is now mostly used to signify trilateral or triangular cooperation where Japan and another country (most often, an "advanced" developing country in Asia) collaborate to help a third country. It is becoming increasingly difficult for Japan to be recognized as a leading, respected donor without contributing to development in Africa—the only continent mostly left behind in the global development trend after the disintegration of Soviet Union. Japan's pioneering efforts to promote triangular cooperation (Asia-to-Africa cooperation with Japanese finance) and its promotion of SSC both bilaterally through JICA and multilaterally through UNDP are part of the grand plans of Japan to claim legitimately that it does contribute to African development and the internationally committed development goals such as poverty reduction and universal basic education.

Redressing imbalances, eliminating poverty, and assuring peace and stability are outstanding challenges that are shared responsibilities. Could SSC be an instrument for ending the division of our world into areas of wealth and material comfort and areas of agonizing poverty? The growing maturity and expansion of markets in the South are being welcomed by the traditional donors from the North as presenting new economic frontiers. At the same time, there are concerns that emerging donors may undercut the position of traditional donors who insist on higher requirements for good governance, environmental appraisal, and human rights standards (see, for example, Manning, 2006). For better or worse, the current UN frameworks to promote SSC are giving the self-designated "prime mover" countries of SSC such as China and India a superb justification for their profit-driven efforts to promote South–South economic exchanges.

NOTES

1. The United Nations Development Programme (UNDP), the United Nations' global development network, is the largest multilateral source of development assistance in the world. The UNDP is an executive board within the United Nations Economic and Social Council (ECOSOC). The UNDP Administrator is the third-highest-ranking member of the United Nations after the United Nations Secretary-General and the Deputy Secretary-General. The UNDP Associate Administrator is the second-highest-ranking member of the UNDP, and during meetings of the UN Development Group (UNDG), which are chaired by the Administrator, UNDP is represented by the Associate Administrator.

2. Japan's reparation issue was resolved by the 1951 San Francisco Peace Treaty and other bilateral treaties that Japan signed. Japan's financial cooperation dates back to October 1954, when the Japan–Burma Peace Treaty and Agreement on Reparations and Economic Cooperation was signed. Following this arrangement, Japan signed reparation treaties with the Philippines, Indonesia, and the Republic of Vietnam, and provided Cambodia, Laos, Thailand, Malaysia, Singapore, Korea, and Micronesia with "quasi-reparations." As MOFA (n.d. (a))

puts it, "[the] historical background of Japan's financial assistance—starting as providing reparations and economic cooperation in tandem therewith to Asian countries—combined with the basic policy of placing emphasis on providing cooperation for Asian countries that have close links with Japan, became the model of the subsequent Asia focus of Japan's ODA." Since the People's Republic of China was not party to the San Francisco Peace Treaty, Japan normalized its relations with China by concluding a joint communiqué in 1972 and a bilateral peace treaty in 1978. China forfeited its reparation rights when it signed the joint communiqué. Partly in compensation for their forfeited reparation rights, Japan has provided a total of US$30 billion ODA to China.

3. "Tied" means that aid funds from donor countries given to a developing country must be used to procure goods and services from companies and/or organizations in a specified country. Under "untied" conditions, no procurement is mandated from any specific country. Until the end of the 1960s, the tied aid rate accounted for almost 100% of Japan's aid.

4. Well-known examples of Japan's educational cooperation projects include Jomo Kenyatta University of Agriculture and Technology (JKUAT) in Kenya and the King Mongkut's Institute of Technology Ladkrabang (KMITL) in Thailand. In 1977, based on the request of the Kenyan government, Japan started technical cooperation for vocational training programs in agriculture and technology, while donating grant aid for building school facilities and providing the necessary equipment for academic work at the school. About 15 years after such "educational cooperation" started, the institution has been turned into the fifth national university in Kenya, JKUAT. In 2002, a new project was launched to transfer JKUAT's achievements to other parts of Africa in the framework of the African Institute for Capacity Development (AICAD). Japan supported the AICAD facilities situated in JKUAT. AICAD is an autonomous institute dedicated to poverty reduction in Africa through capacity development, and it is organized as a joint venture among the three countries of East Africa (Kenya, Uganda, and Tanzania), with the support of the government of Japan.

5. The JOCV program is comparable to the United States' Peace Corps, which was set up in 1961. In fact, on October 25, 2005, JICA and the Peace Corps signed a Memorandum of Understanding to improve their activities by jointly conducting seminars, training programs, and other events (JICA, 2005). Since the launch of the JOCV program in 1965, a total of 28,895 JOCVs (17,111 males and 11,784 females) have been dispatched to 83 countries (as of the end of September 2006).

6. Kamibeppu contends: "In addition to these quantitative expansions, the Japanese government also improved the quality of its aid by making more generous loans and more open the bidding process to foreign firms. Japanese ODA's grant element increased from 70 percent in 1977 to 82 percent in 1989, but it was short of the 90 percent level which the DAC averaged in the 1980s. The government significantly untied Japanese aid from 34 percent in 1974 to 78 percent in 1989, opening the doors to international procurement suppliers. This turned Japan into the most open donor among DAC nations. One major feature of Japanese ODA in sector allocation was its high concentration on economic infrastructure projects, which occupied close to half of the ODA in 1988, more than twice

the DAC average. The technical cooperation share was about 15 percent in 1988, half of the DAC average" (2002, pp. 57–58).

7. The other three principles are as follows: 1) Japan's ODA is provided from a humanitarian standpoint; 2) it is based on the interdependent relationship between Japan and the partner country, and 3) it places an emphasis on environmental conservation in socioeconomic development.

8. For further detail on the Basic Education for Growth Initative (BEGIN), see MOFA (n.d. (b)).

9. According to Nagao (2004, p. 53), "In the year 2000, Japan was not only the largest ODA contributor (US$13.5 billion), accounting for around 25% of total ODA of DAC member countries (ahead of USA with US$9.9 billion) but was also the largest contributor of bilateral educational ODA (around US$515 million, ahead of Germany with US$495 million)."

10. Although it lies beyond the scope of this chapter, Japan has also emphasized the environmental aspect of sustainable development in its ODA program. For example, at the World Summit on Sustainable Development held in Johannesburg in 2002, the government of Japan, together with Japanese NGOs, proposed to start a UN decade on Education for Sustainable Development (ESD). The movement to launch the UN Decade of ESD (2005–2014) originated in the environmental education movement, although the scope of ESD, as defined by the lead agency of the Decade, UNESCO, is much wider than that of environmental education, including all three pillars of sustainable human development (economic development, social development, and environmental sustainability).

11. In July 2005, Japan, together with Brazil, Germany, and India, then known as the Group of Four (G-4), presented a joint proposal to enlarge the Security Council from the current 15 members to 25, and the African Union (AU) submitted a similar Security Council reform resolution. In the end, neither the G-4 nor the AU secured the 128 votes needed for adoption. Both the G-4 and AU wanted the Security Council to be enlarged by six new permanent seats, but the AU wanted veto rights straight away, whereas the G-4 was willing to wait for 15 years. The AU also demanded five additional nonpermanent seats, while the G-4 preferred four.

12. Since Article IX of the Japanese Constitution, the so-called "peace clause," does not allow the country to have military forces, Japan has "Self-Defense Forces," which are, in fact, one of the best-equipped militaries in the world. Notwithstanding suspicious eyes from its Asian neighbors, Japan has been taking steps to enhance its security role overseas since the early 1990s. The government of Japan passed the Peacekeeping Operations (PKO) Law in 1992, which allowed Japanese troops to take part in UN peacekeeping. Since then, Japan has dispatched troops to Cambodia under the UN Transitional Authorities in Cambodia (UNTAC); and to Mozambique, Zaire, the Golan Heights, and East Timor under the PKO law. In late 2001, in its dash to avoid the embarrassment it had experienced in 1991 by failing to send troops to the Gulf War, Japan swiftly passed the Anti-Terrorism Special Measures Law, which enabled it to provide logistical support in the form of refueling and supplies for U.S. forces in Afghanistan.

13. In addition, a $1 million pledge was made by Nigeria to SSC Trust Fund, and $3,510,445 from Algeria, Benin, Brazil, China, Comoros, and Egypt was received for the tsunami-affected countries. The Special Unit for South–South Cooperation (SU/SSC) of UNDP hosts its own website (http://tcdc1.undp.org) and issues two journals, *Cooperation South* and *Sharing Innovative Experiences*, in which the initiatives of SU/SSC are presented and discussed.

14. The full statement is worth reading (see Zhou, 2005).

15. In 1980, the UN General Assembly endorsed the creation of the "High-Level Committee on the Review of Technical Cooperation among Developing Countries" (HLC) (Resolution 35/202, dated December 16, 1980). HLC is comprised of all countries participating in the UNDP system and is held biennially. In 2003, HLC decided in its decision 13/1 to change the name of SU/TCDC to SU/SSC. Likewise, in its resolution 58/220, the General Assembly, endorsing the decision by HLC, decided to change the name of the committee to the High-Level committee on the Review of SSC.

16. The First Cooperation Framework for TCDC (1997–1999) was extended until the end of 2000 (DP/CF/TCDC/1/EXTENSION I) and the Second Cooperation Framework (2001–2003) was extended until the end of 2004 (DP/CF/TCDC/2/EXTENSION I).

17. The 20th Session of G-77 Foreign Ministers Meeting was held in 1996 and issued a declaration in the name of G-77 and China for the first time. In September 1998, Chinese Foreign Minister Tang Jiaxuan participated in the 22nd Session of G-77 Foreign Ministers Meeting and delivered a speech. It was the first time that the Chinese foreign minister attended such a meeting.

18. Yiping Zhou served as senior policy advisor on SSC since April 1997. Before joining the UN system in 1985, Zhou worked as policy officer in the Department of International Relations, Ministry of Foreign Economic Relations and Trade, in the government of the People's Republic of China, from January 1980 to October 1984. He also served as a diplomat in the Chinese Permanent Mission to the UN from November 1984 to October 1985.

19. In the section "Concluding remarks and recommendations" (UN General Assembly, 2003, paragraph 71), the 2003 Report of the UN Secretary-General calls for expanding the scope of SSC within regional and subregional arrangements to "foster economic integration in the South." It also calls for "a more strategic approach" to SSC and further efforts toward "monetary and financial cooperation" (paragraph 72), "proper strategies to avoid counterproductive competition against one another" as more developing countries "enter a highly competitive search for foreign direct investment" (paragraph 73), and "urgent measures . . . to boost the trading capacity of least developed countries" (paragraph 74).

20. See <http://www.cabc.org.cn/english/index.asp> for details of CABC. With initial funding of US$1 million, CABC includes China and five African countries (Cameroon, Ghana, Mozambique, Nigeria, and Tanzania) in its initial 3-year project. Most of its Chinese members are from the China Guangcai Program, which has 14,000 member enterprises. CABC collaborates with government ministries on the Sino-Africa Forum and serves as a practical business tool to assist Chinese

and African companies in achieving investment and trade objectives. As a public-private partnership to facilitate Sino-African ties, the program is expected to help Chinese and African businesses find new markets, partners, and opportunities.

21. Posts held by Koichiro Matsuura include those of director-general of the Economic Cooperation Bureau of Japan's Ministry of Foreign Affairs (1988); director-general of the North American Affairs Bureau, Ministry of Foreign Affairs (1990); deputy minister for Foreign Affairs (1992–1994); deputy director-general, North American Affairs Bureau, Ministry of Foreign Affairs (1990–1992); director-general, Economic Cooperation Bureau, Ministry of Foreign Affairs (1988–1990); director of the Aid Policy Division, Ministry of Foreign Affairs (1988–1990); and director of the Development Cooperation Division, Ministry of Foreign Affairs (1975–1977).

22. For example, the Center for Global Development (CGD), a think tank based in Washington, D.C., has ranked Japan last among 21 developed countries for 5 consecutive years since it started rating developed countries in 2003, based on its own index ("Commitment to Development Index"). This index is calculated on a scale from 0 to 7 and includes the following seven policy areas: aid, trade, investment, migration, environment, security, and technology. Japan's scores for each policy area for 2007 are 1.2 for aid, 1.5 for trade, 5.9 for investment, 1.7 for migration, 4.7 for environment, 1.7 for security, and 6.3 for technology, making its average score for 3.3. (Greece, the country ranked 20th, scored 3.9 on average.) Ironically, according to MOFA (2006), Japanese aid "tailored to local needs" is not highly valued in this index: Japan's technical cooperation and grant aid for Grassroots Human Security are tailored to local needs, thus particularly well-appreciated in developing countries. In this Index, these types of assistance, however, are judged as low-quality aid, compared with large projects, on the grounds that they "overburden recipient governments with administrative and reporting responsibilities." See, for example, Sawamura (2002) for an academic argument characterizing Japanese aid as culturally sensitive.

FIVE

Transnational Corporations as Propellers of Educational Transfer in the Middle East

Zahra Bhanji

Transnational corporations[1] (TNCs) are increasingly entering the education sector—a territory that has been regarded as highly contested and has been viewed as state or national responsibility. In the field of education, corporations have traditionally sold their services or products directly to governments (e.g., the textbook industry) or have donated products directly or through corporate foundations in support of schools (Colvin, 2005). This is changing. New forms of private authority (Cutler, Haufler, & Porter, 1999) in education are emerging as a result of globalization that differ from previous forms of private-sector engagement in education. Cutler, Haufler, and Porter (1999) define *private authority* as "existing when an individual or organization has decision-making power over a particular issue area and is regarded as exerting power legitimately" (p. 5). These new forms of private authority are transnational in scope and mobilize corporate social responsibility norms to legitimize their influence over the broad frame and direction of their activities in education. They require the extra-economic benefits of engaging in social sectors such as education in order to reproduce themselves globally (Bhanji, 2008).

TNCs are entering the education sector through new sustainability models that integrate the poor in developing countries as a market within the core business strategies of a firm (Prahalad, 2005). An unprecedented amount of financial and human resources are being invested as TNCs are becoming key players in conceptualizing, developing, and infusing new educational ideas, norms, and processes. They are facilitating the educational transfer of best-practices from one developing country to another through the delivery of their education-related activities. The engagement of these TNCs in this newly developing terrain is unclear and raises many questions, as there is no global watch guard or monitoring of their activities. Many of these activities originate from corporate headquarters offices in the United States of America and Europe through elaborate worldwide programs, as in the case of some IT corporations. In addition to the increasing ad hoc transnational corporate activity in education that is filling the "governance gap," there is a new multilateralism that is slowly emerging and is embracing the potential contributions of corporate actors—one that is reconstituting a global version of embedded liberalism (Ruggie, 1997) in education. The present multilateral system grew out of World War II to form a specific international order influenced by an interest in sustaining a liberal, international infrastructure of global economic management (Bull & McNeill, 2007). The structure and initiatives of multilateral institutions has evolved with an increasing number of nonstate actors playing an important role in global governance. In recent years, we have witnessed the emergence of social frameworks that are facilitating the engagement of TNCs within a multilateral context. A new form of multilateralism, coined as "market multilateralism," encompasses this new interlinked role of TNCs and nation-states playing a coordinated multilateral role within new "generalized principles of conduct" (Bull & McNeill, 2007). These new "generalized principles of conduct" are based on corporate social responsibility discourse that are mediating the work of the private sector within multilateral institutions (Bhanji, 2008).

This chapter reviews this new "market multilateralism" through the Jordan Education Initiative (JEI) of the World Economic Forum (WEF), as a case of an epistemic community (Haas, 1992) operating in education. The chapter reviews processes and examples of how the WEF and key participating ICT corporations—Cisco, Intel, and Microsoft—are propelling North–North/South–South education and ICT transfer in the Middle East. Cisco Systems develops Internet Protocol-based networking technologies for different sectors, including education. The Intel Corporation was founded in 1968 to build semiconductor processes and introduced the world's first microprocessor in 1971. It develops technologies and products based on silicon innovation (Intel Corporation, 2007). The Microsoft Corporation was established in 1975 and has become a worldwide leader in software development and services (Microsoft Corporation, 2007).

I use a social constructivist (Barnet & Finnemore, 2004) perspective from the field of international relations to critically consider how TNCs are developing and sharing new norms about what is appropriate and legitimate action in education through North–North/South–South transfer. In this chapter, I do the following: 1) trace how TNCs have instituted their expertise and authority by forming a new transnational corporate epistemic community—the WEF's Jordan Education Initiative—by developing new norms and programs to bridge the digital divide in education; 2) review the activities of Cisco Systems, Intel Corporation, and Microsoft Corporation through the JEI and provide examples of how they are advancing their market interests through the transfer of "best-practices" to other Arabic-speaking nations based on the Jordan "experiment"; and 3) critique the entrance of transnational corporate epistemic communities in education and their role as facilitators of North–North/South–South transfer in the Middle East.

THE WORLD ECONOMIC FORUM AND THE JORDAN EDUCATION INITIATIVE AS A TRANSNATIONAL CORPORATE EPISTEMIC COMMUNITY

The World Economic Forum (WEF) is an independent international organization founded in 1971. The aim of the WEF is to improve the state of the world by engaging leaders in partnerships to shape global, regional, and industry agendas, although it is tied to no political, partisan, or national interests. The WEF is based in Geneva and is under the supervision of the Swiss federal government. Membership to the WEF is restricted primarily to the world's leading thousand companies, primarily those ranked among the top companies within their country and/or industry whose activities have a strong global dimension and play a global role in shaping the future of their region (World Economic Forum, 2007b). The WEF is increasingly shaping the global agenda by steering corporations to further their business interests in areas where they traditionally have not been able to enter. These corporations are infusing new corporate social responsibility norms that are circulating to chief executives of the world's most powerful corporations through the WEF. Their authority on solving global problems is also helping them legitimize their role through public–private partnerships[2] (PPPs) to advance business interests in different sectors (Bhanji, 2008).

The WEF's Jordan Education Initiative (JEI) was launched at the annual WEF meetings held in Davos, Switzerland, in 2003. Cisco Systems' president, John Chambers, stood up and challenged the global CEOs to support educational reform in developing countries. Global business leaders from the ICT industry sector, with the support of King Abdullah II of Jordan, made commitments that led directly to the foundation of the JEI. The aim of the program has been to promote educational reform through the effective use of ICTs by teachers and students within Jordan. The intent is to replicate the program in other developing countries (World Economic Forum, 2004). The role of TNCs has been pivotal throughout this project. Corporate support began with a small group of private-sector partners, including Cisco Systems and Computer Associates, that worked closely with the Jordanian government. This group eventually grew to a large group of global private-sector supporters that provided much of the project start-up support, including project management expertise and personnel, leadership, and resources. The JEI is the first PPP of its kind in the world. More than 17 global corporations, 17 local companies, and 11 governmental and nongovernmental organizations are project stakeholders. The primary sources of funding for this project have come from USAID, the Jordanian Ministry of Education, Computer Associates, Cisco Systems, Hewlett Packard, the Krach Family Foundation, Microsoft Corporation, Corning Cable Systems, Dell, and Intel. These and other secondary donors have jointly made investments of over US$22 million for this initiative, of which 50% (US$11 million) come directly from global private-sector corporations (McKinsey Corporation, 2005; Microsoft Corporation, 2003; World Economic Forum, 2004).

The JEI consists mainly of the development of Discovery Schools in Jordan that provide 1) in-classroom technology that fosters new pedagogies in learning through the development of classroom technology models and computer labs, with a particular focus on scalability and sustainability; 2) the development of e-curricula through global–local partnerships to build the local capacity of both the Ministry of Education and Jordan's e-learning industry; and 3) the training of 22,000 teachers over 3 years (Khatib & Cox, 2005). As of 2005, approximately 50,000 students and 100 Discovery Schools have benefited from the program (McKinsey Corporation, 2005). Technology infrastructure has been deployed to the 100 Discovery Schools as well as five different kinds of e-content curriculum (math, Arabic, English as a foreign language, ICT, and science) at different stages. In addition, approximately 1,500 teachers have gone through the International Computer Driving License (ICDL) training, and 1,469 were certified in January 2007 (World Economic Forum, 2007a). ICDL is the world's largest vendor-neutral end-user computer skills certification and is internationally recognized as the global benchmark in this area. The teachers also have a World Links or Intel Teach to the Future qualification (World Economic Forum, 2004).

The conceptualization and implementation of JEI has been instigated by a few key information technology (IT) TNCs that have a relatively long history working in education. Operating as an epistemic community (Haas, 1992), they have been propelling new norms, policies, and expertise through the JEI in Jordan to other Middle Eastern countries.

According to Haas,

> [A]n epistemic community is a network of professionals with recognized expertise and competence in a particular domain and an authoritative claim to policy relevant knowledge within that domain or issue area. (Haas, 1992, p. 2)

In this case, IT TNCs share a set of normative and principled beliefs (Haas, 1992) about the potential use of ICTs in education to overcome the digital divide—referring to the widening gap between those with and without access to computer-based technologies (Perraton & Creed, 2000). For example, there are an estimated 1.5 to 2.5 million sub-Saharan African users of computers. In comparative terms, this means that there is one African user out of every 250–400 African people, one North American and European user out of every two people, and a global average of one user out of every 15 people (Computer Industry Almanac, Inc., 2005). Through the JEI, the CEOs of these companies have rallied around the digital divide policy issue as one that is pivotal to overcome in order to enable countries such as Jordan to become a knowledge-based and competitive economy. The CEOs of IT transnational corporations are using their industry experience, expertise acquired through their worldwide education programs, and extensive resources to legitimize their role as an epistemic community operating in the field of ICTs and education. These corporations have hired leading IT experts and educators to conduct research and to facilitate the sharing of best-practices. Within the JEI framework, they have become leaders through their individual programs to diffuse new norms and priorities in education in the Middle East. The CEOs of these companies have further reinforced their role by making reference to issues of technology through press releases and speeches. For instance, John Chambers, Cisco Systems' CEO, often talks about how "technology will change aspects of our daily lives, including increasing the productivity and standard of living for communities and countries on a global basis" (Chambers, 2005, p. 2). Other examples include Craig Barrett, the chairman of Intel's board, who stated:

> Last year, I traveled to more than 30 developing countries to witness how rural areas are benefiting from technology. In my trips, I've also experienced how private and public organizations can collaborate to amplify opportunities created by technology in the developing world. (Intel Corporation, 2006)

Lastly, Bill Gates, chairman of Microsoft, contended:

> The Global Education Initiative is an unprecedented opportunity to bring government, business and concerned citizens together to focus on one of the

most critical issues of our day, quality education. From young children acquiring basic literacy in elementary school to adult learners striving to acquire new skills in the learning centres that will drive innovation forward. Microsoft is committed to expanding and enhancing educational opportunities. (World Economic Forum, 2007a, p. 17)

In addition to the role played by leading corporate CEO icons in raising awareness about their role in bridging the digital divide around the world, TNCs are also using new policy tools to mediate their efforts. They are increasingly engaging in research and collaborating with educators around the world. They are developing knowledge banks (Steiner-Khamsi, 2007) comprised of educational tools and resources that draw an evidence-based research and best-practices on how most effectively to integrate the use of technology in education. They are leveraging their in-house technical expertise and know-how based on their core business activities within the realm of education. They work closely with teachers and school administrators to develop case studies, lesson plans, and other educational tools that are placed on their company websites. These knowledge banks (Steiner-Khamsi, 2007) are further positioning the IT industry to claim their authority as key sources of quality information related to the use of technology in education.

TNCs are also establishing their expert role by making reference to externalization notions—referring to lessons from elsewhere, such as international standards and benchmarks to compare the level of ICT integration within countries (Schriewer, 1990; Steiner-Khamsi, 2002). Cisco Systems, for example, is increasingly becoming a facilitator of the regional dissemination of ICT benchmarks and indicators in the Middle East (Cisco Learning Institute, 2004). Cisco sponsors the Global Information Technology Report that is developed by the WEF and INSEAD, a leading business school located near Paris with campuses in different parts of the world. The report ranks the impact of ICT on the development process and the competitiveness of nations. The so-called Networked Readiness Index specifically measures the propensity of countries to leverage the opportunities offered by ICT for development and increased competitiveness. It also establishes a broad international framework, mapping out the enabling factors of such capacity. Cisco announced that in 2006–2007, the United Arab Emirates topped the Middle East and North Africa region on the "Networked Readiness Index" (Cisco Systems, 2007b).

As a corporate epistemic community, these TNCs are leveraging their established core IT business competencies and expertise within the sector of education. They are propelling new norms and programs as developers, providers, and implementers of technology in education in Jordan and then to other Middle Eastern countries. On the surface, the mobilization of unprecedented amounts of resources and high-level multi-sectoral partners rallying around improving the ICT skills of teachers and students is impressive. However, this initiative has provided global TNCs with the opportunity to test out new ideas, products, and services within a relatively low-risk framework to develop stronger relationships with educational stakeholders. They have ultimately been able to advance their market interests in Jordan and, through the transfer of "best-practices" regionally within the Middle East, to other Arabic-speaking nations based on the Jordan "experiment" (Bhanji, 2008). The next section reviews the key TNCs engaged as premier partners within the JEI—Cisco Systems, Intel Corporation, and Microsoft Corporation. An overview of their corporate engagement in education and through the JEI is also discussed.

THE TRANSNATIONAL CORPORATIONS UNDER STUDY

Cisco Systems

Cisco Systems has had a long history of working in education as part of its corporate social responsibility efforts worldwide. Under its Networking Academy Program, Cisco Systems established 10,000 nonprofit academies in more than 63 developing countries to teach students and teachers Internet technology skills (Cisco Systems, 2004). The program is a 280-hour web-based course that teaches students a wide array of Internet technology skills that enable them to design, build, and maintain computer networks (Eun-Myo Park, 2001). The curriculum is based on an e-learning model that was developed in the United States and was designed to be scalable and self-sustaining through partnerships with local educational institutions that administer and run the program. The academy program is industry-certified and globally recognized, given similar curricula and assessment programs offered in all countries (Selinger, 2004).

In Jordan, 10 Cisco Networking Academies[3] have opened as part of the *Achieving e-Quality in the ICT Sector* initiative under the patronage of Queen Rania Al-Abdullah, the United Nations Development Fund for Women (UNIFEM), Cisco Systems, Cisco Foundation, and the government of Jordan. Only 11.9% of the women of Jordan are economically active, although they constitute 48% of the population. The program aims to address the low percentage of women's participation in the ICT sector in Jordan and attempts to mainstream women in the field of technology. More than 600 students have enrolled in the program, of which 66% are women. Graduates of the program are linked up to the job market with a job placement program established in conjunction with the public and the private sectors in Jordan. An international conference was held in Jordan in October 2002 to share research that has been conducted to evaluate the ICT sector in Jordan from a gender perspective within Jordan and other nearby countries (Cisco Systems, 2006).

According to Cisco, the JEI is a natural progression of the Networking Academy Program work in Jordan (Chambers, 2005). Cisco has contributed funding, training, equipment, and other resources to JEI, in addition to providing technical and educational specialists for the JEI program management office. Cisco has also funded the development of an e-math curriculum for the K–12 grades in public schools in Jordan. The Cisco Learning Institute (CLI) has worked with Rubicon, a local ICT company in Jordan, to develop more than 2,500 mathematics lesson plans (Cisco Systems, 2007a). Cisco's Learning Institute brought its experiences from the Cisco Networking Academy to the development of the e-math content. The e-math content has been developed in Arabic, based on international standards, to fill the gap existing in the Jordanian curriculum. The math content is a web-based, interactive, and multimedia-rich forum. Cisco Learning Institute and Rubicon jointly worked on the curriculum and then pulled in subject-matter experts, including teachers and supervisors from the Ministry of Education. Cisco has advised the JEI on program design and management, content development, and assessment strategies; technology infrastructure needs; and localization. The Cisco Learning Institute has also conducted a series of best-practices in subject-matter expert trainings, mentoring, and technology transfer to local companies. CLI has worked together with Rubicon and the Ministry of Education to define the appropriate level of support, training, resourcing, and knowledge transfer needed to ensure the successful integration of technology into Jordan (Cisco Learning Institute, 2004). They also conducted trainings for ministry staff on the curriculum matrix, planning and aligning lessons to it, educational theory, and how to storyboard their lessons and media for instructional designers and media experts to create online materials.

Intel Corporation

The Intel Corporation has been working in education since the late 1960s, when the company was founded, and has invested more than US$1 billion to improve education around the world. Intel works with governments and educators in more than 50 countries to improve teaching and learning through the use of technology and to advance mathematics, science, and engineering education and research (World Economic Forum, 2007a).

The Intel Teach to the Future program guides teachers to integrate technology tools and resources into their lessons to promote 21st-century learning and student-centered practices. Through the program, Intel works with local governments to build teacher and student skills, such as digital literacy, critical thinking, problem solving, and collaboration, through quality teaching and learning. The program constitutes an Essentials Course that provides teachers with a foundation of skills to integrate technology fully into existing classroom curricula and promote student-centered learning. Their Thinking with Technology course allows teachers to access free online tools to sharpen student higher-order thinking skills (Intel Corporation, 2007). Through public–private collaborations, Intel has trained more than 3 million teachers around the world with the aim to train an additional 10 million by 2011. In Jordan, the Intel Teach to the Future program has trained more than 15,000 teachers. In 2004, Intel also established an Intel Computer Clubhouse in Jordan, replicating the West Bank model that was the first Clubhouse in the Arab world. The Clubhouse inaugurated by Queen Rania Al-Abdullah is an after-school program set up to provide community-based technology-learning programs in underserved areas. The aim is for youth to acquire the necessary tools for professional success. The Intel Clubhouse is based on a learning model developed by the Museum of Science–Boston and the MIT Media Laboratory in 1993. The Jordan Clubhouse is part of a network of more than 90 Clubhouses worldwide (Intel Corporation, 2004).

Intel Corporation's engagement in the WEF has been through the Intel Teach to the Future program. Intel is partnering with the Jordanian Ministry of Education and has played a leading role in the professional development track by training 80% of the Discovery School teachers. It has also taken the lead on the in-school technology track, building on the Intel IT Innovation Center's experience in technology and content development in schools. The aim was to deploy technology and content in the Jordan Discovery Schools (Intel Corporation, 2006).

Microsoft Corporation

The Microsoft Corporation has been operating in the field of education for close to 30 years. Microsoft's most recent flagship education program—Partners in Learning—offers a range of benefits to schools and colleges through courseware, grants, software licenses for refurbished computers, and special software pricing. The 5-year program was first established in 2004 and operates in more than 100 countries around the world.

Microsoft has been active in the education sector in Jordan. Mark East, Microsoft's Europe, Middle East, and Africa senior director of the Education Solutions Group, states that:

> Microsoft's alliance with the Jordanian government is an extension of our broader commitment to helping individuals, communities and nations in the Middle East gain access to the technology, tools, skills and innovation they need to realize their full potential. (Microsoft Corporation, 2005b)

Microsoft signed a 5-year Strategic Agreement Partnership with Jordan in 2003 to help accelerate the development of the country's IT sector. This has included a significant e-education component that included advanced training for approximately 1,000 engineers, the establishment of electronic libraries for 50,000 children in rural and remote areas, the establishment of IT academies, and the disclosure of source code as part of technology transfer in Jordan (Microsoft Corporation, 2005b).

Through the JEI, Microsoft has led the development of the national ICT curriculum used in state schools in grades 1 to 10. Microsoft has funded and worked closely with a local IT company, Menhaj Educational Technologies in Amman. The curriculum consists of 520 lessons, which have all been written locally, and includes multimedia elements for every lesson (Microsoft Corporation, 2005b). Menhaj has worked with the Jordanian Ministry of Education and Microsoft to develop a localized curriculum in Arabic. The software was deployed to the 100 JEI Discovery Schools, thus enabling them to upgrade and make changes as necessary within an experimental low-risk environment (Microsoft Corporation, 2005a). Microsoft has also funded a few positions at the JEI Program Management Office, as well as provided ongoing support and extensive advice. In addition, Microsoft funded an Innovative Teachers Network in Jordan, which is a peer-based interactive community of practice that includes a digital library of curriculum content. The portal is in Arabic, thus enabling Jordanian teachers to connect with teachers in other Arabic-speaking nations (Microsoft Corporation, 2005b). As part of its Partners in Learning program and involvement in the JEI, Microsoft has also set up a School Technology Innovation Centre (STIC) in 2005 in Jordan.

Microsoft states:

> We (Microsoft) and our partners, through the STIC, will reinforce our "thought leadership," provide a showcase for our products and programmes and through effective utilization to help countries and regions effectively harness the power of information communications technology for school administration, teaching and learning. (Microsoft Corporation, 2007, p. 1)

The Centre is used as a demonstration and learning laboratory for educational institutions in the region to provide information, training, and equipment for teachers to enhance their use of ICT in their classrooms and to share innovative teaching practices (Microsoft Corporation, 2005b).

Microsoft has collaborated with Cisco, Intel, and Hewlett Packard (HP), with each of the partners funding a specific aspect of the center's operations. Microsoft's hope is "that other countries will decide to follow these examples and set up similar centres to encourage the sharing of best-practices" (Microsoft, 2005b, p. 2).

WORLDWIDE STANDARDIZED TO LOCALIZED CORPORATE EDUCATION PROGRAMS IN THE MIDDLE EAST

Each of the cases highlights corporate engagement within the JEI as an extension, for the most part, of existing worldwide standardized programs. Steiner-Khamsi (2004b) states:

> Prepackaged, modularized, and checklisted programs developed at the headquarters of international organizations and subsequently transferred to their field offices are easier to manage than locally developed programs. The design of best-practices evokes associations with principles of efficiency, calculability, predictability, control, and "irrationality of rationality." (Steiner-Khamsi, 2004b, p. 206)

These corporate programs for education have been conceptualized centrally within headquarter offices in the United States and implemented at the local level through company subsidiaries around the world. Cisco's Academies, Intel's Teach for the Future program, and Microsoft's Partners in Learning program have all provided each of these companies with invaluable market intelligence and have also helped them build new markets in the education sector. As these programs mature, corporations are increasingly realizing that in order to truly understand the needs of their customers around the world they need to penetrate the markets they are working in further by establishing relationships and programs closer to potential customers in different geographic regions. The JEI has provided these TNCs the opportunity to build on their already established and standardized worldwide programs in education. The activities through JEI have enabled TNCs to work with local corporations and educational stakeholders to localize curriculum that reflects the Middle Eastern culture and language. Within the JEI framework, TNCs have played an active role as developers, providers, and implementers of technology in education within the Jordan context. Through their concerted efforts, they have participated in the delivery of products and services to the Jordanian education sector through huge investments and the sharing of their technical expertise. They have also conceptualized programs and have directly been involved in developing the capacity of educators and school administrators through systemwide changes to integrate ICTs into the education system at all levels. On the surface, the mobilization of unprecedented amounts of resources and high-level multi-sectoral partners rallying around improving the ICT skills of teachers and students in Jordan is impressive. Ultimately, one may ask, why? What motivated the likes of John Chambers of Cisco, Craig Barrett of Intel, and Bill Gates of Microsoft to participate in this global educational experiment?

The ICT industry represents one of the most lucrative and robust industries in the world today. The global marketplace for ICT was US$3 trillion in 2006 and projections estimate that it will reach almost US$4 trillion by 2009. ICT spending volumes represent 6.8% of global Gross Domestic Product between 2001 and 2005 (WITSA, 2006). TNCs are increasingly looking for new geographic markets to sustain their current levels of growth. The Middle East is emerging as a clear economic bloc. The Gulf area is becoming a multitrillion-dollar economy—a quarter the size of China and as big as South Asia. This presents a real opportunity for TNCs working in the IT industry to develop new markets, first in Jordan and then through Jordan as a potential entry point to the rest of the Arab world. Jordan as a site for the WEF Initiative was a strategic move made by corporate leaders involved in the JEI. The deployment of IT products and services within an experimental and relatively low-risk framework has enabled TNCs to develop stronger relationships with educational stakeholders, including the Ministry of Education, educators, and local corporations, thus providing them with an opportunity to better understand their customers.

THE JORDAN EDUCATION INITIATIVE AND TRANSNATIONAL CORPORATIONS

The aim of JEI from the beginning has been to develop a replicable model through the selection of Jordan as a test bed. There have been similar initiatives launched in Rajasthan and Palestine in 2005 and in Egypt in 2006. Based on the learnings and experiences of the JEI, additional countries have been launched, with several others making similar requests.

The initiative in Jordan itself has propelled the transfer of best-practices to other countries in the Middle East inherently through the way the initiative has been set up. It has had a ripple effect whereby various TNCs and educational stakeholders are now advancing new norms and initiatives in nearby countries, based on the goals and initiatives of the TNCs. One of the aims of JEI was for global TNCs to work closely with local IT companies by sharing their expertise and mentoring them to become regional innovators of educational technology within the Middle East. Five e-content curricula covering more than 6,000 lessons for K–12 schools have been developed locally with global corporate expertise through the JEI. Interestingly, the curriculum content developed is owned by the local private corporations and not the Ministry of Education. Thus, local corporations are reselling the software developed for the Jordan education system to other nearby countries. For example, through the support of Microsoft and the JEI, Menhaj's curriculum and products are now also being used in the educational systems of Bahrain, Saudi Arabia, and the United Arab Emirates (Microsoft Corporation, 2005a). Agreements have been negotiated between the Cisco Learning Institute, Rubicon, and the Jordanian Ministry of Education to license and distribute the e-math curriculum to other Arab League countries, such as Egypt (Cisco Learning Institute, 2004).

Building on its experiences in Jordan, Intel announced in 2006 that it will train 650,000 teachers over 5 years in Egypt in the effective use of technology. The training will take place by expanding the Intel Teach professional development program and will be implemented in close collaboration with the Egyptian government. The program aims to reach 80% of all Egyptian teachers (Intel Corporation, 2006). Intel's involvement in Jordan has provided the corporation with extensive experience working with teachers in schools within the Middle East context. Their initial "experimental" work in Jordan with a relatively small number of teachers has given Intel the opportunity to adapt its training based on lessons learned before transferring these learnings to Egypt, which has a much larger market.

Teachers and students in the 100 Discovery Schools in Jordan have been provided with access to the Internet through the provision of laptop computers and computer labs. TNCs are facilitating another layer of South–South exchange by helping teachers and students to "connect" with others in nearby countries. Microsoft's International Teacher's Network (ITN)—an Arabic portal developed in Jordan—enabled Microsoft to transfer this initiative to other nearby Arabic-speaking countries that serve much larger markets. In 2006, Microsoft launched an Egyptian portal with UNESCO to facilitate the exchange of technology related to teaching and learning best-practices. Teachers from Jordan are now able to share best-practices and resources with teachers in Egypt.

The School Innovation and Technology Center set up in Jordan by Microsoft in partnership with Intel, Hewlett Packard, and Cisco Systems has further assisted these TNCs in facilitating the sharing of educational ICT know-how to the Middle East. Several hundred visitors come to the STIC each year from within and outside Jordan. The center is being used as a forum—for example, for local curriculum developers to demonstrate their new material to schools and for government leaders from nearby countries in the Middle East to view demonstrations on educational products and services that are operating in Jordan.

At the government level, the engagement of TNCs in education in Jordan has developed the skills of the staff working at the Ministry of Education. Staff members have gained substantial exposure and experience to new ways of thinking and working from the staff of some of the most successful corporations in the world. They have acquired new project management, administrative, and technical skills to work more efficiently within government and have gained the skills and expertise to bring technology to schools. The Jordanian Ministry of Education staff is increasingly receiving job offers from other Middle Eastern ministries of education to share and implement best-practices based on their experiences within the Ministry of Education in Jordan.

The new ideas, norms, and programs through the JEI were initiated by a small group of TNCs operating as a new corporate epistemic community within the Jordanian educational landscape. Staff members working for each of these companies share new ideas and knowledge with one another. They meet regularly to discuss milestones, best-practices, and how learnings and experiences in one country can be leveraged in another country within the Middle East. The staffs of each of these companies also collaborate and work very closely together to further perpetuate new educational norms and ideas in the Middle East.

CONCLUSION

The engagement of TNCs as an epistemic community operating in the Middle East presents a new feature of corporations that work in the education sector. TNCs are building on previous corporate social responsibility initiatives to penetrate new markets and pursue material interests by experimenting with new business sustainability models. These new forms of doing business facilitate the development of new markets by "doing good"—in this case, by rallying around the policy issue to bridge the digital divide in education. Bringing technology into schools means greater sales for companies. Cisco's director of marketing for the Internet Learning Solutions Group stated that "the more people are learning online, the more networking gear Cisco can sell" (Galagan, 2001, p. 49).

The Middle East presents a unique, untapped market for IT companies. It is important to note that Jordan was purposefully planned to be a test bed for dissemination in the region and a hub for South–South transfer within the Middle East region. Jordan, for the most part, is seen as the close ally to the North and, thus, was selected as the ideal test bed for subsequent dissemination throughout the region. Jordan's close ties with the United States include "representation" in the royal family—referring to the previous king Hussein's American wife, Lisa Halaby, who became Noor al-Hussein, queen of Jordan. The current king Abdullah II of Jordan has continued the legacy of his father and has been able to maintain strong relations with the North in efforts to play a strategic role in the Middle East. The JEI provides a venue through which King Abdullah and Queen Rania are personally engaged in efforts to build a knowledge economy and expand educational opportunities through technology via the JEI. Under King Abdullah's direction, Jordan has created a very open environment for foreign TNCs to sponsor and promote the use of ICTs in the education sector. In addition, Jordan presents a unique advantage, given the size of the country. A population of 6 million people, including 50,000 teachers, is manageable to pilot new innovations. As a site for the JEI, Jordan presents a strategic advantage whereby TNCs are able to test their products in a supportive educational and political environment. TNCs have been able to obtain quick feedback at different levels before they are transferred to nearby larger markets such as Egypt.

TNCs have been able to propel South–South transfer directly through their activities and programs, but also by instigating various local corporate and educational actors to propel educational transfer to their peers and counterparts in nearby countries. In addition, it is significant to note that the South–South transfer of educational expertise through this initiative has been started and diffused by American TNCs. The TNCs and the other actors through which they operate are legitimizing the South–South transfer based on the "best-practices" learned in Jordan. The cultural nuances and language issues were factored into the development of this initiative; however, the underlying principles forming the conceptualization of the program were based on a Northern worldview to develop a worldwide 21st century skilled workforce that has the access and skills to use technology effectively. Although the initiative, products, and services in this case were developed in Jordan, they were developed by staff and built on experiences of worldwide educational programs that were originally conceptualized in the United States. Jordan's close ties to the United States have enabled it to play a dual role in the Middle East. What appears to be "South" when referring to Jordan is, in fact, biterritorial or in-between spaces. Jordan is, in this case, *both*: It is Northern, the closest Muslim country ally for the United States and Europe, and plays a Northern role in the Middle East. It also can be referred to as a Southern country because of its cultural heritage. In other words, this study suggests that South–South transfer is, in fact, North (United States/Europe)–North/South (Jordan)–South (other Middle Eastern nations) transfer.

This North–North/South–South architecture orchestrated by transnational corporate epistemic community is playing a coordinating role and is influencing the agenda-setting of the educational sector in the Middle East. This new ecosystem is impacting educational expenditures, policies, and priorities toward the use of technology. The financial investment of TNCs infused into the JEI is significant. However, it is really the influence of transnational corporate ideas and norms through the newly formed corporate epistemic community that has truly institutionalized the impact of "Northern" TNCs operating through the North/South–South educational transfer.

NOTES

This work was carried out with the aid of a grant from the International Development Research Centre, Ottawa, Canada.

1. This is an enterprise that controls assets of other entitites in economies other than its home country, usually by owning a certain equity capital stake. An equity capital stake of 10% or more of the ordinary shares or voting power for an incorporated enterprise, or the equivalent for an unincorporated enterprise, is normally considered a threshold for the control of assets.

2. The UN defines *public-private partnerships* as "voluntary and collaborative relationships between various parties, both State and non-State, in which all participants agree to work together to achieve a common purpose or undertake a specific task and to share risks and responsibilities, resources and benefits" (UN General Assembly, 2003, p. 4).

3. The Academies in Jordan are housed within a variety of organizations, including the Jordan University of Science and Technology, Middle East Communications Corporations, the United Nations Relief and Works Agency for Palestine Refugees in the Near East, and Yarmouk University (Cisco Systems, 2007a).

SIX

The New Regionalism in African Education

Limits and Possibilities

Leon Tikly and Hillary Dachi

This chapter considers the possibilities and limitations for developing South–South collaboration as manifested, for example, in the "new regionalism" movement in African education. It takes up and explores key issues in the book, namely, the form and modalities that South–South transfer and cooperation take in the context of the new regionalism, the wider material and discursive conditions that shape possibilities for policy transfer and collaboration in the interests of African-led development, and the possibilities and limitations for transformative change in the interests of the most disadvantaged groups. The focus is on a range of regional initiatives that involve African partners, although in some cases, other international partners are also involved. The decision to focus on the regional level was made as a result of the increasing significance that is attached to this level by African governments, donors, and nongovernmental organizations (NGOs) as a way of managing the globalization process (see Robertson, Novelli, Dale, Tikly, Dachi, & Alphonce, 2007). This is exemplified by the inauguration of Africa-wide organizations, such as the African Union (AU), launch of the New Partnership for African Development (NEPAD), and the Commission for Africa (CFA), as well as establishment of regional organizations such as the East Africa Community (EAC), Southern African Development Community, and a host of other regional initiatives (see NEPAD, 2001a, 2001b, 2001c, 2001d, 2001e; Tikly, 2003b).

The chapter commences with a discussion of the concept of the new regionalism, providing a basis for considering a range of regional initiatives in education. It will be argued that analysis of South–South collaboration in the African context needs to be understood in relation to the material position of the African region in relation to the North, but also to the discursive basis of global educational agendas, the role of indigenous elites, and the specific form of the postcolonial state. These factors ensure the predominance of global agendas and elite interests in shaping policy. Importantly, however, these agendas are both contradictory in their implications and contested. The chapter will consider some of the conditions necessary to develop forms of regional collaboration that reflect the interests of more marginal nongovernmental groups and voices.[1]

REGIONALISM IN THE AFRICAN CONTEXT

Within the broad literature "regionalism" is defined as the body of ideas, values and concrete objectives that are aimed at transforming a geographical area into a clearly identified regional social space whilst the related process of "regionalization" implies a dynamic element, the "creation of a regional system or network in a specific geographical area or regional social space, either issue specific or more general in scope." (Grant & Söderbaum, 2003, p. 7)

Regionalism and the process of regionalization are characterized as having taken place in two main waves. The "first wave" reached its apotheosis in the period following World War II, and focused principally on greater economic integration. The rapid development of regions, including the European Union (EU), North American Free Trade Agreement (NAFTA), Asia-Pacific Economic Cooperation (APEC), and Association of Southeast Asian Nations (ASEAN), during the 1980s is often characterized as a "second wave" of regionalism, or "new regionalism." Whereas the approach of the old regionalism was characterized as "state-centric," with a focus on forms of cooperation between nation-states, the main emphasis of the new regionalism is on the development of regions themselves as an aspect of globalization.

The new regionalism must be understood in historical context and in relation to the new division of power in the world, new forms of global integration, the erosion of the Westphalian nation-state system, and the dominance of neoliberal economic models (Hettne & Söderbaum, 2000). Although this second wave is primarily concerned with developing frameworks to facilitate free trade and commerce, it is also concerned with identity formation and takes on a more overt sociopolitical dimension compared to the first wave. The EU, for example, which is often held up as a model for other regions, represents not only an economic space, but has emerged out of a project of identity construction that goes hand in hand with economic and political integration (Robertson et al., 2007). Crucially, the new regionalism is not confined to formal associations between nation-states but instead includes informal networks and associations between actors in civil society operating at a number of different scales.

Regionalism in Africa exemplifies these broader shifts. First, regionalism on the continent is not a new phenomenon. Regional flows and networks, including the migrations of the Bantu people and the development of trade routes, predate the colonial encounter. Formal efforts to create greater cooperation between African states were instigated under colonial rule, and these associations sometimes formed the basis of fledgling regions in the postcolonial era, such as the East African Community (EAC), which subsequently collapsed, and the Southern African Development Coordination Conference (SADCC), which transformed itself into the Southern African Development Community (SADC). The now-defunct Organization for African Unity (OAU) can also be seen as an example of the old regionalism, because, as was the case with the SADCC and EAC, the key underlying principle was to bolster the sovereignty of the participating nation-states.

By way of contrast, the new-look Southern African Development Community (SADC), the Economic Community of West African States (ECOWAS), the Common Market for East and Southern Africa (COMESA), and the newly fledged African Union (AU) have been overtly modeled along lines similar to those of the EU and are concerned with projecting new macro- and subregional identities as well as encouraging economic integration and development. Important in this regard is the Mbeki-introduced concept of the African Renaissance, which seeks to reassert a positive African economic and cultural message onto the global stage after Africa's marginalization and suppression during the colonial era. Although the concept draws on older forms of Africanist and anti-colonial thought, it has also been criticized for projecting an idealized, elitist, and patriarchal view of African norms and values (Vale & Maseko, 1998; Cheru, 2002).

Like its counterparts elsewhere, the new regionalism in Africa includes informal as well as formal regional networks, including those between NGOs and the private sector. The networks have grown in number and influence in recent years, as we will see in relation to education. War zones and regional conflicts have also proliferated, and represent a darker side of the phenomenon on the continent.[2] Unlike examples of the old regionalism on the continent, the new structures and networks also operate on a range of scales. The Commission for Africa (CFA) and NEPAD, for example, are often portrayed as a partnership between Africa and the rest of the world. In the case of the CFA, its transcontinental nature is reflected in its membership.[3] The AU and NEPAD are perhaps more accurately described as "macroregional" in scope, on a par with other macro regions such as the EU, NAFTA, and ASEAN. SADC and COMESA are variously portrayed as either "macroregions" in their own right or as "subregions" when considered in relation to the AU, NEPAD, and other initiatives.[4]

Although there are clearly differences between the old and new regionalisms in Africa, there is also continuity and overlap. For example, just as the old regions were primarily concerned with economic integration, the new regions have also prioritized economic over sociopolitical and cultural goals (Robertson, 2006; Vale & Maseko, 1998). Indeed, some commentators argue that regional initiatives ought to be principally focused on preemptive national and regional development strategies and economic policy coordination among African countries (Mazrui, 1999; Adedeji, 1998; Mayer, 1998).[5] In this view, Africa's successful integration into global markets lies in the extent to which African economies can diversify their industrial base and export markets and, hence, become less dependent upon domestic markets and foreign imports through participation in regional and subregional trading blocs. The latter are seen as important both for attracting foreign investors and for intervening in the market in the interest of the poor. In these kinds of analyses, the sociopolitical aspects of development are considered important, but follow from the economic ones.

Just as with the new regionalism elsewhere, however, critics have questioned whether the new regionalism in Africa reflects the hegemony of neoliberal economic models that are designed simply to slot Africa into the global market (Simon, 2003; Mittelman, 2000). A consistent criticism directed at both NEPAD and the CFA, for example, has been their supposed neoliberal and market-led underpinnings (Bond, 2001; Labor Resource and Research Institute [LaRRI], 2003; WDM, 2004), which many critics perceive as being against the interests of the poor. These commentators argue that both initiatives see Africa principally as a vast and as yet underexploited marketplace. A criticism leveled specifically at NEPAD is that stronger economies, such as that of South Africa, are more disposed to acting as the agents of globalization, leading other African economies into the global market and providing a "way in" for non-African, and particularly U.S., interests into Africa (Bond, 2001).[6]

These authors argue that since the 1980s, neoliberal policies, associated with structural adjustment, have served to increase rather than decrease poverty and Africa's marginalization (see also LaRRI, 2003). They also argue that the neoliberal model put forward in the initiatives represents a "one size fits all" approach to development that does not take account of the huge differences in the economic and political contexts between countries (LaRRI, 2003; CFA Secretariat, 2005; WDM, 2004). Some critics of neoliberalism advocate a return to more protectionist policies, projecting what Scholte (2006) describes as an "economic nationalist" perspective (ESRC, 2006): that is to say, reassert the need for individual governments to intervene in markets through creating conditionalities that make it much harder for overseas firms and transnational corporations (TNCs) to operate.

In contrast to this position, Scholte (2006) also outlines a global "social market" or "social democratic" approach. This can be seen as characterizing the views of other commentators who have attempted to chart a third, critical but supportive position in relation to regionalism in Africa (Cheru, 2002; Khor, 2002). These authors argue that, whatever one may think of globalization and regionalism, it is unavoidable, and that the task for African economies is to maximize the advantages they bring while minimizing the risks. Ajulu (2001) argues that Mbeki, one of the chief architects of NEPAD, is actually opposed to the idea of untrammeled market forces, and sees a significant role for national, regional, and global regulation and intervention in markets in order to achieve the objectives of ending poverty and underdevelopment. The assumption is that instead of seeing globalization as serving only the interests of the richer nations and global elites, it can also be made to work—to some degree, at least—in the interests of the world's poor. This view is in accordance with what Held, McGrew, Goldblatt, and Perraton (1999) describe as a "transformationalist" view of global flows and networks.[7]

A potential stumbling block, however, is that just as the old regions were sometimes portrayed as representing the interests of elites on the continent and legitimizing unpopular regimes, questions have also been raised about the nature and extent of the democratic process in the new regional structures (Simon, 2003). Many commentators have questioned the democratic credentials of some of the leaders and regimes associated with the new regions. These criticisms have been most vociferous in relation to the AU, NEPAD (Bond, 2001; LaRRI, 2003), and the Commission for Africa.[8] These criticisms must be seen in the context of a discussion of the form of the nation-state that has emerged in Africa.

The development of old and new regionalism in other parts of the globe has been linked to the predominance of the so-called Westphalian state model.[9] Unlike in the Westphalian model, the mode of rule in postcolonial states has variously been described as "personal rule," "elite accommodation," "belly politics," and as a "shadow" or "neopatrimonial state" (Bøås, 2003). These alternative models are relevant for a consideration of the "good governance" agenda in Africa. In the model of the neopatrimonial state, for example, bureaucratic and patrimonial norms coexist. The state is able to extract and redistribute resources, but this process, unlike the Westphalian state model, is privatized:

> In redressing the colonial legacy of racially inherited privilege, the independent states create a specific patrimonial path of redistribution which divides the indigenous majority along regional, religious, ethnic and at times, family lines. (Bøås, 2003, p. 33)

The resulting phenomenon of weak states but strong regimes provides a source of contradiction within the African state system. Through providing a legal framework protecting the sovereign authority of postcolonial states, the OAU and, arguably, the AU and other regional bodies can be seen as complicit in the whole process.

As was the case with the economic critiques of NEPAD and the CFA, some commentators writing about the political aspects attempt to chart a third path. While recognizing the validity of some of the criticism leveled at Africa's leadership and of the NEPAD consultation process, they point out that the framework contains clear commitments to peace, security, democracy, and greater public accountability, but that these aspects, such as the peer review mechanism, need to be further strengthened. Some also suggest that "good governance" should not necessarily rely on Western models (Ake, 1998; Cheru, 2002). Cornwell (1998) argues that the greater accountability of African leaders ought to involve "the creation of voluntary neighbourhood governments and rural grassroots movements that produce alternative institutions of decision making, drawing on customary notions of justice, fairness and political obligation" (p. 14).

In a similar vein, Ake (1998) suggests that involving the vast majority of Africans who live in rural areas in democratic decision-making should include "allowing rural people to build on whatever they consider important in their lives; whatever they regard as an authentic expression of themselves" (p. 35). Cheru (2002) has identified a series of grassroots, civil society organizations, such as peasants' organizations, informal economy and self-help associations, the human rights movement, trade unions, and religious organizations, whose participation in the political process would help to guarantee a form of "democracy from below." Although Cheru is referring here to processes of political representation and voice at the level of the nation-state, these ideas are also expressed in relation to the regional level. They accord with Mittelman's (2000) concept of "transformative regionalism," which refers to the alternative and bottom-up forms of cultural identity and regional self-organization and self-protection, such as prodemocracy forces, women's movements, environmentalists, and other civil society movements. Inasmuch as the new regionalism can be seen from different perspectives, so, too, a conceptualization of South–South transfer and cooperation within a regional framework can permit different understandings of its role, significance, and benefits.

THE NEW REGIONALISM IN AFRICAN EDUCATION

This section provides an overview of some of the more significant regional initiatives in education. Within the framework of this book, they constitute a form of South–South transfer. The initiatives will be briefly described and then analyzed against key themes arising from the above discussion, namely, the general characteristics of the new regionalism in African education, the governance of the initiatives, the role of the region in mediating global policy agendas, the impact of neoliberal ideologies, education, and the development of regional identities. It will be argued that the new regionalism in education demonstrates many of the characteristics as well as the tensions and contradictions of the new regionalism in Africa more broadly. As a result, it serves as a good case study for understanding the possibilities and limitations for educational transformation afforded by the regional level.

Turning first to the overview of the two most influential initiatives, we consider NEPAD and the CFA. Education and training have a critical role to play in relation to both. In NEPAD, education has a role in agricultural development through agricultural extension initiatives, in health education and measures to reduce population growth, in bridging the digital divide, and in developing science and technology. The NEPAD Secretariat has produced four key documents in the area of education and training covering reversing the brain drain (NEPAD, 2001b), bridging the education gap (NEPAD, 2001c), skills development (NEPAD, 2001d), and integrating higher education (NEPAD, 2001e). Likewise, the CFA (2005) report has a considerable amount to say about education and, like NEPAD, perceives it as part of a larger framework of investing in people and capacity building.

Other initiatives, such as the Forum for African Women Educationalists (FAWE), created in 1992, represent a response to the slow pace of implementation of "Education for All" goals in sub-Saharan Africa.[10] The overall aim is to increase access and retention as well as improve the quality of education for all girls within the school system, and for women in higher education institutions. The Association for the Development of Education in Africa (ADEA) was established at the initiative of the World Bank in 1988 (ADEA, 2005).[11] Then called Donors to African Education (DAE), its objective was to foster collaboration and coordination between development agencies in support of education in Africa. ADEA now focuses on developing partnerships between ministers of education and funding agencies in order to promote effective education policies based on African leadership and ownership. The African Virtual University (AVU) also originated as a project of the World Bank, but is now an independent NGO based in

Kenya. Its aim is to build capacity and support economic development by providing "world-class, quality education and training programs" to students and professionals in Africa (African Virtual University, 2007).

The Southern Africa Development Community (SADC) protocol was signed and ratified by the 14 SADC heads of state on September 8, 1997, at Blantyre, Malawi.[12] Whereas the emphasis and priorities of NEPAD, the CFA, FAWE, and ADEA are linked to tackling broader, continentwide systemic issues of poverty reduction and human resource development, the SADC protocol is more overtly related to education's role in supporting regional economic integration, principally through achieving the ultimate objective of equivalence, harmonization, and standardization of education and training systems in the region within 20 years. The Great Lakes Initiative (GLI) is a recent intergovernmental response to civil strife, political instability, and health calamities (such as Ebola and the HIV/AIDS pandemic) in the Great Lakes Region in Central Africa. Even though education is touched upon only perfunctorily in the founding declaration, the members did make some commitments, including a pledge to meet the Millennium Development Goals (MDGs), to develop and promote comprehensive curricula on the culture of peace in their educational systems, and to promote the use of Kiswahili as a working language in the Great Lakes Region.

The Association of African Universities (AAU) and the Inter-University Council for East Africa (IUCEA) are regional bodies representing higher education interests on the continent[13] while the Southern and East African Consortium for Monitoring Education Quality (SACMEQ) developed out of a program of research collaboration between the International Institute for Educational Planning (IIEP) and a number of ministries of education in southern Africa. The focus of SACMEQ has been on establishing long-term strategies for building the capacity of educational planners to monitor and evaluate basic education systems.[14]

General Characteristics of the New Regionalism in African Education

The initiatives of such regional bodies reflect the growing significance of the regional level and serve to illustrate how the new regionalism is currently working itself out in educational terms. For African governments, operating at a regional scale provides an opportunity for linking emerging education and training frameworks and initiatives to regional development projects. The regional level provides unique opportunities for sharing and disseminating effective practice across country contexts, enabling economies of scale in dissemination and other activities. In the case of ADEA, FAWE, AAU, and SACMEQ, organizing at the regional level is important for enabling comparative cross-national research.[15] Distance education initiatives such as the AVU offer significant opportunities for education and training across regions.[16] The SADC protocol on education and training (SADC, 1997) aims to encourage cooperation in policy analysis and formulation, basic and intermediate education and training, research development, lifelong education and training, and publishing and library resources. The ultimate objective of the protocol is to progressively achieve the equivalence, harmonization, and standardization of the education and training systems in the region in order to assist the sharing of resources and to encourage student and staff mobility.

Nonetheless, the above initiatives are extremely diverse in terms of their origins, scope, and objectives. First, although most of the new regional structures developed during the 1990s and, thus, coincide in a temporal sense with the emergence of the new regionalism globally, this is not uniquely the case. The IUCEA, for example, is the last surviving institution of the East African Community, which became defunct in 1977. The continentwide AAU also dates back to the early 1960s and the development of the OAU. Second, they all combine aspects of formal and informal networks. Some, such as the AU and NEPAD, are best described as "formal" because they hinge on governmental cooperation. Others, such as the AAU and IUCEA, are more accurately described as "informal" insofar as they are almost completely nongovernmental in their membership and operations. The situation is more complex with other actors. FAWE, for instance, although rooted in civil society, includes ministers of education and other government officials in many of its senior positions. Likewise, although ADEA and SACMEQ include donors, NGOs, researchers, and other kinds of civil society–based organizations and individuals in their core activities, both are led by government ministers and are based at a national level within ministries of education.

The initiatives also operate at a number of scales in ways that suit their objectives. Organizations such as FAWE, ADEA, the AVU, and the AAU operate at a macroregional level while the SADC protocol on education and training, the IUCEA, and SACMEQ operate across two or more subregions. Although each projects a regional identity, the nature of that identity clearly varies. NEPAD and the CFA, in particular, project a more top-down approach to regionalism. Others, such as FAWE, project a grassroots approach. A feature of all of the initiatives is that they seek to project an indigenous, regional response that is critical for gaining popular support and legitimacy within the continent.

The Governance of Regional Initiatives

With the exception of the IUCEA, the other initiatives include in their leadership and/or in key positions within their governing structures representatives of national ministries. This is significant because it means that national governments exercise ownership and control of the initiatives at least in a formal sense. This helps to give the initiatives political legitimacy in the eyes of the governments themselves and also the donors. Through their controlling stake in initiatives such as ADEA and SACMEQ, national governments also effectively own the intellectual means of production through their capacity to commission research to support policy. The predominance of national governments is also important because, although the regional level is becoming increasingly influential in shaping agendas, the provision of education remains largely a national responsibility. Regional influence over national policy agendas is achieved in slightly different ways, however. Metaregional initiatives, like ADEA, also operate at a subregional level to address issues that arise at that level. In the case of NEPAD and SACMEQ, they also have representatives working within national ministries to implement initiatives. Even a predominantly civil society–based organization, such as FAWE, is organized in terms of national chapters that are then represented at a regional level. This provides an opportunity for FAWE to mobilize and provide a forum for individuals and organizations that operate exclusively at a local and national level to put pressure on national policy agendas. It is also at the local level that FAWE can seek to stimulate innovation in practice that can then be disseminated at national and regional levels.

Crucially, all of the initiatives are substantially donor-supported. A pan-African, regional, or even subregional focus can be attractive to donors because it provides a means for communicating simultaneously with a number of African leaders and influencing developments across a number of country contexts. In this respect, the regional level provides a convenient "way in" outside of the confines of more traditional bilateral mechanisms and relationships. This is seen in relation to the CFA,[17] but also in the AVU, ADEA, SACMEQ, and SADC. However, given the influence of donor-led agendas on regional policy frameworks (see the next section), some question whether donor support for the regional level represents a more subtle form of control by donors over national policy agendas. Furthermore, although initiatives such as SACMEQ and ADEA have large capacity-building components to develop indigenous expertise, their success still depends very much on externally based technical assistance (see below).

For the most part, regionalization in education as in other areas has largely been a top-down affair controlled by national governments and donors. Even the more civil society–based initiatives, such as FAWE and the AAU, have developed mechanisms for influencing policy largely through their collaboration with other regional initiatives, such as the AU and NEPAD. Even in the case of initiatives that target local levels, some critics have argued that these are often hijacked by organized communities and NGOs. Particularly in rural areas, vocal individuals and the rural elite class often benefit more than the intended beneficiaries because they have access to information and resource allocation procedures (Mosha & Dachi, 2004). In this and other respects, questions remain as to whether the civil society–based initiatives have sufficient capacity to influence change and to provide, in Mittelman's (2000) terms, examples of transformative regionalism.[18]

This draws attention to the question of capacity building to support good governance. Some of the regional initiatives make specific recommendations relating to "good governance," which gain support in the wider literature (Cheru, 2002; Ashton & Green, 1996; Carnoy, 1999). However, the emphasis in most of the initiatives is on developing leadership capacity in government. Little, if any, attention is given to the need to develop leadership capacity outside of government, within civil society. In this respect, there is tension between the commitment in NEPAD and the CFA toward developing democratic institutions in Africa and including stakeholders from civil society in decision making on the one hand, and providing training for civil society organizations in policy advocacy work on the other.

The Role of the Region in Mediating Global Policy Agendas

To a large extent, the initiatives reflect dominant discourses in education emanating from multilateral organisations such as the World Bank and UNESCO (see Robertson et al., 2007). The CFA document, for example, defines the role of education as follows:

> Education is a fundamental human right. It is a means to the fulfilment of an individual. It is the transfer of values from one generation to the next. It is also critical for economic growth and healthy populations. . . . The case for education is overwhelming—both in terms of fulfilling human security and as an investment with very high returns. (CFA, 2005, p. 181)

In keeping with developments in human capital theory, the role of education is seen not only in terms of producing the skills required for economic production but also as a means to bring about improvements in the health and welfare of the population. These enlarged understandings of human capital are evident in NEPAD and the CFA, which conceptualize education as an "investment in people." From our perspective, what is particularly interesting is that the initiatives often try to balance the tensions that are evident between economistic and efficiency-oriented emphases of the World Bank that see education as an investment and the approach of organizations such as UNESCO that see education principally as a basic human right. The differing emphases within these global discursive repertoires provide overlapping but also conflicting rationales for education. We will return to this below.

There are also tensions in the initiatives between global agendas and "local" needs and realities. For example, in relation to education access, there is a tension between the emphasis on basic schooling as envisaged in the MDGs and demands for the right to access secondary and tertiary education. A recent synthesis report prepared for the Second African Union Meeting of Experts in Higher Education puts the issues succinctly:

> On the one hand, basic education is seen, both under Education for All (EFA) and the Millennium Development Goals (MDG), as a key factor for the reduction of poverty and the enhancement of social equity. On the other hand, the World Bank's recognition of the critical role of higher education in building the knowledge economy and the renewed campaigns organized around the World Conference on Higher Education (WHCE) have elevated higher education as one of the prime agendas of development. (AU, 2005, p. 2)

Many of the regional initiatives provide support for the Dakar framework and for the MDGs relating to gender parity. This is particularly the case with FAWE. However, while the initiatives emphasize the access of girls to education, there is a relative neglect of other critical issues facing girls and women in Africa, including gendered abuse and exclusion from parts of the curriculum and, in the case of educators, from senior management positions.[19] Furthermore, other forms of social exclusion on the continent besides gender, such as the plight of victims of HIV/AIDS, orphans and vulnerable children, ethnic minorities, people living in rural areas, children with special educational needs, and so forth, are given even patchier treatment (see Robertson et al., 2007).

Many of the initiatives, including the AU, NEPAD, and the CFA, call for the need to reform outmoded curricula so that education systems can better address issues of poverty, insecurity, and disease (CFA, 2005). Unfortunately, it is not clear that many of the solutions suggested by the initiatives are any more relevant for the African context than the approaches they are criticizing. For example, there is tension between an advocacy of more learner-centered approaches, including forms of outcomes-based education derived from Western models, and the reality that these have rarely worked because they have failed to take account of the difficulties of implementing such approaches in many African classrooms (see Chisholm & Leyendecker, 2008). Similarly, many of the initiatives advocate forms of life-skills education to fight HIV/AIDS and to provide basic survival skills, although these have rarely been evaluated. Where they have been evaluated, they have been criticized for not being suited to African contexts (Boler & Aggleton, 2005). As we have indicated, there is also tension in the initiatives between the need to provide skills for a global knowledge-based economy and those skills considered necessary for fighting poverty and disease and supporting sustainable livelihoods.

Linked to the above is the need to address the growing digital divide in African education. Africa lags significantly behind the rest of the world in terms of popular access to technology (UN, 2005).[20] NEPAD, in particular, makes proposals to address the digital divide that the CFA reiterates, and there are several NEPAD initiatives in the area of ICTs as well as a range of similar initiatives in operation in African countries.[21] However, while digital technologies might transform education in the longer term, an exclusive focus on newer ICTs is likely to disproportionately benefit the elites who have access to them and have the effect of exacerbating the divide at least in the short term (see Robertson et al., 2007, for a fuller discussion).

The dominance of global agendas underpinned by Western models of education serves to underline the lack of indigenous[22] research capacity on the continent focusing on African realities (see Ntuli, 1998). This lack of capacity leads to a continued dependence on technical expertise from elsewhere. The problem is even more deeply rooted, however, and can be seen in Foucauldian terms as an aspect of the dominance of the entire Western *episteme* or ground base of knowledge (Tikly, 2004). There is a need to engage critically with dominant agendas (see Chapter 7, for example), their tensions, and contradictions, and to relate these to African priorities and the needs of those most at risk of marginalization by the globalization process.

The Impact of Neoliberalism

Further tensions are inherent in the regional initiatives between support for the privatization and marketization of education on the one hand and support for state-provided and state-led education systems on the other. This tension is growing in significance, given the increasing internationalization of education, particularly at the tertiary level. The privatization and marketization of education has been a feature of education policy in low-income countries since the 1980s, although the policies associated with this process have differed (Whitty, Power, & Halpin, 1998; Bullock & Thomas,

1997). In most African countries, marketization has involved encouraging the policy of cost-sharing, a proliferation of private schools and universities, and the development of a limited notion of "choice" for some students in the urban areas.[23]

The CFA initiative provides support for partnerships in the provision of education and training. It points out that nonstate actors, including faith-based organizations, civil society, the private sector, and communities, have historically provided much education in Africa. Some of these programs, it claims, are excellent, but others are "without adequate state regulation and are of a low quality" (CFA, 2005, p. 186). The CFA is supportive of public–private partnerships, particularly in relation to secondary and tertiary education provision. However, there are tensions inherent between this position and local realities. Cost-sharing had disastrous consequences for primary and secondary school enrollments during the 1980s and early 1990s in many countries (Samoff, 1994). Private education has also been associated with growing educational inequality in countries such as Tanzania (Lassibille, Tan, & Sumra, 1998) and the quality of private schools compared to government schools in Africa has been extremely variable (Kitaev, 1999). The policy of encouraging private provision in secondary and tertiary education since the 1980s has led to only a modest increase in enrollments at these levels throughout sub-Saharan Africa, where secondary school enrollment had risen only slightly from 20.1% in 1991 to 24.3% in 2000 (UNESCO, 2002).

There are also tensions between the CFA and other initiatives. The AU, for example, argues that the privatization of higher education poses risks for what it describes as the

> fulfillment of the broad mission of a university, spanning critical thinking, knowledge generation, innovation, production of different skills, "an enlightened citizenry," laying the foundation for democracy, nation building, and social cohesion. (AU, 2005, p. viii)

This "classical" view of the function of higher education also provides an interesting contrast to the more utilitarian and market-oriented emphasis of the AVU, which has prioritized programs in the area of business administration and computer science during its pilot phase (Naidoo & Schutte, 1999).

The proposed marketization of higher education through the introduction of a General Agreement on Trade in Services (GATS) has also proved controversial in many low-income countries (see Tikly, 2003a). The implication for African countries signing on to such an agreement would be to open up the provision of education to international suppliers evenly.

Consideration of regional responses to the GATS provides us with a further example of the extent to which emerging dominant agendas, although powerful, are contested at a regional level.[24] It is argued that the scope, complexity, and volume of cross-border activities are likely to make it difficult for countries to safeguard the broader cultural, social, and economic contributions of higher education and research (see, for example, AAU, 2004), especially in today's global knowledge society where a few countries, including the major Western industrialized countries, Russia, and Japan, dominate global scientific systems. Many African countries find themselves dependent on the major academic superpowers (Galabawa, 2004; Some & Khaemba, 2004). Some of the initiatives declare their support for an internationalization process that is mutually beneficial, and call on African governments to exercise caution on further GATS commitments in higher education until a more informed position is arrived at on how tradable transnational education can best serve national and regional development priorities. Significantly, as far as the development of South–South collaboration in Africa is concerned, South Africa as the regional hegemon has also begun to increase its provision of international higher education in the region, mirroring the equally rapid spread of South African capital across the continent. This provides a source of potential contradiction for the new regionalism in education, as South Africa stands to benefit disproportionately from initiatives such as the SADC protocol (see Chisholm, 2005).

The Role of Education in Developing Regional Identities

A key feature of the new regionalism is a concern with developing regional identities. However, in the African case, issues of identity and culture have tended to be subordinated to economic concerns in the regionalization process (Vale & Maseko, 1998). Where issues relating to African cultural norms and values have been addressed in the initiatives, their treatment has been characterized by contradictions and omissions. Thus, although some of the initiatives refer to the role of education in transmitting African cultural values and languages, this theme remains relatively underdeveloped. The CFA argues that

> Education systems are often based on inherited curriculum content that is limited to conventional academic subjects.... Curricula should be designed with regional histories, cultures and languages in mind. (CFA, 2005, p. 187)

Elsewhere in the report, there is a suggestion that development must be African-led and informed by African values. Many questions remain unanswered, however. For example, no consideration is given to which cultural values ought to be selected in contexts where there is huge cultural diversity or where more "traditional" norms and values clash with more "modern" ones. It may be that the marginalization of cultural issues reflects the huge political sensitivities surrounding them. This, however, is not a good reason to avoid dealing with them in policy terms.

The relative neglect of the cultural dimension is also evident in relation to the language question. Most of the initiatives are committed to developing and promoting African languages, but shy away from detailed policy recommendations about how this commitment can be realized in practice.[25]

CONCLUSION

The chapter has problematized the notion of South–South transfer and cooperation by examining the complexity of social and political relationships that pertain at the regional level. It would seem that the regions are becoming increasingly important arenas for shaping policy that is then implemented nationally and locally. However, emerging policy frameworks remain dominated by conflicting global agendas. The initiatives to achieve regional integration in and through education have been only partially successful in relating these agendas to African economic, political, and social and cultural needs and realities. A key issue that we have identified is the need to develop indigenous research capacity and technical expertise that is able to inform the development of more locally relevant policy agendas. More powerful countries, such as South Africa, are more able to take advantage of the opportunities that the new regionalism affords, for example, in relation to emerging educational markets. We have argued that there is an important role for capacity building, not only to strengthen existing regional and national leadership, but also to make these structures more accountable. Further, we have argued that the new regionalism in education continues to be dominated by elite interests, but that it also has potential to foster new forms of regionalization from below or, in Mittelman's (2000) terms, transformative regionalism. Grassroots movements and civil society organizations with an interest in education need to grasp the potential for change afforded by the regional level, but these efforts need to be supported if the voices of the marginalized and of those most at risk of being left behind by the globalization process are to be heard. What the above analysis suggests is that, rather than South–South transfer being either all good or all bad in terms of achieving these goals, the concept is increasingly contested in the global era.

NOTES

1. In seeking to develop theoretical understanding, the chapter will draw on evidence from a recent state-of-the-art literature review to which the authors contributed on the impact of globalization on education in low-income countries (Robertson, Novelli, Dale, Tikly, Dachi, & Alphonce, 2007). We have focused on Africa in this chapter because, as a continent, it is most at risk of being left behind by the globalization process (ESRC, 2006).

2. Given the large scope of regionalism in Africa, the analysis below will focus on formal (state-centered), informal (civil society–based), and mixed (state- and civil society–based) examples of educational regionalism.

3. The Commission for Africa was launched by British Prime Minister Tony Blair in February 2004, with the aim of taking a fresh look at Africa's past and present and the international community's role in its development path.

4. An interesting but unexplored dimension would be to consider the implications for education of the proliferation of "microregions" on the continent, i.e., regions that operate within or across national boundaries but at a scale that is between the national and the local. Examples here include conservation areas and spatial development initiatives such as the Maputo corridor (see Simon, 2003, for a discussion of these initiatives).

5. South African President Thabo Mbeki, for example, draws on the idea of "developmental regionalism" as a means of securing African interests.

6. See also Vale and Maseko's (1998) critique of the African Renaissance project, which preceded NEPAD and provided much of the intellectual basis for the program.

7. This kind of view also falls within the grain of more recent calls for instituting new forms of democratic governance and accountability at the global level, including reform of the World Trade Organization (WTO) and a stronger voice for Africa and other low-income countries within the World Bank and other multilateral organizations (Khor, 2002; Atkinson, 2002).

8. A summary of the submissions to the CFA Secretariat collected during the consultation process reveals that, while there was wide praise for the opportunity created and the open nature of the process, there was also criticism of a perceived patronizing tone with too much emphasis on "African leadership" or "African success," which risked appearing to give credibility to current leaders who may not all deserve it. There was criticism of an apparent hesitation to name the ruling class oppression that exists in many places, and the divisive role of ethnicity, tribalism, religion, and regionalism. Others have criticized the fact that the CFA was instigated and led by the British prime minister, which casts further doubt on whether it can be considered a truly African initiative.

9. A particular "ideal type" model of the state as a sovereign authority associated with the peace agreement in Westphalia in 1648 that is characterized by a demarcation between the public and private institutions; the autonomy of the state, which lies in its control over economic resource and a monopoly on violence; the assumption that the rule of law is based on popular support; and that

the state is a nation-state, in the sense that it is governed by an "in-group" based on common cultural and ethnic heritage.

10. FAWE was registered in Kenya as a pan-African NGO in 1993 with a secretariat in Nairobi. Since then, it has grown into a network of 33 national chapters with a wide range of membership that includes women policy-makers and male ministers of education who are associate members (see FAWE, 2000, 2002, 2003).

11. The specific objectives of ADEA are to promote dialogue and partnerships; develop consensus on policy issues facing education in Africa; reinforce African ministries' capacities to develop, manage, and implement education policies; promote the sharing of experiences and successful strategies; and promote nationally driven education policies, projects, and programs.

12. The protocol expresses conviction that "in Education and training a concerted effort by member states is necessary to adequately equip the Region for the 21st century and beyond" (SADC, 1997, p. 2). The SADC heads were further convinced "that concerted effort can only be effected through the implementation of coordinated, comprehensive and integrated programmes of education and training that meet the needs of the Region" (Ibid).

13. The AAU, whose headquarters is located in Accra, Ghana, was formed in November 1967 at a founding conference in Rabat, Morocco, attended by representatives of 34 universities who adopted the constitution of the association. The AAU is the apex organization and principal forum for consultation, exchange of information, and cooperation among the universities in Africa. The Secretary General of IUCEA has also emphasized the resolve to move the council to the center position in cocoordinating and enhancing academic undertakings of both private and public universities in East Africa.

14. The network works closely with the International Institute for Educational Planning (IIEP) to coordinate the delivery of intensive training programs focused on the requirements of the research, and also to facilitate access to advanced technical knowledge and computer-based techniques. The SACMEQ network has completed two major cross-national studies of the quality of education in Southern and Eastern Africa. The SACMEQ I Project (1995–1999) was completed by seven ministries of education (those of Kenya, Malawi, Mauritius, Namibia, Tanzania [Zanzibar], Zambia, and Zimbabwe). The SACMEQ II Project (2000–2003) was completed by 14 ministries of education (those of Botswana, Kenya, Lesotho, Malawi, Mauritius, Mozambique, Namibia, Seychelles, South Africa, Swaziland, Tanzania [Mainland], Tanzania [Zanzibar], Uganda, and Zambia).

15. A good example of this was the recent Female Education in Science and Mathematics in Africa (FEMSA) project, which was conducted across four African countries in West and Eastern Africa. FAWE was a grantee for this project.

16. The recent expansion of the University of South Africa's distance education programs, for example, into Southern and Central Africa also serves to highlight the potential of using information and communication technologies to foster skills formation across national borders.

17. The process allowed for Tony Blair and the other commissioners to interact directly with African leaders. There were 17 members of the commission,

all working in an independent capacity rather than formally representing national governments. Nine of the commissioners were African and included leading government figures such as Benjamin Mkapa, the president of the United Republic of Tanzania, and Trevor Manuel, South Africa's minister of finance. The UK had three representatives besides the prime minister, including the minister for international development, Hillary Benn; the chancellor of the exchequer, Gordon Brown; and the pop singer and activist Bob Geldof. They were joined by representatives from the United States, China, France, and Canada.

18. For example, gender issues are only partially reflected in emerging regional policy frameworks such as NEPAD and the CFA (see below). On the one hand, this may be seen as indicative of a broader "gender-blind" approach to policy on the part of (largely male) policy-makers. On the other hand, it may also indicate the difficulties faced by organizations such as FAWE in influencing these agendas. As we will argue below, a pertinent issue for donors and others interested in developing the gender dimension of policy and giving voice to civil society organizations would be how to boost the capacity of so-called "informal" organizations such as FAWE to influence policy at all levels.

19. For example, girls and women are more likely to experience gendered abuse in African schools (FAWE, 2003; Leach, Fiscian, Kadzamira, Lemani, & Machakanja, 2003) and teenage girls may expose themselves to sexual risk in order to fund their education (Vavrus, 2003, 2005). One of the working groups established by ADEA on female participation in education has concluded that girls face particular difficulties in accessing some areas of the curriculum, such as science, mathematics, and technology education (see also Swainson, 1998). A key issue is the lack of women in senior positions within institutions and at a national policy-making level. For FAWE (2003), gender issues need to be tackled in a holistic way and must be mainstreamed into all areas of policy and practice. There is evidence that globalization is creating the need for new skills training for women and girls that goes beyond the emphasis on primary and secondary schooling and on literacy in the Dakar framework and in the MDGs (Tikly, 2003b). These needs have yet to find a strong expression in regional initiatives.

20. In this regard, and for more details, see Butcher (2001).

21. Besides the NEPAD e-school initiative, there are several other initiatives: Catalyzing Access to ICT in Africa (CATIA), Global E-school and Community Initiative, and Leland Initiative—Africa Global Initiative.

22. We are not using the term *indigenous* here to refer to an essentialized notion of "African culture" or "African knowledge" but rather to research capacity that is African-based, for example, within African universities and research institutes, and that is focused on and rooted in African realities and priorities.

23. The degree of marketization, however—for example, with respect to the proliferation of private schools—has varied considerably across the continent (Bennell, 1997). Without engaging in the debate over "choice," it is apparent that in these countries, there is not much choice or hardly any choice at all where the determinants of education quality are concerned.

24. A negative view of the perceived impact of GATS is expressed in some of the initiatives. For example, the AAU, in collaboration with UNESCO and the

South African Council on Higher Education (SACHE), organized a workshop under the theme *The Implications of WTO/GATS for Higher Education in Africa*. One major outcome of the workshop was the unanimous adoption of the Accra Declaration on GATS and the Internationalization of Higher Education in Africa. In this declaration, participants recalled the significance of and responsibilities for higher education as acknowledged in the Universal Declaration for Human Rights (1948) and the World Declaration on Higher Education for the 21st Century (1998). The participants expressed concern about the perceived commodification of education under GATS.

25. ADEA (2005), however, does provide a summary of research and an overview of some of the key issues facing policy-makers. These are discussed in more depth in Robertson et al. (2007).

SEVEN

Foreign Aid to Education

Managing Global Transfers and Exchanges

Joel Samoff

FOREIGN AID: A PROBLEMATIC RELATIONSHIP

At the core of the common understanding of foreign aid is the idea of a transfer. Primarily resources, but also ideas, technology, and knowledge, are to be made available to those who can use them. Yet, when does foreign assistance actually help? Or rather, who benefits from foreign aid?

In practice, foreign aid may function more often to extract than to deliver resources. Just as the terms for the export of cotton and coffee are largely set by an international system in which the producing countries have limited say, so, too, is the development of their intellectual capacity and advanced skills constrained by a network of relationships that is only partly responsive to their needs and interests. Indeed, many people who are deeply involved in providing and managing foreign aid, including some who are deeply committed to its rationales of transfer and partnership, despair at aid's apparently limited benefits and its major disabilities. The concerns go beyond failed transfers. As aid providers regularly insist, foreign aid is as much concerned with knowledge as with capital. Foreign aid influences not only what knowledge is transferred and how, but also—and more important—the specification of what is knowledge and how it is to be created, validated, managed, and exchanged.

In the context of this discussion of South–South transfer, therefore, it is fruitful to explore the aid relationship, understood broadly to include financial aid and other resources. To do that, it is useful to focus on external support to higher education in Africa.[1] Especially since the 1990 Education for All conference in Thailand, education is expected to have very high priority for external support. If the world agrees that education is critical to development and to poverty reduction, then there is a compelling case for substantially increased and sustained support to countries with limited and weak education systems. As with many of the world's poorest countries, Africa is to be a major focus for that assistance. Although less well studied, higher education is an especially important arena in that regard, both because of its critical role in shaping the overall education system and because modern higher education in Africa has itself been significantly shaped by its external links.

Individuals, organizations, and countries regularly make the case for increased external support to education in poor countries. Major conferences take that as their starting premise or reach it as their principal conclusion. This is especially apparent for higher education in Africa, whose deterioration in the late 20th century was dramatic and obvious. While everyone agrees on the importance of high-quality higher education for development goals, however defined, few African countries can meet its cost. Competent and stable academic staff; high-cost equipment in engineering, medicine, and the sciences; up-to-date information technology; well-functioning and well-stocked libraries and laboratories; and even ordinary classrooms and chalkboards overwhelm national budgets, and are often underfunded or unfunded entirely, as resources are allocated to other activities deemed to be of higher priority. Observers, both African and foreign, regularly report that higher education in Africa simply must have more external support.

At the same time, the critiques of external support are widespread and increasingly sharp. Among the sharpest critics are its providers. Monitors of many sorts note its problems. The global reports on efforts to achieve education for all have shown clearly that the current and projected volume of foreign aid cannot sustain internationally agreed-upon objectives.[2] Systematic evaluations, at both larger and smaller scales, have gone beyond attention to the volume of aid to highlight problems in the aid process.[3] Development cooperation is constrained by inequalities of wealth and power. The promise of partnership is undermined by the persisting assertion of national interests and external expertise. New technologies that are expected to reduce gaps in practice instead increase and entrench them.

Most striking in the monitoring and evaluation is the fact that many of the major impediments to using external support to achieve global, national, and local education objectives are common across diverse settings. They put at risk efforts to expand access, reduce inequalities, and improve quality. Of course, there are important variations. Still, the problems identified are not occasional or ephemeral, and they are not unique to particular programs or countries. Many have been noted and studied over decades, yet they persist.

This combination of the call for increased external support, the unending efforts to modify and refine the objectives and forms of foreign assistance, the imaginative ideas and goodwill of many people involved in providing and receiving foreign aid, and the regular observations that important aid objectives have not been met and seem unlikely to be met confirms that it is the aid process itself that is fundamentally flawed.

From a different perspective, foreign aid can be understood as a tool, or set of tools, for managing international transfers and exchanges. That perspective is particularly instructive for education, where managing transfers and exchanges means not only supporting schools and learning, but also managing the flow of ideas and the accepted procedures for validating knowledge. Understood in this way, the aid relationship clearly has the potential to extend rather than eliminate poverty and to entrench and institutionalize rather than reduce global inequalities.

To contribute to efforts to understand the role of foreign aid in international education transfers and exchanges, especially efforts to support effective collaboration and partnership in a dramatically unequal world, I shall address several dimensions of the aid process. The aspirations here are modest: an initial attempt to explore common patterns that are often obscured by the specificities of particular projects, or support programs, or national education policies. My starting premise is that *the effectiveness and consequences of external support are in significant part a function of the aid process and the aid relationship*. Starting there is not to ignore the intentions, or energies, or goodwill of those involved in providing and receiving external support or to devalue the efforts of some funding and technical assistance agencies to do things differently. Those efforts matter. My starting premise functions to insist that we explore and assess those efforts in an understanding of aid as a structured relationship that often stymies even those who are the most creative, the most tireless, and the best willed. It functions as well to insist that we address the ways in which particular values, assumptions, ideas, interests, and priorities are so deeply embedded that participants and observers fail to notice them or understand their significance and consequences.

To reiterate, the concern here with broad trends and commonalities is not to ignore the differences among agencies and countries (which several authors have studied systematically and critically) or to devalue innovative departures or radical alternatives. Indeed, the point of this discussion is to encourage them. At the same time, it is essential to recognize that what is problematic is the *structure* of the aid relationship, not the misunderstandings or insensitivities or arrogance of a particular agency or individual.

To pursue that exploration of common patterns, I begin with attention to several important dimensions of the aid relationship, including the terminology used to characterize it. To elaborate how the most important pathways of influence may be the least obvious, I report on a recent analysis of World Bank higher education policies and their consequences for Africa. To keep the discussion grounded, my frame of reference is Africa.

HIGHER EDUCATION AS A GLOBAL UNDERTAKING

While higher education institutions are located in particular countries and governed by the policies and laws of those countries, throughout its history higher education has depended on the international exchange of scholars and scholarship. *Globalization* is the current buzzword. But the cross-border exchanges of ideas, science, technology, and those who develop them long preceded the current era.

Modern higher education in Africa (I leave for another discussion higher learning in the precolonial era) has a distinctly dependent history.[4] Most of Africa's oldest universities began as branch or remote campuses of European institutions. Even after the end of colonial rule, the metropolitan institutions continued to provide faculty, curriculum, and external examiners, and to be the arbiter of quality. For most, that dependence has become much less direct, though it has certainly not disappeared. Consider, for example, who specifies the high-status academic journals where publication by African researchers can confer individual and institutional recognition, respect, and remuneration. Consider, too, the overseas programs of respected (and less well-known) universities that bring to Africa learning objectives, curriculum, and examinations that are developed and packaged abroad.

To note that dependence and to see it as problematic is not to argue for African isolationism in higher education. That would surely be short-sighted. What is essential, it seems to me, is to distinguish between exchange and control. Important, too, is the recognition that external control is inimical to developing the sort of higher education that can play a critical role in addressing persisting poverty and dependence in Africa.

To explore how to maintain and expand international exchange, collaboration, and cooperation in higher education without extending dependence requires rejecting the common dichotomy of national = good/ foreign = bad. What is problematic are settings where education communities are unable to specify the fundamental objectives, ethos, and working style of their institutions and, thus, where higher education institutions cannot play a generative role in national development, however that is locally specified. Analytically, what is most challenging is the internalization of external influence, where the articulators and protectors of foreign influence are national citizens who are genuinely committed to improving things in their own country.

TERMINOLOGY

Words matter.[5] The language we use structures the way we think about things. An event or relationship may have multiple appearances, depending on how it is labeled. The cliché is the assertion that a glass can be described as half full or half empty. The point of the assertion is that what really matters is the perspective of the observer. Less often noticed is the fact that a major consequence of the assertion is to distract our attention from the relationship between the fullness of the glass and the need for the liquid. To shift to the development arena, it may be fundamentally misleading to consider a half-completed project good progress toward its ultimate objectives. Partial completion may have displaced people without offering benefits, felled trees without providing alternative firewood, or left the school with walls and no roof. If the local community is injured or alienated, the partial completion may itself be an obstacle to achieving the specified objectives. In this example, partial completion may be an indication of good progress (the glass is half full) or a failed project (the glass is half empty). That is not a matter of the perspective of the observer but of the project and its setting.

Over many years, the development business has spawned a standardized authoritative terminology. Within that terminology are embedded particular conceptions, orientations, prejudices, and policy preferences. Many of the commonly employed terms treat aid as part of the environment: What is "given" and therefore does not require explicit justification and is not subjected to critical attention are important issues that ought to be the focus of policy discussion. All too often, terminology obscures important issues and roles. Not infrequently, it misdirects the search for understanding. Indeed, one of the most powerful mechanisms of influence and control is to be able to specify the words that are used to describe particular events or relationships.

One example must suffice. How should school attrition—that is, learners who begin but do not complete a course of study—be labeled? The common terminology is "dropout," which then leads to "wastage" (misallocated public resources). Understood in this way, wastage is often identified as one of the most serious problems in African education. Surely no one finds high dropout rates desirable. Resources allocated to students who do not remain in school might well be better used elsewhere. "Wastage," however, lumps together disaffected learners who drop out of school, pupils whose poor examination scores lead to their exclusion, and students who score well but who are precluded from continuing by the lack of available places. In many countries, high attrition rates are a normal feature of the education system—not unexpected, or abnormal, or even avoidable waste. Indeed, many education systems are designed to ensure progressively narrower selection of students through their assessment systems.

Note how the words direct attention. Concern with wastage focuses on individual motivation and achievement and on the quality of instruction. Concern with attrition points to the basic assumptions and organization of the education system. Concern with push out or eviction requires attention to which students are not permitted to proceed. Are females or students from a particular region or religion or socioeconomic stratum more likely to be excluded?

Partnership

Prominent in the contemporary terminology is *partnership*. Partnership for international development cooperation is the currently preferred characterization of foreign assistance: no longer the rich uncle helping the indigent and perhaps profligate nephew, but partners working side by side to enable the poor to become more self-sufficient. There have been important conceptual shifts in how aid is described: from charity to technical assistance to cooperation to partnership.

The practice, however, has changed less than the terminology (Samoff, 2004). The term *partnership* is used simply to label whatever is the current pattern of interaction between aid provider and aid recipient.

Why does that matter? Why not accept whatever terms people prefer to employ? Recall that our concern here is the aid relationship, and particularly the ways in which that relationship impedes transfers and exchanges and renders external support ineffective. Applying "partnership" like a whitewash on every weathered and crumbling fence makes it difficult to see whether or not the fence is serving its purpose and, if not, what must be done.

Support for higher education in Africa is particularly plagued by this confusion. Many support programs—public and private, large and small, government-to-government, institution-to-institution—are labeled *partnerships*. Most could be more accurately described as technical assistance. A foreign institution, organization, or government provides specific support—whether it is equipment, staff, or funds for particular activities—to an African university. Initiative, decision-making, monitoring, and control over funding remain largely or entirely overseas. Although there may be extensive consultation, power and authority are generally not shared. Arrangements of this sort may prove to be very useful, but terming them *partnerships* obscures the structured roles that perpetuate inequalities and that may keep them from achieving their stated objectives.

Some higher education support programs go beyond technical assistance (A helping B) to development cooperation (A working with B). Foreign and African institutions undertake joint research projects. Teacher educators in Africa may be paired with foreign counterparts to learn new approaches and improve their skills. Foreign universities may admit and support students from their African partner institution. There are many more modalities. But here, too, the foreign institution generally retains ultimate decision-making authority and control over funding. Once again, the terminology, *partnership*, tends to obscure the structured roles and responsibilities that—notwithstanding the intent of those involved—perpetuate dependence.

The rationales for technical assistance and development cooperation of this sort are clear and regularly reiterated. African higher education institutions are weak and need support. Only later, after they have gained strength, it is argued, can the European institution expect to benefit. Although those rationales are clear, they preclude partnership. They may also impede development.

A strong notion of partnership requires that both partners see clear benefits in the relationship. Put sharply, if the European partner cannot see direct benefits in the relationship, then there may be assistance or support but not partnership.

As I have noted, technical assistance and development support may be very useful. But they can also be debilitating. Terming them *partnerships* obscures the relationships that make them debilitating.

The claim that European institutions have little or nothing to gain from their weaker African counterparts is at best puzzling and frustrating and at worst shortsighted, arrogant, and likely to perpetuate dependence. Surely it is possible to envision relationships between foreign and African universities that provide significant and tangible benefits to the foreign institutions. They may, for example, learn from research conducted in Africa—say, studies of marine biology, plate tectonics, archaeology, linguistics, public health, or democracy. African educators have pioneered innovative approaches to science education, adult literacy, and collecting oral histories. These lists could be much longer.

Until foreign institutions recognize that they have something to learn from their African counterparts, there cannot be effective partnership. Until there is effective partnership, inequalities of power, authority, and wealth will not be managed for mutual benefit but instead will perpetuate relations of dependence. Until there is effective partnership, external support cannot be effective in assisting African institutions to set their own agendas and priorities, to play a generative and constitutive role in the international higher education community, and to contribute significantly to national development.

Ownership

Country-led development is another of the must-use terms in the development discourse. The government must specify development (for our discussion, education) policy, which then must inform and shape how foreign aid is used. The cliché here is a motoring metaphor: Africa must be in the driver's seat. The common rejoinder in Africa is to reject the role of chauffeur.

Notice how the African rejoinder captures a powerful critique. In Europe, the person in the driver's seat decides where to go. In Africa, the person in the driver's seat may well be in the employ of the passenger, who makes the major decisions. While the passenger specifies the final destination, the choice of route, and, thus, ostensibly where and how to go, may be left to the driver.

There are two related issues here. First, does the development agenda reflect national and local needs, interests, and preferences? Second, do national and local authorities and others feel sufficient responsibility for that agenda to commit themselves to achieving it? The understanding of the importance of "ownership" grew out of the recognition that projects, programs, and the development agenda that were imported and perhaps imposed by outsiders withered when the external support declined and could not be sustained.

Formally, all funding and technical assistance agencies regularly reiterate their commitment to that strong national role and their willingness—indeed, obligation—to situate their own activities within a nationally designed and managed framework. Formally, requests for aid come from African institutions and countries. At the same time, many agencies maintain objectives and procedures that reflect their own understandings, goals, priorities, and formal responsibilities. External support continues to carry conditions as well. To receive funding, African countries must agree to make specified changes and set specified targets, both for the management of the national economy and within the education sector. External constraints and influences can, thus, be direct and indirect, obvious and very subtle. Formal conditions for foreign aid are the clearest, but are not the only forms. That should no longer surprise us. External funding agencies are structurally obliged to impose conditions and assert influence. Their training and socialization encourage agency officials to assume, and to expect others to assume, that they are likely to know what is best, what works and what does not, and what ought to be done.

Country-led development requires a strong and assertive national leadership that is willing, on occasion, to terminate aid negotiations or even a funded program rather than acquiesce in external direction. Occasionally, this does occur, as does formal agreement on externally set expectations combined with quiet noncompliance. More common in the aid relationship is the acceptance and internalization of external direction and priorities. Risking the loss of funding that is deemed essential carries a very high political price for government and education officials.

Thus, the uncritical use of the terms *country-led development* and *national ownership* obscures the persistence of the same structured relationships that have characterized the aid relationship over many years. Yes, policies and programs are officially set within Africa. Often, that means that received wisdom appears in local idioms printed locally.

Certainly it is possible to envision a meeting of minds. African authorities may well come to find useful and to own ideas that they imported, borrowed, and adapted. Learning, both individual and institutional, involves exchanging ideas and understandings. That itself is not problematic. But applying "ownership" to every plan, policy, or document signed by an African official obscures what may, under closer scrutiny, prove to be a dramatic lack of ownership.

The claim of ownership can best be tested in circumstances where external funders and national and/or higher education authorities can be expected to have different objectives, priorities, or institutional arrangements. Confirming the claim requires evidence that external agencies have modified their expectations and conditions, have openly and genuinely negotiated their efforts to pursue their own national interests, and have agreed to support programs whose direction, organization, and outcomes they cannot control.

Assessing national ownership also requires critical attention to the common equation that Africa = government. Recall that ownership is deemed important because initiatives and reforms that are not locally owned are difficult to implement and impossible to sustain. What matters, then, is not just the support of national authorities but also the deep involvement of education communities, both individuals and organizations. From this perspective, government's responsibility is not simply to speak on behalf of the country but also to ensure that diverse ideas, perspectives, and interests are addressed. Similarly, even as they work with governments, funding and technical assistance agencies must also assume responsibility for creating space for and listening to multiple voices.

These observations suggest that, as we wrestle with notion of country-led development, we must recognize that 1) aid dependence and country-led development are incompatible, and 2) as long as the heavy reliance on foreign aid continues, making aid more effective requires working on transparency and clarity about roles rather than assuming that external agencies (in the current parlance, "development partners") have no interests, can ignore their interests, or will subordinate their own sense of what must be done to the decisions of national education officials.

APPROACHES AND TOOLS EMBEDDED IN EXTERNAL SUPPORT

External support to education in Africa carries more and less visible direct and indirect conditions. It also carries values, assumptions, and understandings. Education aid brings with it broad approaches and toolkits for encouraging and managing education and development. Three sets of approaches warrant special attention here.

Human Capital Theory

The first approach emerges with the widening influence of human capital theory, which asserts that education ought to be regarded as an investment in developing a country's human resources. In the World Bank's 1995 education policy review, the endorsement is unqualified: Human capital theory has no genuine rival of equal breadth and rigor (World Bank, 1995, p. 21). An extended discussion of the role of human capital theory is beyond the scope of this chapter. It is important to our discussion here because of the ways, often barely noticed and generally rarely challenged, in which its perspective shapes understandings of education reform. Conceiving of education as investment leads us to consider choices among education policies and allocations as alternative investment possibilities whose relative importance (value) can be assessed in terms of their projected return. Within this framework, the primary mechanism for choosing among alternative investment patterns is rate of return analysis. The tools of investment banking, thus, become the appropriate techniques for evaluating and assessing education policies and practices—not learning, not empowerment, not reducing inequality, not other key education objectives, and not education as an interactive process that is continually negotiated and always contextually specific.

Education as Industry

A second approach that is common in the aid relationship understands education as production. Rather than the tools of investment banking, this approach brings with it the logic of manufacturing and, especially, a focus on efficiency. Recall the comments above on wastage, one of the prime measures of what this approach terms *internal efficiency*. Here, too, the adoption of the perspective and its tools is often unnoticed and only rarely addressed critically. Who could object to efforts to become more efficient? But what exactly is efficiency in education? In manufacturing, efficiency seems clear. To produce bottles or cars efficiently, for example, requires finding the lowest-cost raw materials, reducing waste and breakage, training workers to do their jobs quickly and accurately, installing machinery that is reliable, securing low-cost energy, keeping maintenance simple, and making sure that expenditures on marketing are exceeded by income from increased sales. That is, efficiency in manufacturing has to do with reducing the costs of production. Although the production metaphor is occasionally useful, education is fundamentally different from manufacturing. In an interactive process, the distinction between inputs and outputs is consciously blurred. Bottles do not contribute to their own manufacture, but students *do* contribute to their own education. Cars do not suggest improvements in the assembly process or reject the old way of doing things, but learners *are* active participants in their education, not only suggesting improvements and rejecting received wisdom but taking the initiative to chart new paths.

On the face of it, for example, larger classes would increase an education system's efficiency. When the teacher's salary is spread across more and more students, the unit cost goes down. But, of course, the appropriate unit of education is not the student, but the learning. What matters most in an education system is not how many students there are per teacher or even how many teacher hours are allocated to each student, but rather how much and how well those students have learned. It is far from clear that efficiency, however defined, is or ought to be the primary goal to be maximized. Like those responsible for space travel, educators in poor countries may assign higher priority to redundancy.

More generally, the human capital theory approach converts matters of education policy (for example, under what circumstances is repetition pedagogically, socially, politically, even economically desirable) into technical, administrative, or managerial concerns. It also focuses policy attention in the wrong direction. Concern with reducing the unit cost per student is likely to be far less fruitful than focusing on increasing the effectiveness of each unit of expenditure.

A corollary to stress on efficiency is insistence on feasibility and practicality. That orientation may seem quite reasonable, but, in practice, it constrains both education and development. Innovations are inherently risky. Since innovations are risky, funding and technical assistance agencies generally require using older, ostensibly proven and reliable approaches. A major consequence of that orientation, to return to the production metaphor, is that creative departures and the production of new means of production take place in the affluent countries. Those who are poor scramble to catch up as they watch those who are more affluent discard the approaches and technologies that they are told to use. In practice, poverty is deemed to preclude fundamental innovation, which, in turn, is likely to perpetuate the poverty.

Education as Delivery System

A third approach is reflected in the characterization of education as a delivery system. Embedded in that perspective is what Paulo Freire has termed *the banking model of education*. Learners are like empty bank accounts. More or less formally, teachers and others with the relevant capital—wisdom—make deposits into those accounts. Successful students save their resources and complete their education with heads full of knowledge on which they can subsequently draw. At least for younger learners, learning is understood largely as a passive process. Teachers give, provide, or offer, and students receive. Where students play a somewhat more active role, they acquire knowledge and skills. Educators who understand learning as an active process, who situate learners at the center of that process, and for whom learning involves the appropriation, manipulation, and integration of information, have little voice in the policies and programs developed using an approach that understands education as a delivery system.

The terminology used is both instructive and formative. In the documents of the funding and technical assistance agencies, education reforms are regularly termed *interventions*, that is, insertions from outside rather than initiatives from within. Externally funded, externally guided, and often externally managed, specific reform projects are rarely directly responsible to the settings—whether teachers, students, or the local community—in which they function. How are Third World educators to become owners of those reforms when they are the objects of the surgery, not the surgeons? Education is termed a *delivery system*, not an organic process in which learners are the doers rather than the receivers. How do recipients become owners? In practice, this combination of a vantage point external to education (whether national or foreign) and very limited accountability generally proves fundamentally disempowering.

PATHWAYS OF INFLUENCE

My concern here is the aid process and the aid relationship. My general argument is that if the effectiveness of external support is largely a function of the aid relationship, then increasing that effectiveness requires addressing that relationship directly and critically. That, in turn, requires getting inside the commonly used words and approaches to explore the structured patterns that they institutionalize and internalize. There have been important changes in the terminology and forms of foreign aid. The aid relationship itself seems to have changed far less than is often claimed and than is immediately apparent.

I turn now to research on an especially powerful and influential provider of external support, the World Bank. I do so not to suggest that the World Bank is either the sole or always the most important aid organization, or that other organizations always and everywhere follow the World Bank's lead. That is certainly not the case, though several recent comprehensive evaluations have emphasized the centrality of the World Bank's role and the apparently declining role of the United Nations system's education organization, UNESCO. The adoption of sectoral approaches has apparently increased cooperation among other agencies, sometimes including shared representation. Yet we find very few situations where that cooperation has directly reversed the agenda articulated by the World Bank or has reduced World Bank influence. A few agencies have energetically sought to strengthen partnership and reduce external direction—the Nordic and Dutch agencies stand out—but they, too, have generally been enmeshed in a structured aid relationship that permits only limited local direction and ownership. Not infrequently, even those agencies have preferred to acquiesce in World Bank leadership rather than challenge it. Over several decades of external support, there have been some aid agencies and projects with radically different conceptions of roles and responsibilities. Most often, however, these have been exceptions to common practice, swamped by the powerful tide of the aid process. Hence, it is important to focus on the World Bank, remaining attentive to the circumstances in which other agencies follow or depart from its lead.

Within the World Bank, debate is often intense, sometimes acrid. Accordingly, in this attention to the World Bank and its policies and practices, it is essential to recognize the critical voices, critiques, and innovative departures that emerge within the institution. The story here is not about heroes and villains, but about structured relationships.

For the present, the World Bank has asserted and assumed a central and often dominating role in education and development in Africa. Accordingly, it is useful for our concern here with the aid relationship to explore exactly how that role works. How does an external organization so profoundly influence education policies and programs in Africa, even where its own funding—in practice, since the World Bank lends not its funding but the resources of recipient countries themselves—is a very small part of total spending on education? To address that, let us consider the multiple pathways of the World Bank's influence in higher education in Africa.[6]

Notwithstanding the important transitions in the World Bank's orientation toward education, there have been significant continuities in its education policy, including increased student fees, privatization, reduced public support for nonacademic activities, and a generally diminished government role. How has it sought to make that agenda the agenda for the development of education in Africa?

In the 1960s, the World Bank insisted on the importance of post-primary education. For many countries, the influence was quite direct. Years later, the World Bank has changed its mind and methodology and assigned highest priority to basic education.[7] So, too, have many countries in Africa—indeed, around the world. Causality? In part, surely. But not everywhere, and often not direct. Tanzania provides a useful example. It was Julius Nyerere and the Tanzanian African Union (TANU), not the World Bank, that rejected the manpower planning orthodoxy in favor of basic education. In that setting, and in others influenced by Nyerere's notion of education for self-reliance, the World Bank followed, not led. Only occasionally is a simple linear causality between World Bank pronouncement and African practice tenable. More common is what has been termed a *funnel of causation*, in which major and minor influences that tend in the same direction become mutually reinforcing and ultimately lead to a common outcome. That funnel helps focus attention beyond the fact and extent of influence to its process.

Viewed closely, World Bank policies emerge from a tangled mix of ideas, experiences, research, powerful individuals, and shifting alliances. Similarly, viewed closely, World Bank education lending and conditionalities are buffeted and shaped by political currents inside and outside the institution. Every project, every loan, every interaction is a local tale with infinite details, all seemingly significant. Yet there are broad patterns, and they do matter. The funnel metaphor helps clarify how diverse actions and divergent perspectives are organized into a common policy direction. At the wide end of the funnel are the debates, discussions, coalitions, and power brokers. Educators, politicians, evaluators, researchers, specialists of all sorts, community organizations, students, parents, and others may all be active. As the funnel narrows, the specific setting shapes the interactions. In different settings, arguments and negotiations about, say, the priority assigned to teacher education or the role of decentralized management may take different forms and reach different conclusions. Outcomes are, in that sense, conjunctural. But they occur within the confines of the funnel itself, which represents the values, assumptions, and understandings of the World Bank's global role and the world's political economy. Diverging currents, churning confrontations, and local particularities manifest a striking commonality. What flows through the narrow end of the funnel is surprisingly homogeneous.

How do external and internal pressures intersect? Patterns of influence have been varied and have evolved with changing global and local circumstances. Outsiders, from the World Bank to the former colonial powers and other governments to the philanthropic foundations as well as governments, have long had a strong sense of how education in Africa should function. With a similarly strong sense of how instruction and research should be organized in African universities, they have regularly sought to shape departments, faculties, and institutes according to their vision. Simultaneously, there have been local visions and initiatives. The two spheres overlap. Educated and socialized overseas, African decision-makers, educators, and academic staff brought home not only new skills and understandings, but also strong views on the appropriate mission (intellectual and developmental), domain (academic and political), and methodology (instruction and research) for higher education in Africa. With a few exceptions, local circumstances and external funding agencies have been inhospitable to the most radical higher education voices. Foreign aid in general and institutional cooperation in particular have tended to reinforce particular perspectives and orientations and thereby strengthen their advocates and to disparage and devalue others. It is not the case that all external influence is problematic or that external ideas and preferences are invariably implemented faithfully and uncritically. African universities have innovated and insisted on their own direction, and overseas institutions acknowledge learning from Africa. It does seem clear that, from their creation, modern higher education institutions in Africa have been strongly influenced, both directly and indirectly, by intellectual and political currents from abroad, and that their organization and orientation reflect the internalization and local articulation of particular ideas about what should be their mission and focus. It also seems clear that there is little evidence of Mazrui's notion of counter-penetration—powerful African influences in the overseas institutions that educate and employ Africans or in the funding agencies for which they consult (1975).

Direct Advice and Conditions

World Bank influence can be explicit and direct, both in advice and in recommendations, and embedded in the conditions required for the provision of funds. While the World Bank has always provided advice with its funding, in recent years, it has insisted ever more forcefully that its development expertise is even more important than its loans. This is the first pathway of influence. In large and small ways, the World Bank instructs loan recipients on what they should and should not do, when, and how. Those instructions may come from the World Bank's president or other senior officials, from midlevel managers, and from young staff who have barely completed their own education. The resources associated with those instructions make them loud and forceful, however they are articulated. That the World Bank increasingly acts as the lead funding agency or on behalf of other funding agencies makes its messages even more compelling. That the World Bank is a primary designer of aid forms and modalities enables it to set the rules that govern the aid process more generally. In this way, even as it insists that it is not imposing its will, the World Bank seeks to achieve its objectives by specifying those rules in ways that require some behaviors and preclude others.

The World Bank also exercises influence through its extensive reports and publications. Loans are enmeshed in a web of documents from early studies to pre-appraisals to sector analyses to public expenditure reviews to implementation and management reports to narrower and broader evaluations and more. Embedded in nearly all of those reports (there are occasional exceptions) is the World Bank agenda of the moment. Although their specific purposes and focuses vary, those reports specify what has been done and what is yet to be done. African countries and education ministries put their loan eligibility at risk when they ignore or reject the findings and recommendations of those reports.

Historically, the authors of many of those reports have been non-Africans deemed to have relevant expertise. Increasingly, in part in response to persistent critiques on this score, the World Bank has involved African researchers and evaluators in its analytic efforts. Recognizing this transition helps us understand that the nationality of the report author is far less consequential than the origins of the approaches and methodologies employed. African economists of education who employ rate of return analysis uncritically reach the same conclusions and make the same recommendations as their non-African counterparts. Rate of return analysis, however, was developed in particular settings outside of Africa, and may or may not yield the same insights or have the same utility in African settings. More important, rate of return analysis may be an inappropriate tool for assessing the relative value of alternative decisions about priorities and the use of resources in education. In this example, the World Bank's influence is incorporated in analytic tools and does not depend on the nationality of those who use the tools. Indeed, the tool and the consequences of its use gain credibility and legitimacy when they are cloaked in African cloth.

Beyond its loan-related reports and associated studies, the World Bank's massive publications program directly enhances its influence. Its documents are of all sorts, from small reports on individual projects to major studies of sectors and countries to analyses of aid and its consequences to periodic reports on the state of the world. Formerly, many of the World Bank's documents remained confidential, available only to its staff and a small circle of others. More recently, more of its publications are being broadly circulated, and many are now instantly accessible on its massive website. Effectively, the World Bank has become a global point of reference for the major issues in which it is involved. Even resource-starved African university libraries and bare shelf bookshops may have an ample supply of World Bank publications. Most recently, the World Bank has organized and managed online discussions on studies and policy papers in preparation. The World Bank's annual *World Development Report* has become a standard reference for nearly everyone, including many of those who decry the assumptions, values, and orientation written into it. World Bank studies, analyses, reviews, and policy guides address all major development domains. They, too, are widely regarded as reliable points of reference, even though it is often difficult to cross-check their findings. Generally readable and well presented, World Bank major publications frequently do not cite their sources or rely nearly entirely on research undertaken or commissioned by the World Bank itself. Colorful boxed inserts provide vignettes and examples that should be treated as illustrative, but that are commonly regarded as demonstrative or confirming. Far too often, what emerges are assertions that are accepted as facts largely because the World Bank says they are facts.

Like many dimensions of the World Bank, this information and publishing role has a dual edge. On the one hand, it is desirable that World Bank analyses, policies, and recommendations be widely available. It is especially helpful to be able to trace thinking from initial drafts and preliminary papers to final documents. On the other hand, the very profusion of documents and their authoritative character makes the World Bank the center and focus of discussion and often the term-setter, manager, and arbiter of the discussion itself. The World Bank is not, however, a neutral discussion organizer, but rather an institution with a strong agenda. Notwithstanding the plethora of publications, those mixed roles do not ensure transparency or accountability or even equitable access to a debate in which the issues are fully aired and critics have effective time at the microphone.

The World Bank also exercises direct influence through its certifying role. How are aid providers to determine whether or not a country is making progress along an agreed-upon trajectory, implementing the activities for which it has received foreign support, or fulfilling its commitments to modify spending patterns or decentralize authority or democratize political competition? Often, other funding agencies tie their own support to the satisfaction of expectations and conditions determined by the World Bank and the International Monetary Fund. Consequently, where the World Bank or the IMF has not certified that actions are appropriate or that progress is adequate, all aid stops. Even countries that prefer to seek assistance from other sources—for example, Tanzania in the late 1970s and early 1980s—find all funds blocked until they have satisfied World Bank and IMF terms.

Conditionalities, too, must be understood as a mode of direct influence. In their initial form, conditionalities had to do with increasing the likelihood of loan repayment, which, in turn, required increasing the likelihood of success in the activities financed by the loan. More recently, conditionalities have become a major component of policy-based lending. If the goal is to encourage particular behaviors, then attaching conditions to loans is a major way to achieve that. Structural and sectoral adjustment loans carry explicit requirements, both at the macroeconomic level and within the education sector.

The World Bank and other funding agencies stoutly defend the conditions they impose, not only in terms of the requisites of development but also to achieve desired social goals. We see here a manifestation of the expanding role of the World Bank. Initially, imposed conditions were intended to ensure loan repayment and were defended in those terms. Over time, providing development advice became both a purpose and a rationale for direct influence and explicit conditions. Girls' education is a clear example. For many years, girls' education was a barely visible or a low-priority objective in African education strategies and plans. By the 1990s, no policy paper, proposal, or project could ignore it. The major funding agencies simply insisted. Even more, they presented themselves as more active and more effective defenders of the disadvantaged than Africa's governments and organizations. "How do you get girls educated in the Sahel, except through conditionality?" the World Bank vice president for Africa asked (Samoff, 1995).

Note here the delicate dance that the World Bank must perform as it sets loan conditions. Note, too, the tacit negotiations about conditions between the World Bank and recipient governments. Formally, the World

Bank must lend to and negotiate with governments. At the same time, the World Bank believes that it knows better than those governments what their countries need and that it is more effective than those governments in advancing the interests of the poor, women, ethnic minorities, and other disadvantaged groups. From that perspective, it is reasonable for the World Bank to impose conditions with which government must comply. Yet those very governments must agree to the conditions. Hence, the fan dance with obscuring veils and feathers. Even as it insists that the governments change their behavior, the World Bank insists that its conditions reflect African government preferences and decisions. Sometimes, though probably less often than the World Bank claims, the governments themselves find the conditions reasonable but unpalatable to strong local political interests. From that perspective, too, it is reasonable for the World Bank to impose conditions, since it is helping the government do what it thinks must be done but for which the Bank cannot appear to be taking the initiative. The government can blame the World Bank for unpopular action and claim credit for beneficial results.

Although it is powerful and influential, the World Bank is not omnipotent. African governments ignore or reject World Bank instructions at the risk of reduced funding, not only from the World Bank but from other agencies as well. Yet African governments can create room to maneuver and can decide not to implement World Bank instructions without necessarily becoming ineligible for future funding. To understand the influence of the World Bank, and of other funding and technical assistance agencies, we must explore how that influence is mediated and negotiated.

Indirect Conditions

Although they may be intrusive and onerous, direct conditions are visible. Where funding is conditional on, say, the commitment of a specified percentage of education spending to basic education, or on the privatization of textbook production and distribution, everyone involved can see and address whatever is expected. The conditions may be regarded as unpleasant and unreasonable, but they are apparent and can be confronted directly.

Far less visible and, therefore, often far more insidious and powerful are indirect conditions, the second pathway of influence. These indirect conditions may be imposed and monitored in several ways. Among them are the conditions embedded in the administration and management of the aid relationship. The expanded terrain of the analysis and planning required to support a funding request provides a clear example. For many years, the World Bank has required what it terms *education sector work* as part of the preparation for a project proposal or loan application. The concept is straightforward. To assess the proposal for a specific activity, whether physical facilities or the learning process, as the lender, the World Bank wants to be sure that what is proposed has a reasonable prospect of achieving its objectives and, thus, contributing to the income generation necessary to repay the loan. Education sector studies, historically undertaken by expatriate-led teams with brief, intense fieldwork, addressed those and related issues, intended both to provide the foundation for the loan proposal and to strengthen its preparation.[8]

As critics pointed to the external orientation of those studies, to their reliance on expatriate researchers, and to their distance from national education planning and management, the World Bank and other funding agencies increasingly employed African researchers and presented results in government-led forums. At the same time, however, a different set of pressures both entrenched the external orientation of education sector studies and made them more onerous for African governments.

First, the World Bank and other funding agencies began to shift their focus away from discrete projects and toward sectorwide support.[9] That necessarily broadened the scope and, often, the intrusiveness of their preparatory studies. Second, the World Bank's overarching attention to poverty leads it to insist that education be understood as part of a broader antipoverty strategy. The required studies and other preparatory documents must, therefore, address not only the education sector but the entire national development strategy. Ironically, the critique that the education sector work required by the World Bank was not well integrated into national education planning and management has fostered the expectation that, in order to receive funding, the countries must themselves produce studies and plans in a form and manner that are acceptable to the World Bank. Currently, the most visible and the most imposing of those documents are the Comprehensive Development Framework (CDF) and the Poverty Reduction Strategy Paper (PRSP). PRSPs have been adopted by the World Bank and the IMF, and with their leadership, by other funding and technical assistance agencies, as the major framework for development cooperation:

> Poverty Reduction Strategy Paper (PRSP) will be broadly endorsed by the [World] Bank and [International Monetary] Fund Boards as the basis of concessional assistance from the two institutions. (World Bank, 2002)

> The World Bank has enormous influence over the shape and pace of Indonesia's policies and reform in its own right, but also through its production of the economic analysis that serves as the information base on which other creditors and donors rely to make decisions. (International NGO Forum on Indonesian Development, as cited in Wilks & Lefrancois, 2002, p. 11)[10]

> If the PRS process were a government-led process, why would the Bank and Fund send numerous missions to the country to develop the PRS? Why would the Bank develop a 1,000 page Sourcebook to tell developing country groups how to create a PRS? (Abugre, 2001, as cited in Wilks & Lefrançois, 2002, p. 11)[11]

Effectively, the approach and major tenets of structural and sectoral adjustment—a broad development agenda commonly characterized as neoliberal and as the Washington consensus—have now had their lives extended in the form of PRSP development and approval. Note that PRSPs provide a rationale for broadened external intervention. Poverty reduction is a widely shared goal. The process of developing a national poverty-reduction strategy can permit greater transparency and wider participation in debating national policies. In practice, however, that process can also broaden, extend, and legitimize external influence, and can deflect and defuse the critiques of community groups even as it positions them as cosponsors of its outcomes. Many more people can board the aid train. They can speak forcefully and loudly about where it should go. They may even sit in the driver's seat. They may determine its speed and fuel economy. The national government and community organizations are responsible for what happens. But they are proceeding along tracks whose directions and technical specifications have been set elsewhere.

Ostensibly the products of national deliberations and analysis, the CDF, PRSP, and related documents are heavily shaped by the explicit and implicit expectations of the external agencies and by national interpretations of those expectations. That extends not only to the content of the planning and analytic documents but also, and more importantly, to their assumptions, constructs, and tools. For example, to accept uncritically that rate of return analysis is the preferred tool for setting education priorities, or that student attrition should be addressed in terms of the efficiency of schooling, or that attention to the gendered character of power and authority in society is inappropriate in an education planning document is to exclude vital issues of education policy from discussion without debate. A political perspective that is embedded in the selection of analytic tools and the organization of research and planning documents thereby becomes a condition of receiving funding. Internalized, institutionalized, and often not fully recognized, that condition is all the more powerful for its near invisibility.

> PRSPs from wildly divergent countries reveal great universality in vocabulary, process, form, content and even prescription. With some exceptions, PRSPs provide a good deal of evidence of the macro still driving the national, the global the local, the rational the practical, the technical driving the political and economic. (Craig & Porter, as cited in Wilks & Lefrançois, 2002, p. 21)[12]

The point here is not that it is undesirable to base decisions on extensive data collection and careful analysis. Of course not. Well-grounded decisions are certainly to be preferred. Rather, what is important here is that the extent, form, and frequency of required education sector work overwhelm African capacities and come to rely on external staff, and that when they are embedded in education sector work, assumptions, preferences, and conditions are both difficult to discern and sharply constraining.

Influence on Other Funding and Technical Assistance Agencies

A third pathway of World Bank influence is through other funding and technical assistance agencies. The international and national providers of financial and technical support are numerous and diverse. Each defines its own role and agenda. Each is responsible to its own governing body or national government. None can keep up with the World Bank. That was not always the case. Earlier, the World Bank credited UNESCO for the recognition of the importance of basic education. Now, the World Bank has explicitly and implicitly assumed some of the roles of UNESCO and other agencies. Across Africa, the World Bank's professional capacity exceeds that of most other agencies, though the situation varies from country to country. Even though it may not be the largest aid provider in a particular country, the World Bank's macroeconomic leverage is unparalleled. It sets the pace and largely controls the form for education sector work. Not infrequently, it oversees the provision and use of other agencies' funds. Its energetic development of CDF, PRSP, and related holistic strategies effectively makes the World Bank the primary point of reference for how to organize and manage development assistance.

Recent years have seen increased efforts to coordinate foreign aid. In many African countries, a committee or working group of funding and technical assistance agencies meets periodically to share information, address divergent expectations and practices, and speak with a single voice to the national government. Commonly, the World Bank's own voice carries great weight in those settings. Its message shapes or becomes the common message. This is especially so for higher education, since most other agencies, in part following the World Bank's lead, have shifted their attention to basic education.

Periodically, the World Bank has created new organizations to strengthen this pathway of influence. A clear example is the Association for the Development of Education in Africa (ADEA), originally Donors to African Education (DAE). Initiated and centered at the World Bank, which provided its rationale, organizational priorities and structure, and secretariat, DAE brought together funding and technical assistance agencies that were involved in education in Africa. To increase its influence and effectiveness and ensure its legitimacy required the involvement of Africa's education ministers. That has taken a momentum of its own. Over time, the organization has strengthened the ministers' roles and African participation in working group activities, relocated its secretariat to the International Institute of Educational Planning (UNESCO) in Paris, and changed its name to ADEA.

ADEA is also a useful example for understanding the complexities of influence. While its origins are clear, currently ADEA is not solely or perhaps even primarily a vehicle for promoting World Bank ideas. Its working groups maintain a good deal of autonomy, often reflecting the interests and expectations of their own lead agencies and other participants, and periodically spawning or supporting still other organizations with their own agendas (for example, the Forum for African Women Educationalists). Its biennial meetings permit active, sometimes acerbic, exchange between agencies and governments in a relatively informal setting. The African education ministers use ADEA to forge their own common messages and deliver them to funding and technical assistance agencies. At the same time, having moved beyond its origins and having acquired greater legitimacy as it did so, ADEA remains an important vehicle for transmitting and reinforcing ideas and practices with roots in Washington.

ADEA may also have played an unintended role within the World Bank. Precisely at the moment when its basic education message was the most forceful, the World Bank assumed formal leadership of ADEA's (then DAE's) Working Group on Higher Education (WGHE), with funding from the Ford Foundation. In practice, that increased the visibility for higher education in Africa inside the World Bank. As WGHE focused heavily on commissioning research and publications on higher education in Africa (more than 25 to date), it spoke a language well understood and difficult to ignore within the World Bank. Here, too, there is no linear causality. However, it seems reasonable to infer that WGHE, the child of a World Bank effort to influence others, has contributed to the continuity of attention and lending to African higher education in a context of unsupportive institutional policy and in the face of strong objections.

New Participants in the National Education Policy Process

Aid dependence has fostered another, fourth, pathway of influence. Africa has seen a wide range of strategies for generating, debating, and adopting national education goals and programs.[13] In many settings, presidential initiatives, national commissions, *États-Généraux*, stakeholder forums, and other approaches have fostered vigorous debate about directions, priorities, and practices.

Education policy is perhaps always a muddy morass of conflicting interests and alternative orientations. The process matters. Who has participated? Which ideas have been considered and which have been discarded without examination? Whose interests are reflected? Aid dependence has brought two new participants to the African education policy table: external agencies and finance ministries.

The external agencies, and the World Bank in particular, have become direct participants in national policy-making. Although it is careful to defer formally to the national government, in practice, the World Bank regularly makes clear what it regards as good and bad education policy, and equally regularly makes clear that the adoption of what it regards as poor policies will limit the availability of funds. It is, of course, not unreasonable for the World Bank to make decisions about what it will or will not support and to communicate its preferences to African governments. What has changed, however, is that aid dependence has effectively made the World Bank an insider in those discussions. In part, that participation in policy debates is formal and direct. Also in part, the World Bank sows the seeds through its contacts with and support for key individuals or by funding the preparation of policy briefs. As those seeds germinate, they take on national colors.

Like most forms of external support, World Bank loans are made to governments, not directly to education institutions or the education sector. As a result, they are commonly administered by the finance ministry, which also secures a seat for itself at the policy table. Along this pathway, the World Bank's messages are presented in education policy debates by the national finance ministry.

Thus, as the reliance on foreign funds increases, so does the influence of both the finance ministry and the external agencies. Representing the government in negotiations with those agencies, the finance ministry tends to become much more directly involved in policy and programmatic details across all government departments. This increased role may suit the external agencies well. Especially concerned with reducing government spending, those agencies are likely to see the finance ministry as their ally, in contrast with ministries of, say, health or education, whose general mandate requires them to be more concerned with spending than with saving. The alliance between external agency and finance (and perhaps planning) ministry may be structured as a powerful lever for influencing national policy.

As this occurs, the concerns, orientations, and priorities of the funding agencies are internalized in the policy process, both in the analyses and diagnoses that become the platform for policy and in the recommendations that shape the policy itself. As the distinction between insider and outsider becomes blurred, the homogenization of perspective and the adoption of universal verities, ostensibly with sound research support, proceed apace.

The World Bank distinctly prefers a rational-technical orientation to policy-making, with unambiguous policy directions, systematic planning, and orderly implementation, all supported by applied research. Education itself, however, is more process than product. A rational-technical orientation to education policy disdains interactive and participatory policy-making that is necessarily clumsier, muddier, and slower. As they work in an aid-dependent setting, often without being fully aware of the transition, African educators and decision-makers discard education as the vehicle for national liberation, for reducing inequality, and for constructing a new society in favor of education that consists of upgraded facilities, more textbooks, better-trained teachers, and improved test scores.

Commissioned Research

External support to higher education in Africa is increasingly associated with research in several important ways. The ironies are painful. Even as African universities are less able to support sustained research programs, research on education has become one of the major forms of influence on education in Africa.[14] In this fifth pathway of influence, the World Bank and other funding and technical assistance agencies have become research entrepreneurs. As I have noted, education sector work—studies required as part of the project approval process and, more recently, for broader sectoral support—continues to be an important, though less visible, component of the aid relationship. Formally intended to inform and guide, education sector studies in practice often serve to justify and legitimize. Ostensibly technical and functional, they carry values, assumptions, analytic frameworks, and constructs, and are, thus, another pathway of influence.

The specific examples are too numerous to detail here. As I have noted, rate of return analysis is presented and employed as an ostensibly neutral technique, thereby obscuring the values and assumptions embedded in its development and use. Important issues of education policy, like the circumstances in which repetition is educationally desirable, are treated as matters of efficiency. The egalitarian objectives of residential education are obscured by narrow notions of cost and benefit. The terminology can be particularly obfuscating, as increased fees become "cost recovery."

The near invisibility of this path of influence renders it particularly powerful. The World Bank controls a desired good that is highly sought by African educators. To release funds, it commissions research. Although African researchers are increasingly involved in those studies, the research bears the strong imprint of those who have commissioned it. Their assumptions, understandings, and expectations are embedded in the framing questions and the detailed terms of reference. This combination of funding and research constitutes a financial-intellectual complex that is difficult to challenge or deflect (Samoff, 1996a). The World Bank and, to a lesser extent, other funding agencies no longer need to announce imperiously what is to be done. Rather, they attach their funding to strategies and programs based on research findings that they regard as relevant and solid. Notwithstanding the efforts of some researchers to adopt a critical posture, the commissioned research presents a strikingly coherent and self-reinforcing picture. What might be controversial becomes unexceptional as it is incorporated into frameworks and ostensibly technical questions, with no explicit or direct link to the source of the constructs or their ideological content. Some questions simply never get asked. External support guides education policy in part by shaping the research that is policy's justification.

Influence by International Conference

By the 1970s, the World Bank had already begun to argue the importance of basic education in Africa. The challenge for the World Bank's education advocates was to show that education is a productive sector and, thus, an appropriate focus for lending and not simply a service. After all, the World Bank had argued earlier that education was a luxury to be enjoyed only after expanded production generated sufficient revenue to fund it. The theoretical lever was human capital theory. Spending on education could be understood as an investment in future productive capacity, like investment in new technology and equipment. But the education sector is broad, with many claimants for resources. Rate of return analysis, it was argued, showed clearly that investments in basic education yielded better societal results.[15] The World Bank has championed both the method and the message for more than 2 decades.

The late 1980s saw the effort to make that message a global campaign, leading to the 1990 Education for All conference, followed by a 1995 midterm conference in Jordan, and the follow-up 2000 World Education Forum in Senegal. With major international support (the World Bank was one of four sponsoring organizations), a substantial commitment from the national funding agencies, and some engagement by nongovernmental education organizations, the 1990 conference and follow-up activities became another, sixth, important pathway of influence. Ultimately, notwithstanding what its leaders or educators might say privately, no country wanted to be the lone and lonely naysayer, arguing an alternative perspective or different priorities. If the major players were putting their money on basic education, those seeking funds clearly had to do likewise. Not only the broad basic education message but also interpretations and implementation were communicated and given official sanction through the conference process. Education for All was to focus on expanding access, primarily to formal schools. Although they were mentioned, preschool and adult education were clearly lower priorities. So, too, were equity and quality issues, although girls' education achieved some prominence. Critics quickly raised these and other concerns with an even louder voice at the 2000 conference. The evidence suggests, however, that the original framework has proved to be quite durable, even though the funding agencies have apparently not provided the resources needed to achieve agreed-upon goals (UNESCO, 2002).

The implementation strategies associated with these international conferences further entrenched particular understandings and approaches. For the 2000 conference, countries were required to report on their progress toward EFA goals using an outline that specified topics to be addressed and data to be included. Following that conference, an even more elaborate monitoring process also specified the constructs and categories that were to be used to report on and talk about EFA.[16]

International conferences have many purposes and forms. They may or may not have influence beyond their participants or even beyond the few days that they meet. Conferences provide opportunities for debate and disagreement and for challenging those who organize them. Sometimes conferences take on a life and momentum of their own. What is important for this discussion is to recognize the extent to which the World Bank has used the international education conferences for developing and communicating a particular message about basic education and for pressing national governments and organizations of all sorts to modify their behavior in accordance with that message. Equally important is to recognize the ways in which the major message, along with its values and assumptions, are embedded in the procedures of the conferences and their follow-up. Once again, the ostensibly technical is, in practice, strongly ideological and fiercely political.

On a smaller scale, the same pattern is discernible in seminars, colloquia, and task forces. The deep agenda may be more about how to approach issues than about the issues themselves or their consequences. Participants return home with a thesaurus and a toolkit. The former influences how they understand their own education sector. For example, "student attrition" becomes "dropout," which, in turn, becomes "wastage," obscuring the many social, economic, educational, and other pressures that push students out of school in favor of a notion of individual failure to continue. The toolkit includes a spanner for tightening some connections and loosening others, but generally not a wire cutter or acetylene torch for severing links entirely.

Study tours can play a similar role. The World Bank identifies settings where its recommendations have been effectively implemented and then brings others to see. World Bank staff are quick to note that study tours of this sort are far more influential than even the most carefully documented study, cogently presented analysis, or coherent policy recommendations.

Recruitment of African Professionals

In this review of pathways of influence, I have been especially concerned with what is not obvious, particularly routes and vehicles that are less visible and the ways in which values and ideas are institutionalized and internalized. Another such pathway, the seventh identified here, is through the recruitment of African professionals.

For its work in and on Africa, the World Bank has relied heavily on non-Africans, including professional staff and longer- and shorter-term consultants. At the same time, its multinational personnel has increasingly included Africans in senior positions. Especially as it has expanded its poverty focus and its work on education, and as it has been challenged to be less Washington-centered, the World Bank has assiduously sought to hire Africans and other Third World professionals at various levels. In itself, that is not problematic. Indeed, many see this as a positive development, with benefits for the individuals employed and the countries where they work, both during and after their World Bank employment and with at least some prospect that they will have some influence inside the institution. There are individual stories that support all of those expectations. Still, another dimension of this process warrants critical attention.

The World Bank is a particularly powerful socializing institution that is generally more resilient, more persistent, and more penetrating than its individual employees. Irrespective of their politics, professionals recruited to work at the World Bank, whether as interns or as temporary or permanent employees, often carry with them particular assumptions, frameworks, and expectations that are (more or less consciously) influenced by World Bank policy and that, in turn, influence behavior in Africa. This observation refers not to employees' motives, intentions, or ethics, but rather to the analytic orientations—core ideas not only about what makes a good education system, but even more important, how to study and assess an education system—that inform their observations, findings, and recommendations. First-person accounts of World Bank employment are replete with references to how things must be stated or presented to secure approval from managers and, eventually, the Board of Governors. Ultimately, the World Bank remains a bank, managed largely by people with expertise and experience in economics and finance. Access to funding requires requests and rationales to be formulated according to its standards, which effectively structure the education and development discourse. Humanist notions of the intrinsic value of education and educators' support for child-centered learning are simply never as persuasive as detailed cost-benefit and rate of return analyses for securing authorization for an education sector loan. To reiterate, the point here is not the intentions, goodwill, or morality of World Bank staff, but rather the occasionally direct but often much more subtle ways in which the institution shapes their ideas and their approaches. This also occurs through advanced education programs, in which young scholars adopt ideas, perspectives, frameworks, and research methods that then shape what they do when they return home. For some, these include, eventually, national education policy and practice. Once again, the pathways of influence are indirect, difficult to discern, and, in this case, particularly delicate to challenge.

Recruiting African professionals brings legitimacy to the World Bank's agenda, even when their work is formulaic, unimaginative, and insubstantial. One example must suffice. In 1990, the World Bank published a series of discussion papers that sought to provide a comparative overview of education reform efforts in eastern and southern Africa. Eight case studies (Ethiopia, Kenya, Lesotho, Swaziland, Tanzania, Uganda, Zambia, and Zimbabwe) were complemented by a brief general overview by the series editor and a literature review (see Psacharopolous, 1990, and Samoff, 1993). Individually, notwithstanding the experience and competence of their authors, the eight case studies say little that is new, oversimplify complex issues of policy and practice, confuse policy pronouncements with actual behavior, employ constructs and categories uncritically, and do not substantiate their findings.

The process of embedding influence in approach is particularly clear in these papers. All of them manifest the assertion of the positivist faith. Studies that are not principally concerned with testing hypotheses—indeed, all other approaches to knowledge and understanding—are fundamentally flawed. The conjunction of funding and research becomes the vehicle for imposing orthodoxy. A particular approach to knowledge is characterized as social science itself. Detached from its context and shorn of its ideology, the scientific method is transformed into an atheoretical straitjacket. Positivist proselytizing parades as injunctions for good research. And only good research should guide the allocation of funds and the specification of activities to be supported.

For whom was this series produced? Informed readers surely found the case studies superficial. Readers with little background on African education found the jargon frustrating and confusing. Policy-makers were not likely to find these papers much more useful. Other sources provided clearer, more concise summaries and more substantial analyses. Nearly all of the authors had published more insightful, better-supported and better-documented, and more rigorous and stimulating analyses elsewhere. Yet, reading these papers does prove instructive. They reflect both the World Bank's willingness to accept insubstantial work from competent Third World scholars and its effort to institutionalize a particular set of understandings and constructs in research on education. While those constructs do not significantly enrich these papers, it is their uncritical acceptance that is striking. Within the accepted terminology are embedded particular conceptualizations, conceptions, orientations, prejudices, and policy preferences. That discourse-structuring terminology treats as part of the environment—what is "given" and therefore does not require explicit justification and is not subjected to critical attention—important issues that ought to be the focus of policy discussion. That terminology also obscures important issues and, thereby, far too frequently misdirects the search for understanding. The quasi-official status of these constructs in a setting where the same agency oversees both funding and research effectively diverts attention from and often precludes consideration of alternatives that warrant serious exploration, systematic elaboration, and critical evaluation.

This series of publications highlights two consequences of this pathway of influence. First, the use of the constructs, frameworks, and terminology was clearly deemed more important than the substantive content of the studies. Second, the fact that African scholars were the messengers rendered more legitimate both the message and its originating institution.

Cross-National Achievement Assessments

Yet another, eighth pathway might be termed *influence by examination*. Here, we move beyond the World Bank to funding and technical assistance agencies more generally. Coincident with the funding agencies' increasing attention to quality and outcomes has been an expansion in efforts to compare learning achievement across national borders. The common strategy relies on standardized tests, more or less modified to suit local conditions, to assess competence in specific subjects among generally comparable groups of students in different countries. Results often catch public attention, appearing as newspaper headlines that proclaim the improvement or decline of education in a particular country.

Assessments of this sort may provide useful information on education approaches and strategies and their implementation in diverse settings. The challenges, however, are enormous. There are major differences in understandings of what education is to accomplish and how to measure that. The tests used necessarily embed some of those understandings and discard others. Critics charge that the international comparative analysis is generally insensitive to the importance of local variations and their consequences, both in explaining test results and in comparing outcomes. For those who understand effective learning as interactive and, therefore, necessarily local, the problems of cross-national testing are structural and can never be satisfactorily resolved.

Like tests everywhere, cross-national assessments incorporate curriculum understandings and can shape teachers' behavior. Commonly, and especially when they regard themselves as underprepared, teachers teach to the test. Indeed, some reformers use modifying national examinations to change education practice. In this role, cross-national assessments become another pathway for external influence. Although there are some African initiatives of this sort (Naudet, 1999), the principal impetus and locus of control are external to Africa. With more or less African participation, and always proclaiming the universality of their approach, outsiders specify what are reasonable learning objectives for Africa, how to measure them, how to interpret the measures, and what to do when the scores are low.

OBSTACLES TO AID AS TRANSFER AND EXCHANGE: THE AID RELATIONSHIP

The modern history of African universities began with dependence, formally institutionalized in the links between European universities and subordinate institutions in Africa. External support has been significant throughout their history, combining the rhetoric of development, closing the gap, protecting national initiatives, capacity building, and empowerment with the practice of continued dependence. That dependence seemed to lessen in the energy and excitement of the immediate postcolonial era. Dynamic debates within higher education were increasingly Africa-oriented and Africa-focused and decreasingly driven by the disciplines and discourses of their overseas counterparts. Although they were listening to and watching the flow of events overseas, African academics were less often following and accommodating.

Just as economic and financial crisis threatened national development plans and constrained national courses of action, so, too, it reinforced external direction within higher education. As structural adjustment became the order of the day, universities also found that access to (rapidly declining) funds was dependent on reorganizing in accord with externally set priorities and agendas.

Coexisting with and periodically undermining intellectual independence, intellectual dependence is maintained in several ways. At the broadest level, the global system of academic recognition—especially publication, invitations to professional seminars and conferences, and research grants—is controlled outside Africa. At a very deep level, external influences on the intellectual structure and priorities of African universities continue to be profound and often unrecognized: What constitutes high-quality social science research? What is the appropriate balance between curative and preventive medical education? What is the recognized corpus for comparative literature or music or poetry? To what extent should legal education focus on the social consequences of constitutions and laws? In immediate and practical terms, external influences are once again directly visible in the increasing use of curriculum developed and packaged overseas, for which the most recent but not sole examples are web-based units and modules.

Foreign aid plays an important role in maintaining that external orientation. Foreign aid is always a relationship. While that relationship is shaped by dramatic inequalities of power and influence, it can neither survive nor function without direct and active African participation. We, thus, find a curious dance of the mutually dependent. Funding agencies, including the World Bank, and African leaders need one another to pursue their agendas. Where governments rely more for their programs and tenure on external funds than on a mobilized citizenry, the funders retain the upper hand.

Recall our starting point: The effectiveness of external support is a function of the aid relationship. The disabilities of the aid relationship are deep and enduring. Consequently, organizing aid to permit effective transfers and exchanges cannot be achieved by modifying forms and terminology, but rather requires structural transformations.

The deep context—the national interests of both providers and recipients of foreign aid and the current configuration of the global political economy—is constraining but not fully determining. There is room to maneuver, and even to make substantial changes, at all levels, from very local settings to the international arena.

Seizing the initiative requires analyses of the aid relationship that proceed well beyond what is easily visible and readily observed. With that in mind, I have sought here to outline patterns of influence whose power is, at least in part, a function of their invisibility and, thereby, to render more accessible the internalization of external influence.

My concern has not been to demonize funders or to lionize recipients. As I have said, this is not a story of heroes and villains but of structured relationships and complex interactions. In developing that story, we must be careful not to romanticize Africa or particular countries. In the effort to explore and create partnership and ownership, just as we subject the relationship between aid providers and aid recipients to critical scrutiny, so must we develop a critical approach to the relationships between government and the education community and between government and its citizens.

Higher education institutions in Africa and their governments energetically seek external funds. With those funds come both direct conditions and indirect influences on the evolution of higher education and on African society more broadly. Terms such as *partnership* and *ownership* become standard jargon that obscures the actual locus of authority and decision-making. Foreign aid becomes another tool, or set of tools, used by powerful forces to manage not only the movement of education resources but, more important, the flow of ideas and the specification of which ideas matter. Ironically, as Africa's universities work to secure external support, they become responsible for the internalization of the values, assumptions, and precepts that accompany foreign aid, thereby entrenching their own and national dependence. Scrambling for those funds without a corresponding critical analysis of the funding process and well-informed efforts to transform it may yield short-term benefits even as it renders longer-term changes even more difficult.

NOTES

1. An earlier draft of some of the ideas developed here was presented at the Nuffic Expert Meeting on a Changing Landscape: Making Support to Tertiary Education and Research in Developing Countries More Effective at The Hague, in May 2005, and included in the conference proceedings by Boeren and Holtland (2005).

2. The annual Education for All Global Monitoring Reports provide extensive detail, especially UNESCO (2002).

3. Several recent evaluations, differing in scope, focus, and style but complementary in their attention to problems in the aid relationship, were presented at a colloquium organized by the Netherlands Ministry of Foreign Affairs in The Hague in March 2004 (see The Hague, 2003; Mercer, Gosparini, Melchiori, Orivel, Sirtori, & Steinback, 2002; Sack, Cross, & Moulton, 2004).

4. For the development of this theme, see Samoff and Carrol (2004b).

5. I summarize here themes that I have developed in several publications. Among them, see Samoff (1996a, 1996b, 2004).

6. The following discussion is drawn from a study commissioned by the UNESCO Forum on Higher Education, Research, and Knowledge: Joel Samoff and Bidemi Carrol, *From Manpower Planning to the Knowledge Era: World Bank Policies on Higher Education in Africa* (Samoff & Carrol, 2004a).

7. Note that there is strong evidence of renewed interest in secondary education. This reflects both a more holistic approach to the education sector and more focused attention on the increased demand for secondary education that is one of the consequences of increased primary enrollment.

8. For a critical review of education sector studies in Africa in the early 1990s, see Samoff and Assié-Lumumba (1996) and Samoff (1999a, 1999b).

9. The literature on this claimed transition is expanding rapidly. For a start, see Buchert (2002) and Samoff (2004). A recently completed evaluation confirms both increased sectorwide support and, at the same time, the persistence and utility of the project orientation (The Hague, 2003).

10. Although the country discussed is Indonesia, the comment is equally relevant for Africa, where few countries have Indonesia's size or presence in the global economy.

11. Abugre's (2001) paper reports on PRSP preparation in Kenya and Ghana. Besides the *PRSP Sourcebook* (World Bank, 2002), the World Bank has also made other PRSP-related documents publicly available on the PRSP web page, http://www.worldbank.org/poverty/strategies/index.htm, including a PRSP Document Library, located at http://poverty.worldbank.org/prsp/. For the World Bank/IMF review of the PRSP process, see International Development Association and International Monetary Fund (2002). Wilks and Lefrançois (2002) list the analytic reports prepared for each country and sector considered for World Bank funding.

12. Other recent analyses of the PRSP process and its consequences include Fraser (2003); Gould, Ojanen, and McGee (2003); Hanley (2002); Kanbur and Vines (2000); McGee, Levene, and Hughes (2002); Randel, German, and Ewing (2000).

13. Instructive are the case studies of education policy-making reported in Evans (1994) and the Association for the Development of African Education (1996).

14. I draw here on Samoff (1999b) and Samoff (2003).

15. It is important to note that critics of this use of rate of return analysis were inside as well as outside the World Bank. For the use of rate of return analysis to reach the opposite conclusion—in Kenya, secondary, not primary, education has the higher rate of return—see Knight and Sabot (1990). For the more general critique, see Bennell (1996).

16. See the World Education Forum website, www2.unesco.org/wef/. For detailed guidelines on the preparation of national EFA country plans of action, see www.unesco.org/education/efa/country_info/country_guidelines.shtml. For the EFA observatory, which is to develop standardized indicators, see www.unesco.org/education/efa/monitoring/efa_observatory.shtml.

EIGHT

The Strategic Triad

Form and Content in Brazil's Triangular Cooperation Practices

Adriana Abdenur

In March 2000, the Brazilian Cooperation Agency (ABC), an office within the country's Ministry of Foreign Relations, signed the Japan–Brazil Partnership Program, in which the two nations pledged to collaborate in providing technical assistance to Portuguese-language countries in Africa and to East Timor. One of the program's key projects entailed training educators for remote training in public health, in partnership with Brazil's renowned public health foundation, Fundação Oswaldo Cruz (FIOCRUZ). Five years later, when President Inácio Lula da Silva of Brazil made an official visit to Japan, he and Japanese Prime Minister Junichiro Koizumi issued a joint statement lauding the agreement's accomplishments and stressing the importance of triangular cooperation in technical assistance (Ministry of Foreign Affairs, Japan, 2005).

Triangular cooperation, in which a developing country partners with either another developing country or an industrialized counterpart to lend technical assistance to a third country, is a growing model of technical cooperation in the developing world. Despite the spread of these tripartite arrangements, we still know little about their form and function within the global network of cooperation relations. Why do developing countries participate in triangular cooperation, and how are these arrangements different from bilateral and multilateral linkages?

Most of the literature on technical cooperation focuses either on bilateral relations or on multilateral channels, offering only clues as to why countries might sometimes prefer to partner up to lend assistance to a third party. This chapter analyzes both the form and content of technical assistance within triangular cooperation. What motivates developing countries such as Brazil to engage in triangular cooperation? How do those governments justify lending resources through triangular cooperation when those countries are themselves recipients of aid and technical assistance?

To help answer these questions, I draw on the social networks perspective. I begin examining this new configuration of technical assistance by drawing on Simmel's (1950) microsociological distinction between dyads and triads and transposing this framework to the macro level of South–South technical assistance. I apply Simmel's emphasis on the need for understanding the *form* of social interaction in order to grasp the *content* of interaction, analyzing both the configuration and meaning of triangular cooperation.

BACKGROUND

Technical assistance between developing countries is not a new phenomenon. In 1974, the General Assembly created a Special Unit within the United Nations Development Programme (UNDP) to boost technical cooperation among developing countries. Until the 1990s, however, South–South cooperation was carried out primarily through bilateral agreements. In the 1990s, a network began to emerge among Southern countries, facilitated by international organizations. This emerging network was characterized by the appearance of regional nodes—primarily India, Brazil, and South Africa—with the frequent participation of China. For example, in November 1997, the UNDP's Special Unit for Triangular Cooperation convened a meeting for 23 countries that had become key nodes of South–South cooperation, including China, India, Brazil, and South Africa. Over the next few years, some of these pivotal countries launched network-formation initiatives of their own. In 2003, Brazil teamed up with India and South Africa to launch a joint program for cross-regional poverty alleviation. In March 2007, the foreign ministers of the three countries met in New Delhi to further the New Delhi Agenda for Cooperation, the main charter of the India–Brazil–South Africa (IBSA) Forum. The agenda included not only clauses to strengthen trade among the three countries, but also provisions to boost cooperation in tackling poverty.

In addition to the emergence of this node-heavy network of South–South cooperation, over the past 10 years, new configurations of cooperation have emerged within the network. One such new form is triangular cooperation,[1] which has gained ground over the past 5 years. A joint document by Japan and the UNDP provides a definition of the arrangement:

> Triangular South–South cooperation is becoming increasingly popular as a way of fostering development by leveraging the best features of cooperation between developing countries with assistance from developed countries. A Tri-

angular South–South cooperation activity can be the initiative of one or more Southern countries that wish to cooperate with one another. In order to maximize their financial, logistical and technical resources, such countries can ask for the support of a Northern donor as a third partner. Alternatively, a donor can partner with a developing country willing to provide technical cooperation to other Southern partners and whose initiative will make triangular cooperation the Northern donor's priorities and interests. The Northern donor would then offer to support South–South cooperation through a triangular approach by providing financial and/or technical support. (UNDP, 1999)

In 2004, the UNDP's report *Forging a Global South*, published by its Special Unit for South–South Cooperation (the new name of the Technical Cooperation among Developing Countries unit), stressed the rapid spread of this configuration and emphasized its growing importance for developing human resources and for building research and institutional capacity. In its report, the UNDP emphasized the potential of triangular cooperation to tap into centers of excellence and knowledge networks within the developing world. Understanding the politics behind these cooperation arrangements, however, requires a grasp of both form and content.

BUILDING A FRAMEWORK

Why do developing countries lend assistance to other developing countries, and how do they justify this lending to their constituencies when their own resources are often scarce? Similarly, how do states justify borrowing from another country that is frequently labeled as developing? And how are these dynamics affected by triangular cooperation, more specifically? While this chapter does not aim to provide full answers to these questions, I propose a framework for analyzing those issues.

Answering these questions requires an understanding not only of the form of networks and linkages, but also of the politics of lending and borrowing in technical cooperation. The scholarship on education transfer has shown that institutions (agencies, governments, organizations) that engage in education lending must also justify their lending activities, especially when their own resources are scarce. For instance, Steiner-Khamsi (2004b) has identified three reasons why international organizations lend education models. First, they hope to show their constituents that their own projects are effective and desirable. Second, the cost of education transfer might, in fact, be relatively low, given the division of labor in international organizations. And third, cookie-cutter programs developed at headquarters are generally easier to implement than custom-designed programs.

Agencies and governments also have various motivations to engage in education lending. For instance, Japan's growing involvement in lending technical assistance was triggered in part by the country's superior performance on the Third International Mathematics and Science Study (TIMSS) (Steiner-Khamsi, 2004c). The enhanced legitimacy that comes with such results gives high scorers added visibility on the international scene.

Assistance between developing countries also entails complex politics and modes of justification. For instance, government initiatives for student exchanges between African countries and China present political and strategic opportunities for both parties. China can use these exchanges to boost its political influence in Africa, and African countries can use them to challenge the colonial heritage within their education systems (Gillespie, 2001).

The networks perspective in sociology can add to the understanding of technical cooperation accumulated through the literature on education transfer. The relevance of the networks perspective to education transfer has already been acknowledged (Steiner-Khamsi, 2004b). Education transfers take place through ties among social actors, such as governments, institutions, agencies, and individuals. These social ties are established and maintained through student exchanges, technical cooperation programs, and the diffusion of institutional organizational forms, educational materials, and other concrete innovations. In addition to analyzing the structure of education transfers, the literature has also begun to examine the content of those ties, highlighting asymmetrical relationships and power dynamics.[2]

The social networks perspective within the social sciences can help shed light on these forms and dynamics. Broadly put, the social networks perspective has two key traditions. The sociocentric perspective focuses on the structural properties of relations rather than the individual relationships themselves. Methodologically, social scientists working within this tradition rely primarily on quantitative approaches, using matrices, cluster- and graph-based analyses, and network visualization. The second tradition—the egocentric perspective—focuses instead on the networks of specific social actors, starting with a single individual or institution. Studies adopting this perspective tend to rely heavily on survey methods.

The sociocentric perspective builds on Georg Simmel's work on the configuration of social ties and the implications of form for the content of interaction. Simmel (1950) argued that the size of a social group was key to understanding the interactions among the group's constituents. Simmel (1950) argued that dyads are the most basic form of interaction and exchange, involving immediate reciprocity between the two social actors involved.

When a third social actor transforms a dyad into a triad, the norms of reciprocity are weakened; within this configuration, actors may pursue strategies that generate competition, alliances, or mediation. In this sense, a triad (and any larger group) is far more than the sum of its individual parts.[3] Simmel argued that social interaction within a triad differs from the dyad in that the triad offers greater possibilities in strategies, competition, alliances, and mediation. Thus, far more than in a dyad, a triad develops a group structure that is independent of its individual components.

In contrast to Weber and Durkheim, who tended to focus on larger social groups or society as a whole, Simmel's distinction between dyads and triads was microsociological—an observation about social interaction at the level of individuals and small groups. Here, we transpose this theoretical framework to a higher level of aggregation: that of organizations and states. One key caveat: Norms of reciprocity between individuals are not necessarily equivalent to those between governments, whose interaction is constrained by official treaties and regulations as well as informal rules of international conduct. Nevertheless, even at a higher level of analysis, the form of social groups offers clues as to the content of interaction.

Thinking systematically about the differences between dyadic and triadic arrangements within international cooperation relations will help clarify the unique characteristics of triangular cooperation arrangements. Thus, we can ask: Why do governments engage in triangular cooperation? And, more specifically, does this particular configuration offer Southern lending countries more space for maneuvering within the international arena?

DATA AND METHODS

To examine the dynamics of triangular cooperation, I focus on the case of Brazil. Not only has Brazil been proactive in building South–South relations over the past 10 years, but it has also played a significant role in the dissemination of triangular cooperation as a form of technical assistance. The Brazilian Cooperation Agency (Agência Brasileria de Cooperaração, or ABC) includes a special division devoted exclusively to technical cooperation between developing countries (TCDC), and this division has initiated some triangular cooperation projects that are being implemented in South and Central America, Africa, and Asia.

I analyzed documents pertaining to technical cooperation that have been published by the ABC, including texts outlining Brazil's strategy for pursuing international partnerships and documents about specific treaties and projects, available through the agency's triangular cooperation DC

Projects Database (ABC, 2005b). I analyzed the content and language of these official documents to identify the triangular cooperation arrangements in which Brazil participates, as well as the different types of justification offered by the Brazilian government for engaging in triangular cooperation. Finally, I complemented this analysis of Brazilian documents by examining documents published by Brazil's counterparts in triangular cooperation.

By focusing on Brazil as a key player, I aim to clarify both the form that triangular cooperation arrangements take, and a key aspect of their content: namely, the range of justifications offered by a state that is participating in triangular cooperation.

FINDINGS

Form

Configurations in international technical cooperation range from dyadic arrangements, in which states or agencies enter into bilateral agreements, to multiplex arrangements, in which a number of countries or agencies form a network of cooperation agreements (sometimes within the scope of international organizations, such as the UN). Triangular cooperation, which entails a triadic arrangement, can be seen as an intermediate between bilateral and multilateral technical cooperation arrangements. The case of Brazil offers insight into these types of arrangements.

Brazil's role in triangular cooperation is reflected in the institutional history of government agencies that deal with international technical assistance. In the late 1980s, Brazil's federal government established the ABC. The agency, a part of the Ministry of External Relations, coordinates Brazil's international technical cooperation—both that received from foreign donors and that provided to other countries. The ABC has a special division devoted entirely to South–South cooperation carried out by Brazilian government agencies, universities, and NGOs. As of this writing, the agency was coordinating 86 TCDC projects, of which approximately 50% were in Latin America, 25% in Africa, and 25% in East Timor. Moreover, the number of projects grew fast: In 2003 alone, the agency launched an additional 36 new projects. Around 70% of ABC's South–South projects relate to education, agriculture, health, and the environment (ABC, 2005a).

The ABC has also been participating in a growing number of programs that deal specifically with triangular cooperation by partnering with key industrialized countries to maximize its capacity for triangular cooperation projects. As of 2007, Brazil has established triangular cooperation treaties with several industrialized countries. The main partners as of 2007 were Japan, through the Japan International Cooperation Agency (JICA); Germany, through the Deutsche Gesellschaft für Technische Zusammenarbeit (GTZ); and the United Kingdom, through the Department for International Development (DFID). Most projects focus on public health (mainly HIV/AIDS prevention), education, and a variety of agricultural issues. One pilot project, for example, involves a partnership between Brazil and the United Kingdom to fight the HIV/AIDS epidemic in Bolivia. Another partnership with JICA taps into Brazil's FIOCRUZ Institute to train East Timorese distance-learning tutors in public health education.

More recently, Brazil has been partnering with other Southern regional leaders in technical assistance, notably South Africa and India, to expand and extend triangular cooperation into a wider-reaching network for South–South cooperation. The India–Brazil–South Africa (IBSA) Forum has recently established a fund—to be managed by the UNDP—to help pool resources in the fight against poverty. India and Brazil have each so far committed US$100,000, and South Africa has added $50,000 to the pot (Devraj, 2007). Areas of cooperation include health, information technology, civil aviation, and defense.

The spread of triangular cooperation arrangements involving these regional leaders reflects a change in the network configuration of technical assistance, with interconnected regional nodes emerging as alternatives for partnerships with industrialized countries. This represents not only a change in the form in which cooperation occurs among developing countries, but it also signals a shift in the reasons (explicitly and implicitly) why developing countries engage in these activities. As Simmel (1950) wrote about small social groups, the form of social ties yields clues as to the content of social ties. The next section examines in greater detail one aspect of content: the justifications provided by countries engaging in triangular cooperation, focusing once again on the case of Brazil.

Content: Justifications for Engagement

How does the Brazilian government justify its participation in triangular cooperation? Government documents refer to the ABC's triangular cooperation efforts as part of Brazil's foreign-policy strategy. In 2004, the ABC's South–South Cooperation Division (*Cooperação Técnica entre Países em Desenvolvimento*, CTPD) stated that its objectives included "prioritizing technical cooperation programs that strengthen Brazil's relations with its partners in development, especially with those countries that are priorities for Brazil's foreign policy" (ABC, 2007a). Thus, the Brazilian government explicitly acknowledges that participation in triangular cooperation is not only a goal unto itself, but also serves the broader purpose of furthering international relations.

In fact, CTPD identifies a number of priorities in its mission statement:

> To honor commitments made by the President and the Minister of External Relations during trips abroad; South American countries; Haiti; African countries, especially Portuguese-language countries and East Timor; other Latin American and Caribbean countries; to support the Community of Portuguese Language Countries; to expand Brazil's triangular cooperation initiatives with industrialized countries (through their respective agencies and international organizations). (ABC, 2007a)

These priorities reflect Brazil's aspirations to boost its relations with (and influence upon) not only its neighbors in Latin America, but also countries elsewhere with which it shares historic or linguistic ties. In addition, the mission statement recognizes that a more visible stance within the international arena in turn opens up more possibilities for technical cooperation. A section of the ABC website dealing with triangular cooperation states that "As Brazil attains a higher position within international forums, it becomes a central country for this type of cooperation policy" (ABC, 2007b).

These explicitly stated priorities show that the Brazilian government uses technical cooperation to further a number of broader foreign-policy goals. As the ABC mission statement for South–South cooperation states, "The actions of the General Office for Cooperation between Developing Countries constitute an important instrument for foreign relations, which Brazil has drawn on to secure a positive and growing presence in countries and regions of primary interest" (ABC, 2005b).

A more nuanced analysis of the ABC charter and documents reveals that Brazil pursues this goal of enhancing its standing in the international arena through cooperation with developing countries—including triangular cooperation—by drawing on five broad modes of justification. These are ideal types rather than mutually exclusive categories. Boundaries are imprecise, and types often overlap; still, it is useful to create a typology for analytical purposes.

Pragmatism

Like other developing countries, Brazil has pragmatic reasons for engaging in South–South technical cooperation. Countries and agencies that have undergone equivalent experiences often have a great deal of accumulated practical knowledge to share. Moreover, some countries have developed niches of expertise that help legitimize the lending and borrowing of programs and projects from other developing countries.

This niche expertise might come from private initiative or from the public sector. Even in countries whose state apparatuses deviate in large part from Weberian ideals of meritocratic and coherent bureaucracy, there may exist "islands of competence" that generate successful development programs (Evans, 1995). The ABC states on its website, "Brazil has an important stock of technical knowledge and imaginative solutions that can be applied in countries that need resources and 'know-how'" (ABC, 2007a). Thus, within this mode of justification, the Brazilian government posits programs that have been deemed as successful as "a better fit" for other developing countries than solutions proposed by industrialized countries:

> Many developing countries face problems similar to ours in the fields of public administration, health, education, agriculture, environment, small enterprises, among others, and our experience in finding appropriate solutions to them is frequently sought. . . . [Brazil] has a significant number of institutions of excellence in various areas of knowledge. (ABC, 2007b)

The same logic appears not only in bilateral and multilateral cooperation agreements, but also in triangular cooperation. In 2001, the United Nations Population Fund forged a partnership with the ABC, aimed at tapping into the expertise that Brazilian public health institutions have developed in the prevention and treatments of sexually transmitted diseases, particularly HIV/AIDS (in 2003, Brazil received the Gates Award for Global Health for its comprehensive response to the epidemic). The program seeks to facilitate the transfer of Brazilian knowledge in these areas to other Latin American and Caribbean countries, Portuguese-speaking Africa, and East Timor.

Altruism

In addition to (and sometimes alongside) instrumental justifications for engaging in triangular cooperation, Brazil also posits itself as an altruistic lender of knowledge and experience. The ABC stresses that Brazil's technical cooperation with other developing countries "occurs through the transference of Brazilian technical knowledge and experience, on a non-commercial basis, in order to promote the autonomy of its partners" (ABC, 2005b). It goes on to assert that:

> The main strategy of Brazil's technical cooperation lending—which is not assistentialist, has no profit goals, no commercial objectives and focuses on the institutional strengthening of our partners, a fundamental condition for the effective transference and absorption of knowledge. (ABC, 2005b)

By highlighting the noncommercial aspect of these cooperation agreements, Brazil seeks to enhance its positive image and boost its legitimacy as a nonexploitative participant in international relations. Triangular cooperation offers the Brazilian government one more way of promoting its claims of altruism.

Strengthening Cultural Ties

As ABC's list of priorities for South–South transfer indicates, the Brazilian government also relies on technical cooperation as a concrete way of strengthening ties with other countries in the Community of Portuguese Language Countries (CPLP), as well as its Spanish-speaking neighbors in Latin America: "[Brazil] maintains cultural ties of friendship with other developing countries, and it has a history of overcoming problems that are typical of countries of the so-called 'Third World'" (ABC, 2007a).

Justifications for international exchanges based on cultural affinity are not a novelty. Since the 1970s, Brazil has promoted trade relations with Portuguese-language African countries, and its foreign ministers repeatedly have highlighted ethnic ties between Brazil and those countries as a driving force behind these exchanges. Cultural affinity might also serve pragmatic ends: Shared culture may facilitate labor mobility and technology transfer, since experts share language and can, thus, collaborate on projects without having to overcome significant linguistic barriers.

In addition to citing cultural affinity with certain developing countries, the Brazilian government also cites cultural ties in justifying partnerships with industrialized countries. For example, the ABC mission statement mentions that, in its triangular cooperation partnership with Japan (JBPP), Brazil's government "takes into consideration the historically friendly relations, close economic ties, and the presence of some 1.4 million Japanese immigrants and their descendants in the Federative Republic of Brazil" (MRE, 2005).

Driving this justification is the belief that common historical and cultural heritage facilitates the exchange of experience and knowledge:

> Over the past three years, the Brazilian government has placed special emphasis to the strengthening of its technical cooperation with the Portuguese speaking countries of Africa, with East Timor and with South and Central American countries. (ABC, 2007a)

This logic extends to triangular cooperation. The JBPP was originally designed to implement triangular cooperation programs in African Lusophone countries. More recently, it has grown to encompass non-

Portuguese countries in the region, such as Ghana, but the emphasis remains on fellow members of the Lusophone community.

Regional Leadership

A key component of Brazilian foreign relations over the past few years has been the goal of regional leadership (Soares de Lima & Hirst, 2006). Brazil also uses South–South transfer, including triangular cooperation, to further its goal of consolidating a position of regional leadership in Latin America and the Caribbean. In 2004, Brazil led the United Nations peacekeeping mission to Haiti, sending 1,200 troops—Brazil's largest foreign military deployment since World War II. Initiatives like leadership of the Haiti peacekeepers deployment sharply contrast with the inward-looking foreign policy that characterized Brazil during the latter half of the 20th century.

President Luiz Inácio Lula da Silva, elected through the Workers Party in October 2002, has made regional leadership one of the key goals of Brazilian foreign policy. In 2005, during one of his radio "Coffee with the President" broadcasts, Lula declared that, because it is the largest economy in South America, "Brazil has an obligation to provide the conditions for the economic growth of neighboring countries" (Crispim, 2005, p. 1).

Technical cooperation with other developing countries is seen by the Brazilian government as another way to further the goal of regional leadership. As one of the ABC directives for TCDC states, the agency seeks to "prioritize technical cooperation programs that allow for the intensification of Brazil's relations with partners in development, especially with those of primary interest for Brazil's foreign policy" (ABC, 2007a). On ABC's list of priorities for TCDC, strengthening ties of cooperation with other South American countries comes second only to the top item of honoring "commitments made by the President and the Minister of External Relations during trips abroad."

Given this goal, the links with industrialized countries in some triangular cooperation arrangements might provide Brazil with added legitimacy as a lender of technical assistance within Latin America. This seems to occur despite the arguable loss of legitimacy of industrialized countries as lenders of aid. The supposed enhanced added legitimacy is seen to help compensate for the long history of affable yet distant relations that Brazil has maintained with most other countries in the region (Costa Vaz, 2004).

Networking with Other Regional Leaders

Yet the foreign relations ambitions of Lula's administration extend far beyond South America. In addition to trying to make Brazil a regional leader, since 2002, the Brazilian government has attempted to become a spokesperson for developing countries. Initiatives linked to this goal include the founding of the G-20 Group, which lobbies for industrialized countries to lower agricultural subsidies, and seeking a permanent seat on the UN Security Council. So far, these efforts have had limited success, but more specifically, the Brazilian government has been trying to forge and strengthen ties with leaders of other regions—the so-called "pivotal countries" (South African Permanent Mission, 2003). The India–Brazil–South Africa, or IBSA, Forum, is arguably the most active of such alliances. Russia and China are also entering a cooperative coalition (known informally as BRICS), although it has not yet been formalized. Through triangular cooperation arrangements related to these alliances, Brazil works to amplify its influence overseas.

Within this mode of justification, triangular cooperation serves as an efficient way to expand Brazil's network (and, more broadly, the network of South–South cooperation) because regional hubs are multiplex: They feature a large number of localized ties. By strengthening its links with regional leaders elsewhere, Brazil can tap into those many ties and, thus, reach into a broader territory, directly or indirectly.

CONCLUSION

This chapter set out to explore the form and content of an emerging type of technical cooperation arrangement within the network of international cooperation ties: triangular cooperation. Research on Brazil's technical cooperation ties showed that triangular cooperation has emerged as an intermediary form between two traditional forms of cooperation: bilateral and multilateral. More specifically, the appearance of regional nodes of cooperation (not just Brazil, but also India and South Africa) marks a shift both in the configuration of the international network of cooperation and in the politics involved in participating in this network.

This shift can be understood in terms of both form and content of the ties in technical assistance. As the sociologist Simmel (1950) noted in his study of small social groups, understanding the form of a social configuration can yield clues about the content of social interaction. A triad differs from a dyad in that it offers participants many more options for strategies and alliances. Thus, both form and content shift as a social group grows in size from two to three members.

In terms of form, triangular cooperation is an intermediary between bilateral technical cooperation and the direct utilization of broad multilateral channels. Pivotal countries such as Brazil, South Africa, and India in particular act as nodes for the growth of South–South transfer network, and triangular cooperation is emerging as a major strategy to strengthen this network. This new configuration allows regional nodes and their partners to tap into localized knowledge and sources of innovation that might be overlooked in more traditional forms of cooperation and technical assistance. Brazil's experiences with HIV/AIDS education might provide other developing countries with suitable approaches to the problem.

In addition to offering pragmatic solutions to common problems in South–South transfer, triangular cooperation constitutes a specific tactic for national self-promotion within a broader strategy of foreign relations. States seldom, if ever, engage in technical cooperation within a political vacuum; rather, they typically forge cooperation ties at least in part to advance broader regional or global ambitions.

The motivations behind participation in triangular cooperation agreements yield clues as to how they fit within a state's broader foreign policy goals. An analysis of the language of documents related to triangular cooperation reflects the multitude of strategies available to Brazil as a participant in triangular cooperation arrangements. The documents reveal a multitude of frequently overlapping justifications for participating in triangular cooperation, ranging from pragmatism to altruism, cultural affinity, aspirations to regional leadership, and efforts to link up with regional leaders elsewhere.

Together, these different justifications reflect Brazil's desire to expand its presence within international arenas. Engagement in triangular cooperation has served to further the Brazilian government's broader goal of consolidating Brazil's position as a "pivotal" Southern country in the international arena. These findings are consistent with recent efforts by the Brazilian government outside the arena of technical cooperation—for instance, by leading the UN peacekeeping mission to Haiti or attempting to secure a permanent seat on the UN Security Council. Yet triangular cooperation allows the Brazilian state to engage with other developing countries more directly than through multilateral channels.

Notably absent from these justifications is the desire to substitute triangular cooperation, and, more broadly, South–South relations, for the traditional links to industrialized countries. Because it partners an industrialized country with a developing counterpart to lend assistance to a third country, triangular cooperation represents a departure from the autarkic rhetoric of leftist developing states in earlier decades. Instead, triangular cooperation reflects a new compromise: a willingness by certain developing countries to supplement assistance from the "North" with assistance from other developing countries.

Further research on the role of triangular cooperation in international cooperation ties would benefit from three complementary approaches: a case study, an institutional analysis, and a network analysis. First, an in-depth study of a specific triangular cooperation arrangement, with insight into the participation of all three parties, would shed light on the political strategies of members. Such a study might establish the extent to which the rhetoric of individual members coincides, and whether this rhetoric matches the actual practices of technical assistance implemented through the agreement.

Second, an institutional perspective on triangular cooperation would clarify the historical and political forces that led to the emergence and recent spread of this particular form of cooperation. A longitudinal analysis would thereby enhance our understanding of how technical cooperation among developing countries fits within the shifting landscape of regional and global politics.

Finally, a bird's-eye view of cooperation networks, placing triangular cooperation within the broader scheme of international cooperation network, would give students of international relations and cooperation a better sense of how these nodes are evolving across time. Recent developments in network analysis, including quantitative methods, could be applied to either a regional or the global network of technical cooperation to identify key nodes and the role that triangular cooperation plays in the network.

Research along these lines will supplement the extant—and surprisingly scant—academic literature on triangular cooperation as well as technical assistance in general.

NOTES

1. The idea of triangular cooperation is not entirely new. Wai's (1982) book *Interdependence in a World of Unequals: African-Arab-OECD Economic Cooperation for Development* endorses triangular cooperation among those three country groups, highlighting the complementarity of their resource endowments.

2. Although recent methodological advances in quantitative network analysis have not yet been employed within education transfer literature, there are probably enough data on transnational exchanges that such studies can now be undertaken.

3. As Ritzer (1992) has noted, small groups tend to restrict the behaviors of their members, whereas, in larger groups, members enjoy greater individual freedom. When the size of a group increases, the direct ties between members are diluted, and a greater number of relation types is possible.

PART THREE

Contradictions, Complexities, and Ambiguities

NINE

Reclaiming the Empire

Turkish Education Initiatives in Central Asia and Azerbaijan

Iveta Silova

Since the collapse of the Soviet Union in 1991, Turkey has emerged as an important actor in post-Soviet Eurasia because of its strong historical, religious, cultural, and ethnolinguistic connections with the newly independent countries of the southern Caucasus (Azerbaijan) and Central Asia (Kazakhstan, Kyrgyzstan, Tajikistan, Turkmenistan, and Uzbekistan). The role of Turkey in the post-Soviet transformation of these countries was extensively discussed by policy-makers in the West, Central Asia, and Turkey. Western countries were concerned that radical Islam might fill the power vacuum created by the collapse of the Soviet Union and, therefore, strongly encouraged these states to adopt a "Turkish model" of secular democracy combined with liberal economy (Aydin, 1996; Demir, Balci, & Akkok, 2000; Sander, 1993). Central Asian politicians were interested in developing closer relations with Turkey to construct a new network of external relations beyond the Soviet Union, hoping that closer ties with Turkey could ease their entry into the Western world (Demir, Balci, & Akkok, 2000). Finally, Turkish policy-makers felt the need to redefine the role of Turkey in the international arena, shifting away from its role as "a buffer state" between the Soviet Union and the West during the Cold War to becoming a more active player in a global arena by reclaiming a pan-Turkic empire in Central Asia and the Caucasus after the collapse of the Soviet Union.

International development assistance became an important part of geopolitical reorientation policies pursued by the Turkish state. While remaining an aid recipient itself,[1] Turkey took on a new role of an "emergent donor in the Muslim world," particularly in the largely Turkish-speaking Central Asian region (Marinova & Novak, 2006). In 1992, the Turkish government established the Turkish International Cooperation

Agency (TIKA),[2] which became an important instrument for the government's foreign-policy agenda by providing development assistance to neighboring countries, the Turkic states, as well as the countries where the Turkish language is spoken by sizable minorities.[3] While aspiring to be a "global provider of significant humanitarian aid and technical assistance" (Gül, 2006), Turkey's international development efforts have been primarily focused on the post-Soviet republics of Central Asia and the Caucasus. Excluding the contributions and membership fee payments to international organizations, Turkish Official Development Assistance (ODA) to Central Asia and the Caucasus reached US$332.49 million in 2005, constituting more than half of the entire amount of ODA. In addition to state efforts, technical assistance was actively provided by a number of private agencies, charity institutions, and nongovernmental organizations in Azerbaijan and Central Asia.

Education has become one of the most important parts of Turkey's international development assistance. Highlighting the link between education and identity, Turkish officials perceived education as a powerful mechanism of creating the "Turkic identity" among the elites from the Turkic republics of the former Soviet Union (Yanik, 2004). The educational campaign had two goals. First, Turkish elites thought that educating today's students would create the elites who later would be in charge of the transformation to a market economy and democracy in their countries. Second, and more important, the goal was to create a stratum of people who would be well versed in Turkish culture and language, acting as "a bridge between their countries and Turkey" (Yanik, 2004, p. 294). The students coming out of this educational experience were expected to become "the foundation stones for the common cause" and "the architects of the great Turkish world" (former Minister of Education Köksal Toptan, quoted in Yanik, 2004, p. 294).

Turkey's educational development assistance followed two main trends, including organizing educational exchanges for university students and establishing Turkish schools in the former Soviet republics of Central Asia and the Caucasus (Yanik, 2004). The "Great Student Exchange Project" aimed to educate the future generation of elites through scholarships to Turkey's secondary schools and higher education institutions. In the first 10 years of educational exchange (1992–2002), a total of 21,871 scholarships were distributed to students from Eurasia (Yanik, 2004). Although the success rate of the educational exchange program was estimated at approximately 50%,[4] it nevertheless presented a unique opportunity to expose many students from the former Soviet republics of Central Asia and the Caucasus to Turkey's educational and cultural life. In addition to educational exchanges, the Turkish Ministry of Education and various private foundations established a number of Turkish schools in Central Asia and the Caucasus. Among the most popular schools were the ones known to have ties to Fethullah Gülen's Islamic reform movement—a movement promoting Turkish nationalism, the free market, and modern education (Gülen, 1997). Although these schools were funded by private institutions, they were strongly supported by the Turkish government, which perceived the Gülen community to be helping the state to create "a Turkish world" in the former Soviet republics (Balci, 2003, p. 166).

Given that the Turkish government generally keeps a tight monopoly on culture and national identity issues, the involvement of the Gülen community as a nonstate actor in Turkey's international development assistance presents an interesting case (Yanik, 2004). There is a sharp contrast between the attitude of the Turkish authorities toward the Gülen community in Turkey and their attitude to the community abroad. Some state authorities in Turkey consider the movement to be dangerous in their own country, while the same authorities support it in Central Asia (Balci, 2003). This chapter examines the role of Gülen schools (also referred to as Turkish schools) in education development in Central Asia and the Caucasus by discussing questions related to the South–South transfer of the "Turkish education model." In particular, why was the transfer of the "Turkish schools" so successful in the post-Soviet republics of Azerbaijan and Central Asia? Why was it so appealing both to the Turkish education policy lenders and the Central Asian education policy recipients? Why was a controversial educational model exported to other countries? What were the politics and economics of the South–South transfer?

FETHULLAH GÜLEN'S ISLAMIC MOVEMENT FROM TURKEY TO CENTRAL ASIA

Fethullah Gülen's Islamic reform movement has its origins in the teaching of Said Nursi (1873–1960), who emphasized the importance of scientific knowledge in raising religious consciousness. Nursi's death splintered the movement into several different groups, with the most important of these groups being led by Fethullah Gülen, a former state-appointed preacher who presides over some 3 million followers and many sympathizers across the world. Fethullah Gülen sees the economic and moral decline in the Muslim world as a result of spiritual and intellectual decline, and aims to renew the Muslim tradition (Solberg, 2005). Compared with other Islamic social movements, the Gülen movement stands out because of its emphasis on Turkish nationalism, the free market, and modern education. In particular, Yavuz (2003) argues that the Gülen movement pursues three main goals: 1) raising Muslim consciousness, 2) reexamining the connection between science and religion in order to refute the dominant intellectual discourses of materialism and positivism, and 3) recovering collective memory by revising the shared grammar of Islam (p. 7). The overall purpose is "to create a 'golden generation' that is armed with the tools of science and religion" (Agai, 2003, p. 57).

The Gülen's movement builds on the idea that education is key to raising a generation both deeply rooted in Islam and able to participate in the modern, scientific world. The assumption is that only in combination with knowledge (especially secular education) can society benefit from the religious principles, because it is secular education that enables the follower to shape society (Agai, 2003). By emphasizing the importance of modern education, Gülen produced an Islamic discourse that links Islam so closely with education that one can speak of "educational Islamism" as opposed to political Islamism (Agai, 2003, p. 50). Outside of Turkey, however, Gülen schools have broader cultural and political agendas. The schools in Europe, for example, attract Turkish families who prefer to raise their children in the "Turkish way" (Turam, 2003, p. 188). In the developing countries, they appeal to students because of better technology and higher standards of education. Finally, the high concentration of Gülen schools in Central Asia is often perceived as an important part of the pan-Turan ethnic politics that Gülen pursues in that region (Turam, 2003).

Importantly, Gülen's schools have not been accepted universally, particularly in his native Turkey. Some critics have regarded his educational philosophy as an intellectual cover for forming cadres who conceivably might pose a threat to the established secular order in Turkey (Michel, 2003). In particular, many left-leaning journalists accuse Fethullah Gülen of having a secret agenda of trying to undermine the secular system in Turkey by encouraging his followers to aim for central positions within institutions such as the military and the police. Furthermore, some critics fear that internationalization of the Gülen movement, especially the establishment of many schools in the former socialist bloc (Russia, Central Asia, the Caucasus, and the Balkans), aims to build a "Green Belt" around secular Turkey (Michel, 2003). Other commentators, however, perceive Fethullah Gülen as someone who is putting "Turkey on the map" by promoting Turkey and Turkish values abroad (Solberg, 2005, p. 5).

THE EMERGENCE OF FETHULLAH GÜLEN SCHOOLS IN AZERBAIJAN AND CENTRAL ASIA

The Fethullah Gülen movement was originally geographically limited to Turkey, but it evolved from an isolationist Turkish to an international movement with the collapse of the socialist bloc in 1989. During the 1990s, the group succeeded in opening more than 100 schools and universities in Azerbaijan, Kazakhstan, Kyrgyzstan, Turkmenistan, and Uzbekistan, as well as in Russia's Turkic republics of Daghestan, Karachai-Cherkessiya, Tatarstan, and Bashkotorstan. Gülen's schools also appeared in Ukraine, Georgia, Moldova, and Tajikistan—all countries with sizable Turkic minorities. The Gülen community also expanded in the former socialist countries of Southeast Europe, including Albania, Bosnia-Herzegovina, Bulgaria, Macedonia, and Romania. Today, the group supervises an estimated 150 educational institutions abroad, approximately the same number as in Turkey (Balci, 2003).

Gülen's education institutions in Central Asia operate alongside Turkish schools funded by the state. They include mainly secondary schools, but also some universities, including a university named after former Turkish president Suleyman Demirel in the former Kazakh capital of Almaty, the Ahmet Yesevi University in the southern Kazakh city of Turkistan, the Kyrgyz-Turkish Manas University in Bishkek, and the International Turkmen-Turkish University of Ashgabat (Aypay, 2004). Kazakhstan has the largest number of Turkish schools, followed by Turkmenistan and Kyrgyzstan (see Table 9.1.). One factor favoring the growth in the number of schools in Kazakhstan is that the country is administratively less centralized than the other Central Asian republics and regional governors have the prerogative of reaching educational agreements with foreign companies (Balci, 2003). Turkish schools are also numerous in Kyrgyzstan and Turkmenistan. The Gülen community is especially active in Turkmenistan because two of its members serve as advisors to President Niyazov himself (i.e., the Minister of Textiles and the Minister of Education). In Uzbekistan, which had the second-largest number of Turkish schools in Central Asia in the early 1990s, President Islam Karimov ordered most "fcthullahcı" teachers out of the country in 1994 and closed all Gülen schools in 2000, thus completely forbidding any activities of the Gülen community in the country. While the main reasons for the closure of Gülen schools were political,[5] Uzbekistan's state authorities feared that the Islamization of the society (including the teaching of Islam in Gülen schools) could threaten the new state.

In Central Asia and Azerbaijan, all Gülen schools were established in accordance with the individual agreements between the countries in which they are located and education companies set up for this purpose. Each school is an independently run institution, but most of the schools rely on the services of Turkish companies to provide educational supplies and human resources (Michel, 2003). In Central Asia and the Caucasus, these schools are run by private companies and institutions that sympathize with the thinking of Fethullah Gülen.[6] For example, these schools are run by a private nonprofit education institution, "Şebat" in Kyrgyzstan, "Başkent Education Company" in Turkmenistan, "Feza et Şelale" in Kazakhstan, and "Cag Oyrertim Isletmetleri" in Azerbaijan (see Table 9.1.). As a result, Gülen schools offer students relatively better equipment and opportunities compared to those available in public schools. Generally, the host governments provide the buildings and infrastructure, while the Gülen community appoints teachers, education and counseling specialists, administrators, and principals.

Gülen schools select students through competitive entrance examinations. In the beginning of the 1990s, Gülen schools were free and enrolled students from all ranks of society, including orphans, gifted children

Table 9.1. Schools of the Fethullah Gülen Movement in Azerbaijan and Central Asia (1997/98–2006/07)

Country	Number of schools		Number of students		Name of company
	1997/1998	2006/2007	1997/1998	2006/2007	
Azerbaijan	12	11	3023	3000	Cag Oyrertim Isletmetleri
Kazakhstan	29	23*	5644	5613*	Feza et Şelale
Kyrgyzstan	12	15	3100	4287	Şebat
Tajikistan	5	7	694	1874	Şalola
Turkmenistan	13	16	3294	×	Başkent
Uzbekistan	18	×	3334	×	Silm

Sources: Data for 1997/98 from Balci, 2003; data for 2006/07 retrieved from digital databases made available by the Ministry of Education of the Republic of Azerbaijan (personal communication, October 2, 2007); Ministry of Education of the Republic of Kazakhstan (personal communication, October 15, 2007); Ministry of Education of the Republic of Kyrgyzstan (personal communication, September 5, 2007); Ministry of Education of the Republic of Tajikistan (personal communication, September 17, 2007); and the Ministry of Education of Turkmenistan (personal communication, November 3, 2007).

* Information from the Ministry of Education of the Republic of Kazakhstan for the 2005/2006 academic year.

× Information not available.

from poor families, and children from rural areas. However, admission to these schools became more selective throughout the 1990s, with most schools introducing increasingly high tuition fees. The amount of tuition varied among the countries, usually depending on the number and the wealth of the Turkish companies that supported the schools. In the beginning of the 2000s, for example, parents in Turkmenistan had to pay US$1,000 a year for the education of one child (Balci, 2003), while parents in Azerbaijan paid up to US$2,000 a year (Bakı Özəl Türk Litseyi, 2006). Undoubtedly, Turkish schools became "elite schools," primarily enrolling children of wealthy parents and/or government officials, and often leaving out children from poor, rural areas.

As in Turkey, a strong emphasis of Gülen schools in Azerbaijan and Central Asia is on sciences, ethics, and self-discipline. Education is provided mainly in English, but also in Turkish, local languages, and, occasionally, Russian. Although many assume that Turkish schools focus on the teaching of religious subjects because they are part of an Islamic educational movement, the unique feature of these schools in Central Asia is that they do, in fact, follow the state curriculum. Religious values are taught more indirectly, through the hidden curriculum such as the behavioral patterns of teachers, administrators, and students; their preferred clothing style; and the magazines, books, and TV channels that reveal more implicit cues about their Islamic orientation (Demir, Balci, & Akkok, 2000, p. 151). Furthermore, most Gülen schools operate as boarding schools and are not coeducational institutions, which could also be perceived as tools to internalize certain values and lifestyles (Demir, Balci, & Akkok, 2000).

SOUTH–SOUTH TRANSFER: REASONS, RATIONALES, AND REALITIES

Recent research into the activities of the Gülen community in Central Asia shows that it is a real missionary movement. The mission of the *fethullahcı* is "to reestablish Islam in an area that was dominated for 70 years by an atheist power" (Balci, 2003, p. 162). Schools play a key role in achieving this mission. In particular, Turam's (2003) research reveals that many teachers working in Gülen schools feel that they "shelter subaltern Turkic people who were suppressed and oppressed many years under the Soviet rule." They claim to help Central Asian students in revitalizing commitment to their own origins, implying that Turkish Islam is "a recognized and living aspect of the region," despite the fact that the repressive Soviets attempted to bury it (Turam, 2003, p. 200). According to Gülen himself, the main motive for establishing schools in the former socialist countries was to fill the value vacuum that was created in the aftermath of the Soviet disintegration:

> We could enter the education world [in these countries] before anybody else ... and we could fill the gap and leave no place neither for Iran [as a representative of official Islam] nor for Turan [ideas of unrealistic pan-Turkism]. ... I saw the Turkic states of the former Soviet Union as oppressed and unjustly treated. As the son of a great state, I could never digest this humiliation. (quoted in Yanik, 2004, p. 300)

However, the Gülen community has faced difficulties in trying to pursue its mission openly in the Central Asian republics, because of the deep-rooted distrust of Islam in this post-Soviet region. Instead of overtly practicing their Islamic proselytism, the Gülen schools have used less conspicuous ways of Islamizing the younger generation (Balci, 2003). For example, teachers try to set a good example by embodying their ideals in their way of life rather than preaching about them. At the same time, Islamic goals are often pursued more covertly through extracurricular activities, cultural events, and a nonformal elementary Islamic education outside of schools (Balci, 2003). Publicly, however, schoolteachers avoid mentioning to students and their parents that the schools are associated with the Islamic group. Their concern is mainly not to lose credibility because of lingering Soviet-inflicted negative feelings against religion (Turam, 2003). In Kazakhstan, for example, the Gülen schools are usually presented simply as "Turkish schools," with the schools' national affiliation being emphasized in everyday use, while their community affiliation is practically omitted (Turam, 2003). Similarly, Balci (2003) notes that none of the local people in Central Asia talks about "Nurcu" or "*fethullahcı*" schools, but always about the "*turestky litsey*" or the "*turk maktabi*" (Balci, 2003, p. 166). Across the region, most of the non-Turkish students in the Gülen schools know only that the schools are Turkish, extremely successful, and competitive, and that the main language of instruction is English (Turam, 2003). In other words, the primary mission of the Gülen schools is usually downplayed (i.e., re-Islamization of Central Asia), while the more patriotic element in the movement ideology is emphasized (i.e., spreading the Turkish education model).

It is specifically the emphasis of the Gülen schools on Turkism (i.e., Turkish identity) that has made them attractive to both the Turkish state and the Central Asian governments, thus increasing the schools' credibility at the international level. The Turkish state and nonstate actors (i.e., the Gülen community) have, in fact, shared a goal—the emergence of liberal Islamic-Turkic identity in the former Soviet republics of Azerbaijan and Central Asia. The official Turkish vision of Turkism is that Turks (of

Turkey), Uzbeks, Kazakhs, Kyrgyz, Turkmen, and others are different branches of the same, larger Turkish ethnic family (Turam, 2003). Because of a strong presence of Gülen schools in Central Asia, and because Turkish diplomacy has difficulty exporting its own definition of a Turkish identity internationally, the Turkish government has used Gülen schools as a foreign-policy tool in its efforts to make the Turkish language an international tool of communication and contribute to the development of ethnic unity in the "Turkic world" (Turam, 2003). As a result, the Gülen community has become one of the strongest "lobbyists" carrying Turkish culture and the idea of "Turkicness" abroad through education and the postmodern face of Islam. This symbiosis between the Gülen community and the Turkish state in achieving their goals was clearly articulated by Fethullah Gülen himself, who stated that "the success of these schools was also becoming the success of Turkey" (quoted in Yanik, 2004, p. 300).

Creation of a new national identity was similarly important for the Central Asian governments in the aftermath of the Soviet disintegration. In particular, the Central Asian governments have favored cooperation with the Gülen community, believing that it would help them speed up the process of creating new national identities and reducing the extensive Russian influence. For example, Turam (2003) explains that Kazakhstan's ethnic politics emphasize pride in "Turkicness," proudly celebrating—and, to some extent, inventing—commonality between Kazakhs and Turks. For example, the affirmative sayings of this celebrated commonality are often heard in sayings such as "We have the same roots" (in Kazakh), "The same mother nursed us" (in Turkish), or "We are blood brothers" (in Turkish) (Turam, 2003, p. 189). In Gülen schools, students learn not only the notion of Uzbek, Kazakh, Kyrgyz, or Turkmen identity, but also the concept of "Turkism." According to Balci (2003), these schools thus help the formation of a common Turkish identity, linking Turkey and the Turkic republics of Central Asia.

Undoubtedly, the existence of shared goals between the Gülen community, the Turkish state, and the Central Asian governments—creating new national identities and reducing excessive Russian influence—was central in the successful establishment of the Gülen schools in the post-Soviet region. However, this "South–South" transfer was favorable for several other reasons, highlighting the economics and the politics of the transfer process. First, Turkish schools were established at the time when public education systems across the region began to lose their credibility due to chronic underfunding, rampant corruption, and declining education quality. Insisting on higher education standards and transparency, Turkish schools became "model schools" in the region, revealing the great academic potential of students from Central Asia and Azerbaijan in a global education market. Second, the establishment of Turkish schools was politically beneficial for the state authorities in Azerbaijan and Central Asia, who were struggling with severe economic crises during the 1990s. These schools were fully funded by the Turkish private agencies and NGOs, functioning without the imposition of any political conditionalities on the governments of Azerbaijan and Central Asia. Furthermore, Turkish schools reinforced new political ideologies of their host countries, thus legitimizing these regimes nationally and internationally. In a way, Turkish schools have become international ambassadors for the Central Asian regimes, promoting their culture and history in Turkey and, thus, legitimizing some of these authoritarian regimes abroad.

THE ECONOMICS OF THE SOUTH–SOUTH TRANSFER: IMPORTING TURKISH MODEL SCHOOLS AT A TIME OF EDUCATIONAL CRISIS

The first Gülen schools were established at a time when post-Soviet republics of Central Asia and Azerbaijan were experiencing an education crisis, resulting from the loss of traditional economic networks and the end of budget subsidies from Moscow. Although the Central Asian regimes have repeatedly made rhetorical commitments to maintaining the Soviet indicators of educational achievement, the decline in national incomes, the lack of central subsidies, and shifting budget priorities have led to steadily decreasing education expenditures across the region. By 2000, the percentage of GDP spent on education fell by approximately one-third in Uzbekistan and by one-half in Azerbaijan, Kazakhstan, and Kyrgyzstan, compared with pre-independence levels. Tajikistan had the lowest education expenditure as a percentage of GDP, constituting 2.3% of GDP in 2000, compared to 3.2% in Kazakhstan, 3.7% in Kyrgyzstan, 6.8% in Uzbekistan, and an average of 4 to 6% in OECD countries (Silova, Johnson, & Heyneman, 2007).

The political, economic, and social hardships of the transition period have made it practically impossible to provide basic education for all children, let alone to undertake a fundamental reform of the national educational systems. As a result, the capital infrastructure has rapidly deteriorated; pedagogical materials, equipment, and textbooks have fallen into short supply; and many qualified teachers and faculty have left the profession for more lucrative employment in the private sector, or have simply emigrated. As a consequence, the issues of access and equity in education have become more pronounced: Women and girls are worse off, rural areas are more marginalized, and students from low socioeconomic levels are more under threat. In the case of Turkmenistan and increasingly in Uzbekistan, school curricula are dominated by cults of personality, xenophobia, and a strident nationalism, where foreign degrees and international standards are being rejected or marginalized.[7] Perhaps most important, public education systems across the region have, by all accounts, been corroded by endemic corruption.

Given these multiple challenges, the quality of education has been steadily declining throughout the 1990s. The 2005 study of Monitoring of Learning Achievement (MLA) in Kyrgyzstan (Ministry of Education of the Kyrgyz Republic, 2006) showed that only 44.2% of all surveyed fourth-graders passed the minimum literacy test and 58.5% passed the mathematics test. In Tajikistan, the same study showed that 63.1% of all surveyed students failed the literacy test and 50% failed numeracy tests (Ministry of Public Education of the Republic of Tajikistan, 2002; see also UNICEF Regional Office for CEE/CIS, 2007). In both Kyrgyzstan and Tajikistan, students from urban areas scored the highest, while students from the remote rural areas scored the lowest. Furthermore, the study results revealed significant variation in student achievement depending on the language of instruction in school. In Tajikistan, for example, students from Tajik-language schools performed the worst (with 72.3% of the surveyed students failing the literacy test), while students from Uzbek and Russian language schools performed better (39.4% and 22.5% failing the test, respectively) (Ministry of Public Education of the Republic of Tajikistan, 2002). In Kyrgyzstan, students attending Russian-language schools scored significantly higher than students attending Kyrgyz schools (Ministry of Education of the Kyrgyz Republic, 2006). As the MLA reports explained, learning achievement has been negatively affected by factors such as insufficient teacher qualifications, lack of appropriate textbooks and teaching/learning materials, inappropriate teaching/learning methods, and a lack of education support at home.

In the context of serious education decline and an increasing lack of trust in public education system, Turkish schools have been perceived by many parents as an opportunity for their children to receive education of considerably higher quality than that available in public schools. As Demir, Balcı, and Akkok (2000) point out, curricula implemented at Turkish schools are generally perceived to be "at world standards" and significantly more up-to-date than the curricula implemented in public schools (p. 144). In particular, Turkish schools strive to ensure that their students are fluent in four languages (English, Turkish, Russian, and the state language), are computer literate, and are scientifically competitive. Drawing on qualitative data from the Kyrgyz and Turkmen samples, Demir, Balcı, and Akkok (2000) confirm that both the Kyrgyz and Turkmen parents would like to send their children to Turkish schools, because these schools provide an opportunity to learn four languages (English, Turkish, Russian, and the state language) and develop computer skills, as well as provide the necessary materials and equipment.

Public perceptions about the high quality of education in Turkish schools are generally based on the statistical data about the number of students from Turkish schools continuing their studies in higher education institutions. Across the region, Turkish schools report remarkably high rates of students' admission into higher education institutions. In Kazakhstan, for example, Turkish schools have reported a consistently high university acceptance rate (over 90%) among their school graduates throughout the 1990s and 2000s (see Figure 9.1.). In Azerbaijan, some Turkish schools have reported that almost 100% of their school graduates successfully enter higher education institutions (Azernews-Azerkhabar, 1999). Furthermore, data from the State Student Admission Commission (2004) in Azerbaijan reveal that graduates of Turkish schools are generally more successful at centralized university entrance examinations, receiving on average 20%

Figure 9.1. Turkish School Graduates Who Were Admitted to Higher Education Institutions in Kazakhstan (1996–2001)

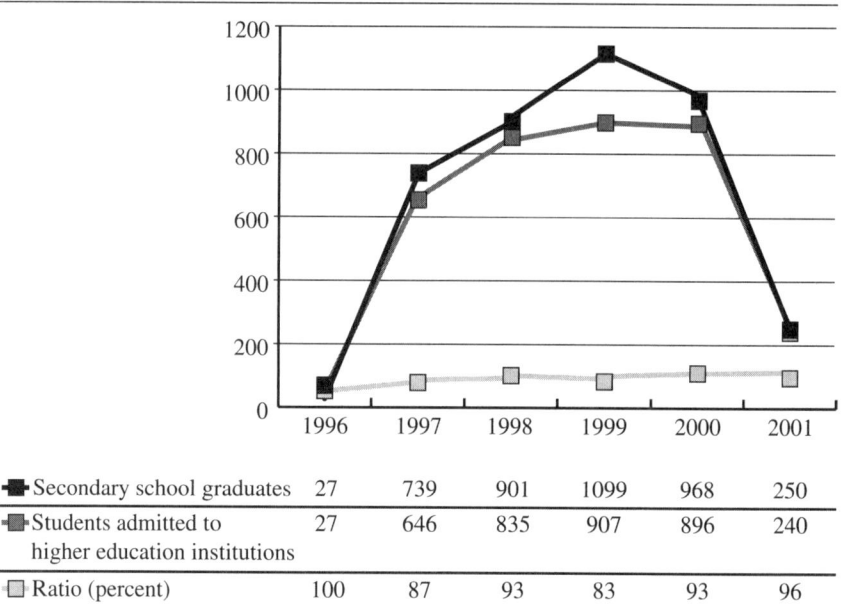

	1996	1997	1998	1999	2000	2001
Secondary school graduates	27	739	901	1099	968	250
Students admitted to higher education institutions	27	646	835	907	896	240
Ratio (percent)	100	87	93	83	93	96

Source: KATEV, 2006

more correct answers on examinations in Azerbaijani language/literature, mathematics, physics, chemistry, biology, history, and geography, compared to students from other public and private schools. In addition to high acceptance rates to higher education institutions, students from Turkish schools across the region regularly participate in various national and international scientific Olympiads, often receiving the highest awards for their achievements in sciences (KATEV, 2006).

In addition to offering higher-quality education, Turkish schools are often praised for their commitment to "training well-bred individuals," who "accept and develop the moral values of Islam and the Turkish culture," including respecting elders and caring for younger people, respecting and obeying parents and teachers, having good relationships with friends, and being honest (Demir, Balcı, & Akkok, 2000, p. 145). Of all the problems and dilemmas faced by educators today, the absence of purpose is often singled out as the largest challenge by teachers from public schools (de Young, 2006). As one teacher said,

> For many years we lived under the ideology of the USSR. When the country fell apart there was nothing to replace it. Young people today fill that emptiness with what they call "values." But I don't call them values. The students have a consumer mentality, even in their relations with each other. (Quoted in Heyneman, 2006, p. 2)

Given the existing value vacuum in many spheres of public life (especially in education), many parents commend Turkish schools for their efforts to enforce discipline and instill morality in their students—the values that are often overlooked by public schools.

Combined, the dual mission of Turkish schools—providing high-quality education and teaching moral values—distinguishes these schools from other public and private schools in Azerbaijan and Central Asia, which have been seriously corroded by a lack of funding, declining education quality, and rampant corruption during the post-Soviet transformation process. In the context of a declining credibility of public education across the region, Turkish schools have been perceived as "model schools," which strive to raise the quality of education in order to prepare "citizens who are able to cope with the requirements of market economy and the modern world" (Demir, Balcı, & Akkok, 2000, p. 153). Importantly, Turkish educational assistance has been perceived positively by most of the governments of Azerbaijan and Central Asia. On the one hand, it has helped the host countries to deal with educational crises by encouraging private investments in education and by setting higher educational standards for all schools. On the other hand, it has helped the host countries disguise the depth of the crisis facing their educational systems by showcasing the achievements of students from the Turkish schools internationally, often presenting these academic achievements as the ones produced by the national educational systems and failing to acknowledge student affiliation with Turkish schools.

THE POLITICS OF THE SOUTH–SOUTH TRANSFER: EDUCATIONAL ASSISTANCE WITHOUT POLITICAL CONDITIONALITIES

The post-Soviet transformation processes of Azerbaijan and Central Asia have been accompanied by an immense international financial and technical assistance, which increased steadily through the 1990s and then jumped sharply after September 11, 2001. Major international organizations—such as the Asian Development Bank, the World Bank, UNICEF, UNESCO, Aga Khan Foundation, Save the Children, and the Open Society Institute/Soros Foundations network—"moved to support development, promote democracy, and buttress stability in Central Asia" (Open Society Institute, 2002, p. 18). With very few exceptions, international educational assistance aimed at democratization of the educational systems across the region, urging the host governments to internalize education policies and practices necessary for developing civic activism and creating open, democratic societies. Although some of the most authoritarian regimes of Central Asia (e.g., Uzbekistan and Turkmenistan) have openly resisted outside interference in education reform and have insisted instead on local ideological control of education, most governments have welcomed Turkish technical assistance in education. This was true even for the most authoritarian country in the region, Turkmenistan, which has prohibited any international interference in education reform altogether, yet has allowed a network of Turkish schools to function effectively in the country.

What made the Turkish educational assistance so appealing for Central Asian political leaders? The answer to this question unveils the politics of South–South transfer, highlighting the importance of personal connections with the politicians in Central Asian republics and the conformist, pro-state attitude of the Gülen community in dealing with the post-Soviet governments in the region. In particular, some members of the Gülen community have personal ties to the government representatives of the Central Asian republics, which is key in initiating and implementing education projects in highly bureaucratized education environments of Central Asia, where any outside education initiatives commonly face strong opposition and sometimes high suspicion among the local education policy-makers. For example, Balci (2003) explains that the Gülen community is very active in Turkmenistan (the most closed society in Central Asia) because two of its members serve as advisors of President Niyazov (i.e., the Minister of Textiles and Minister of Education). Having direct access to the sole decision-maker in this authoritarian country ensures the success of the Turkish schools in Turkmenistan. Similarly, personal connections with the national, regional, and local authorities allow the Gülen community to run its schools successfully in other republics of Central Asia and the Caucasus.

In addition to cultivating personal contacts with local decision-makers, the Gülen community is known for its conformist, pro-state attitude toward local governments, including Turkmenistan, which is classified as "the only remaining neo-Stalinist regime in the world, along with North Korea" (Freedom House, 2006). To guarantee its presence in Central Asian countries, the Gülen community employs "the strategy of seduction" toward local governments (Balci, 2003, p. 165). Commonly, this means that the Gülen community offers its support for the government's policy and post-Soviet ideology in exchange for an undisturbed existence of its schools across the region. For example, Gülen's followers teach their students to love the new independent state, the president, the flag, the new institutions, and the new heroes who have been chosen by the new regimes (Balci, 2003). Furthermore, some schools supported by the Gülen community are known for translating some of the presidents' books and distributing them in Turkey. In Turkmenistan, for example, the general director of Turkmen-Turkish missionary schools, Nedim Polat, translated President Niyazov's "holy" book *Ruhnama*[8] into Turkish (Mamedov, 2005). As Balci (2003) points out, the Gülen schools thus become "ambassadors to Turkey for these Central Asian regimes" (p. 165), promoting their culture and history in Turkey and, inadvertently, legitimizing these authoritarian regimes abroad.

While promoting the values of the new regimes is an important part of the mission of Gülen schools, it is often deemed unacceptable by other international actors involved in education reform in the region. In particular, some international agencies may perceive the values of the new Central Asian regimes as conflicting with their own missions. For example, educational programs initiated by the Open Society Institute (OSI) and the United States Agency for International Development (USAID) call for democratization of the educational systems across the region—developing critical thinking, active student participation, and community involvement in school life—which often contradicts educational policies pursued by some of the new regimes, especially in Turkmenistan and Uzbekistan. It is not surprising, therefore, that some Central Asian governments are more supportive of educational initiatives promoted by the Gülen community (which supports the political ideology of the Central Asian regimes by teaching students patriotism toward their home countries) than by other international agencies (which often question the legitimacy of the new regimes in Azerbaijan and Central Asia and teach students to think critically about their governments' policies).

TURKEY AS A NEW BIG BROTHER IN POST-SOVIET CENTRAL ASIA

In the early 1990s, there was the question whether Azerbaijan and Central Asian countries would adopt a "Turkish model of development," the context being that of a "reunion" of "Turkic brothers" (Balci, 2003, p. 154). In particular, the Turkish authorities aspired to reconnect Central Asians with the Turkic origins by spreading Turkish Muslim culture and morality to the region. This goal was realized largely through the "civil society projects" of education—education exchanges, schools, dormitories, and summer camps—as well as through business and trade networks inside and outside of Turkey (Turam, 2003, p. 187). While some Central Asian state officials feared that the Turks were simply "replacing the Soviet hegemony" and taking advantage of the power vacuum to dominate the region through their missionary agendas, the initial suspicion was soon replaced with trust and cooperation from the Central Asian governments, who believed that Gülen schools helped students in Central Asia and Azerbaijan to revitalize (or perhaps create) a commitment to their own origins, such as learning and appreciating their own languages, culture, and religion, which had previously been suppressed by Soviet rule (Turam, 2003, p. 200).

Of all international education assistance in the region, Gülen schools have been perceived most favorably by the majority of local education stakeholders in Azerbaijan and Central Asia. This "South–South" transfer was favorable for several reasons, the most important being the existence of shared goals among different players involved in the transfer process— the Central Asian governments, the Turkish state, and Turkish private institutions. In particular, these key players collectively aimed to fill the gap that resulted from the collapse of the Soviet Union by creating common "Turkic" identities and de-Russifying the former Soviet republics of Azerbaijan and Central Asia. Importantly, Turkish state and nongovernmental institutions worked together to use educational assistance as a foreign-policy tool to redefine the role of Turkey in the international arena by reclaiming a pan-Turkic empire in Central Asia and the Caucasus after the collapse of the Soviet Union. In this context, Gülen schools emphasized a more patriotic element of the movement, i.e., promoting the Turkish language as an international tool of communication and, thus, contributing to the development of ethnolinguistic unity in the new "Turkic world," while downplaying their main mission of Islamizing the young generation in Azerbaijan and Central Asia.

Although the existence of shared goals between the Gülen community, the Turkish state, and the Central Asian governments was one of the key elements in the successful establishment of Gülen schools in Azerbaijan and Central Asia, this "South–South" transfer was favorable for two other reasons. First, the establishment of Gülen schools was economically beneficial for the state authorities in Azerbaijan and Central Asia, which had been struggling with severe economic crisis, corruption, and declining education quality throughout the 1990s. On the one hand, the establishment of Gülen schools helped the host governments deal with educational crises by encouraging private investments in education and by setting higher education standards for all schools. On the other hand, the existence of Gülen schools—offering higher-quality education compared to public schools—helped the state authorities in Azerbaijan and Central Asia to disguise the depth of the educational crises in the region by showcasing the achievements of students from Gülen schools nationally and internationally and presenting these academic achievements as the ones produced by national educational systems.

Second, the transfer of Gülen schools was politically beneficial for the governments of Azerbaijan and Central Asian republics. In particular, Gülen schools strongly reinforced the new ideologies of their host countries, teaching students to love their countries, flags, presidents, and new heroes. This pro-state, conformist attitude of the Gülen schools was exactly what made these schools appealing to the new post-Soviet regimes of Azerbaijan and Central Asia. In fact, most state authorities in Azerbaijan and Central Asia (with the exception of Uzbekistan) were much more supportive of educational initiatives promoted by the Gülen community (which supported the political ideology of the new regimes and, thus, legitimized them both nationally and internationally) than by other international agencies (which often questioned the legitimacy of these new regimes).

This case of the South–South transfer examined the local policy constellations in Azerbaijan and Central Asia at the time of education borrowing and found a plethora of political and economic reasons why the "Turkish model" was successfully imported to the post-Soviet region. More important, however, it uncovered how different actors—the Turkish state, Turkish private institutions, and the state authorities in Azerbaijan and Central Asia—used this South–South transfer to pursue their own, often diverging interests. For example, the Turkish government supported private schools founded by the Gülen community because of its perception that the Gülen community was helping the state to create a "Turkish world" in the former Soviet republics. The Central Asian governments supported the Gülen schools because of their unconditional support of Central Asian governments, which helped legitimize some of these authoritarian regimes nationally and internationally. Finally, as long as the Gülen movement was able to oblige the Turkish state (by emphasizing the patriotic element of their movement through the creation of Turkic identities) and the Central Asian governments (by supporting new political ideologies and, thus, legitimizing some of these authoritarian regimes abroad), Gülen schools were able to pursue their main mission of Islamizing the new generation in the post-Soviet region. Understanding the political and economic gains that were associated with the establishment of Gülen schools in Azerbaijan and Central Asia during the post-Soviet transformation period was, therefore, central in assembling the complex puzzle of this South–South transfer.

NOTES

1. According to the European Investment Bank (2007), total lending in the country as of December 2006 stands at €6.8 million (of which €4.9 billion since 2001).

2. TIKA aims to 1) contribute to sustainable social and economic development in partner countries through technical projects, 2) support development programs in line with the Millennium Development Goals of the United Nations, 3) support capacity-building activities and promote institutional development by facilitating the transfer of know-how and expertise of Turkish institutions, 4) improve human resources in partner countries, and 5) coordinate development cooperation activities of Turkish institutions (Baktir, 2007).

3. TIKA has Program Coordination offices in Afghanistan, Albania, Azerbaijan, Bosnia-Herzegovina, Ethiopia, Georgia, Kazakhstan, Kosovo, Kyrgyzstan, Macedonia, Moldova, Mongolia, Palestine, Sudan, Tajikistan, Turkmenistan, Ukraine, and Uzbekistan.

4. Yanik (2004) reports the total number of scholarships distributed to students from Eurasia, including the Turkic republics, between 1992 and 2002 as 21,871. During this period, of the 21,871 scholarships distributed, 11,017 were revoked, making the success rate approximately 50%.

5. During the 1990s, the Uzbek and Turkish government authorities developed hostile relationships. As Balci (2003) explains, the first crisis arose because Uzbek opposition leaders Muhammad Salih, chairman of the political party Erk, and Abdurrahman Polat, chairman of the Birlik party, fled as refugees to Turkey when they were threatened by the Uzbek government. President Karimov demanded that the Turkish authorities expel them, fearing that they would influence Uzbek students in Turkey, but met with a refusal. Karimov was also hostile to a strong Turkish foreign policy in Uzbekistan, refusing to deal exclusively with

Turkey and aiming to develop relationships with other countries, including Russia. There is a third reason for Karimov's hostility to the Gülen movement. In Uzbekistan, the state authorities saw Islam becoming powerful in the Fergana valley and feared that it would threaten the new state. They decided to limit the Islamization of society by closing some mosques in Fergana and a couple of Turkish *fethullahcı* schools, which tried to openly proselytize their students and recommended that young girls wear headscarves (Balci, 2003).

6. The community is not a tightly controlled hierarchical organization, but rather a loose network of schools, study centers, foundations, companies, and other organizations, some of which are closely affiliated with Gülen himself, and others who merely regard him as a source of inspiration.

7. In Turkmenistan, the cult of personality of President Niyazov is imposed in schools via the compulsory and almost exclusive study of his book, the *Rukhnama*. In Uzbekistan and Turkmenistan, this stultifying control is producing a generation that is fearful of open discussion and seldom able to form independent opinions.

8. The *Rukhnama*, or "Book of the Soul," is a moral code supposedly authored by President Niyazov and now mandatory reading for every Turkmen schoolchild and university student.

TEN

BRAC Goes Global

Colette Chabbott

BRAC, the largest international NGO based in the global South, has been sharing its Non-Formal Primary Education (NFPE) model with many government and nongovernment organizations in the global South for almost 20 years. Many involved in the global Education for All (EFA) initiative (Chabbott, 2003) hoped that the BRAC NFPE model, which had scaled up to more than 30,000 low-cost, one-classroom primary schools in Bangladesh in less than 10 years, might similarly help scale up quality primary education at similarly unprecedented rates in other high-priority, less industrialized countries. Many of BRAC's international sharing activities have been encouraged and financially supported by UNICEF and other international donors. BRAC has, however, also undertaken many activities at the invitation of organizations based in the global South, at times, at its own expense. This chapter explores several of the mechanisms that BRAC has used to share its model and how experience with those mechanisms has informed BRAC's own recent efforts to "go global" in countries such as Afghanistan.

The story told here is largely informed by interviews with BRAC and UNICEF staff who were involved in sharing BRAC's NFPE model in one or more countries. It also draws on public and internal BRAC reports. It is an insiders' account, lacking the critical perspective that outside partners and former employees might bring to the narrative. In an effort to get down as much of BRAC's perspective as possible in these pages, I do not engage in any more critical reflection—celebrating or criticizing South–South transfers or Third Country Development Cooperation—than my informants did.

WHAT IS THE BRAC MODEL?

When the World Conference on Education for All (EFA) was held in Jomtien, Thailand, in 1990, the Bangladesh Rural Advancement Committee (BRAC) had been involved in relief and community development for almost 20 years. BRAC was generally recognized as among the most dynamic NGOs in Bangladesh (Lovell, 1992), soon to become the largest indigenous NGO in the world. In 1989, Bangladesh was slightly larger in area than Greece, with about 10 times the population and only about 1/30th the income per capita, and with few natural resources besides land, water, and people. In this context, BRAC focused on identifying low-cost, high-impact innovations in health, agriculture, and micro-enterprise, and on scaling them up quickly. By the time of the EFA conference in 1990, BRAC's NFPE (B-NFPE) program, although only 5 years old, had grown from 22 to almost 4,000 schools, and its expansion showed no signs of slowing down (Ahmed, Chabbott, Joshi, & Pande, 1993).

In 1985, with less than 25% of girls in rural areas completing primary school, BRAC's approach was to keep capital and salary costs low in order to reach the largest number of students. NFPE centers were started only in villages with at least 30 children who had dropped out of school or had never attended. Classes met in one-room buildings made of thatch and corrugated tin, rented part-time, where 30 children sat in a U-shape on mats on the floor, with slates on their laps. BRAC recruited a village woman with eight or more years of education to serve as a paraprofessional teacher for 3 to 4 hours a day for a small stipend. A School Management Committee (SMC) selected the times and days the school would meet according to the needs of the parents, with no long vacations. Parents, teachers, students, and the SMC all lived in one small village, resulting in high levels of attendance and timeliness, eliminating appropriate concerns with girls' safety, and eliminating many of the hidden opportunity costs of schooling for both students and teachers. The teacher received brief preservice training that focused on child-centered methods of instruction to a greater degree than did formal teacher training in Bangladesh. In addition, teachers also received weekly visits from BRAC staff, monthly refresher training, and annual grade-up training. The same teacher worked with the same students for one 3- or 4-year cycle. At the end of the first cycle, if 30 out-of-school children were found in the village, a second cycle would begin; otherwise, the school would close.

In contrast with its approach to salaries and capital infrastructure, B-NFPE spends more on supervision and management than do most formal schools in the global South. Clusters of 10 to 15 schools receive weekly visits from high school– or college-educated Program Officers (POs) who live in the rural area near the schools they supervise. BRAC provides these POs with training, transportation (bicycles or motorcycles), and lodging, and they, in turn, organize monthly parents' meetings for each school, deliver supplies, and provide monthly inservice training to teachers. The

POs submit monthly reports, which are reviewed by managers at two higher levels. The results of these reviews may redirect attention to schools that need more support or to parts of the curriculum that need improvement. Over time, BRAC's Curriculum and Teacher Education Unit at headquarters has produced—and revised—teaching and learning materials that are more appropriate to the rural milieu, including G1–G3 texts in second languages for ethnic minorities. Other BRAC departments, not specific to NFPE, also provide support for research and evaluation, procurement, finance, personnel, and commercial printing. As a result, despite lower costs for teacher salaries and buildings, the cost per child enrolled in NFPE is on par with formal schools in more accessible areas with less disadvantaged students. However, because of higher repetition and lower completion rates in the formal system, BRAC's cost is low relative to the costs of formal schools in terms of completers (Rahman Rahman Huq, 1992).

In the early years of B-NFPE, BRAC students performed poorly, relative to their formal school peers on tests of the formal Bangla, mathematics, and environmental studies curriculum (Begum, Akhter, & Rahman, 1988). In 1992, UNICEF funded the development of an Assessment of Basic Competencies (ABC) by BRAC's Research and Evaluation Division that focused on the basic literacy, numeracy, and life skills reflected in BRAC's original 3-year, three-grade model. The first large-scale application of the ABC found that more 11-year-olds in BRAC schools achieved all four basic competencies relative to their peers in formal rural primary schools (United Nations Children's Fund, 1992). Since then, BRAC has tracked the performance of its system annually, first using the ABC and later using an examination based on the more than 50 competencies covered in the government's primary school curriculum.[1]

The performance of BRAC students was particularly impressive, given their low socioeconomic status relative to their peers in formal schools. Much to the surprise of BRAC staff, many of the earliest NFPE graduates subsequently gained entry to grade three or four in formal primary schools. However, confronted with some of the same obstacles that had discouraged their earlier enrollment—mainly the cost of school in terms of travel time, clothing, books, materials, foregone labor, and tutoring fees—many NFPE graduates did not persist (Nath, 2002). In response, BRAC expanded the curriculum of NFPE to cover the formal grades one through five primary curriculum in 4 years, added English instruction, and provided promising BRAC graduates coaching in preparation for the secondary school scholarship examination.

Finally, BRAC continues to adapt its model to serve more hard-to-reach groups. By June 2006, B-NFPE was operating 20,000 preschools and about 32,000 one-room primary schools of four different types:

- Original BRAC Primary Schools, for children ages 8–11
- BRAC Adolescent Primary Schools, for children ages 11–14
- Education Support Program schools, implemented by other NGOs and supervised by BRAC
- Education for Indigenous Children

After a brief, unsuccessful experiment with collecting user fees in the 1990s, BRAC now includes the full cost of its classroom and management models in its proposals to foreign donors. To minimize the cost of reporting to multiple donors, BRAC has persuaded many donors to join a consortium, which accepts common proposals, quarterly reports, and evaluations. In addition, BRAC uses income from several large commercial enterprises to cover NFPE activities for which it has found no donor to date.

BRAC AND UNICEF

Although UNICEF dropped the term *Emergency* from its original name (United Nations International Children's Emergency Fund) in 1952 and has branched out into many development activities, it remains determined to work in disaster-struck and conflict areas, and to do so, it must find partners capable of operating there. In 1971, following a devastating liberation war, during which most of Bangladesh's infrastructure was destroyed and millions of people were killed or permanently disabled, UNICEF, along with many other donors, directly funded a burgeoning community of international and national emergency relief organizations, including the newly formed BRAC.

Adult literacy was among BRAC's first programs, but not until the early 1980s, at the request of members of its adult literacy classes, did it begin to experiment with basic education classes for children. Initially, BRAC gained some early inspiration from a UNICEF report about and a visit to a nonformal primary education model in Pune, India (Naik, 1980). UNICEF's office in Dhaka was, therefore, one of several funders for the B-NFPE efforts and, in 1988, UNICEF headquarters commissioned a brief report on the model, which was distributed at the 1990 World Conference on EFA (Lovell & Fatema, 1989). Nothing in the 1989 report, however, suggests that BRAC's model should be used to do anything beyond improving and providing better primary education delivery in rural Bangladesh; the report does not discuss potential replication or adaptation of B-NFPE in other countries.

Following the Jomtien Conference in 1990, however, UNICEF Executive Director James P. Grant proceeded directly to Dhaka to see the BRAC model for himself and to discuss its possible adaptation in other countries. Nothing in Grant's approach in other sectors suggests that he might have considered the BRAC model directly transferable to other countries. Rather, he argued, the BRAC model proved that it was possible to develop and quickly expand contextually appropriate primary education models in even the poorest countries. Nonetheless, Grant's intense enthusiasm for the BRAC model was such that he was referred to at BRAC as "our personal ambassador."

BRAC's NFPE model was highlighted again as one of five innovations particularly relevant to EFA in the 1992 UNICEF report *What Are We Waiting For?* (Anderson, 1992). By 1992, however, NFPE had grown and changed in so many ways that UNICEF and USAID funded an expanded study of NFPE (Ahmed et al., 1993), publishing it in time to be distributed at the 1993 Summit on EFA for the Nine High-Population Countries. The 143-page report, based on a village-level census, independent cost surveys, financial analyses, and field visits, like the 1989 report, finds the potential for achieving universal primary education (UPE) in Bangladesh through NFPE schools promising. The report, however, highlights several conditions that are apparently vital to the success of NFPE in Bangladesh that were unlikely to be found in other high-priority EFA countries, particularly in Africa:

- Relative political stability
- Cultural and linguistic homogeneity
- A large and capable NGO community
- High levels of educated unemployment among women in rural areas
- Dense populations in underserved areas

The section summary states:

> Worldwide experience indicates repeatedly ... that wholesale transplanting of an innovation from one country to another, without substantial "ownership" and sense of origination by the recipient country is "doomed" to failure. (Ahmed et al., 1993, p. 123)

These three reports, in addition to NFPE case studies in anthologies and other donor reports (Cummings, Dall, Fiske, & Al-Husainy, 1993; Little, Hoppers, & Gardner, 1994; Rugh & Bossert, 1998; Sweetser, 1999; Wolf, Kane, & Strickland, 1997), circulated widely among education experts working in international development organizations in Africa and elsewhere. None of these reports or case studies suggests that the BRAC model could be transferred more or less directly to another country. Nonetheless, many of these authors assumed that BRAC's NFPE program at least served as proof that a poor country with a largely dysfunctional formal education system serving only a small fraction of school-age children could find a way to expand primary schooling rapidly.

By the end of the 1980s, as BRAC's NFPE program scaled up and the overall situation in Bangladesh became less of an emergency, UNICEF encouraged BRAC to seek more funding from other development donors and, by the end of the 1990s, UNICEF/Bangladesh had become a minor funder for B-NFPE. UNICEF headquarters, however, continued to promote South–South sharing into the current decade, as described below.

SHARING BY SHOWING, TELLING, ADVISING, AND COACHING

In response to the studies and reports described in the previous section, a thousand or so visitors have traveled to Bangladesh to see BRAC's NFPE model firsthand. These study tours, in turn, prompted a series of pilot community school efforts in Africa and Asia for which BRAC staff provided short- and long-term technical assistance, as described below. BRAC's most recent efforts to establish freestanding BRAC offices in Afghanistan and elsewhere are described in the following section.

Study Tours: Show and Tell

Most of UNICEF's education staff in sub-Saharan Africa traveled to Bangladesh for exposure to the BRAC NFPE model in the 1990s and, in turn, sent many national delegations from African countries in the mid-1990s. Other groups from China and Ethiopia visited on their own initiative, and BRAC accommodated many other unsponsored visitors at its own expense. Over the years, the volume of visitors to NFPE and other BRAC programs was such that BRAC had to create several programs to manage them. Neither BRAC nor UNICEF maintained a comprehensive list of the individuals and groups that visited NFPE. However, various NFPE reports include illustrative lists. For example, the 1997 NFPE annual report mentions visitors from Britain, Japan, Vietnam, Canada, India, France, Pakistan, the United States, the Netherlands, Myanmar, Nepal, Bhutan, Iraq, China, Sudan, Uzbekistan, and Azerbaijan.

As his most difficult foreign delegation, a former BRAC public affairs officer describes a group of education ministers organized by the Association for Development of Education in Africa who came in 2003 or 2004.

Several ministers expressed outrage at the lack of the most basic amenities associated with formal schools, such as ceiling fans, benches, tables, and latrines. The ministers' insistence that BRAC meet "African" standards of acceptable infrastructure represents the reverse of a problem that several BRAC staff had already encountered in efforts to implement NFPE outside of Bangladesh: Some visitors were loath to change or adapt any aspect of the BRAC school model once they returned home. For example, in Ethiopia, BRAC staff noticed that the adolescent girls sat in the traditional U-shape, around the perimeter of the classroom, with their legs stretched out stiffly in front of them, taking up most of the space in a classroom of the usual size. Much taller and less comfortable on the floor than their Bangladeshi peers, they obviously needed more space or something to sit on. However, when the staff member asked why the teacher didn't arrange the students or the classroom differently, the teacher is reported to have said that the BRAC model required that the girls sit on the floor in a U-shape and the management did not want to deviate from that model.

Given the volume of visitors, surprisingly few returned home and attempted to launch NFPE-like one-room schools. One BRAC staff member reflected that many visitors from the global South, both governmental and nongovernmental, may have found the scale and degree of organization of BRAC's NFPE overwhelming. He suggested that some visits to BRAC's Education Support Program (ESP), through which BRAC provides training, supervision, and curriculum development to smaller Bangladeshi NGOs that want to run NFPE schools, might have been more appropriate. This, however, begs the question of how small NGOs in other countries would have managed NFPE-like schools without this sort of help from a BRAC-like organization. In Mali, one of the best-documented examples of an attempt to adapt the BRAC model to another country without direct input from BRAC, the international NGO Save the Children played this role. This dramatically raised the per pupil cost of the model, but also enabled the Mali model to scale up more than any other NFPE model in Africa (Boukary, 2004; DeStefano, 2006; Laugharn, 2001; Muskin, 1999).

Sharing NFPE with the rest of the world, therefore, involved more than showing and telling and encouraging visitors to go home and do likewise. Beginning in the early 1990s, BRAC senior staff served as short-term consultants to groups experimenting with NFPE in many countries. From the perspective of BRAC staff, these consultancies led, more often than not, to recommendations to deviate from, rather than stick closely to, the original BRAC classroom model. If local implementers were reluctant to change any aspect of the school model, onsite BRAC consultants could encourage them.

Short-Term Consulting: Advising

Following the Jomtien conference, UNICEF invited the originators of both the Escuelas Nuevas (EN) and BRAC NFPE to join the UNICEF education staff. The EN originator subsequently served for several years as UNICEF's regional advisor for Education in the Americas, which provided her with a platform for promoting EN there and in the Caribbean. The BRAC originator, however, declined UNICEF's offer of employment, agreeing instead to a handful of short consultancies in Africa and Asia. In addition, the former country director for UNICEF/Bangladesh in the early 1990s moved to Nairobi in the mid-1990s to become regional director for UNICEF in the Eastern and Southern Africa Office (ESARO). During this period, Bangladeshi nationals working for UNICEF, or other UNICEF staff who had previously worked in Bangladesh and were familiar with BRAC, served in key roles in eastern and southern Africa. In addition, one senior member of the BRAC NFPE program was seconded to ESARO for about 12 months in 1997 in order to help identify promising locations for piloting adaptations of the BRAC model.

UNICEF was by no means the only client for consulting services from BRAC staff. At the instigation of governments or national NGOs, senior BRAC education staff participated in pro bono delegations to several countries, including Ethiopia, Pakistan, and India. As was the case for visitors to BRAC, neither BRAC nor its clients have maintained systematic records of all their international consulting work. The following illustrative cases, therefore, are based largely on interviews with BRAC staff.

Oxfam-America in India. Among the people from dozens of countries coming to look at BRAC NFPE in the first half of the 1990s, one of the earliest was the regional representative for Oxfam-America in South Asia. Following her visit to BRAC, the representative proposed that Oxfam support NFPE in many NGOs in India as soon as possible. Oxfam's board, however, only agreed to fund a pilot adaptation of the BRAC NFPE model by two local NGOs in two districts in India. In addition, Oxfam contracted for a study comparing the B-NFPE model with 15 existing Indian nonformal primary education efforts, including the Pune model that had provided early inspiration for BRAC. The study collected data on 38 variables, less than eight of which addressed management capacity (Varma & Malviya, 1996).

While the study was ongoing, a BRAC consultant traveled twice to India to provide advice to the two pilot projects. In the process, she noted that the Indian equivalent of POs and their supervisors were working on projects in more than one sector at a time. She emphasized that NFPE needed full-time POs and supervisors. This represented an attempt to bring the implementation process more in line with the BRAC's management model, ensuring that paraprofessional teachers received far more practical supervision than was typical in most schools in rural South Asia.

By the time the study of 15 Indian NFPE programs was wrapping up, 1,800 children in 30 Oxfam-supported, BRAC-modeled nonformal centers were finishing grade three and preparing to transfer into government school. Although the students in the centers were mainly dropouts and nonstarters, Varma and Malviya (1996) reported that 90% of them—70% of them girls—had "successfully" completed primary education and continued their education in secondary schools. This achievement, however, was not directly compared with the results achieved by the other 15 Indian NFPE programs.

Whether the success of this pilot project led to an expansion of community schools in India is not known. As was the case with almost all countries described below where BRAC provided short- or long-term consultants, BRAC has lost contact with the two Indian NGOs that were adapting its NFPE model.[2]

UNICEF in Sierra Leone. During a workshop with regional UNICEF education staff in Senegal, a BRAC consultant was approached by a UNICEF national staff person from Freetown, Sierra Leone. The consultant recalls that the staff person was very excited by the presentation and persuaded UNICEF to bring the consultant to Freetown to help launch an NFPE pilot. During the ensuing short-term consultancy, the BRAC consultant found that the UNICEF staffer had "thousands" of photocopies of the UNICEF-sponsored Lovell and Fatema book (1989) stacked in her office. The staff person showed a keen appreciation of both the elements of BRAC's management model and the need to adapt them to Sierra Leone. For example, she worked closely with the government curriculum institute to design appropriate curriculum and textbooks, and assembled a strong team of trainers. However, the consultant noted the lack of "the right kind of NGOs" and expressed doubt that the government could maintain the flexibility necessary to implement an NFPE model. The UNICEF officer was still looking for the right kind of NGO when civil war started in Sierra Leone and BRAC's work with the NFPE effort in Sierra Leone was curtailed.

A BRAC consultant returned to Sierra Leone in 2001 or 2002 with a testing expert to help evaluate the state of the NFPE schools that had survived or had been started after the war. Tests showed that NFPE students were doing better than the formal school students. The consultant commended the UNICEF officer for modifying the model to fit the Sierra Leone context, including hiring unemployed formal teachers to teach in NFPE schools. In 2005, UNICEF reported that 400 of the community schools covering grades 1 to 3 had served approximately 19,000 children and that by 2009, 900 more such schools would be established (Chiejine, 2005). As was the case in India, BRAC has not maintained contact with the Sierra Leone project.

Of the overall short-term consulting experience, one BRAC consultant reflected, "In a short visit you cannot study things properly. I felt frustrated everywhere I went." Short-term consultancies did not permit sufficient time for BRAC staff to fully imagine the best ways the NFPE model might be adapted in other countries, particularly with respect to the complex management model. Moreover, without high-speed Internet and e-mail access during the 1990s, and often with limited English as the only common language, following up short consultancies in writing was not practical. Long-term consultancies, described in the next section, seemed to offer a better chance to help local organizations adapt and establish new NFPE models and stay with them long enough to get both school and management models on a solid footing.

Long-Term Consulting: Coaching

In the late 1990s, several UNICEF staff moved directly from water and sanitation projects in Bangladesh to staff UNICEF's Operation Lifeline Sudan (OLS). Because at that time Southern Sudan lacked a formal government, UNICEF took an unusually active, hands-on role in OLS. The head of OLS was unsatisfied with the "lack of new ideas" in Southern Sudan and dispatched a group of 10 to 12 officials from the Ministries of Education and Health on a study tour to Bangladesh, Nepal, and India. The UNICEF field program coordinator for education in OLS was impressed with the BRAC NFPE program and was determined to support it in Southern Sudan.

The area where the field program coordinator asked the BRAC consultants to begin work, Rumbek, was extremely remote; a small plane flew international relief agency staff and materials from Kampala to a small town on the Uganda/Sudan border where most agencies maintained offices. From there, a UN plane made the trip to Rumbek less frequently. Rumbek had few buildings or even building materials beyond handmade mud bricks; roofing material, furniture, and most supplies had to be flown in. BRAC consultants lived in tents, and water was rationed. In 2002, there was only one girl enrolled in the secondary school in Rumbek. In the widely dispersed, sparsely populated rural communities, most inhabitants with 8 or more years of education had left for the cities, draining the already small pool of paraprofessional teacher candidates.

In mid-2001, three short-term BRAC consultants participated in a 3-day strategic planning symposium organized by UNICEF and the Southern Sudan Education Authority. One of the BRAC consultants said that the presentation UNICEF asked them to prepare felt "like we were selling our program to them." The first longer-term BRAC consultant visited Rumbek in November and returned to begin a 6-month consultancy in March 2002. UNICEF invited potential staff to a seminar that the consultant prepared on the BRAC model. From the seminar participants, the consultant selected two program officers, one materials developer, and one team leader. Together, these staff set up 10 G1–G3 schools during the first 6-month consultancy, with the consultant working alongside the staff to identify communities, students, teachers, and supplies, and to conduct training.

The Sudan environment demanded many adaptations of the BRAC classroom model. For example:

- Educated women were hard to find in rural communities. Of the first 10 schoolteachers selected in Southern Sudan, only four were women.
- All buildings were in full-time use. Consultants organized communities to make mud-brick shells and UNICEF flew in roofing material.
- No large mats of any material were available. Parents were asked to send small mats for their children to sit on.
- Low population density meant that few communities had 30 eligible students eligible for enrollment within a 1-mile (1.6-km) radius. Selecting only communities meeting this criterion meant the distance was 40 miles (65 km) between some schools. After trying this and finding it impractical, the minimum number of students was reduced and the catchment area was increased.
- Because of the distance between schools and the lack of roads, POs could not reach all schools weekly. POs who were responsible for very distant communities were issued camping equipment and arranged to spend several days at a time per month in harder-to-reach communities.

In addition, many of the support services needed to make the POs effective were lacking. For example:

- Rumbek had no professional printers to produce learning materials. Staff photocopied and collated many materials by hand.
- UNICEF made Dinke textbooks available, but teachers' guides and other teaching and learning materials that BRAC considered essen-

tial were not available. A short-term consultancy by a BRAC materials developer translated some materials from Bangla into English, but there was no one to translate them into Dinke.

In total, four consultants, all of whom had 10 or more years of experience with BRAC, served for up to 6 months over a 2-year period. Together with the newly hired Southern Sudan Education Authority staff, these consultants helped establish 120 to 200 "Village Girls' Schools" in three areas. In addition, BRAC consultants also trained CARE and Save the Children staff in the BRAC NFPE model, with the expectation that the three organizations together would be operating 600 schools by the end of 2004. Some or all of the CARE and Save the Children schools were expected to be funded by USAID, under the Sudan Basic Education Program.

In the absence of a permanent government, BRAC consultants serving in Southern Sudan kept the UNICEF/OLS education program officer, who was based in Kampala, informed. She praised their professionalism and commitment. She said that the BRAC staff provided good role models for national development workers in that they didn't impose their ideas and they spent a lot of time in the communities, modeling more "child-friendly" ways of relating to children.

The UNICEF/OLS education program officer returned to Bangladesh in 2003 to request a memorandum of understanding that would establish a steady stream of BRAC consultants into Southern Sudan for several years. Sufficient senior staff members, however, were not available to fulfill this request, as BRAC itself was in the process of scaling up new types of NFPE in Afghanistan and a new preprimary model in Bangladesh. Moreover, without guaranteed OLS funding for the 2 years necessary to complete one cycle of NFPE in the Sudan, BRAC was not willing to undertake the work. In retrospect, one of the BRAC consultants estimated that the education program in Southern Sudan would need at least 10 years before it could operate without substantial technical assistance from BRAC staff, a period to which no partner was prepared to commit.

When the UNICEF education program officer transferred out of Southern Sudan in the middle of 2004 and was not replaced by someone similarly inspired to press the BRAC connection, BRAC staff lost touch with the program. Despite the advent of high-speed Internet and e-mail access after 2000, written follow-up of the long-term, onsite coaching did not occur. This may have been at least in part a problem with limited English, as mentioned above. It was certainly exacerbated by the workloads in the new jobs awaiting the long-term consultants after they returned to BRAC, including long-term contracts in Afghanistan, the subject of the next section. Meanwhile, USAID funding for nonformal community schools also lapsed within a year or two of the BRAC training provided to CARE and Save the Children staff. Some of those staff members have continued to work in nonformal education in Southern Sudan; however, the status of the schools started by BRAC with UNICEF funding is not known.

In summary, reflecting on various short-term advising and the Sudanese long-term coaching experience, BRAC staff emphasized the importance of individual initiative within the requesting organization, Northern or Southern, governmental or nongovernmental. They concluded that someone had to have both vision and stamina to create and maintain the momentum necessary to launch the adaptation process and follow it through. In the next section, I look at BRAC's efforts to circumvent the need for visionary individuals in donor organizations by setting up a BRAC office in another country, staffed with multiple experienced managers who hire national staff, who are then mentored and trained as BRAC staff.

SHARING BY DOING AND MENTORING

At the beginning of the 21st century, BRAC was arguably the largest national nongovernmental organization in the world. In 2005, BRAC's revenue from commercial projects (such as the BRAC Bank) and program support enterprises (such as handicrafts retailing) and service charges for loans to village organization members totaled almost US$ 140 million,[3] more than 200% of the value of the international donor grants received that year (BRAC, 2006). This gave BRAC rare flexibility as a Southern NGO to pilot its own ideas and launch new programs without reference to Northern funders, at least in the initial stages. This streamlined BRAC's work in microfinance, where interest can render a new program in a new country self-sustaining within a matter of years. It is less helpful, however, in the education sector, where, historically, there are no precedents for self-financing mass, first-generation universal primary education.

Some Bangladeshis maintain a strong sense of cultural and historic solidarity to Afghanistan and compare the demolished condition of dry, mountainous, sparsely populated Afghanistan in 2002 with the condition of low-lying, densely populated Bangladesh at the end of its Liberation War in 1972 (Chowdhury, Alam, & Ahmed, 2006). Shortly after the fall of the Taliban in 2001, the chairman of BRAC sent a group of senior managers on a fact-finding visit to Afghanistan. On a second visit later that year, the chairman and the executive director of BRAC met with the minister for Rural Reconstruction and Development, who requested BRAC's help with a 5-year strategic plan. Later that year, BRAC began the process of registering as an international NGO, piloted programs in several sectors in two Afghan provinces (Parwan and Balkh), and conducted the surveys that helped determine BRAC's three priority sectors: microfinance, health, and education. BRAC funded most of these efforts with income from its profit-making enterprises in Bangladesh.

In 2002, BRAC launched 24 pilot schools for older girls in two Afghan provinces with funds from the Swedish International Development Cooperation Agency (SIDA). In addition, the UNICEF-funded Accelerated Learning (or Winter) Program (ALP, December 2002–March 2003) provided BRAC with an opportunity to demonstrate the range of its capabilities in primary education to the government of Afghanistan. Through the ALP, BRAC helped about 15,000 older children to advance one grade in 4 months by developing teacher training material, master trainers who would then train 159 grade-two teachers and 318 grade-one teachers during the winter months, and mathematics training for 500 teachers. In addition, it established regular coordination with the Ministry of Education and UNICEF, and it trained and dispatched local supervisors to visit each school twice weekly (BRAC Education Programme, 2002).

In each of these endeavors, BRAC created a somewhat new school model, using different combinations of formal curricula and outside materials, and finding new ways to train female teachers in communities where women may not be allowed to spend 12 days away from home at a training center. Bangladeshi staff reported that Afghan women were willing and able to do much more than their male colleagues were prepared to ask of them, much as had been the case in Bangladesh 20 years earlier. BRAC also had to adjust the pace of the curriculum for Afghan children who, having grown up in refugee camps and only recently returned to rural areas, had a broader exposure to the world and to print than most rural Bangladeshi children had.

Based on the track record established by ALP, BRAC has been working much more closely with the Ministry of Education in Afghanistan than it has been able to do with its counterpart in Bangladesh. Initially, the priority areas for primary education identified by the Ministry—establishing formal primary school buildings and recruiting and paying professional teachers—appeared to clash with BRAC's commitment to minimal infrastructure, part-time paraprofessional teachers, and serving overage girls in rural areas. Later in 2004, UNICEF's former senior advisor to education, now working with BRAC, conducted a strategic education planning meeting for teachers and government officials, during which a complementary role for BRAC within the formal government system began to emerge.

According to its annual report, by the end of 2005, BRAC had established 52 area offices in 26 districts in 13 provinces and had operated or was operating three types of schools: 608 2-year classes covering 3 years of the formal primary curriculum for older girls; 216 feeder schools, providing 1 year of school readiness for young children; and 24 nonformal primary education schools. Under the Accelerated Learning Program, BRAC was continuing to provide basic teacher training to primary school teachers and mathematics training to 158 teachers. Under all these programs, 80% of the students were female, and over 80% of the teachers were female (BRAC, 2006). Because many of its schools exist for only 1 or 2 years, to help overage children catch up and rejoin formal primary schools, the exact number of schools that BRAC continues to operate is difficult to estimate. In April 2006, BRAC announced the opening of 5,000 new schools (Chowdhury, Alam, & Ahmed, 2006).

Building a primary education system in Afghanistan will require massive international assistance for a decade or more. In the context of international NGOs (INGOs) in Afghanistan, BRAC stands out as a low-cost partner with a good track record with key donors, such as the European Community, the Nordic donors, DfID (UK Department for International Development), the Aga Khan Foundation, and CIDA (Canadian International Development Agency). As was the case in the Sudan, BRAC's Bangladeshi managers live simply, in the Afghan rather than the expatriate community. In contrast with Western INGOs, BRAC spends little on security and it pays Bangladeshi staff just twice their normal salary—a small fraction of a Western expatriate's salary supplemented by danger pay. The program has had some tragic setbacks,[4] but continues to expand. Over the next few years, as Afghans pick up experience, confidence, and something of the BRAC organizational culture, senior BRAC staff say that they plan to increase the number of Afghan managers and reduce the number of Bangladeshi staff in Afghanistan.

In summary, the size of BRAC's independent operating budget and the size of its staff in Bangladesh have given it the luxury of diverting staff and resources to a new country, to set up operations first and find donor funding later. In connection with tsunami relief, BRAC has also set up a small international office in Sri Lanka, and other offices in Uganda and Tanzania will be managing an East African health initiative for the Gates Foundation. In contrast with Afghanistan, however, no donors in these places are looking for partners in basic education. However, BRAC has been invited to open an office in Pakistan, where more international support for education is likely to be forthcoming. The work in Afghanistan and other countries in Asia and Africa helps nationals experience not just the BRAC NFPE school model, but also its management model. Self-financing means that BRAC can afford to keep experienced Bangladeshi managers in these countries until such time as nationals are deemed ready to take over operations, even if it takes, as BRAC staff suggested in Southern Sudan, a decade or more.

CONCLUSION

Thousands of reports have been written, thousands of person days of study tours have been undertaken, thousands of consultancy days have been spent, and yet few countries have produced nonformal primary education systems of the scope and efficiency of BRAC's in Bangladesh. Specifically, Africa was subjected to a full-court press by UNICEF for more than 10 years, yet, with the possible exception of Mali, there has been no rapid expansion of NFPE on a significant scale anywhere in sub-Saharan Africa to date.

Those involved offer a wide range of explanations. One frustrated former UNICEF senior staff person attributes the inability to sustain and scale up NFPE activities at least in part to a lack of imagination among UNICEF staff and to the tendency for African education ministries to perceive any school that does not meet the standard of elite schools during colonial times as "second rate." Others attribute the failure to produce lasting NFPE programs to the short-term nature of UNICEF's assistance in education as well as changes in strategy by the executive directors who followed James P. Grant and adopted a more comprehensive approach, versus Grant's targeted approach to EFA.

This extended discussion of UNICEF's relationship with BRAC's international work in the late 1980s and early 1990s highlights how BRAC may have been more important to UNICEF's program than UNICEF was to BRAC's. UNICEF saw in BRAC's NFPE a rare opportunity to fulfill its commitment to provide children in especially difficult circumstances—such as Sierra Leone and Southern Sudan—with a basic education. But BRAC had many other partners, both governmental and nongovernmental, Northern and Southern. All of them seemed to grasp and adapt the classroom model more easily than they did the management model. There is no doubt that those who visit BRAC for just a day or 2—and few visit longer—carry away striking image of a simple, one-room building with a tin roof, filled with smiling children and a bashful young female teacher. But few visitors grasp the significance of the young man in a neatly pressed white shirt and Western-style trousers—the Program Officer—standing just off to the side. And those who stay longer are often, as one BRAC staff member reflected, overwhelmed by the scale and complexity of it all.

BRAC staff members are justifiably proud to be part of a Bangladeshi organization that is now in a position to be a provider rather than a one-way recipient of international assistance. Henry Kissinger's characterization of Bangladesh as an "international basket case" still galls. BRAC's program in Sri Lanka, much smaller than the Afghanistan program, was launched with the contribution of one day's salary from every BRAC employee. In addition, having witnessed heavy-handed Western assistance at home for decades, senior BRAC staff members appear to be fully cognizant that if the B-NFPE model has any hope of being useful in other places, both parts of the B-NFPE model—classroom and management—will need to be thoroughly contextualized. A BRAC consultant to Pakistan told me that she was struck speechless when a Pakistani official announced, "We are ready to launch NFPE; we have trained the teachers and sent them back to the field." She exclaimed, "As if all it was about was training teachers once!"

The reasons why the centrality of BRAC's management model has been so frequently overlooked by the many Northern donors who have supported efforts to share BRAC's "innovative," large-scale health, microcredit, and education programs are the subject of another essay. For now, the natural experiment with BRAC International in Afghanistan and elsewhere may provide the opportunity to test how much time and how many experienced BRAC managers may be needed to adapt and transfer some variation on the BRAC management model to national employees—if only in one very difficult context.

Returning to one of the premises of this volume, even if BRAC succeeds in introducing a viable adaptation of its school and management models in Afghanistan and other least-industrialized, high-priority EFA countries, BRAC's approach is unlikely to reduce these countries' dependence on Northern funding. After all, BRAC assumes that, however cost-efficient, modern schools for the first generation of literates must be externally funded. Successful future adaptations of the BRAC NFPE model are only likely to put available international funding to better use than it is at present and, with every success, increase pressure to provide more funding.

NOTES

1. Several of the annual *Education Watch* reports (see http://www.campebd.org/content/about_EW.html) provide results of primary-level competency-based assessments for different types of schools in Bangladesh. Note that the nonformal schools category created by *Education Watch* contains several types of nonformal school models and does not represent a valid sample of BRAC schools. The comparisons cited here, therefore, draw on two sources: a separate annual study of BRAC schools conducted by BRAC's Research and Evaluation Division and the results of *Education Watch* reports for formal rural primary schools, both conducted using the same research team and methodology.

2. Later, many staff from Lok Jombish, an Indian rural development NGO with a well-known community school model included in the Oxfam-supported Varma and Malviya study, would visit BRAC often. I have found no evidence, however, that the BRAC Education Program was involved in these visits.

3. Official exchange rate (2005): 64.328 Taka = US$1 (U.S. Central Intelligence Agency, 2007).

4. In April 2005, three Afghan women associated with BRAC were found stoned in Baghlan, and in January 2006, an Afghan engineer working for BRAC was also killed. As a result, in July 2006, BRAC withdrew from southern Afghanistan (see UN Office for the Coordination of Humanitarian Affairs, 2006).

ELEVEN

African Students in China

Past and Present

Sandra Gillespie

Since its establishment in 1949, the People's Republic of China has made a concentrated effort to forge close ties with African nations. Part of this effort has included establishing educational ties by providing African students with the opportunity for higher education. The life these students have typically encountered on a Chinese university campus has some rather striking characteristics. First, a complete society exists within the parameters of the university grounds. A wall defines these parameters and surrounds this entire society. All staff and students live within this wall. Two smaller walls stand inside the main wall; these smaller walls surround the foreigners. The first wall surrounds the foreign experts (mainly Western professionals); the second wall surrounds the foreign students (mainly African men). These walls divide the society twice. The walls separate the Chinese from the non-Chinese and the foreign experts from the foreign students. Thus, three distinct societies live inside the school grounds: the Chinese, the Westerners, and the Africans. In a way, each group plays a different role in relation to the others. The Westerners, as foreign experts, teach local Chinese students; the Chinese professors, as local experts, teach the foreign African students. In the first case, the more commonly discussed First World to Third World (North–South) educational exchange occurs; in the second case, the lesser-known phenomenon of Third World to Third World (South–South) exchange takes place. This study explores South–South aspects of educational cooperation by asking: What are the "essential elements" in the lives of African students in China?

Emmanuel John Hevi provided some answers to this question in his 1963 publication, *An African Student in China*. Since then, no other intensive work has focused exclusively on this topic. In his text, Hevi relates his journey, which began in November 1960 as he traveled from Ghana to China in the hope of studying medicine. Hevi chronicles his personal experience and the experiences of 118 other Africans who arrived in Peking in 1961–1962. Reactions to this study have been mixed and, at times, emotional. Snow (1988, p. 199) judges the text to be "savagely polemical" and characterizes Hevi as "a toady . . . soured by his inability to find a girlfriend . . . [and] spoiling for revenge. . . ." Sautman (1994, p. 414) refers to the text as "hostile." Larkin (1971, p. 142) and Hutchison (1975, p. 186), finally, describe the text as "polemical," but add that the allegations Hevi makes have never been disproven. In fact, Hutchison confirms that actually these allegations "were substantiated by Zambian students . . . in 1972." Findings in my study also share key points and tend to support Hevi's account.

My study thus complements Hevi's work (Hevi, 1963, 1967) and attempts to contribute to a larger understanding of international academic relations by further examining this South–South dimension of cooperation. In order to do so, I supplemented quantifiable data, obtained from surveys of African students in China, with more qualitative information gathered through individual and group interviews. From September to December 1997, I visited 14 different sites in four cities: Shanghai, Hangzhou, Nanjing, and Beijing. I held seven interviews with 12 participants from six different countries and collected survey data from 133 students from 29 countries. Twenty-four of the 133 students who completed the questionnaire were Burundians. This overrepresentation had to do with the fact that Burundians assisted me in all stages of this project. These colleagues garnered interest and participation from the larger African community and from their own community in particular. Of the 133 students, 85.7% (114) were male and the median age was 29. The majority of students, 64.7%, first attended university in their own country, and of these, most—38.3% —held a bachelor's degree. On average, they had lived in China for 3.29 years. In all, I spoke with current undergraduate and postgraduate scholars, graduates living in China, and three embassy counselors. These participants wrote and spoke in a remarkably consistent manner, joining to articulate a collective discourse clearly and unanimously situating the concepts of "color and money" at the center of this South–South transfer.

CHINA'S FOREIGN POLICY AND AFRICA

China Quarterly authors, like the participants in this study, have raised questions about race and class in China, which, to date, have been largely ignored. For example, Dikötter (1994) points out that, while a considerable body of scholarly work has revealed much about the historical and contemporary dimensions of racial identities in the West, comparatively little is known about racial identities elsewhere, and "virtually nothing is known about the articulation and deployment of racial frames of reference in China" (p. 403). Dikötter (1994) argues that racial identities in the modern world are framed in exclusively Western terms, which marginalize and trivialize other discourses. Yet, in fact, the discourse of race in China has far-reaching significance. This is especially true as China, host of the 2006 Forum on China–Africa Cooperation, celebrated the 50th anniversary of diplomatic relations and commits to further cooperation with more than 48 African nations.

In many ways, the voices of African students in China may be seen as a reflection of the evolution of China's worldview and a gauge of its foreign-policy orientations. In the early 1960s, when African students first arrived in Beijing, they brought with them a Maoist-inspired image of the world that embodied the spirit of Bandung and an emerging revolutionary zeal that symbolically linked China's fate with the Third World and heralded the nations of Asia, Africa, and Latin America as a revolutionary force that would unite to end the dominance of the First World and transform the existing international order (Sautman, 1994). Although this projection of a new world order had a strong appeal, most African students in Maoist China found that the vision had little grounding in reality. John Hevi's (1963) account of 118 African students in China between 1961 and 1962 reveals that disillusionment and discontent grew so massively and so rapidly that, within 9 months, 90% of students (96 of the 118) returned to Africa. He details the factors that caused this mass exodus:

> undesirable political indoctrination, language difficulty, poor educational standards, restriction on social life, general hostility, spying, and racial discrimination. (Hevi, 1963, p. 183)

Hevi (1963) identifies racial discrimination as "the first item on our list of grievances" (p. 183), but at the same time, this item appears to have been one among many factors.

Hevi's account reflects an environment that may be attributed to a Maoist view of the world that was marked by an ideological inversion: Racial and social hierarchies were stratified in a thesis that extolled the virtues of "colored" people and the poor. These ideals were featured in posters of Third World revolutionaries and in photographs of Mao surrounded by exchange students of all races. Racial solidarity was particularly highlighted in Mao's pronouncements on anti-colonial and revolutionary movements in Africa and the black diaspora. At a time when the Chinese government officially justified its African aid projects on grounds of racial solidarity and the Red Guards rallied to support African causes, few would have dared to express hostility openly to people from the Third World (Sautman, 1994).

With the death of Mao Tse-tung (1976) and the ascension of Deng Xiaoping (1978), China's worldview changed. In December 1978, the Third Plenum of the Eleventh Central Committee of the Communist Party (CCP) initiated the post-Mao era of reform, heralded the rise of Deng Xiaoping, and signified the acceptance of his open-door policies (Hayhoe, 1989). The open-door policies shifted attention from the promotion of international solidarity to the promotion of trade with advanced capitalist nations. While these social and political shifts brought about tremendous openness and political reforms, they also resulted in a reemergence of social stratification and a rejection of Third World solidarity. As the preeminence of the poor was quickly replaced by the preeminence of national and individual enrichment, many began to equate humiliation—not solidarity—with the Third World. Mao's Three-Worlds Theory, which symbolically linked China's fate with that of the Third World, was quickly abandoned for a reform-era vision that argued that China's destiny lay with the West (Sautman, 1994; Sullivan, 1994).

This reform-era vision was immediately manifested on China's university campuses. In July 1979, just 7 months after the Third Plenum, a confrontation between Chinese and African students at the Shanghai Textile University set a pattern for a decade of conflict across campuses in Shanghai, Shenyang, Guangzhou, Beijing, Tianjin, Xian, Hangzhou, Wuhan, and Nanjing. Although many commentators focused on the motives behind the conflict, for others, these conflicts raised deeper concerns regarding the emerging world vision among China's future elites.

In the 1979 clashes, Chinese students began to voice their support for the government's decision to cut interest-free loans and technical assistance to the Third World, but at the same time, began to voice their opposition to the government's decision to continue educational aid. Students argued that the government should not "waste" its resources on others, and particularly objected to the policy of "spoiling" African students while Chinese citizens suffered on lesser means and in worse conditions because of the failed economic policies of the Mao era (Sullivan, 1994, p. 444). University administrations also began to react adversely to government policies that sent universities a quota of scholarship students but not the necessary financial resources (Cheung, 1989). What the Chinese students and school authorities largely regarded as means to indulge, the African students regarded as means to control, isolate, alienate, and segregate them from the local community. Resentment built on all sides across many campuses.

Administrators' attempts to defuse the tensions by dispersing African students across provincial universities only enlarged the problem. Hostilities rose to such an extent that, eventually, Africans across China boycotted classes and ultimately demanded protection from the university administrations. In addition to security, the students insisted that authorities eradicate negative images of Africa through educational programs. University administrators considered these demands unwarranted and refused (Sautman, 1994; Sullivan, 1994).

In 1988–1989, these problems caught international attention when they culminated in the Nanjing Anti-African protests. During a weeklong demonstration, 3,000 Chinese students marched in the streets, chanting anti-black, human rights, prodemocratic, and nationalistic slogans. Moral indignation, sparked by racially motivated rumors, led Nanjing students to "take the law into their own hands" (Sullivan, 1994, pp. 456–457). Four months later, this indignation and determination, combined with patriotism and antigovernment sentiment, erupted into the most serious challenge to the Committee of the Community Party's (CCP) rule since 1949. From this view, the Nanjing Anti-African protests heralded the prodemocracy movement of 1989, as Chinese "democrats" used the anti-African sentiments to direct protest against the party regime (Sautman, 1994, p. 426).

Since 1989, no protests—either against the regime or against African students—have been publicly staged. This does not mean, however, that such opposition has dissipated. In fact, as this study reveals, problems of racial hostility and social isolation continue to plague African students, as they have in various forms and intensities since the Maoist era. Now in the second decade of reform, these problems have been exacerbated by economic impoverishment at a time when, ironically, China has established itself as the world's third-largest economy. The reform-era view of the world, like the Maoist view of the world, has been marked by yet another ideological inversion; this time, however, racial and social hierarchies have been restratified by a worldview that holds economic prosperity, in addition to race, as a key indicator of status. Thus, "color and money," as will be shown below, are the essential elements in the lives of African students today, as China shifts its view of the world and its position in the world system.

DIFFERENTIAL TREATMENT OF AFRICAN STUDENTS

"The most important issue facing foreign students is the question of racial discrimination and the class consciousness of the local people," wrote one Ghanaian. A Burundian student specified, "the Chinese have the bad habit of looking down on black Africans." "Even teachers," according to one Ethiopian, "don't believe blacks can be good enough." A Benin man observed that "the Chinese unconsciously think of an African as someone they should set straight." Another simply noted, "they are critics of black skin." A Cameroonian woman elaborated, "The Chinese present a masked xenophobia towards foreigners, especially the Africans, therefore, they pretend to love us, but in reality, they despise us." As a result of these attitudes, one Namibian woman declared: "African students are seriously molested and embarrassed in China." (These notes come from seven questionnaires, with nationality mentioned for context.)

Students linked how they are perceived individually to how the entire African continent is understood. "Our continent is the most damned according to their conception," wrote one Burundian. A Ugandan added that the "Chinese simply associate Africa and any country in it with disaster, poverty, wars, and all the bad things you can imagine." Another Burundian asserted that "Regardless of what is meant in political speeches by Chinese officials in Africa, . . . when you are from a small country, they don't respect you anymore, and . . . [if you are] from a poor country, then [you are] not an important person." And yet another student acknowledged these same biases when he wrote, "Without denying the slow development of Africa, the Chinese seem to look down on Africa. As a proof of that, just look at the rare television programs. For them, all the bad things are African, nothing good comes from there." One student seemed to summarize these sentiments when he wrote, "If you look at the whole thing, our feeling, inside is that we are/I am not satisfied by these attitudes of many Chinese [who] look down on African students as [if] we came from nowhere"(notes from five questionnaires).

Students largely attributed these "attitudes" to "a lack of knowledge of the African realities." This ignorance is a result of the fact that, as a society, "the Chinese are not open to the outside world, and they are taught things totally contrary to Africa." Again and again, this sentiment about the local population being "ill informed" and deliberately "misinformed" about African realities emerged. One student noted that "African[s] . . . are maltreated by the lack of information," and, to another, this "lack of information" explains why "there is always confrontation between Africans and Chinese." In short, students recognized that "The existence of several bad prejudices on our countries of origin and ourselves . . . makes the connection between Chinese and foreigners difficult" (notes from 10 questionnaires). The nature and impact of this "difficult connection" became clearer in the interviews.

During the interviews, students talked at length about the "daily frustrations" encountered when walking down the street, taking a bus, or entering a building. As a matter of course, students felt insulted, shunned, and feared.

> Every day, everywhere I go, [I] get the same thing. Someone is calling, "Hey black devil, . . . you are dirty, you are poor, you have

nothing. . . . Black devil, black stupid, you are. . . ." Whatever—all dirty words. You leave one corner and then the next one. . . . Let's say you're walking a hundred meters . . . you can get the same thing ten times. (Group of 4 Graduates)

Black devil, *hei gui*, is the most common epithet students reported encountering. Sullivan (1994, p. 448) explains: "The meaning of 'devil' (gui) is derogatory in that it expresses various degrees of hostility toward foreigners, treating them as 'non-humans' (i.e., without having the Chinese 'heart and mind')." In adding the word black (*hei*) to *gui*, the epithet takes on a racial meaning.

One embassy counselor observed that "they do speak things like that":

People in the street will say, . . . You come here [because] you need assistance, but you can't give anything. . . . You come for something, but you are not bringing in anything. . . . Black stupid, black poor, black strange, black very ugly, AIDS. . . . Things like that. . . . Black—any negative adjective you can put on it. (Embassy Counselor B)

Most "don't say it straight," assuming that the students don't understand Chinese. However, "99, 98% of Africans here, they [do] understand the language" and those who don't can "read and "see" people's reactions. This type of nonverbal reaction is evident when students encounter another daily frustration—taking the bus.

People always stand in the bus when there is a seat next to me. I don't see any [reason why] someone could not sit next to me. . . . Then, of course, if . . . I sit next to [a person] . . . then he will, she will, feel like trapped. And then, if there is another spare seat, . . . she or he will move to another [seat], . . . but most [of the time], . . . I will sit, like in two seats, and no one will come to sit next to me. (Group of 4 Graduates)

These daily verbal and nonverbal affronts, though clear, leave the students mystified:

I see someone digging a, a street and laughing at me, like poor, black devil. They insult me. . . . He thinks I'm, I'm, I'm really meaningless because I'm a black devil. . . .
    He's allowed to be proud of himself . . . more [than] . . . I'm allowed to be proud. . . . I don't understand where, where all this

pride comes from. And, I do not get [why] someone who has been digging the road and who has dirty clothes [and] I have a clean jacket or trousers, he cannot sit next to me. (Group of 4 Graduates)

Perhaps even more perplexing than such "pride" is the reaction of fear. One student described entering an office building:

I had an appointment with the general manager. . . . The secretary . . . came to open the door [and] ahh! she screams, she jumps . . . [as if she met] a tiger or a lion in the corridor. (Group of 4 Graduates)

The secretary's fearful recoils "shamed" this student and shook his confidence:

Why is she so scared? What does it mean? Why are you acting like this? Am I an animal or what? Why, am I something like a devil, or am I something that is coming from the other planets or Mars or what? I have a head, I have two eyes, I have a nose. . . . I do ask myself, what does she or he think I am?
     The only thing different is the color. . . . It's because of my color, they're not used to this. . . . So for me, he or she should know firsthand, I am a human being. (Group of 4 Graduates)

Students felt they were perceived as "creatures [from other] planets." People "do not seem to understand why and how an African could possibly be in China. Nothing can explain or can tell them why a black man is walking in the Shanghai streets or Nanjing streets." The sensation of being perceived as "some kind of alien that's dropped down from Mars" or an "extraterrestrial, like ET" intensifies during "certain times [when] the way people stare almost [becomes] scare[y]." One woman initially dismissed this staring in that it came from "just students," but then became disturbed when she realized, "Even the teachers don't care. [Teachers] can see [the students staring at us] but will not even bother to stop [these students] and say, 'what are you doing?'" Another woman could understand "if it was the first time they are seeing me but [they] see me every day." For her, it became a matter of "just showing rudeness to me, or [showing me] . . . I am not accepted in your land. . . . It is really humiliating" (Three Undergraduates). The staring becomes so "depressing," so "uncomfortable," that, at times, it is "very difficult to even go outside" and especially difficult to conduct research. Students emphasized that the inability to know "how to react or handle the situation" came from all levels of society.

Students linked this attitude to ignorance and issues of language, economy, and development. Students pointed out that, in the Chinese language, *Africa* translates to *Fei zhou*; "*zhou* means continent and *fei* means nothing." Thus, students were "refusing the word *Fei zhou* . . . [because] *Fei zhou* means the continent of nothing!" Students asserted that the perception of the country affects the perception of race.

Sautman (1994, p. 421) reports that after the anti-African outbreak in Nanjing (1988–1989), African students also requested that the Chinese name for Africa be changed. Sautman points out that *feizhou*, a homophone for "Africa," can be translated as "evil continent," whereas homophones of other countries, such as America (*meiguo*, or "beautiful country") and England (*yingguo*, or "brave country"), are, by contrast, complimentary.

The insinuations of *feizhou*, however, do not necessarily apply to the whole continent. Students attributed attempts to "minimize" them to concepts held regarding the level of economic prosperity and development of their home nations. South Africa, for example, garners respect because it is considered economically developed. Scholars attribute the tendency to look down on foreigners from poorer parts of the world to the concept of *minzu*, "nation-race" (Fisher, 2003).

An embassy counselor expressed bewilderment and an overwhelming sense of the resultant negativism and resentment toward anything Chinese among Africans. He felt that African students consequently have very little knowledge of or insight into Chinese culture. The counselor revealed that some students, in China for 10 years and fluent in the language, remain at the same level of cultural understanding as newcomers because they "have never been let in. . . . They have never been given the chance to understand the culture . . . [nor] participate in any of the Chinese way of life . . . [because] it has always been closed to them." The impact of these barriers on personal relationships was further revealed in discussions about social contact.

Typically, when students spoke about their friends, they were referring to fellow foreigners because their "Chinese friends [were] very few" (Post Graduate B). This reality perplexed many. A counselor asked:

> Why, why, why, can you stay years in a country and you don't have a single friend? I often ask these fellows, "You know, you have been here 8 years, where are your friends? I want to meet them, and we will talk, and we get to know China." And they say, "Ah, you are joking. You can never have a Chinese friend" . . . Why? (Embassy Counselor A)

Students reported "a very clear barrier between the foreign students and the Chinese students. It is really difficult to make good friends among our comrades." One attributed this difficulty in making friends to "reasons of openness" and another to the fact that authorities "do not allow [local people] the chances of being in permanent contact with the foreigners." Others suggested that "the closure of the Chinese society" and the "interdiction of access to many places for foreigners (recreation, work)" separates people (notes from five questionnaires).

Many expounded on the difficulty of friendship in light of these barriers. Students frequently spoke about the separate living and eating quarters for foreign students. Generally speaking, in a Chinese university, all students and many of the staff live on campus. Students attend class, eat, and stay together in the same dormitories. Foreign students may attend the same classes, but they live and eat in separate quarters. Students in this study not only reflected upon their "own building" and "own dining hall," but at one institution in Shanghai, students also spoke about "their own floor." They contend that until a violent protest a few years ago, foreign students were further segregated within their dormitory, by floor, according to their place of origin: Africans on one floor, Arabs on another, Koreans on another, Europeans on another, and so on.

That being said, the living conditions given to all foreign students are fundamentally better than those of their Chinese colleagues. For example, most foreign quarters have daily hot water, heat in the winter, and more space. Although students may enjoy these higher standards of living, some view these conditions as means to enforce segregation. More than 30 years ago, Chen (1965, p. 177) detailed the nature and consequences of this "privileged segregation enforced upon them." Hevi (1963) also commented on this situation and noted that segregation bred mutual ignorance. He stated,

> Through no fault of our own, we foreigners formed a segregated colony in the school, eating, studying, sleeping separately and even having separate entertainment, with the result that, though living in the capital of China, we knew extremely little about what the Chinese were really like. (Hevi, 1963, pp. 130–131)

Students also spoke about the regulations for receiving visitors. Guests must check in with the guard, sign in a registry, and note the time and purpose of the visit. When leaving, guests must sign out and again note the time. Guests from outside the university were generally not permitted. Students described the environment in which guests must register, visitations are timed, and purposes are monitored as "frustrating," "restrictive," and "strange." Above all, such conditions were not conducive to developing close friendships and mutual understanding.

Students and counselors alike spoke about the risks of seeking friendships and challenging the rules: "If these rules are not respected, and students don't stay put, there are sanctions" (Embassy Counselor B). One responsibility of the Foreign Affairs Office (the *waiban*) was "to protect [and] to prevent too much involvement of African students in Chinese [lives]. Too much involvement in Chinese affairs can be one of the reasons of bad relation between Chinese, the *waiban*, and the students." According to the counselor, "too much involvement" was "suspect," especially "too many friends, too many visitors, and ladies"(Embassy Counselor B).

Students and counselors broached the sensitive issue of relations with women. Students revealed that "It is difficult to feel at ease with a Chinese girlfriend because of the . . . Chinese law, and also the Chinese society itself considers girls who go out with Africans as being prostitutes." Another reiterated this exact point: "Even though we are obliged to spend here in China more than 4 years, an African student who entertains relations with a Chinese woman, simple friendship or not, that means the practice of prostitution in China." As a result of these reactions, any relationships that may exist are kept out of the public eye. The same interviewee added that it is more than a question of "foreign relations . . . between a man and a woman; [it is] a question of color first":

> For a Chinese here, it's more acceptable to see a white man going out with Chinese ladies. It's more acceptable to see a Chinese man going out with a white lady than seeing a Chinese and an African. . . . There are people who still [do] not understand that such a relationship can exist because he's black. (Embassy Counselor B)

Hevi (1963, p. 131) reported that Chinese women who associated with African students were "packed off to prison or to the commune farms for hard labour, . . . their only crime being that they dared to make friends with Africans, contrary to Party's orders." Scott (1986) reported on a Liberian student who, in 1985, ended up alone in a jail cell for 4 days because of contact with a Chinese girl. At the time of this study, however, sanctions seemed to be primarily social, not legal.

Although intimate relationships may be the most complex, the separation between the local people and the students extends into everyday social contact. Counselors and students agreed that students were welcome to pursue academic endeavours but were expected to confine their pursuits to their studies. One counselor summed up the situation as follows:

> Our students come to study the Chinese language, get a Chinese education, but they find they are limited in the interaction they have with the Chinese counterparts. They live apart. They are not allowed to mix freely. They don't visit each other freely. Actually,

the social intercourse is so, so, so, limited, at the end of the day you wonder, ... what the objective was all about. ... The objective has not been achieved. (Embassy Counselor A)

He added, "They don't want the Chinese to be influenced by the foreigner, [but] they want the foreigners to be influenced by the Chinese" (Embassy Counselor A).

Like the counselor, students also raised the lack of mutuality as being at the heart of many conflicts:

Why this segregation? ... If African students and Chinese students ... are fighting each other, it's because ... this conflict is created, ... is built by the whole system. ... We are sharing classrooms, but we cannot share a social life. (Group of Postgraduates)

One doctoral candidate from Guinea Conakry, now in China for over 10 years, commented on this estrangement: "Under any circumstances, I always feel [like] a foreigner in China." This feeling of being perpetually foreign was echoed in an interview:

I've been already in this country for already the last 7 or 8 years. ... I have been accustomed to the food, to the language, to everything, ... but I don't belong here. ... I asked myself, when ... can I feel like I have entered this culture? ... What will it take? ... I don't know, but it's something I cannot help because I cannot get used to it. Every single day I wake up, and ... I feel like a stranger. (Group of 4 Graduates)

Feelings of social alienation were further exacerbated by financial marginalization.

SCHOLARSHIPS AND TUITION

For the majority of students (71.4%) the so-called scholarship is "woefully inadequate." One of the students concluded that students "[are] not getting anything that was spelled out in our letter, ... so they are deceiving us" (notes from eight questionnaires). Students felt misled and confused about what a full scholarship entailed and required information. At the same time, they were disappointed that their own governments did not support them on a consistent or regular basis (notes from nine questionnaires). Again, counselors were aware of the problem, but were unable to help the students beyond providing moral support.

This misery comes at a time of "exceptional growth," when China is "developing every day." With China's "economic evolution" and the ensuing "skyrocketing inflation," students noted that "Prices change every year, but the resources don't change." Another specified: "Prices for all products and services have gone up about 400% [and the] level of life has changed, [but] the bursary remains the same" (notes from seven questionnaires).

With inadequate scholarships, little support from home, and economic inflation of 400%, students were unable to afford the "basic necessities." They expressed further frustration that, unlike local people and other foreigners, African students have "no access to part-time jobs." They described the "impossibility of carrying out lucrative work . . . even during holidays to make up for the low allowance received as stipend." Again and again, students lamented that there was "no possibility of earning extra income" (notes from five questionnaires). Students characterized their financial situation as "desperate," and wrote about problems of "surviving," with "not even enough [money] for food to eat" (notes from 19 questionnaires).

Feelings of being stuck and cut off were exacerbated by being unable to afford "any communications (telephone or fax)." One African student said: "I have not even once called my parents, even I cannot frequently write a letter to them because I cannot afford [it]." A Tanzanian woman felt that her inability to afford communication "add[ed] to her loneliness, depression, and homesickness" (Questionnaire Note).

African students expressed further distress because they were "not tourists . . . but are supposed to live like tourists, i.e., accommodation in designated hotels, soft seater in trains, and expensive air tickets, not to mention expensive visa renewals. . . ." In addition to these costs, students pointed out the "differences made between foreigners and Chinese citizens [in terms of the] prices of goods." Students felt "swindled," especially when shopping, because "[merchants] multiply the prices by two" (notes from four questionnaires).

Other discrepancies were raised when they wrote and spoke of "realizing" that there was "a certain injustice toward the Africans, if we compare what China does for the Asians, Europeans, or Americans." A woman explained: "The amount of allowance given to African students [is] less than what [is] given to others." Chen (1965), Goldman (1965), and Hevi (1963) all reported on this same discrepancy in fund allocation.

One student detailed this claim:

> All foreign students are not getting the same allowance. They give African and Arab students less money compared to the same students under the same scholarships from Europe, America,

Korea, and Japan. These students from these countries are given more money, more facilities, and [are] more highly respected than the Africans. (Response in Questionnaire)

Respect was an issue for several students. According to one, "The respect to scholarship students is getting less. . . . Self-finance[d] students are welcome[d] at high[er] respect." Respect was also on the mind of another student, who wrote, "According to the Chinese, Africans . . . come to beg here in China . . . only because they do not have enough food in their own countries, which are very poor" (notes from three questionnaires). While this student focused on the negation of African cultures, another directly attributed the negation of individual African students to economic changes:

The most recent Chinese economic reform/economic miracle is creating a big problem in how they treat African students. [Because] Africa [is] an economically left-behind continent, African students are considered globally, like by a Chinese national moral [*sic*], . . . from a poor continent, then not an important person—regardless of what is meant in political speeches by Chinese officials in Africa. (Questionnaire Note)

In a succinct statement, one counselor corroborated these observations. For African students, life in China was getting progressively more difficult: "Before it was a question of only color. . . . Now it is a question of color and money."

CONCLUSION

In this study, a total of 133 undergraduates, postgraduates, and graduates from 29 African nations, pursing degrees in more than 12 disciplines, in 14 sites, across four cities, spoke volumes in a remarkably consistent voice. "Color and money," above all else, were the essential elements in their lives. This chapter has argued that the question of "color and money" can best be understood within the context of China's changing foreign policy. The realities presented above need not diminish the accomplishments and future possibilities for Sino-African relations. Both governments and individuals in China and African nations consider these exchanges to be a source of considerable value and have gone to great lengths to secure opportunities to train, be trained, and, thus, sustain Sino-African relations. Sustained relations for China represent a continued strategic opportunity. For many African nations, sustained relations with China represent an opportunity to begin to realize what is, for many, a political priority: to overcome the colonial traces in the content and substance of their educational experiences (Weiler, 1984). A decolonized pedagogical paradigm offers an opportunity to ensure, in the words of Amadou Mahtar M'Bow, "the full development of cultural identity" (M'Bow, Senegalese educator and former director-general of UNESCO, as cited by Weiler, 1984, p. 192).

China holds the potential to make a significant contribution to an alternative pedagogy and rethinking of international academic cooperation. However, as this study reveals, this opportunity has not been fully embraced and the potential not fully realized. Similar to the experience of other Third Word nations, China's integration into the capitalist world order underscores the power of the dominant mechanisms that maintain the international status quo (Hayhoe, 1989, p. 97). This reality highlights what Weiler (1984, p. 189) considers part of the most critical aspects of "underdevelopment": the dominant mechanisms of economic, cultural, scientific, and professional control that have been generated and sustained, in part, by systems of knowledge production and higher education in the center countries. China's self-reliant economy and strong socialist institutions make it less vulnerable to the economic dependency, cultural alienation, and social divisiveness threatening many other societies of the Third World. However, its integration into the capitalist world order is nevertheless similar in that China currently plays more of a supporting than a transforming role in international power relations (Hayhoe, 1986, 1989). This notwithstanding, hope for emerging strategies that promote structural transformation to greater equality may be revealed through future investigations.

And finally, as Dikötter (1994, p. 405) has argued, the discourse of race in China cannot be minimized as a consequence of the "hegemonic powers" of Euro-American imperialism. This is so for three reasons. First, it perpetuates a unitary conception of racism that is universal in its origins (the West), its causes (capitalist society), and its effects (colonialization). Second, it disregards the historical specificities of racial identities and reduces a variety of cultural groups into the West and the Rest. Third, it represents people in China as passive subjects devoid of free thought, critical analysis, and intellectual autonomy. The "Western impact–Chinese response" approach imposes "eurocentric" distortions and negates historical transformations that occurred in China long before its prolonged exposure to foreign thoughts (Dikötter, 1994, p. 409). Dikötter's (1991) *The Discourse of Race in Modern China* is perhaps the most systematic investigation of the topic to date, but it is an area that requires much more work, especially in the context of China's growing influence within Africa. As a result, this chapter argues for an understanding of South–South relationships in all their complexity, by giving due recognition to the social construction of new hierarchies of power and inequality within "the South," on terms dictated in part by changes in a globalized world order and in part by history.

TWELVE

India and South Africa

Diaspora and Transfer

Crain Soudien

The Indian subcontinent has long been a site of interest and comparison for the South African and the broader African anti-colonial and postcolonial experience. The motivation for this in the case of South Africa derives from three key sources: The first is the almost-synchronous history of British colonial occupation that the two countries share; the second is the life and work of Gandhi, which straddles and informs their anti-colonial histories; and the third is the presence of a large community of people of Indian descent in South Africa. More recently, moreover, as India, in the context of its history of poverty and social segmentation, has gone through a sustained period of economic growth, it has become a source of increased significance for Africa and for South Africa in particular. This significance has manifested itself in a number of bilateral agreements into which the two countries have entered, the most important of which was the establishment of the India–South Africa Joint Ministerial Commission.

Against this backdrop, predictably, exchanges of all kinds—personal, family, business, political, and academic—have developed between India and South Africa. Most interesting, for the purposes of this chapter, are those of an intellectual and academic nature. What the substance, nature, and potential of these exchanges consist of has become an important subject of scholarly interest, especially for understanding what is deemed to be of value between and for the two countries, and how two countries from the global South or the periphery of the metropolitan world conduct academic relationships between themselves.

Underpinning this interest, as recent initiatives reflect, are questions about the comparative anthropologies, sociologies, histories, and economies of the two countries, and indeed the regions in which they are set, and the potential for these comparisons to shed light on the respective internal social dynamics of each country.

This chapter develops a meta-analysis of the politics of transfer—including bilateral intellectual and knowledge production and its exchange—through an analysis of the issues that might lie behind some of the relations between the two countries. How might one undertake such an analysis? Two articulated lines of investigation will be pursued in this chapter. First, and more conventionally, the chapter introduces the concept of knowledge transfer and questions the suitability of this framework for understanding South–South relationships and those of South Africa and India specifically. The chapter then looks at the case studies of two recent bilateral initiatives to see what in them—the characteristics of these cases—might lend itself to developing a way of understanding how one might analyze knowledge transfer between sites of relative underdevelopment.

KNOWLEDGE TRANSFER THEORY

In the context of globalization and development, Castells, *inter alia*, has argued that social development is determined by the

> ability to establish a synergistic interaction between technological innovation, and human values, leading to a new set of organizations and institutions that make possible positive feedback loops between productivity, flexibility, solidarity, safety, participation and accountability. (Castells, 2000, p. 1)

He goes further to say that it is easy to agree about these goals, but there is a difficulty in our capacity to "share the policies and strategies" that are necessary for the implementation of goals such as these (Castells, p. 1). Castells's caution is important for us take heed of, given his insistence that "the availability and use of information and communication technology is a pre-requisite for economic and social development in our world" (Castells, p. 2).

The process of knowledge transfer needs to take place in order for the synergistic interaction that Castells speaks of to take effect. Knowledge transfer, however, as multiple scholars of the process of globalization have pointed out (Appadurai, 1996; Carnoy, 1974; Hoogvelt, 1997; Soudien, 2005), is a process fraught with conceptual problems. Sarker (2005, p. 1), speaking within an information technology environment, makes the point simply and clearly: ". . . sharing of knowledge becomes especially problematic when team members are distributed in time and space." The core issues, according to Sarker, have to do with what he refers to as capability differences, credibility, extent of communication, and culture. Much of this discussion has been dominated by key commentators such as Hofstede

(2001). Unfortunately, the trajectory that this iteration of the discussion has taken under the guidance and leadership of Hofstede and reproduced by scholars such as Sarker (2005) is to present the knowledge transfer process as a primarily cultural matter. While accepting the critical significance of that, I suggest in this discussion that the version of culture appropriated here, and underplayed by scholars such as (and even) Castells (1997), is a weakened and apolitical form of the term. As Feenberg writes in *Critical Theory of Technology*,

> modern technology is no more neutral than medieval cathedrals or the Great Wall of China: it embodies the values of a particular industrial civilization and especially of its elites, which rest their claims to hegemony on technical mastery (Feenberg, n.d., p. 3).

When elites meet across contexts of difference, it is important to understand how they bring their histories with them, how aware they are of their own and one another's histories, and how these histories collude with or contradict one another's power hierarchies.

I use the general orientation of Feenberg in this argument and suggest, with Chatterjee (1997), that although we need to understand the value of knowledge transfer, we need, simultaneously, to be aware of its dangers and particularly of the ways in which it brings with it inappropriate and oppressive forms of knowledge that are obstructive for processes of social development. The work of Stromquist and Monkman (2000) is useful in helping us understand the implications of inequitable forms of knowledge transfer. They argue, borrowing from Amin, that the most powerful industrial nations hold five monopolies: technology, worldwide financial markets, global natural resources (in terms of access), media and communications, and weapons of mass destruction. They produce the classic asymmetries and inequities that have long been associated with metropole-satellite and dependency-type analyses. Poor countries emerge as the victims rather than the beneficiaries of processes such as these.

Stromquist and Monkman (2000, p. 20) ask how these monopolies might be broken: "Can we change the nature of these monopolies?" I suggest here that part of a process of disrupting these monopolies involves weakening the dependence of developing countries on them. How this might be done is a strategic question: It includes making assessments of need, of local and national priorities, and of developing relationships and solidarities with others who are alert to the sensitivities of difference. An important arena of possibility is that of operating within the developing world itself, of building what one might call South–South relationships. This possibility, however, is not unproblematic itself. It remains susceptible, given the dominance by elites driven often by self-interest, to all the issues that arise between economically developed and economically developing countries.

INDIA–SOUTH AFRICA RELATIONS

Important initiatives to break out of the stranglehold of the countries of the North have been begun recently in the world's global South. Third World countries have come together in important new coalitions and have begun to revive others that had become more or less moribund, such as the Non-Aligned Movement. A critical initiative amoung South Africa, Brazil, and India has seen the leading nations of the South commit themselves to developing their internal capacity in a series of trilateral meetings (see also Chapter 8). A leading objective of these new relations is trade and "improved market access for developing countries." Indian multinationals such as Mittal Steel have invested in and taken control of critical South African industries, have moved considerable financial capacity into the country, and have placed social development high on their list of priorities. In 2005, the three ministers of foreign affairs from India, Brazil, and South Africa endorsed South–South cooperation. A ministerial communiqué from the South Africa government recorded the agreement the three nations arrived at as follows:

- The ministers emphasized that South–South cooperation was an essential and fundamental component of international cooperation for development, especially in terms of global, regional, and country-level efforts to achieve the MDGs [Millennium Development Goals] and reaffirmed cooperation under IBSA [India–Brazil–South Africa] to promote these objectives.
- The ministers committed themselves to work together to strengthen the political will of the UN membership to maintain the momentum of the 2000 Millennium Summit, in order to translate commitments into concrete action—in particular, the areas of development and poverty eradication.
- The ministers recognized the strong multiplier effect of poverty eradication strategies targeting women and children, and agreed to reflect this approach in IBSA programmes and initiatives. (Republic of South Africa, Department of Foreign Affairs, 2005)

Practically, this agreement has facilitated the achievement of significant gains for the African continent. A Joint India–South African Commission has, for example, been established, and the Indian government has committed ZAR1.5 billion (US$200 million) in funding to the New

Economic Programme for African Development (NEPAD) initiative. Outside of trade, several cultural initiatives have also taken shape. The Bollywood film industry has regularly used South African locations for the making of new films (Ebrahim, 2006). High-level academic initiatives have been instituted, such as the Nelson Mandela Chair at Jawaharlal Nehru University in Delhi and the Dadoo Memorial Lecture in New Delhi in honor of Dr. Yusuf Dadoo, a leader of the South African Indian Congress. Large new cross-country partnerships have been established involving South Africans and Indians, often by themselves, but just as often in the company of larger multilateral initiatives. The Center for Higher Education Trust (CHET) initiated and published an important comparison of higher education and diversity in South Africa and India (see Beckham, 2000). The University of Cape Town, with the assistance of scholars at Princeton University in the United States, has recently looked at discrimination in India and South Africa. The Institute of Development Studies at Sussex has initiated a number of such collaborations, one of which is reviewed below, looking at development issues such as citizenship and education. The University of London's Institute of Education has also recently initiated an India–South Africa–Brazil and UK collaborative network. Individual South African scholars have developed partnerships with Indian academics in specialist projects at a number of universities, as have scholars working at the Human Sciences Research Council in South Africa. At the University of the Witwatersrand in the last 5 years, at least a dozen collaborative projects have emerged in a range of disciplines (see the discussion below in the Case Studies section). The University of Pretoria has regularly, over the last 3 years, brought an Indian voice alongside the more predictable North American voice into its integration and diversity forums. Important policy experts have moved between the two countries, particularly in the areas of education, communication technology, and finance.

Significant about all these developments is that they have taken place in the context of a process of rediscovery of the historic links that bind South Africa and India, such as their shared heritage of Gandhi, Gandhi's influence on the African National Congress, the support of India for the anti-apartheid struggle, and so on. For the record, important in this process of discovery has been the fascinating unveiling of Indian Ocean relationships between early Indian wayfarers and communities along the East African coastline, and the recognition that cultural exchanges were already taking place in the region a thousand years ago, long before the Portuguese made their entry into this part of the world (see Gupta, 2006; Pinto, 2006).

While these developments have been greeted with great enthusiasm, the inevitable question about what they mean remains. What have they come to stand for? Are we seeing a new trend in the field of knowledge transfer? Are we seeing in this South–South cooperation elements of what Castells refers to as synergistic interactions framed in mutually acceptable human values, which are leading to what he describes as productive feedback loops, participation, and accountability? In the rest of the chapter, I look at two examples of academic collaboration between India and South Africa and ask to what degree, as South–South partnerships, they represent a qualitatively different approach to North–South relationships.

THE CASE STUDIES

The first project is the Inclusion and Exclusion Project and the second is the South Africa/India: Reimagining the Disciplines Colloquium. In looking at these two case studies, the issues of how projects involving knowledge transfer are conceived, funded, executed, and then mediated into the public arena are important to understanding the power valences that lie within them. Key is locating the political economies that give character and substance to the questions of symmetry, mutuality, and interdependence, and that might allow us to make judgments about equality and respect in the interacting countries. Equally important is asking how self-reflective the projects are of the nature of their interrelationship and the ways in which they transfer into new contexts. In terms of this, it is important to look for the "self-reflective" dimension in the project.

The Inclusion and Exclusion Project

The first project came into being at the University of Sussex and the Institute of Development Studies at Sussex, where a South African and an Indian colleague began a discussion about the comparability of exclusion processes in the two countries. They developed a proposal that successfully secured the support of the UK Department for International Development (DfID), a matter that is, of course, not inconsequential in this analysis. The purpose of the study, "Learning About Education Inclusion and Exclusion in India and South Africa," was to look at the similarities and differences in and between race and caste at school and community levels in carefully selected sites in India and South Africa (see Subrahmanian, 2003). The conceptual framework used in the study of inclusion/exclusion sought to enable the research teams to show how at different levels—the macro, institutional, and individual—experiences of inclusion and exclusion were mutually shaped, and how policies of inclusion, while attempting to generate inclusionary effects and practices, invariably produced, often in unanticipated ways, new forms of exclusion or different forms of old exclusionary measures (Sayed & Soudien, 2003).

Although the study was an important academic exercise in its own terms and has yielded important insights with respect to the project's major objective—that of showing how much inclusion and exclusion are involved—there are features of it that we need to pull out here for our focus on transfer.

First, the project was developed, deliberately, as a South–South collaboration. It was proposed to DfID that the virtue of the project would be that it would shift the center of gravity in the political economy of knowledge and knowledge transfer from its traditional North–South axis to that of a relationship within the developing world. This orientation and point of departure was facilitated by the environment within which the principal investigators worked, where the issues around knowledge transfer were being debated.

On the strength of the motivation that the project was an attempt to build South–South relationships, the project was, importantly, initiated with its conceptual and operational bases in the two subject countries. This movement toward the South, and locating the project within the countries, was not without its difficulties or without its detractors. The terms of the grant that was received from DfID stated that the principal investigators would be located at Sussex and that they would have ultimate accounting responsibility. This meant that all the power for the disbursement of funds remained, so to speak, within the metropole, or the North, which thus remained the center. Critically, however, the principal investigators, based in the United Kingdom (UK), sought to relocate and devolve responsibility for financial accountability, as far as they could, to the sites where the study was to take place. This constituted, for both India and South Africa, an important commitment. Flowing from this, and what it made possible, was a range of developments that saw the project develop a particular "Southern" character. Project coordinators were appointed in each country and they were given primary responsibility for the conceptualization, development, and implementation of the project. Their institutions, moreover, became the lead institutions for the study.

The resultant process of developing the project conceptually took place in one of the countries in the presence of, and with the participation of, a large number of local Indian and South African researchers who provided input into the overall design. Once the design was determined, the project was then implemented and executed by the local researchers. During the execution of the plan, significantly, regular exchanges took place between the teams operating in the two countries. A South African went to India when the team there went through a midterm review and joined the field work for a short while in local schools. Reciprocally, members of the Indian research team spent periods of time in the South African schools and joined in some of the field work processes. At the end of the project, a large meeting took place in India, which involved many of the South African field workers and some of the stakeholders in the research, with their Indian counterparts.

These localizing initiatives were key in giving the study and the relationship its particular character. When the study was concluded in each country, it carried the clear imprint of the local participants. It came to be understood in each country as an important locally based study and was accorded that respect in each.

Significantly, this localization of the project impacted strongly on the conditions of transfer of knowledge. In the process of working across the two countries, the important interlocutors of the project—the principal investigators, the coordinators, and the researchers—came to realize the following: first, the distinctive sociologies of their two spaces and the differences and similarities that characterized these two spaces; second, the necessity, therefore, of having to proceed with caution in understanding what the two countries could teach each other.

One of the lessons learned was that difference is animated by deep sociostructural conditions and particularly that the histories of race and caste have come to produce two distinct societies, the two countries' common colonial heritage notwithstanding. Drawing out the comparisons, the researchers were only able to discern similarities between themselves at high levels of generality. To be sure, class, within the dynamic environment of globalization, was an important factor in each country. In the context of globalization, the formation and reproduction of a common transnational and even metropolitan class identity was evident in each country. This elite in the two countries—and this was also evident in the second case study discussed below—had very similar cultural, economic, and social investments. Strikingly, individuals in the two places could invoke very similar social and cultural experiences that were familiar to one another. But their status articulated with, and also rearticulated, race and caste in different kinds of ways. Critically, in each country, this elite culture and even its metropolitanism took form and character in the dynamic context of the older social interests and power valences of each context. In each, for example, the interests of older and established social formations were always pertinent and consequential.

Illustrating these complexities was the way in which decentralization and devolution of project funding and management took shape in the two contexts: as political spaces in which new elites were coming to express themselves and as incorporating important and common policy choices made in each country. While new elites (the researchers who were themselves often graduates from previously disadvantaged communities) were very much in evidence in both countries, having moved, for example, to occupy important positions of influence in relation to the schools that were being studied, their institutional and sociostructural settings conditioned their maneuverability in very different kinds of ways. An important observation to be made about the way in which the project unfolded, and which reflects the shift of its center of gravity from the North to the South, was how the configuration of issues that arose in the project came to gravitate around local politics as opposed to the politics of the North–South axis. Although the presence of the metropole by no means disappears in this collaboration, its determinative role in deciding how and whether the project is to be disseminated as a formal publication of DfID is an ongoing issue—for example, it is much more interesting to write on how the internal politics of India and South Africa have affected the project.

Significantly, and therefore contributing to our larger understanding of how transfer relations work, these issues were featured not only as empirical elements of the data that emerged out of the study but also impacted on the project itself. Race and class in South Africa and caste and class in India presented themselves as important logistical and organizational issues in influencing how the projects were prosecuted, such as dictating how entry into particular kinds of research sites should be managed racially and in caste terms, how to manage the composition of research teams, and so on. These were important "realities" to which the project constantly found itself having to respond. In both countries, for example, issues had arisen at key moments around compromises that had been made regarding the nonracial and noncaste nature of the research project. In the South African field work, to illustrate the point, field workers at one point had to be deliberately redistributed on racial grounds to secure access to schools. In the Indian example, these tensions were less obvious, but they were present nonetheless as the dynamic of the caste system surfaced in the project management team. The most important outcome of the project, in some ways, was that it demonstrated how strongly local realities, and, in particular, the sociologies of domination in each context, configured the basic architecture of and substance of the transfer process.

Reimagining the Disciplines Colloquium

As important a milestone in India–South Africa relations as the experience of the Inexsa project was, the Re-Imagining Disciplines project was in many respects an even more significant initiative for India–South Africa relationships. Interestingly, the Re-Imagining Disciplines project was a self-

India and South Africa 235

conscious attempt both to build on the sweep of collaborations that were developing across South Africa and to reflect on what it meant to be engaged in a collaborative exercise. The project, crucially, was imagined in the South, at the University of the Witwatersrand (Wits), in contrast to the Inexsa project, which had its origins in a South–South relationship conceived in the North.

Toward surfacing the extent of the South Africa–India relationship, a professor of African literature at the University of the Witwatersrand approached the National Research Foundation (NRF) to fund a colloquium that would draw together scholars working on connections between South Africa and India (Hofmeyr, 2006). The intention was also that the colloquium would include the signing of an agreement between the NRF and the Indian Council for Social Science Research, with a view to furthering and promoting exchanges between the two countries in the humanities and the social sciences.

A specific objective of the conference was to highlight the fact that a distinct field of knowledge transfer was taking shape. It recognized the similarities and divergences between the two countries and the fact that they were often in competition with one another. Both countries manifested stark disparities between its elites and its poor. There were real prospects for the exchange of skills and scarce resources to take place between them. In the proposal to the NRF, the following was noted:

> Occupying a fundamentally intermediate/liminal position within current debates around globalization, both countries thus offer fruitful ground for exploring the dimensions and tensions—the roughness and texture of the superficially smooth process of globalizing markets. . . . In addition to the strategic factors outlined so far, there are compelling intellectual reasons to pursue this project. The top sectors of the South African and Indian academy are outstanding and produce internationally competitive work. If we can harness the power and capacity of these two national streams of scholarship, we can spark innovative theoretical insights in the humanities, social sciences, economics and law and lead the way in promoting scholarly excellence in, and through the South. (Hofmeyr, 2005, p. 2)

The proposal made clear that it sought to make the big questions the focus of its work, namely, those of "pushing back disciplinary boundaries rather than just filling in gaps of knowledge" (Hofmeyr, 2005, p. 2). It argued strongly that the two countries' common experience of diversity and development, democracy and social movements, affirmative action, and their similar power status in the regions in which they found themselves made them appropriate subjects for developing intellectual comparisons. The issue of transnational studies was central to the proposal:

"Transnational studies seek to understand the processes across and between different spaces without assuming that national boundaries are the critical factor" (Hofmeyr, 2005, p. 3). For the short term, the proposal sought to energize existing and new research between South Africa and India, and in the longer term, to develop teaching modules, transfers between the two countries, and, most ambitiously, a center to be called the Center for South African–Indian Studies.

The first phase of this plan was the colloquium itself. The colloquium was an important event that drew seven scholars from India and 15 South African scholars who had worked in collaborative projects, most of them from Wits.

As a way of developing the discussion begun in relation to the first case study, and also bringing the analysis of this second case study to a close, I would like to highlight the significance of the workshop. An important contribution of the workshop was that it was deliberately constructed as an attempt to reflect on the nature of the knowledge transfer process between South Africa and India. In making this commitment, the nature of the discussion at the colloquium was extraordinarily rich. It critically came to show up the major characteristics—the strengths and weaknesses—of the South Africa–India knowledge transfer relationship.

- Very apparent was the dominance of Gandhi in the history and political studies dimensions of the relationship. A large proportion of the work of both Indians and South Africans exploring what one might refer to as the "zone of interaction" took its point of departure from the experience of Gandhi.
- The keynote address by Uma Mesthrie (2006) pointed to the degree to which collaborative work in its focus on South African "Indianness" had homogenized South African Indians and looked at them in isolation from their South African context.
- The criticism was also made that there was no attempt to show how complicit the state of India itself was in promoting the separation and, indeed, the special treatment of Indians in South Africa.
- The observation was made that most of the scholarship tended to focus on the movement of people, ideas, and goods from India to Africa. Mesthrie (2006), for example, called for work that recognized the multidirection flows and movement of people and ideas between South Africa and India.

The Wits colloquium was a significant moment in the political economy of the South Africa–India knowledge relationship. What it sought to do, in ways that did not explicitly arise in the Inexsa project, was ask the question: What would the features of an equitable relationship be? It set itself up as a deliberately reflective space. Out of it came a clear commitment to mutuality and a recognition of interdependence.

OUTSTANDING QUESTIONS

This notwithstanding, two problems need to be highlighted. These, it is suggested, operate almost below the surface of the discussion. One of them, interestingly, had arisen explicitly in the Inexsa project. The first, which manifested itself earlier, concerned not the issues of mutuality and inter-country civility, but the degree to which the politics of the local assert themselves, sometimes imperceptibly, on the terrain of the interrelationship. In both encounters, particularly during the first visit, issues of race and caste were hard to evade. At a joint report-back in Delhi of the Inexsa project, a Dalit academic, who was to come to South Africa shortly afterward as a guest of a South African academic, spoke from the floor about the presumption of the Indian researchers to address the issues of caste, given their own largely upper-caste status. Significantly, although this critique did not arise publicly in the Wits meeting, it was present as an issue in the Indian delegation. The issues of race had arisen within the Inexsa project when the South African team criticized the employment of a white researcher who had, on an earlier occasion, associated himself with a homophobic critique of an important education policy that sought to extend gender rights to children. The argument had been made that it was not appropriate for a boundary-crossing initiative such as Inexsa to employ a researcher who was known to support explicitly conservative causes.

The point is that the formal frame of the encounters allows a particular level of scrutiny of the collaboration and its commitments to take place. Given who the people are in each case, this is almost to be expected. But the effects of these local political conditions and dynamics—and this is where knowledge transfer discussions are approached somewhat statically—are often difficult to process and manage in the act of reflection. The major problem in both the Inexsa and the Wits colloquium was recognizing and engaging with the complex ways in which relations of dominance insinuate themselves into the relationships within the projects. These relations, particularly those of race and caste, are profoundly difficult questions to manage, because they require levels of self-awareness and discussions of the significance of such self-awareness in ways that are not the conventional substance of even politically progressive initiatives. The closest one gets to this in the field of knowledge production is in gender studies, where there is the challenge of how, as Grossberg (1997, p. 373) puts it, one is asking those who "are caught up in lines of power" to recognize and define the nature of that very power. With respect to this, the argument that I am making here takes me in a different direction from that suggested by the transfer theory discussed above. This approach to transfer continues to work with a binary understanding of relationships with fixed and homogenized cultures standing on either side of the knowledge transfer encounter. Why it works in this fashion is understandable, and has much to do with prevailing functionalist theory that invokes, uses, and projects human subjects and the collectives in which they find themselves as whole, coherent, and unitary forms. Thus, an idea of "South Africanness" or "Indianness" is used, which compresses the contradictions of identity into a single construct. In the process, the complexities of race, class, gender, place, language, political orientation, and a host of other factors that influence the making of identity are not taken into consideration. These functional imaginaries are not far from the surface in the ways in which expertise and knowledge of subject matter is presented and discussed. As Owen Sichone, a recent incumbent of the Nelson Mandela chair at J. Nehru University, said, in the course of commenting on the perspective of his Indian colleagues in his report following the visit,

> [the Indian colleagues] are very well read and knowledgeable about Africa with a particularly Indian perspective that focuses on the Indian diasporas and views Africa as a younger cousin requiring Indian technical help. (Sichone, 2006, p. 2)

This approach, in many ways, validates the approach of the knowledge transfer theorists, insofar as India imagines itself and takes on the identity of an intact, coherent, single new metropole in relation to an equally coherent, homogenized, and comprehensible African satellite. In this process, there is little historical sense of how the African and Indian identities that are invoked have been socially constructed. Forgotten is the sense of the very colonial history of the production of both an Indian and African identity, and the hierarchies instantiated in that process through the politics of colonial knowledge-making. One sees in the Indian conceit experienced by Sichone an uncritical appropriation of the racialized discourses of difference that emanate out of dominant North American and European sociologies and histories.

Clearly, as this experience shows, there are elements of the familiar asymmetry of transfer networks in the relations between the two countries. But it is more complex, because this asymmetry and the power levers, residues, and opportunities do not pivot around only one dimension of the relationship. Asymmetrical features pertain in a number of dimensions of the relationship, such that one is seeing a matrix in which certain actors are dominant in some moments and distinctly less so in others. There is a real sense, for example, that Indian technical expertise is sought after and courted by South Africa within a metropole–satellite relational framework. This contains, as the public statements around the Indian donation to NEPAD show, intimations of a donor–recipient mentality. But this development is advanced and counterbalanced by the unspoken and often opaque historical presence of colonial domination, which has a deep racial character to it. There remains active in the dynamic between the two countries the significant trope of "Britishness," which is unarticulated, but always pertinent. This Britishness, often stereotypically attached to but also perhaps actively cultivated among South African English-speaking white people, and even other South Africans of color, remains a subject of influence in the relations of South Africans with themselves and with their Indian counterparts. At its core is an attitude of racial and cultural superiority of "white" people over "backward" India. It needs to be recognized that these kinds of factors add layers of complexity to the relationships between the two countries, and configure dominance and subordination in interesting ways to which conventional transfer theory is not particularly alert. New postcolonial psychologies of dominance and subordination are emerging that are interesting and rich in complexity.

Some of this complexity might be extrapolated from Sichone's concluding comments to his report. He explained that

> African students studying in India . . . tend to have difficulties adjusting. South African and Namibians in Delhi were particularly poor at adapting and a few returned home without completing their studies. The culture shock, racism and harsh living conditions were some of the reasons cited. (Sichone, 2006, p. 2)

What might be happening in the Indian context, and there is insufficient discussion of this, is that the apartheid histories of the South Africans make themselves felt in the new cultural spaces of the Indians, which themselves are complex amalgams of experience. The possibility is strong that the kind of shock Sichone refers to is a product of the narrow self-understandings that apartheid could have produced among disadvantaged layers of the South African population. Entering any new social space could have resulted in the same outcomes. But the possibility is also there that colonial racisms (and, one needs to acknowledge, other indigenous prejudices that are endemic to the country itself) are activated in India in the presence of black Africans. This racism is real, but the history of its production is complex. This commentary recognizes that this kind of politics—in

India, and, to put it bluntly, in South Africa—against the romantic view that both South Africans and Indians exist in a new world of civility and mutuality, is of consequence in shaping the terms of the terrain of transfer. The ways in which these local attitudes condition the nature of each group's participation in these local spaces is important to recognize and to begin to understand who has been selected as the objects of the study and who has been entitled to analyze them.

In terms of this explanation, I am arguing, therefore, for an approach that recognizes how power relations are reconstituted in contact situations to yield instances of domination and subordination that are not amenable to easy reading. What is not addressed, in both the case studies discussed in this chapter, is how these factors, in the process of managing transfer, are of consequence. I am suggesting that, in relations between India and South Africa, we need to be aware of the ways in which privilege is reconstituted at new levels. Important in making sense of this is understanding how the process of knowledge transfer works with the factors determining privilege and beginning to ask how those involved in those processes themselves are able to deconstruct their positions inside of those situations. In neither project has that stage yet been reached. This constitutes an important area for further investigation in knowledge transfer study.

THIRTEEN

Conclusion

A Way Out from the Dependency Trap in Educational Development?

Gita Steiner-Khamsi

Social researchers have good reasons for being both fascinated by, and skeptical of, concepts that suddenly enter popular speech. Excessive use detaches ideas from their original context, as they take on entirely different meanings. These meanings depend upon the identity of the speakers and—perhaps more importantly—the audience. Like the term *globalization* that preceded it, the term *South–South cooperation* means different things to different individuals and institutions. These groups continuously update or adapt their definition in response to new political, social, and economic realities. Skeptics, however, are quick to point out that the idea of South–South cooperation is not new. It can be dated back to the postcolonial period of the Cold War, or even, as I would like to suggest, to the colonial period itself.[1]

One can argue that countries that are exploited and deemed peripheral have always collaborated with one another. Core countries supported cultural, social, and technological cooperation among peripheral countries as a means to legitimize centrally organized political and economic power. Whether we accept the formation of the Non-Aligned Movement at the Bandung Conference in 1955 in response to U.S. and Soviet domination (see Chapter 3 by Morais de Sá e Silva) as the first signpost of South–South cooperation, or the transnational alliances between oppressed groups during the colonial era, it would be absurd to claim that South–South cooperation is either new or funded by only a few states. Although skeptics argue that South–South cooperation is merely a myth created by the global North to appease the South, the authors in this book believe it is vital to examine the context in which it reemerged, the actors who have advocated it, and the impact it has had on development work. Ultimately, we are interested in learning whether South–South cooperation has replaced earlier, asymmetrical forms of cooperation, and if it is a way out of the dependency trap in educational development.

WHY NOW?

Several scholars have argued convincingly that to understand the receptiveness toward new ideas, we must investigate the changes, context, or environment of the country where they are promulgated. Similar to David Phillips's theory of cross-national attraction (Phillips, 2004; see also Ertl, 2006), and Jürgen Schriewer's consideration of the "socio-logic" of external references (Schriewer, 1990; Schriewer & Martinez, 2004), I have scrutinized policy constellations to understand why reforms are borrowed from elsewhere. I also examine how policy-makers generate pressure for reform by referring to "globalization" or vaguely defined "international standards" (Steiner-Khamsi, 2004c; Steiner-Khamsi & Stolpe, 2006). In my study, a protracted policy constellation emerged around a contested issue at the local level that explained why "traveling reforms," or reforms from elsewhere, resonated in the domestic context. In these particular moments, policy borrowing had a salutary effect on the protracted policy conflict. This method of inquiry, embedded in system theory (Niklas Luhmann), emphasizes local contexts and changed environments. Within this interpretive framework, a concept such as South–South cooperation resonates because it appears, or rather, is presented as, a solution to new problems. As a corollary for understanding the general acceptance of the concept of South–South cooperation, one must identify areas that are perceived as new challenges or problems. By asking how the "aid" environment has changed in recent years, who the new donors are, and what their logic is, we can understand why South–South cooperation is currently presented as a panacea in development work.

There has been unprecedented growth and diversification in funding sources for international projects in the past few years. It is ironic that precisely at the moment when all multilateral donors (UN organizations, World Bank, and so forth) and bilateral donors (U.S. Agency for International Development, U.K. Department for International Development, and so on) have finally been brought in line to provide only loans and grants to low-income countries if certain rigorous conditions are met, a new class of "unruly donors" has emerged. These donors—philanthropists, businesspeople, and celebrities—do not abide by international agreements, such as Education for All (EFA), the Millennium Development Goals (MDG), or the Indicative Framework of the EFA–Fast Track Initiative. They are also not concerned with what the education sector strategies of donor–

recipient governments promise to accomplish over the next 5, 7, or 10 years. Their decisions are guided by encounters with statesmen and peers at the Economic Forum in Davos and on Wall Street, rather than by international agreements reached in Jomtien, Dakar, Monterrey, or Washington. Although "unruly donors" are given little attention in development studies literature, the significance of their emergence should not be underestimated.

At the end of 2006, the Bill and Melinda Gates Foundation had US$33 billion in endowment assets for charitable activities (Gates Foundation, 2007). Having been developed from the income of just two men—Bill Gates and Warren Buffett—the foundation plans to disburse US$3.2 billion a year by 2009. This amount equals one-third of the US$9.8 billion that the U.S. government, with a population of more than 300 million taxpayers, thought it could afford annually for USAID. The volume of aid provided by newly emerging philanthropies, such as the Gates Foundation, is—with the exception of the Official Development Assistance (ODA) of the United States, Japan, United Kingdom, France, Germany, and Sweden—greater than the ODA of any other loan- and grant-providing government (OECD, 2007). It is also several times the amount donated by earlier philanthropists, including the Rockefeller Foundation established in 1913 (endowment of US$3.4 billion), and the Open Society Institute established by George Soros in 1979 (average annual giving of US$400 million). Arguably, the size of the endowments of newly established philanthropies reflects the widening gap between the extraordinarily rich and the extremely poor.

The influence of individuals or businesspeople on aid priorities, entirely detached from governments' foreign-policy goals, is not only manifested in philanthropies. It has become fashionable for celebrities and other public figures to donate money to people they consider to be "the neediest," especially if the media cover their donations with much glamour and fanfare (see *Vanity Fair*, 2007). The willingness to donate has also trickled down to the individual consumer. Arguably, the glamorization of aid goes hand in hand with the commercialization of aid. The licensing of Bono's product Red Initiative to American Express, Apple, Converse, Emporio Armani, Gap, Hallmark, and Motorola is perhaps indicative of a new era in which it has become profitable for businesses to get involved in charity. By the end of 2007, however, the dollar amount spent on publicity for Red still exceeded the donations made for the Global Fund to fight AIDS, tuberculosis and malaria, and to raise public awareness about HIV/AIDS in Africa (Global Fund, 2007). However, as these examples demonstrate, a new class of donors, composed of philanthropists, businesspeople, and celebrities, has emerged.

Some new donors do follow the script established by the Millennium Development Goals (MDGs), but they are a minority. The UN Millennium Villages project, managed by the Earth Institute at Columbia University and directed by Professor Jeffrey Sachs, is an exception to the rule in that it does commit itself to the MDGs. It is a public–private partnership that includes sponsors such as the United Nations Development Programme; celebrities such as Bono, Madonna, Brad Pitt, and Angelina Jolie; as well as philanthropies, exemplified by George Soros's recent pledge of $50 million. These new types of donations are distinct in being almost exclusively channeled into health and, to a smaller extent, education projects in Africa. Another new phenomenon, perhaps unique to U.S. foreign policy, is the militarization of economic and humanitarian aid in conflict zones.[2]

These new donors (aside from the military) see themselves as cosmopolites representing global capital and a global community, rather than their governments in the North. Unlike conventional bilateral and multilateral donors, their donations are not linked to foreign-policy priorities, nor are they contingent on specific conditions that the recipient governments must fulfill (e.g., structural adjustment, poverty alleviation, good governance). South–South cooperation and other debates within the field of development studies are irrelevant to them: They give as they please. Given that governments closely tie their loans and grants to foreign-policy goals, multilaterals make assistance contingent on specific conditions (structural adjustment, poverty alleviation, good governance), and international agreements such as EFA and MDG are biased in their exclusive focus on primary school education, philanthropies may be the last glimmer of hope for aid. Not being part of the "cartel of good intentions" (Easterly, 2002) can be beneficial for individuals and institutions that receive funding from philanthropies. They fill the void left behind in international and bilateral agreements.

Nevertheless, some of the new forms of giving are not only ineffective, but harmful for development. However, since they operate in a vacuum of accountability, they are exempt from professional and academic scrutiny. This is not the case for governments and their bilateral and multilateral agencies, which are held accountable by their constituents and competitors. Conventional donors are in the position of having to reinvent themselves continuously and they are pressed to reflect on their mistakes. Today, international organizations emphasize lesson-drawing, that is, learning from "good practices" or "best-practices" that they have already funded in the global South, to influence national reform more effectively. This is the motivation for their emphasis on South–South collaboration.

THE STANDARDIZATION OF AID

South–South cooperation has resonated with the conventional donors, at least rhetorically, for one particular reason: Aid has become standardized. The means that governments in the global South use to achieve the standards or targets established by the North have become secondary. The new logic of the conventional donors consists of rigorous enforcement of international benchmarks for development, along with verbal acknowledgment of national ownership over reforms that help achieve internationally established standards.

From the first international agreement, Education for All (1990), to the EFA–Fast Track Initiative (2002), which prescribes how educational systems must be reformed to achieve universal primary completion by 2015, governments receiving ODA loans or grants have had less room to maneuver. Since the direction, content, or reform "package" is predetermined by international agreements, latecomers in development are encouraged to learn from, cooperate with, or adopt "best-practices" from early adopters situated in the global South. Benchmark-oriented reforms are coercive in terms of content and the timeline of reform. However, they are discrete when it comes to choosing appropriate strategies for achieving benchmarks. Constant monitoring and evaluation is a feature of this new donor logic, because it enables international donors to stay involved. Despite the assurance of national ownership, the establishment of annual targets enables international donors to keep governments in line if the donors find that the governments did a poor job in implementing reforms.

Donors have set up knowledge banks as an elaborate apparatus for developing country-specific benchmarks. In the education sector, the World Bank has taken the lead in developing and drawing upon its knowledge bank to influence national reforms. In an era of evidence-based educational policy research and policy-making, knowledge banks constitute more sophisticated versions of databanks. They include data on the educational, economic, and social development of a country, and comprise a package of reform ideas or "best-practices" that have already been tested in other ODA recipient countries. Most grant proposals to multilateral organizations refer to a crisis, outlined with an abundance of statistical information, followed by ideas on how to remedy said crisis through the adoption of "best-practices" such as EMIS (Education Management Information System), pro capita financing, outcomes-based education, standardized student assessment, and a host of other traveling reforms funded by multilateral organizations.

Educational statistics provide the foundation for the standardized approach to assessing development needs and targeting aid outcomes.

Unsurprisingly, in recent years, every international organization, including international nongovernmental organizations, has established its own databank with indices that measure regress or progress in categories such as children's rights and economic stability in the areas where they intervene. Indices, ranging from 0 to 1, or from 0 to 100, enable cross-national comparison and the construction of league tables. Naming, shaming, and ranking have become powerful tools to generate or alleviate reform pressure. At the same time, UNESCO's resurgence in the international arena can be, to some extent, attributed to its regained capacity for collecting and analyzing data (see Heyneman, 1999; Cussó, 2006; see also Cussó & D'Amico, 2005), or monitoring progress toward Millennium Development Goals.

The development of knowledge banks is also significant. The concept of an international knowledge bank was first discussed by the Board of Governors of the World Bank in March 1996 (Jones, 2004; Jones with Coleman, 2005). One of the options considered was whether financial lending operations should be delegated to regional development banks (Asian Development Bank, African Development Bank, and so forth), while the Bank itself focused on the lending of ideas. Three years later, in 1999, the World Bank's Global Development Network (GDN) was launched at a conference in Bonn (see Stone, 2000). The idea was to treat local best-practices as a "public good" (Stiglitz, 2000, p. 29) and make them globally available. As a result, policy transfer would ideally occur within and among the countries of the South, replacing the practice of transplanting reform packages from the First to the Third World. Although the World Bank has maintained its financial role, it has also increasingly, during the past decade, acted as a global monitor and lender of "best-practices."

The World Bank has not been alone in constructing and using international knowledge banks to gain leverage at the national level. As mentioned earlier, other international organizations, such as Transparency International in the general public sector or UNESCO (with its annual *Global Monitoring Report*) in the educational sector, have followed suit by acknowledging that monitoring national development against internationally set standards is a powerful strategy for influencing national policy. Used as an advocacy tool, the ranking and scoring of nations along specific indices generates far greater reform pressure on low-income countries than more conventional strategies such as making grants and loans contingent on externally imposed conditions (structural adjustment, poverty alleviation, good governance). The previous approach of imposing conditionalities externally has been rendered obsolete by more subtle strategies of inducing reform pressure from within. In retrospect, imposing conditions on ODA recipients, a practice that was in place for over 20 years, not only makes donors look bad, but also fails to accelerate reform. In ODA recipient countries benchmark-oriented reforms may be even more coercive. However, unlike earlier approaches to pressuring recipients, their framework is pseudo-scientific, rather than political and economic. In the next section, I will describe the agenda-driven, evidence-based approach underlying the EFA–FTI Indicative Framework.

THE WHAT-WENT-RIGHT APPROACH

Of all knowledge banks, the Education for All–Fast Track Initiative (EFA–FTI) best illustrates the politics and economics of statistical knowledge. In 2002, the EFA–FTI was launched at a meeting of the G-8 in Monterrey, Mexico. The FTI was supposed to help reform-minded governments of poor countries implement universal primary education by the year 2015. The goal of achieving universal primary education by this date was inscribed in the 1990 international agreement Education for All (EFA), and confirmed in the UN Millennium Development Goals of 2000. A major priority shift occurred between 1990 and the new millennium: Whereas the emphasis in EFA (1990) was on universal access to primary education, the focus of the MDGs (2000) and the EFA–FTI (2002) is on *completion* of primary school education. The question for policy-makers became not only how to attract children to school, but also how to keep them there for at least 4 to 6 years. The new priority implied more consideration of how to improve the quality of education. A new and compelling approach to this issue was taken up by a group of World Bank economists (see Bruns, Mingat, & Rakotomalala, 2003) who decided to study the educational systems of ODA-recipient governments that had or were likely to achieve universal primary completion by 2015. By asking what these countries had done right that would be worth emulating, they provided the foundation for the EFA–FTI Indicative Framework.

The ideas underlying the EFA–FTI were sensible and compelling to policy-makers: Governments from low-income countries need to be given incentives for borrowing "best-practices" from other comparable educational systems that succeeded with universal primary completion. In order to reward reform-minded governments, the international donor community would commit itself to securing and providing the necessary funds for reforms, placing such governments on the "fast track" to development. In 2002, 18 countries were invited by the G-8 to submit proposals for consideration in the initiative.

FTI has grown exponentially since its inception. As of October 2007, 36 education sector plans have been endorsed, and the EFA–FTI Secretariat expects that seven countries will qualify for FTI funding in 2008, followed by 13 more in 2009 (EFA–FTI Secretariat, 2007, p. 9). The Education Program Development Fund (established in November 2004) added substantial resources to the already-existing Catalytic Fund. However, pledges for the Catalytic Fund and the Education Program Development Fund are smaller than the EFA–FTI Secretariat had expected, calling into question whether the eligible incoming countries will receive the same level of funding as the ones already approved during the first FTI cycle, 2002–2005. Apart from the Netherlands and the United Kingdom, which contributed 75% of the total pledges in the Catalytic Fund, the donors have shown weak enthusiasm. Norway is the lead donor for the Education Program Development Fund ($34.8 million out of $53.32 million), followed at much lower participation levels by the United Kingdom ($5.9 million) and Canada ($3.4 million). The United States is, as of 2007, entirely absent. It has not contributed to the Catalytic Fund or the Education Program Development Fund of FTI. Other large donors, such as Japan, Germany, and France, have only contributed cosmetically to the EFA–FTI funds (EFA–FTI Secretariat, 2007, p. Annex 2 and 3). Even though more than 30 bilateral, regional, and international agencies and development banks have supported the initiative, the World Bank is the lead coordinator and host to the EFA–FTI Secretariat. The spirit advocated in FTI is "harmonization," in that all 30 donors are supposed to be "using common arrangements for aid, sharing their technical and analytical work, and joining together on field missions" (World Bank, 2005, p. 2).

The 2015 benchmarks of the FTI Indicative Framework (Bruns, Mingat, & Bakotonalala, 2003, p. 73) address three areas: service delivery, system expansion, and system financing. For example, one benchmark determines that the average annual teacher salary should be 3.5 times the annual per capita GDP by the year 2015. Another benchmark requires that the student-teacher ratio should be 40:1. According to the World Bank, these benchmarks have been determined on the basis of empirical evidence. First, researchers at the World Bank examined 155 developing countries and identified 69 top-performing educational systems with regard to universal primary education completion rates. These 69 countries were deemed to be "on track," because they either already have, or are likely to achieve, universal basic education by the year 2015. Second, researchers focused their analyses on the 69 countries and asked what they "did right" in the areas of service delivery, system expansion, and system financing (Bruns, Mingat, & Rakotomalala, 2003, p. 58). Table 13.1. lists the resulting standards, or FTI benchmarks, that were established in 2002 based on the study of 69 top-performing educational systems in developing countries mentioned above.

A Way Out from the Dependency Trap?

Table 13.1. The EFA-FTI Indicative Framework

Variables That Affect Primary Education Efficiency and Quality	2015 Benchmarks
SERVICE DELIVERY	
Average annual teacher salary (as multiple of per capita GDP)	3.5
Pupil-teacher ratio	40:1
Spending on inputs other than teachers (as % of primary education recurrent spending)	33
Average repetition rate (%)	10 or lower
SYSTEM EXPANSION	
Unit construction cost	$6,500–$12,600
SYSTEM FINANCING	
Government revenues as % of GDP (staggered targets proportional to per capita GDP)	14/16/18
Education recurrent spending as % of government revenues	20
Primary education recurrent spending as % of total education recurrent spending (benchmark is 50% for a 6-year primary cycle; 42% for a 5-year cycle)	50/42
Private enrollments (as % of total)	10

Source: Bruns et al., 2003, p. 73.

Apart from a $1 billion shortfall in pledges during the period 2008–2010 in the Catalytic and Education Sector Development Funds, mentioned above, there are also three problems highlighted by the EFA–FTI World Bank Secretariat (2007) at the country level: incongruence of statistical data between international and national databanks, inconsistencies between the international Indicative Framework and the national education sector plans, and an inability to measure *good* primary education. First, according to the EFA–FTI Secretariat (2007) the gap between what Ministries of Education report in terms of enrollment figures and what the

UNESCO Institute for Statistics determines is more than three percentage points. In some cases, it is as high as 20. For a donor strategy that relies so heavily upon benchmarking and monitoring annual targets, the incongruence of statistical information is so grave that it calls into question the very foundation of evidence-based planning.

Second, Ministries of Education are supposed to use the Indicative Framework and the EFA–FTI Appraisal Guidelines as a foundation to develop their education sector plans. The standards provided by the two international documents, however, are only reluctantly applied by the Ministries of Education. Of those countries approved for EFA–FTI, only 64% referred to the Indicative Framework. Naturally, for EFA–FTI, such a disregard for international standards is a cause of great concern, and a series of corrective measures has been put in place, including funds to provide a "quality support review from external experts" (EFA–FTI Secretariat, 2007, p. 21). Such measures are meant to ensure that the national education sector plans comply with the reform areas predetermined in the country-specific EFA–FTI appraisals, prepared by international consultants, and the international Indicative Framework.

Finally, commitment to completion of—rather than just access to—primary education requires greater attention to improving quality. According to EFA–FTI, a quality assessment can only be made by means of international student achievement tests. To date, seven ODA-recipient governments have participated in TIMSS (Trends in International Mathematics and Science Study), PIRLS (Program in International Reading Literacy), and PISA (Program in International Student Assessment), and EFA–FTI envisions that many more countries will, with external financial assistance, participate in internationally standardized tests in the future. The multilateral and bilateral donors are attempting to increase the number of countries that bring their education sector plans in line with EFA–FTI and expand the Indicative Framework to include other relevant benchmarks that relate to quality of primary education. They also hope, in the near future, to increase the number of countries that endorse education sector plans that move beyond primary education into early childhood and secondary education (EFA–FTI Secretariat, 2007, p. 31).

The study of knowledge banks as a new education policy tool is an emerging field in international and comparative education. As mentioned earlier, Phillip Jones (2004) explains in detail the various stages of policy development at the World Bank, identifying the most recent as the era when the Bank envisioned itself both as an education policy lender and as a loan provider. Other scholars have also investigated the transformation of multilaterals—in particular, the World Bank—into knowledge banks. However, they sometimes restrict their analyses to technology and

A Way Out from the Dependency Trap? 251

knowledge transfer, i.e., the Global Gateway (King, 2002, 2005), or to the World Bank's Knowledge for Development (K4D) and Knowledge Assessment Methodology (KAM) programs (Robertson, 2008). It might be more accurate to see the proliferation of global databanks and knowledge banks as a consequence of the standardization of aid.

Of all recent initiatives, the EFA–FTI manifests most visibly the strategy of international target-setting as a means to influence domestic policy. The haste and carelessness with which the FTI grant proposal was prepared (e.g., 3 months in Tajikistan and Kyrgyzstan) and approved was noticeable. Moreover, some reforms were already funded by other donors. Certain countries, such as Mongolia, were approved for EFA–FTI even though they were considered, with a primary completion rate of 95%, to be "on track." However, in contrast to ODA loans and grants, there are fewer strings attached. EFA–FTI, along with the emergence of new donors, has changed the aid environment in major ways. The pace at which low-income countries receive funds from the EFA–FTI Catalytic Fund or the Education Development Fund is breathtaking. The ease with which EFA–FTI proposals are approved is astounding, given that, for more than 2 decades, the Cartel of Good Intentions (Easterly, 2002) and development banks imposed rigid and ambitious conditions (structural adjustment, poverty alleviation, good governance) for their loans and grants. Even though the Monterrey Consensus of 2002, which marked the beginning of the new EFA–FTI era, continues to list 73 actions that ODA recipient countries must undertake, nobody seems to take them seriously. William Easterly explains why:

> Meanwhile, the U.N. International Conference on Financing for Development held in Monterrey, Mexico, in March 2002 produced a document—"the Monterrey Consensus"—that has a welcome emphasis between rich donor and poor recipient nations. But it's somewhat challenge for poor countries to carry out the 73 actions that the document recommends, including such ambitions as establishing democracy, equality between boys and girls, and peace on Earth. (2002, p. 40f)

TARGET-SETTING IN PRACTICE

The EFA–FTI proposals seem highly analytical in that a host of statistical material is presented to demonstrate the need for immediate action. The authors hired to prepare the EFA–FTI proposal are expected to make the case that the educational sector is in crisis, and in need of major and immediate external funding. It is also assumed that they will say that the government has the capacity to implement major reforms. The greater the deviation from the MDG target—universal primary school completion—the greater the crisis, and in practice, the greater the willingness of donors to cover the funding gap.

Once the sense of crisis is invoked, the analyses follow a script like the one illustrated by the data on dropout rates. The dropout problem during primary school is supposed to be eradicated by the year 2015. International consultants determine the dropout rate for the base year (the year EFA–FTI is launched), and then set targets for each subsequent year until the rate reaches zero. The simulation includes vague considerations of what must be undertaken in the next few years to actually produce a reduction in dropouts, and the costs are calculated with implausible precision. As a final step, the "funding gap"—the amount the recipient government is not able or willing to finance for the vaguely formulated reforms of the next couple of years—is determined. The gap is then closed with the Catalytic Fund and the Education Development Fund, established to provide external financial assistance.

The donor logic reflects a new way of doing development business. However, it would be wrong to assume that the standardization of aid, propelled by EFA–FTI, has significantly transformed the way administrators and teachers operate at the school level. One example is Mongolia, a country in the East that, along with more than 30 other post-communist countries, has become part of the new global South. Countries with centralist governance structures, like Mongolia, are perfect for examining how standardization plays out in practice. They tend to demand that the lower levels of administration (province level, district level, school level) tailor their plans to the national agenda to achieve, at least on paper, universal primary school completion by the year 2015. In Mongolia, these multiyear plans, which already existed during the socialist period, are today reframed as education sector plans, or the "Master Plan." The school's Master Plan is supposed to conform to the 650-page Master Plan of Mongolia 2006–2015, formulated in 2006 by Mongolian experts, with substantial input from international consultants hired by the Asian Development Bank (Government of Mongolia, 2006).

Throughout 2007, the School Master Plan was discussed daily, and schools eagerly shared what they had produced for the Ministry of Education, Culture, and Science.[3] The School Master Plans typically consist of four sections: assessment of the schools' current situation, the school's mission, the school's vision, and the priorities of the plan (with benchmarks and indicators). The following is an example from a rural school in Undur-Ulaan in the Arkhangai province. I will confine my description to excerpts from the first section (assessment of the school's current situation), and the last section (priorities of the plan). The first section reads like a narrative from any school in the South that has to operate with very limited resources:

> *Assessment of School's Current Situation:* High number of children who are out of school, underdeveloped learning environment, textbook shortage, limited opportunities for inservice training, weak collaboration between school and parents, insufficient number of student desks and chairs, shortage of teachers, unqualified teachers, difficult/poor living conditions of teachers, low quality and limited access to nonformal education for the illiterate, lack of comprehensive support for teachers to implement the new education standards. (Undur-Ulaan school, 2007)

The last section is disingenuous, composed of parts reflecting what the Ministry of Education, Culture, and Science wants to read (e.g., benchmarks for enhancing enrolment), and what schools want to express as their needs and the funds they desire to meet them from the Ministry of Education, Culture, and Science. The School Master Plan is identical to the EFA–FTI framework. It uses the same "façade of precision" (Samoff, 1999a, p. 261) to establish presumably exact, but ultimately unpredictable, benchmarks for enrollment figures over the next few years, while it also incorporates the concrete needs assessment developed by the school. The first two points are the ones that the Ministry of Education, Culture, and Science wants to read. The façade of precision manifested in such plans is quite specific, with decimal points denoting future developments in a school with just a few hundred students:

> *Priorities of the Plan:* . . . Goal 2: To increase enrollment. To increase the net enrollment to cover 98% at primary level, 93.4% at secondary level and 95.6% at high school level. Timeline: 2007–2010.
> (Undur-Ulaan school, 2007)

Of the 11 points listed in the section Priorities of the Plan, only two relate to the national Master Plan and to EFA–FTI. The other nine points summarize what schools actually need. The next excerpt is from the same section that deals with what the school really requires:

> *Priorities of the Plan:* . . . Goal 3: To improve the material conditions for learning: (a) to supply all classrooms with new tables and chairs, (b) to repair a roof of the school building that accommodates 320 students and stop the roof leak, (c) to improve the looks of the school's outside area, to repair the outdoor sports area and to ensure that the annual repairs of the school are well executed.

Other goals include "to build a hot shower for students accommodated in the school dormitory," "to fully repair the kitchen facilities and buy necessary machines and kitchen tools," and "to rehabilitate the vacant school building for 120 students as an additional school dormitory for students." It is noticeable that the list of priorities that reflect a school's needs (hot shower, new tables and chairs, fixing the leaking roof, and so forth) are supplemented with an action plan, and are far more concrete than the priorities derived from the national Master Plan. Of the 11 priorities listed in the Master Plan of Undur-Ulaan school, only the first two deal with the EFA–FTI benchmarks. The remaining nine are written as requests and correspond to the old genre of 3-year financial plans that schools were required to submit. In other words, EFA–FTI benchmarks have made it onto paper at the school level, but have very little consequences in practice.

Given schools' disregard for decisions made between the government and donors at the central level, there is no great cause for concern that they are coerced into externally exposed reforms. Neither governments nor schools are helpless victims or passive recipients of reform packages. Even if they were, the goals pursued in EFA–FTI, including gender parity or elimination of nonenrollment and dropout rates, are hard to disagree with. But there is a legitimate concern, expressed by Jansen (2005) and others, that internationally set targets neglect, and thereby distract from and de-invest in, much-needed reforms at the national level. Notable among these are nonformal education, early childhood education, lower and upper secondary education, vocational education, and higher education.

For many educational systems, the exclusive focus on primary schooling, which international donors have pursued blindly for almost 20 years, has become outdated. The education sector strategies of Burkina Faso and Kenya, to name just two countries in Africa that tend to be unfortunately showcased by donors to justify the primary school focus, went on to outline planned reforms at the secondary school level. In the part of the world I work—Mongolia and Central Asia—EFA did not have any relevance in 1990 when it was conceived. At that time, most of the (post-) communist countries had achieved universal access to primary schooling, and were in the midst of completing multiyear plans for ensuring universal access to general secondary education (preschool and grades 1–10). Internationally established goals assume that all educational systems in ODA-recipient countries face the same challenges. What if primary school completion is not an issue, or what if gender parity is a problem because boys—rather than girls—are discriminated against? Mongolia is not alone in having an "inverse gender gap," whereby girls outperform boys at all levels of schooling.

Government officials are quick to discover the political and economic gains that come with speaking the universal language of educational reform. In my studies on educational import in Mongolia (e.g., Steiner-Khamsi & Stolpe, 2006), I noticed that government officials take a different take when they address local constituents. Rather than labeling this practice doubletalk, I prefer to call it policy bilingualism, where one set of reforms is advanced with funding from donors ("global speak"), while another, sometimes diametrically opposed set of reforms, is promoted with local or national support. More often than not, money made available from international donors is redirected and channeled into supporting locally developed reforms, which in Mongolia are referred to as "national programs." Governments of aid-recipient countries are not victims. Rather, they deal creatively with their economic dependence by redirecting funds into locally developed programs, adopting the language but not the content of an imposed reform; decline to implement an imported reform; or only adopt the reform selectively.

As mentioned earlier, international knowledge banks also contain a portfolio of "best-practices" that are transferred along with loans and grants. The ODA-recipient governments have no choice but to select from an existing portfolio. But how a government deals with the "best-practices" once they have been imported is a different issue. In my study of educational import in Mongolia, I analyzed structural adjustment programs in the educational sector that were implemented in the mid-1990s. Ten years later, one reform was still in place (tuition-based higher education), one was at first advanced and then was retreated (decentralization of educational finance and governance), and one had partially reverted to a structure that was in place prior to the structural adjustment reforms (rationalization of staff and reorganization of schools). It is important to understand how Mongolian government officials managed, with some reforms more than others, to undermine, adapt, or modify the educational import to the needs of the country. We lack studies that analyze reforms initiated and funded by international donors retroactively after 10 years or more. We would perhaps find, as in the case of Mongolia, that ODA-recipient governments have their own ways of selectively implementing reforms that had been externally financed. Which reforms they actually implement, which they modify, and which they subvert have been key research questions for research on policy borrowing and lending.

NORTH–SOUTH–SOUTH?

The emphasis on knowledge banks in this concluding chapter, the EFA–Fast Track Initiative in particular, has served to illustrate that lesson-drawing, or *South–South transfer*, is currently central to the operations of international donors. Countries that the World Bank identified as "off track" and "seriously off track" with regard to universal primary completion are supposed to learn from other poor countries that are "on track" (Bruns, Mingat, & Rakotomalala, 2003; EFA–FTI Secretariat, 2007). This commitment to South–South transfer is asserted in the EFA–FTI Framework:

> Globally, the FTI also aims to promote: *mutual learning on what works* to improve primary education outcomes and advance EFA goals. (EFA–FTI Secretariat, 2004, p. 3; italics in original)

The EFA–FTI Framework treats its commitment to promote "mutual learning on what works" as a priority, followed by the other "guiding principles of the Fast Track Initiative" (EFA–FTI Secretariat, 2004, p. 4): country-ownership, benchmarking, support linked to performance, lower transaction cost, and transparency.

In the case of the EFA–Fast Track Initiative, South–South transfer, or "mutual learning on what works," is clearly defined. The "best-practices" of on-track countries are inscribed in the Indicative Framework of EFA–FTI. Ministries of Education are supposed to bring their education sector plans in line with the "best–practices" of systems that perform well. From this, they can learn how much to spend on primary education, what to pay teachers, how big class sizes should be, what are acceptable repetition rates, and so forth.

There has been tremendous growth in the number of knowledge banks that include both statistical information on indicators and portfolios of "best-practices." The World Bank and other multilateral organizations are not alone in establishing such banks. In the wake of evidence-based policy-making, each and every major international organization resorts to its own data and "best-practices" for areas that matter to them. South–South transfer is not restricted to conventional donors, but also applies to "new donors," such as the Millennium Villages Project of the Earth Institute, Columbia University, which draws from a private–public partnership and is heavily engaged in evidence-based lesson-drawing. The project selected 79 villages, clustered into 12 groups across 10 African countries (Ethiopia, Ghana, Kenya, Malawi, Mali, Nigeria, Rwanda, Senegal, Tanzania, and Uganda), and developed a sectorwide reform package that attempts to end poverty in these countries. These 79 villages will serve as showcases for neighboring villages, the 10 countries will serve as models for neighboring countries, and Africa will set an example, possibly, for the entire Third World. As the Millennium Villages claims:

Individual villages are now exporting their successful interventions to neighboring villages in their districts, and the result is a transforming Africa. (Millennium Villages, 2007)

South–South or East–East transfer occurs, but from where did the benchmarks, targets, and interventions emanate? In most cases, we deal with a North–South–South transfer or a West–East–East transfer, whereby donors in the North or West, respectively, have designed a standardized reform or intervention package for the global South. Nevertheless, it is striking that international organizations increasingly endorse South–South transfer or, to frame it differently, encourage lesson-drawing from other countries that have already successfully implemented externally financed reforms. International donors have also endorsed, at least rhetorically, South–South cooperation.

The authors of this book have contributed greatly to a better understanding of South–South cooperation by analyzing the phenomenon from different angles. As Linda Chisholm summarizes in her introductory chapter, several authors in this book examined changing notions of "South," and with it, changing constellations of countries that used to be seen as "peripheries." Another group of authors examined the modalities of transfer and cooperation as reflected in policies and practices of bilateral and multilateral aid, national governments, and nongovernmental organizations, as well as multinational businesses. Finally, the book concludes with several chapters that question whether South–South cooperation really is a way out from the dependency trap in educational development.

As with transfer, cooperation among the individuals and institutions in the South reflects a changed environment for aid. It is an environment that has become increasingly standardized, prescriptive, and coercive for national governments. The new emphasis is on benchmarks, standards, and targets. How governments in the South achieve these benchmarks, established in the North, is secondary. In fact, "national ownership" has become the buzzword of the new millennium. How governments choose to implement reforms in line with internationally set targets is left, to some extent, up to them. In this new era of evidence-based policy-making and standardized aid, South–South cooperation can be seen as a vehicle to accelerate the accomplishment of development targets established by the North. Perhaps we need to curb our enthusiasm for this revitalized concept in development and acknowledge instead that South–South cooperation is part and parcel of standardized aid, designed, funded, and monitored by the North. The Cartel of Good Intentions has strengthened and expanded its global governance and is now granting some leeway to ODA-recipient governments in the South. The purpose, however, is to achieve the standardized targets, determined in the North, in a more efficient and, if possible, cost-effective manner.

NOTES

1. In an earlier study on Achimota in colonial Ghana (Steiner-Khamsi & Quist, 2000), we examined the "technical assistance" provided by African American elites to schools under British colonial rule during the first 2 decades of the 20th century. The idea that South–South cooperation is particular to the 21st century is regularly advanced by the UNDP and UNESCO. For the notion that it is funded by only a few states, notably Japan, see Mochizuki's chapter in this book.

2. Two sources of U.S. overseas loans and grants, in particular, reflect the blurred line between military and humanitarian assistance: the Economic Support Fund ($3.8 billion in 2006) managed by USAID and the State Department, and the Department of Defense Security Assistance fund ($4.7 billion in 2006). The Greenbook *U.S. Overseas Loans and Grants* provides a more detailed description of how these funds are disbursed (U.S. Government, 2006).

3. My collection of school-level Master Plans comes from two program evaluations that I conducted on behalf of the Danish International Development Agency DANIDA (Rural School Development Project II) and the NGO Mongolian Education Alliance (Rural Education and Development Project, component classroom libraries, funded by the World Bank).

References

Abugre, C. (2001). *Still sapping the poor? A critique of IMF poverty reduction strategies*. Retrieved June 6, 2006, from www.wdm.org.uk/cambriefs/Debt/sappoor.pdf

Adedeji, A. (1998). African renaissance, economic transformation and the role of the university. *Indicator South Africa, Winter*, 64–70.

African Union [AU]. (2005). *Revitalizing higher education in Africa: Synthesis report*. Accra, Ghana: Department of Human Resources, Science and Technology.

African Virtual University [AVU]. (2007). *About African Virtual University*. Retrieved September 7, 2007, from http://www.avu.org/about.asp

Agai, B. (2003). The Gülen movement's Islamic ethic of education. In H. Yavuz & J. Esposito (Eds.), *Turkish Islam and the secular state: The Gülen movement* (pp. 28–68). Syracuse, NY: Syracuse University Press.

Agência Brasileira de Cooperação [ABC]. (2005a). *Coordenação geral de cooperação técnica entre países em desenvolvimento*. Retrieved December 7, 2005, from http://www.abc.gov.br/abc/abc_ctpd.asp

ABC. (2005b). *Pesquisa de projetos de cooperacão tecnica entre paises em desenvolvimento*. Ministerio das Relacoes Exteriores, Brasilia DF, Brazil. Retrieved December 5, 2005, from http://www.abc.gov.br/ct/pesquisa_projetosctpd.asp

ABC. (2007a). *A cooperação triangular*. Retrieved June 21, 2007, from http://www.abc.gov.br/abc/abc_ctpd_triangular.asp

ABC. (2007b). *Histórico: CGPD—Coordenação geral de cooperação técnica entre países em desenvolvimento*. Retrieved June 21, 2007, from http://www.abc.gov.br/abc/abc_ctpd.asp

Ahmed, M., Chabbott, C., Joshi, A., & Pande, R. (1993). *Primary education for all: Learning from the BRAC experience*. Washington, DC: Academy for Educational Development.

Ajulu, R. (2001). Thabo Mbeki's African renaissance in a globalizing world economy: The struggle for the soul of the continent. *Review of African Political Economy, 87*, 27–42.

Ake, C. (1998). Building on the indigenous. In P. Fruhling (Ed.), *Recovery in Africa: A challenge for development co-operation in the 1990s* (pp. 19–21). Stockholm: SIDA.

Alzona, E. (1932). *A history of education in the Philippines, 1565–1930*. Manila: University of the Philippines Press.

Amin, S. (1980). Collective self-reliance or national liberation? In K. Haq (Ed.), *Dialogue for a new order* (pp. 153–169). New York: Pergamon Press.

Anderson, M. B. (1992). *Education for All: What are we waiting for?* New York: UNICEF.
Appadurai, A. (1996). *Modernity at large: Cultural dimensions of globalization.* Minneapolis: University of Minnesota Press.
Arias de Saavedra Alías, I. (1987). *Las sociedades económicas de amigos del país del reino de Jaén.* Granada, Spain: Diputación Provincial de Jaén/Universidad de Granada.
Arnove, R. F. (1980). Comparative education and world-systems analysis. *Comparative Education Review, 24*(1), 48–62.
Ashton, D., & Green, F. (1996). *Education, training and the global economy.* Cheltenham, UK: Edward Elgar.
Association for the Development of African Education. (1996). *Formulating education policy: Lessons and experiences from sub-Saharan Africa. Six case studies and reflections from the DAE biennial meetings.* Paris: Association for the Development of African Education.
Association for the Development of Education in Africa [ADEA]. (2005). Learning, but in which language? *ADEA Newsletter, 17*(2), 1.
Association of African Universities [AAU]. (2004, April 27–29). Accra Declaration on GATS and Internationalization of Higher Education in Africa and Participants Declaration from *Workshop on the Implications of WTO/GATS for Higher Education in Africa.* Accra: Ghana.
Atkinson, T. (2002). Is rising income inequality inevitable? A critique of the transatlantic consensus. In P. Townsend & D. Gordon (Eds.), *World poverty: New policies to defeat an old enemy* (pp. 25–53). Bristol, UK: The Policy Press.
Aydin, M. (1996). Turkey and Central Asia: Challenges of change. *Central Asian Survey, 15*(2), 157–177.
Aypay, A. (2004). Turkish higher education initiatives toward Central Asia. In S. Heyneman & A. deYoung (Eds.), *The challenge of education in Central Asia* (pp. 81–96). Greenwich, CT: Information Age Publishing.
Azernews-Azerkhabar (1999, July 22). *Turkish world education.* Retrieved October 1, 2007, from http://www.geocities.com/ai320/education.htm
Bakı Özəl Türk Litseyi (2006). *School profile.* Retrieved October 1, 2007, from http://en.wikipedia.org/wiki/Baku_Private_Turkish_School
Baktir, Y. (2007). *Turkish development policy and Turkish international cooperation and development agency (TIKA).* Presentation at the UNDP regional workshop "Emerging Donors Initiative" in Budapest, Hungary.
Balci, B. (2003). Fethullah Gülen's missionary schools in Central Asia and their role in the spreading of Turkism and Islam. *Religion, State & Society, 31*(2), 151–177.
Barnet, M., & Finnemore, M. (2004). *Rules for the world: International organizations in global politics.* Ithaca & London: Cornell University Press.
Bashkin, O. (2006). When Mu'awiya entered the curriculum: Some comments on the Iraqi education system in the interwar period. *Comparative Education Review, 50*(3), 346–366.
Beckham, E. (Ed.). (2000). *Diversity, democracy and higher education: A view from three nations.* Washington, DC: Association of American Colleges and Universities.

References

Begum, K., Akhter, S., & Rahman, S. (1988). *An evaluation of BRAC's primary education program*. Dhaka, Bangladesh: World Bank.

Bell, A. (1797). *An experiment in education, made at the Male Asylum of Madras. Suggesting a system by which a school or family teach itself under the superintendence of the master or parent*. Edinburgh, Great Britain: Cadell & Davies.

Bennell, P. (1996). Rates of return to education: Does the conventional pattern prevail in sub-Saharan Africa? *World Development, 24*(1), 183–190.

Bennell, P. (1997). Privatisation in sub-Saharan Africa: Progress and prospects during the 1990s. *World Development, 25*(11), 1785–1804.

Benot, E. (1857). *Observaciones sobre la educación*. Cádiz, Spain: Imprenta de la Revista Médica.

Bergesen, A. (1984). The critique of world-system-theory: Class relations or division of labor? *Sociological Theory, 2*, 365–372.

Bhanji, Z. (2008). Transnational corporations in education: Filling the governance gap through new social norms and market multilateralism? *Globalisation, Societies and Education, 6*(1), 55–73.

Binns, H. B. (1908). *A century of education, being the centenary history of the British and Foreign School Society 1808–1908*. London: Dent.

Bøås, M. (2003). Weak states, strong regimes: Towards a "real" political economy of African regionalization. In J. A. Grant & F. Söderbaum (Eds.), *The new regionalism in Africa* (pp. 31–46). Aldershot, UK: Ashgate.

Boeren, A., & Holtland, G. (Eds.). (2005). *A changing landscape: Making support to higher education and research in developing countries more effective*. The Hague: Nuffic. Retrieved September 22, 2007, from www.nuffic.nl/pdf/os/em/samoff.pdf

Boler, T., & Aggleton, P. (2005). *Life skills education for HIV prevention: A critical analysis*. London: Save the Children and ActionAid International.

Bond, P. (Ed.). (2001). *Fanon's warning: A civil society reader on the new partnership for Africa's development*. Lawrenceville, NJ: Africa World Press.

Boukary, H. D. (2004). The village schools of Save the Children—US in Mali: A case study of state–NGO relations in the provision of basic education. In M. Sutton & R. F. Arnove (Eds.), *Civil society or shadow state?: State/NGO relations in education* (pp. 71–109). Greenwich, CT: Information Age.

British and Foreign School Society [BFSS]. (1817). *Manual of the system of teaching reading, writing, arithmetic, and needle-work, in the elementary schools* (1st American ed.). Philadelphia: Benjamin Warner.

Broadman, Harry G. (Ed.). (2006). *Africa's Silk Road: China and India's new economic frontier*. Washington, DC: World Bank Publications.

Bruns, B., Mingat, A., & Rakotomalala, R. (2003). *Achieving universal primary education by 2015: A chance for every child*. Washington, DC: World Bank.

Bryant, C., & Kappaz, C. (2005). *Reducing poverty, building peace*. Bloomfield, CT: Kumarian Press.

Buchert, L. (2002). Towards new partnerships in sector-wide approaches: Comparative experiences from Burkina Faso, Ghana and Mozambique. *International Journal of Educational Development, 22*(1), 69–84.

Building Resources Across Communities [BRAC]. (2006). *BRAC 2005* (Annual Report). Dhaka, Bangladesh: BRAC.

BRAC Education Programme. (2002). *Technical assistance outside Bangladesh for replicating NFPE*. Dhaka, Bangladesh: BRAC.
Bull, B., & McNeill, D. (2007). The rise of public–private partnerships in the multilateral system. In B. Bull & D. McNeil (Eds.), *Development issues in global governance: Public–private partnerships and market multilateralism* (pp. 1–22). New York: Routledge.
Bullock, A. & Thomas, H. (1997). *Schools at the centre: A study of decentralisation*. London: Routledge.
Burgess, H. J., & Welsby, P. A. (1961). *A short history of the National Society 1811–1961*. London: National Society.
Bustos Rodríguez, M. (2005). *Cádiz en el sistema Atlántico: la ciudad, sus comerciantes y la actividad mercantil (1650–1830)*. Madrid: Sílex.
Butcher, N. (2001). *Technological infrastructure and use of ICT in education in Africa: An overview*. Paris: Association for the Development of Education in Africa.
Butrón Prida, G. (2001). Fiesta y revolución: Las celebraciones políticas en el Cádiz liberal (1812–1837). In A. Gil Novales (Ed.), *La revolución liberal* (pp. 159–178). Madrid: Ediciones del Orto.
Calderón España, M. C. (2001). Las Reales Sociedades Económicas de Amigos del Pais y la educación. In M. C. Calderón España (Ed.), *Las reales sociedades económicas de amigos del pais y el espíritu ilustrado: Análisis de sus realizaciones* (pp. 87–120). Sevilla, Spain: Universidad de Sevilla.
Candido, S. (2001). La Revolución de Cádiz de Enero de 1820 y sus repercusiones en Italia, en los Reinos de Nápoles y de Cerdeña (1820–1821). In A. Gil Novales (Ed.), *La revolución liberal* (pp. 251–256). Madrid: Ediciones del Orto.
Carnoy, M. (1974). *Education as cultural imperialism*. New York: David McKay.
Carnoy, M. (1999). *Globalization and educational reform: What planners need to know*. Paris: UNESCO.
Cartaya Cotta, P. (2005). La Sociedad Económica de Amigos del País in: Revista Vitral, No. 69. *Revista Vitral*. Retrieved April 8, 2006, from www.vitral.org/vitral/vitral69/nhist.htm
La Cartera Cubana. (1839). Apuntes para la historia de la Isla de Cuba. Educación primaria. De los métodos que se observan en las escuelas de la Habana, las de los pueblos de su jurisdiccion y el resto de las isla, *2*(1), pp. 146–154.
Caruso, M. (2004). Locating educational authority: Teaching monitors, educational meanings, and the import of pedagogical models: Spain and the German states in the 19th century. In D. Phillips & K. Ochs (Eds.), *Educational policy borrowing: Historical perspectives* (pp. 59–87). Oxford, UK: Symposium Books.
Caruso, M. (2007a). *Der unterrichtsorganisatorische Übergang zur modernen Elementarschule. die Rezeption des wechselseitigen Unterrichts aus England im Vergleich (Deutsche Staaten—Spanien, ca. 1808–1868)*. Berlin: Humboldt-Universität zu Berlin.
Caruso, M. (2007b). Disruptive dynamics: The spatial dimensions of the Spanish networks in the spread of monitorial schooling (1815–1825). *Paedagogica Historica, XLIII*(2), 271–282.
Castells, M. (2000). *The power of identity*. London: Blackwell.

Chabbott, C. (2003). *Constructing education for development: International organizations and Education for All.* New York: Routledge Falmer.
Chambers, J. (2005). How technology can lift the world. *Global Agenda Magazine.* Retrieved February 1, 2006 from http://newsroom.cisco.com/dlls/2004/ts_012104.html
Chandler, D. S. (1976). Jacobo de Villaurrutia and the Audiencia of Guatemala, 1794–1804. *The Americas, 32*(3), 402–417.
Chatterjee, P. (1997). *A possible India.* Delhi, India: Oxford University Press.
Chen, T. H. (1965). Government encouragement and control of international education in communist China. In S. Fraser (Ed.), *Governmental policy and international education* (pp. 111–133). New York: John Wiley and Sons, Inc.
Cheru, F. (2002). *African renaissance: Roadmaps to the challenges of globalization.* London: Zed Books.
Cheung, T. M. (1989, February 16). Frayed welcome mat. *Far Eastern Economic Review, 32.*
Chiejine, I. (2005, December 30). *Taking community schools to children in rural Sierra Leone.* Retrieved March 10, 2007, from http://www.unicef.org/infobycountry/sierraleone_30628.html
Chisholm, L. (2005). The politics of curriculum review and revision in South Africa in regional context. *Compare, 35*(1), 35–100.
Chisholm, L., & Leyendecker, R. (2008). Curriculum reform in post-1990s sub-Saharan Africa. *International Journal of Educational Development, 28,* 195–205.
Chowdhury, A.M.R., Alam, M. A., & Ahmed, J. (2006). Development knowledge and experience—from Bangladesh to Afghanistan and beyond. *Bulletin of the World Health Organization, 84*(8), 677–681.
Cisco Learning Institute. (2004). *Case study: Jordan education initiative.* Retrieved May 4, 2007, from www.ciscolearning.org
Cisco Systems. (2004). *Cisco networking academy program data sheet.* Retrieved September 26, 2004, from http://cisco.netacad.net/public/academy/DS_CNAP.pdf
Cisco Systems. (2006). *Success story: Women take up the challenge to accelerate Jordan's economy.* Retrieved April 30, 2007, from www.cisco.com/edu/academy
Cisco Systems. (2007a). *Jordan education initiative.* Retrieved May 4, 2007, from http://www.cisco.com/web/about
Cisco Systems. (2007b). *UAE tops the network readiness index in the Mena region.* Retrieved May 4, 2007, from http://www.cisoc/com/web/ME/about/news/2007/070331
Colvin, R. (2005). The new philanthropists. *Education Next, 5*(4), 34–41.
Commission for Africa [CFA] Secretariat. (2005). *Summary of main points emerging from consultation.* Retrieved July 1, 2006, from http://www.commissionforafrica.org/french/consultation/consultation-pdfs/review_of_consultation.pdf
Computer Industry Almanac, Inc. (2005). *PCs in-use surpassed 820m in 2004, PCs in-use will top 1b in 2007.* Retrieved April 5, 2005, from http://www.c-i-a.com/pr0305.htm
Cornwell, R. (1998). The African renaissance: The art of the state. *Indicator South Africa, Winter,* 9–14.
Corts Giner, M. I., & Calderón España, M. C. (1995/96). El método de enseñanza

mutua. Su difusión en la América colonial española. *Historia de la educación, XIV-XV*, 279–300.

Costa Vaz, A. (2004). *Brazilian foreign policy under Lula: Change or continuity?* Friedrich Ebert Stiftung Brazil Briefing Papers: Dialogue on Globalization. Berlin: Friedrich Ebert Stiftung.

Crispim, D. (2005, May 3). Presidente diz que lideranca regional e obrigacao do Brasil. *O Estado de São Paulo Nacional*, 1.

Crónica Científica y Literaria (November 1818). Educacion, *172*, 7.

Crónica Científica y Literaria. (February 1819). Enseñanza mutua. *Real sociedad económica de Cádiz, 199*, 5–6.

Crossley, M., & Watson, K. (2003). *Comparative and international research in education: Globalization, context and difference.* London: Routledge Falmer.

Cuesta Mendoza, A. (1946). *Historia de la educación en el Puerto Rico Colonial (1508–1821).* México: M. L. Sanchez.

Cummings, W. K., Dall, F., Fiske, E., & Al-Husainy, S. M. (1993). *BRAC appraisal: Feasibility of first [NFPE] expansion phase.* Dhaka, Bangladesh: UNICEF–Dhaka.

Cussó, R. (2006). Restructuring UNESCO's statistical services—The "sad story" of UNESCO's education statistics: 4 years later. *International Journal of Educational Development, 26*, 532–544.

Cussó, R., & D'Amico, S. (2005). From development comparatism to globalization comparativism: Towards more normative international education statistics. *Comparative Education, 41*(2), 199–216.

Cutler, C., Haufler, V., & Porter, T. (1999). The contours and significance of private authority in international affairs. In C. Cutler, V. Haufler, & T. Porter (Eds.), *Private authority and international affairs* (pp. 333–376). Albany: State University of New York.

Daniels, C. (Ed.). (2002). *Negotiated empires: Centers and peripheries in the Americas, 1500–1820.* New York: Routledge.

David, J. P. (1967). *L'établissement de l'enseignement primaire au XIXe siècle dans le département de Main-et-Loire (1816–1879).* Angers, France: L'imprimerie de l'Anjou.

Debt AIDS Trade Africa [DATA]. (2006). The DATA Report 2006: Keep the G8 Promise to Africa. Retrieved October 10, 2007, from http://www.thedatareport.org/pdf/DATAreport.pdf

de la Sagra, R. (1826). *Aperçu statistique de l'Ile de Cuba, précédé de quelques lettres sur La Havane.* Paris: Chez P. Dufart.

del Marmol, M. M. (1821). *Manifiesto que demuestra los sucesos respectivos a la escuela mutua del Carmen.* Sevilla, Spain: Imprenta de Anastasio López.

del Monte, D. (1838). Educacion primaria en la Isla de Cuba. *El plantel, 1*(2), 35–40.

Demir, C., Balci, A., & Akkok, F. (2000). The role of Turkish schools in the educational system and social transformation of Central Asian countries: The case of Turkmenistan and Kyrgyzstan. *Central Asian Survey, 19*(1), 141–155.

DeStefano, J. (2006). *Meeting EFA: Mali community schools* (EQUIP2 Case Study). Washington, DC: USAID.

Devraj, R. (2007). *India, Brazil, South Africa ready to lead the global south.* Inter Press Service. March 5, 2006. Retrieved May 1, 2007, from www.ipsnews.net

Dewey, J. (1929). *Impressions of Soviet Russia and the revolutionary world: Mexico-China-Turkey.* New York: New Republic.
de Young, A. (2006). *The erosion of Vospitanye (social upbringing) in post-Soviet Kyrgyzstan.* Lexington: Department of Educational Policy Studies and Evaluation, University of Kentucky.
Diabre, Z.(2002). *Statement at the Johannesburg world summit on sustainable development, side event on "Global transmission of the 'East Asian Development Approach.'"* 1 September 2002. Japan Pavilion. Retrieved October 10, 2007, from http://www.mofa.go/jp/policy/environment/wssd/2002/event1-6.html
Dikötter, F. (1992). *The discourse of race in modern China.* London: Hurst & Company.
Dikötter, F. (1994, June). Racial identities in China: Context and meaning. *The China Quarterly, 138,* 404– 410.
Dolowitz, D., & Marsh, D. (1996). Who learns what from whom: A review of the policy transfer literature. *Political Studies, 44*(2), 343–358.
Domínguez Ortiz, A. (1986). *Sociedad y estado en el siglo XVIII español.* Barcelona, Spain: Ariel.
Dunn, H. (1828). *Guatemala or, the United Provinces of Central America, in 1827-8 being sketches and memorandums made during a twelve months residence in that republic.* New York: C. & G. Carvill.
Easterly, W. (2002). The cartel of good intentions. *Foreign Policy, July/August,* 40– 49.
Ebrahim, H. (2006, May 19–21). *Bollywood in South Africa.* Unpublished paper delivered at the South Africa/India: Re-imagining the Disciplines Colloquium, Johannesburg, South Africa.
Economic & Social Research Council [ESRC]. (2006). *Africa after 2005: From promises to policy.* Retrieved July 1, 2007, from http://www.esrc.ac.uk/ESRCInfoCentre/Images/africa_after_2005_tcm6–13210.pdf
The Economist. (2007, January 27). Dr. diplomat. *The Economist, 382*(8513), 35.
Education for All–Fast Track Initiative (EFA–FTI) Secretariat. (2004). *Education for All–Fast Track Initiative. Accelerating progress towards quality universal primary education. Framework.* Washington, DC: EFA–FTI Secretariat.
Education for All–Fast Track Initiative (EFA–FTI) Secretariat. (2007). *Quality education for all children: Meeting the challenge. Annual report 2007.* Washington, DC: EFA–FTI Secretariat.
Edwards, M. (1999). *Future positive: International cooperation in the 21st century.* London: Earthscan Publications.
Ertl, H. (Ed.). (2006). *Cross-national attraction in education. Accounts from England and Germany.* Oxford, UK: Symposium Books.
Escobar, A. (1995). *Encountering development: The making and unmaking of the Third World.* Princeton, NJ: Princeton University Press.
Espigado Tocino, G. (1996). *Aprender a leer y a escribir en el Cádiz del ochocientos.* Cádiz, Spain: Universidad de Cádiz.
Eun-Myo Park, K. (2001). Networking with Cisco systems. *United Nations Chronicle,* 4 [online edition]. Retrieved May 10, 2007, from http://www.un.org/Pubs/chronicle/2001/issue4/0104p61.html

European Investment Bank. (2007). *EU enlargement: Turkey.* Retrieved July 1, 2008, from http://www.eib.org/projects/regions/enlargement/turkey
Evans, D. (1994). *Education policy formation in Africa: A comparative study of five countries: Technical paper.* Washington, DC: United States Agency for International Development.
Evans, P. (1995). *Embedded autonomy: States and industrial transformation.* Princeton, NJ: Princeton University Press.
Exercicios de Enseñanza Mutua, practicados el día 3 de octubre de 1818 en la Escuela Gratuita establecida por la Real Sociedad de Amigos del País de la Ciudad de Cádiz y su Provincia. (1818). Cádiz, Spain: Imprenta de Carreño.
Feenberg, A. (n.d.). *Critical Theory of Technology.* Retrieved October 12, 2007, from http://www.rohan.sdsu.edu/faculty/feenberg/CRITSAM2.HTM
Fernández Bulete, V. (2001). Los amigos del país sevillanos ante la enseñanza mutua. In M. C. Calderón España (Ed.), *Las Reales Sociedades Económicas de Amigos del País y el espíritu ilustrado* (pp. 310–316). Sevilla, Spain: Universidad de Sevilla.
Ferrer Benimeli, J. A. (1986). *La masonería española en el siglo XVIII.* Madrid: Siglo XXI ed.
Fisher, R. (2003, April 17). Racism in China. *Shanghai Star.* Retrieved December 13, 2003, from http://app1.chinadaily.comcn/star/2003/0417/cu18-1.html
Fontana, J. (2002). *La quiebra de la monarquía absoluta, 1814–1820.* Barcelona, Spain: Crítica.
Food and Agriculture Organization of the United Nations [FAO]. (2007). South–South cooporation. In *The Special Program for Food Security.* Retrieved January 20, 2007, from http://www.fao.org/spfs/south_en.asp
"The Foreign Work" [author not noted]. (1906/1909). A Retrospect. The Foreign Work of the British and Foreign School Society. *The Educational Record, XVII,* 134–145, 217–228, 287–299, 355–368, 474–494, 560–573, 631–645, 698–705.
Forum for African Women Educationalists [FAWE]. (2000). FAWE strategic plan. *FAWE News, March,* 1.
FAWE. (2002). *The ABC of gender responsive education policies.* Nairobi, Kenya: FAWE.
FAWE. (2003). Engendering EFA: Is Africa on track. *FAWE News, 11* (January-June), 1.
Fraser, A. (2003, September). *Poverty reduction strategy papers: Now who calls the shots?* Paper presented at the Review of African Political Economy Annual Conference.
Freedom House (2006). *Nations in Transit: Turkmenistan.* Retrieved October 1, 2007, from http://www.freedomhouse.hu/nitransit/2006/turkmenistan2006.pdf
Freire, P., & Guimarães, S. (2003). *A África ensinando a gente: Angola, Guiné Bissau, São Tomé e Príncipe.* São Paulo, Brazil: Paz e Terra.
G-77. (2000). *Havana Programme of Action. Group of 77 South Summit, Havana, Cuba, 10–14 April.* Retrieved May 1, 2008, from http://www.nam.gov.za/documentation/southact.htm
G-77. (2003a). *Marrakech Declaration on South–South Cooperation.* Retrieved May 1, 2008, from http://www.g77.org/marrakech/Marrakech-Declaration.htm

G-77. (2003b). *Marrakech Framework of Implementation of South–South Cooperation*. Retrieved May 1, 2008, from http://www.g77.org/marrakech/Marrakech-Framework.htm

G-77. (2005). *Second South Summit of the Group of 77, Doha, Qatar, 12–16 June*. Retrieved May 1, 2008, from http://www.g77.org/southsummit2/index.htm

Gaceta de Madrid. (1818, November 7). Cádiz, 24 de Octubre, *135*, 1123–1125.

Gaceta de Madrid. (1819, September 18). Circular del consejo real, *115*, 942–943.

Gaceta de Madrid. (1820, January 4). Baeza 8 de Diciembre, *2*, 12–13.

Galabawa, J.C.J. (2004, August 26–27). *Implications of the World Trade Organization (WTO)'s GATS on higher education delivery in Tanzania*. Presentation from Role of Higher Education in the Development of Tanzania: Prospects and Challenges Higher Education Accreditation Council [HEAC] Workshop, Dar es Salaam, Tanzania.

Galagan, P. (2001). Mission e-possible: The Cisco e-learning story. *Training and Development, 55*(2), 46–56.

García Fernández, M. N. (2005). *Comunidad extranjera y puerto privilegiado: Los británicos en Cádiz en el siglo XVIII*. Cádiz, Spain: Universidad de Cádiz.

Gates Foundation. (2007). *Bill and Melinda Gates Foundation. Annual Report 2006*. Retrieved December 27, 2007, from http://www.gatesfoundation.org/nr/public/media/annualreports/annualreport06

Gillespie, S. (2001). *South–South transfer: A study of Sino–African exchanges*. New York: Routledge.

Gil Novales, A. (1975). *Las sociedades patrióticas (1820–1823). Las libertades de expresión y de reunión en el origen de los partidos políticos*. Madrid: Tecnos.

Gil Novales, A. (1980). *El Trienio Liberal*. Madrid: Siglo XXI.

Gil Novales, A. (1991). *Diccionario biográfico del Trienio Liberal*. Madrid: Ediciones el museo universal.

Global Fund. (2007). *(Product) Red. Investing in our future. The Global Fund to Fight AIDS, Tuberculosis and Malaria*. Retrieved December 27, 2007, from http://www.theglobalfund.org/en/partners/private/red

Goldman, R. (1965). The experience of foreign students in China. In S. Fraser (Ed.), *Governmental policy and international education* (pp. 135–140). New York: John Wiley and Sons, Inc.

Gould, J., Ojanen, J., & McGee, R. (2003). *"Merging in the circle": The politics of Tanzania's poverty reduction strategy*. Helsinki, Finland: Institute of Development Studies, University of Helsinki.

Government of Mongolia (2006). *Master Plan to Develop Education of Mongolia in 2006–2015*. Ulaanbaatar, Mongolia: Ministry of Education, Culture and Science.

Grant, J. A., & Söderbaum, F. (Eds.). (2003). *The new regionalism in Africa*. Aldershot, UK: Ashgate.

Grindle, M., & Thomas, J. (1991). *Public choices and policy change*. Baltimore, MD: Johns Hopkins University Press.

Grossberg, L. (1997). *Bringing it all back home: Essays on cultural studies*. Durham, NC: Duke University Press.

Gül, A. (2006, April 19). *Speech delivered by H. E. Mr. Abdullah Gül, deputy prime minister and minister of foreign affairs at the luncheon for the candidacy of Turkey* to the UN Security Council for the term 2009–2010. Retrieved October 1, 2007, from http://www.un.int/turkey/page17.html

Gülen, F. (1997). *Prizma,* (Vol. 1). Istanbul, Turkey: Zaman.

Gupta, P. (2006, May 19–21). *Mapping Portuguese Decolonisation: From Goa to Maputo and Beyond.* Unpublished paper delivered at the South Africa/India: Re-imagining the Disciplines Colloquium, Johannesburg, South Africa.

Haas, E. B. (1991). *When knowledge is power: Three models of change in International Organizations.* Berkeley: University of California Press.

Haas, P. (1992). Epistemic communities and international policy coordination. *International Organization, 46*(1), 1–35.

The Hague. (2003). *Local solutions to global challenges: Toward effective partnership in basic education. Final report.* The Hague, Netherlands: Netherlands Ministry of Foreign Affairs for the Consultative Group of Evaluation Departments.

Hanley, E. (2002). Thinking and doing things about poverty II: The poverty reduction strategy process in Africa. *Progress in Development Studies, 1*(2), 47–51.

Hayhoe, R. (1986). Penetration or mutuality? China's educational cooperation with Europe, Japan, and North America. *Comparative Education Review, 30*(4), 532–559.

Hayhoe, R. (1989). *China's universities and the open door.* New York: M. E. Sharpe, Inc.

Held, D., McGrew, A., Goldblatt, D., & Perraton, J. (1999). *Global transformations: Politics, economics and culture.* Cambridge, UK: Polity Press.

Hettne, B., & Söderbaum, F. (2000). Theorising the rise of regionness. *New Political Economy, 5*(3), 457–472.

Hevi, E. J. (1963). *An African student in China.* New York: Praeger.

Hevi, E. J. (1967). *The dragons embrace.* New York: Praeger.

Heyneman, S. P. (1999). The sad story of UNESCO's education statistics. *International Journal of Educational Development, 19,* 66–74.

Heyneman, S. P. (2006, November). *Higher education and social cohesion.* Paper presented to the American Society for the Study of Higher Education, Anaheim, CA.

Hofmeyr, I. (2005). *South Africa/India: Connections and Comparisons. A Proposed New Research Thrust.* Proposal presented to the National Research Foundation, Pretoria, South Africa.

Hofmeyr, I. (2006, May 19–21). *Report on a colloquium entitled "South Africa/India" Re-imagining the Disciplines.* Report presented to the University of the Witwatersrand, Johannesburg, South Africa.

Hofstede, G. (2001). *Culture's consequences: Comparing values, behaviors, institutions and organizations across nations.* Thousand Oaks, CA: Sage.

Hogan, D. (1989). The market revolution and disciplinary power: Joseph Lancaster and the psychology of the early classroom system. *History of Education Quarterly, 29*(3), 381–417.

Hoogvelt, A. (1997). *Globalization and the post-colonial world: The new political economy of development.* Baltimore, MD: Johns Hopkins University Press.

Hopman, S. (1990). The monitorial movement and the rise of curriculum administration: A comparative view. In H. Haft & S. Hopman (Eds.), *Case studies in curriculum administration history* (pp. 13–30). London: The Falmer Press.

Huerta Martínez, A. (1992). *La enseñanza primaria en Cuba en el siglo XIX (1812–1868)*. Sevilla, Spain: Expo.

Hutchison, A. (1975). *China's African revolution*. [Place of publication not specified], UK: Hutchinson & Co.

Intel Corporation. (2004). *Intel computer clubhouse: Queen Rania inaugurates first Intel computer clubhouse in Jordan*. Retrieved May 10, 2007, from www.intel.com/education/teach

Intel Corporation. (2006). *Intel expands teacher training to support Egypt initiative*. Retrieved May 10, 2007, from http://www.intel.com/education/worldahead/Headline2.htm

Intel Corporation. (2007). *The world ahead starts here: Intel teach program*. Retrieved May 10, 2007, from www.intel.com/education

International Centre for Trade and Sustainable Development [ICTSD]. (2004, March 10). India, Brazil, South Africa strengthen South-South cooperation. *Bridges Weekly Trade News Digest, 8*(9). Retrieved October 14, 2006, from http://www.ictsd.org/weekly/04-03-10/story3.htm

International Development Association & International Monetary Fund. (2002). *Review of the Poverty Reduction Strategy Paper (PRSP) approach: Early experience with interim PRSPs and full PRSPs*. Retrieved June, 6, 2003, from www.worldbank.org/poverty/strategies/review/earlyexp.pdf

Ishikawa, S. (2006). *Kokusai kaihatsu seisaku kenkyu*. Tokyo: Toyo-Keizai Shinpo-Sha.

Jansen, Jonathan D. (2005). Targeting education: The politics of performance and the prospects of "Education for All." *International Journal of Educational Development, 25*, 368–380.

Japan International Cooperation Agency [JICA]. (n.d.). *JICA's support for South–South cooperation*. Retrieved October 17, 2007, from http://www.jica.go.jp/infosite/issues/ssc/pdf/sout_eng_01.pdf

JICA (2005, October 30). *JOCV and US Peace Corps sign memorandum of understanding*. Retrieved September 22, 2007, from http.//www.jica.go.jp/english/resources/announce/2005/oct.html

JICA (2006, March). *Final report of thematic evaluation on south-south cooperation*. Third-party evaluation by Kaihatsu Management Consulting, Inc. Retrieved September 22, 2007, from http://www.jica.go.jp/english/evaluation/program/thematic/pdf/2006_06_04.pdf

Jervis, R. (1976). *Perception and misperception in international politics*. Princeton, NJ: Princeton University Press.

Jiménez Gámez, R. (1991). *La Sociedad Económica gaditana y la educación en el siglo XIX*. Jerez de la Frontera, Spain: Caja de Ahorros de Jerez.

Jiménez Gámez, R. (1992). El método de enseñanza mutua en la historia del currículum en España. *Bordón, 44*(2), 153–159.

Jomo, K. S., & Fine, B. (Eds.). (2006). *The new development economics: After the Washington consensus*. London and New York: Zed Books.

Jones, P. W. (2004). Taking the credit: Financing and policy linkages in the education portfolio of the World Bank. In G. Steiner-Khamsi (Ed.), *The global politics of borrowing and lending,* (pp. 188–200). New York: Teachers College Press.

Jones, P. W., with D. Coleman. (2005). *The United Nations and education. Multilateralism, development and globalization.* London and New York: Routledge Falmer.

Jones Shafer, R. (1958). *The economic societies in the Spanish world (1763–1821).* Syracuse, NY: Syracuse University Press.

Junta general de la sociedad económica de amantes del país de Puerto-Rico, celebrada en 2 de enero de 1821. (1821). Puerto Rico: Imprenta Nacional.

Junta general de la sociedad económica de amigos del país de Puerto-Rico. (1825). Puerto Rico: En la oficina del Gobierno á cargo de D. Valeriano de Sanmillan.

Junta general de la sociedad económica de amigos del pais de Puerto-Rico, celebrada en 2 de enero de 1824. (1824). Puerto Rico: En la oficina del Gobierno.

Junta Protectora y Directora de la Enseñanza Mutua. (1820). *Método de enseñanza mutua, según los sistemas combinados del Dr. Bell y de Mr. Lancaster: para uso de las escuelas elementales o de primeras letras.* Madrid: Imprenta Real.

Kaestle, C. F. (1973). *Joseph Lancaster and the monitorial school movement: A documentary history.* New York: Teachers College Press.

Kamen, H. (1985). *Inquisition and society in Spain in the sixteenth and seventeenth centuries.* Bloomington: Indiana University Press.

Kamibeppu, T. (2002). *History of Japanese Policies in Education Aid to Developing Countries, 1950s–1990s.* New York: Routledge.

Kanbur, R., & Vines, D. (2000). The World Bank and poverty reduction: Past, present and future. In C.L. Gilbert & D. Vines (Eds.), *The World Bank: Structure and problems* (pp. 87–107). Cambridge: Cambridge University Press.

KATEV. (2006). *KTL [Kazakh-Turkish Lyceums].* Retrieved October 1, 2007, from http://www.KATEV.org/official/Rus/rus1.htm

Khatib, S., & Cox, A. (2005, November). *Transforming education with technology: The experience of Jordan.* Paper presented at the World Summit for Information Society, Tunis, Tunisia.

Khor, M. (2002). *Rethinking globalisation: Critical issues and policy choices.* London: Zed Books.

King, K. (2002). Banking on knowledge: The new knowledge projects of the World Bank. *Compare, 32(3),* 312–326.

King, K. (2005). Knowledge-based aid: A new way of networking or a new North–South Divide? In D. Stone & S. Maxwell (Eds.), *Global knowledge networks and international development. Bridges across boundaries* (pp. 72–88). London and New York: Routledge.

Kitaev, I. (1999). *Private education in sub-Saharan Africa: A re-examination of theories and concepts related to its development and finance.* Paris: UNESCO.

Knight, J. B., & Sabot, R. H. (1990). *Education, productivity, and inequality: The east African natural experiment.* Oxford, UK: Oxford University Press for the World Bank.

Kuroda, K., & Yokozeki, Y. (2005). *Kokusai ky iku kaihatsu-ron: Riron to jissen* (International Educational Development: Theory and Practice). Tokyo: Y hikaku.

Labor Resource and Research Institute [LaRRI]. (2003). *Nepad: A new partnership between rider and horse?* Retrieved July 1, 2007, from http://www.sarpn.org.za/documents/d0000406/index.php

Lana, X., & Evans, M. (2004). Policy transfer between developing countries: The transfer of the Bolsa Escola Program to Ecuador. In M. Evans (Ed.), *Policy transfer in global perspective* (pp. 190–210). Burlington, UK: Ashgate.

Lancaster, J. (1803). *Improvements in education, as it respects the industrious classes of the community: Containing, a short account of its present state, hints towards its improvement, and a detail of some practical experiments conducive to that end* (1st ed.). London: Darton and Harvey, J. Mathews, W. Hatchard.

Larkin, B. D. (1971). *China and Africa 1949–1970: The foreign policy of the People's Republic of China.* Los Angeles, CA: University of California Press.

Lassibille, G., Tan, J., & Sumra, S. (1998). Expansion of private secondary education: Experiences and prospects for Tanzania. *Working Paper Series on Impact Evaluation of Education Reforms* (Vol. 12). Washington, DC: World Bank.

Laugharn, P. A. (2001). *Negotiating "Education for Many": Enrollment, dropout, and persistence in the community schools of Kolondièba, Mali.* Unpublished doctoral dissertation, University of London, London.

Leach, F., Fiscian, V., Kadzamira, E., Lemani, E., & Machakanja, P. (2003). An investigative study of the abuse of girls in African schools. *Education Research Report No. 54.* London: DfID.

Lightfoot, C. (2002). *Havana: A cultural and literary companion.* Oxford, UK: Signal Books.

Lindt, A., Aksornkool, N., & Heisohn, N. (2006). *Cuba's literacy methodology: Yo si puedo.* Unpublished manuscript. Paris: UNESCO.

Lira González, A. (1970). Las escuelas de primeras letras en la municipalidad de Guatemala hacia 1824 (Un intento para orgnizar la educación elemental). *Latinoamérica: Anuario de estudios latinoamericanos, 3,* 117–140.

Little, A., Hoppers, W., & Gardner, R. (Eds.). (1994). *Beyond Jomtien: Implementing primary education for all.* London: MacMillan.

Lluch, E. (1973). *El pensament económic a Catalunya, 1760–1840.* Barcelona, Spain: Edicions 62.

Lovell, C. (1992). *Breaking the cycle of poverty: The BRAC strategy.* Hartford, CT: Kumarian.

Lovell, C. H., & Fatema, K. (1989). *The BRAC non-formal primary education programme in Bangladesh* (Assignment Children). New York: UNICEF.

Lynch, J. (1994). *Latin American revolutions, 1808–1826: Old and new world origins.* Norman: University of Oklahoma Press.

Madeley, J. (2003, September 18). Beyond WTO, will South–South cooperation bite? *Panos Features,* 2048. Retrieved January 27, 2007, from http://www.panos.org.uk/global/featuredetails.asp?featureid=1139&ID=1023

Mamedov, N. (2005). *Ethnocultural practices in post-Soviet Kyrgyzstan and Turkmenistan: A comparative perspective.* Unpublished master's thesis, Central European University, Budapest, Hungary.

Manning, R. (2006). *Will "emerging donors" change the face of international cooperation?* Speech by Richard Manning, OECD DAC Chair. Retrieved September 22, 2007, from http://www.oecd.org/dataoecd/35/38/36417541.pdf

Manual of the system of primary education, pursued in the model schools of the British and Foreign School Society. (1934). London: Longman and Co. Retrieved January 20, 2008, from http://dickens.stanford.edu/images/Hard%20Issue%201/School-at-borough-Road.gif

Manuale del sistema di Bell e Lancaster. (1819). Naples, Italy: Dalla Tipografia di Luigi Nobile.

Marinova, B., & Novak, A. (2006). Turkey as an emerging donor in Central Asia, the Middle East and the Balkans. [Online]. Retrieved October 10, 2007, from http://www.trialog.or.at/docs/tk_emerging_donor.doc

Maxwell, K. R. (1999). Hegemonies old and new: The Ibero-Atlantic in the long eighteenth century. In J. Adelman (Ed.), *Colonial legacies: The problem of persistence in Latin American history* (pp. 69–90). New York: Routledge.

Mayer, M. (1998). Towards an African renaissance: The role of trade integration in the southern African development community. *Indicator South Africa, Winter*, 27–31.

Mazrui, A. (1975). The African university as a multinational corporation: Problems of penetration and dependency. *Harvard Educational Review, 45*(2), 191–210.

Mazrui, A. A. (1999, November 23). The African renaissance: A triple legacy of skills, values and gender. In *The African renaissance: From vision to reality conference*. London: The Barbican Centre.

McGee, R., with Levene, J., & Hughes, A. (2002). *Assessing participation in poverty reduction strategy papers: A desk-based synthesis of experience in Sub-Saharan Africa.* Retrieved September 9, 2003, from server.ntd.co.uk/ids/bookshop/details.asp?id=677

McKinsey Corporation. (2005). *Building effective public–private partnerships: Lessons learnt from the Jordan education initiative.* London: McKinsey & Company.

Mehnert, K. (1980). *Kolonialisierung und Entkolonialisierung des Lernens: Die Anwendung der Erziehungskonzeption Paulo Freires in Guinea Bissau.* Frankfurt/Main, Germany: Haag und Herchen Verlag.

Meneses, M. P. (2004). Agentes do conhecimento? A consultoria e a produção do conhecimento em Moçambique. In B. S. Santos (Ed.), *Conhecimento prudente para uma vida decente. "Um discurso sobre as ciências" revisitado* (pp. 721–755). São Paulo: Cortez.

Mercer, M., Gosparini, P., Melchiori, P., Orivel, F., Sirtori, M., & Steinback, T. (2002). *Evaluation of EC support to the education sector in ACP countries. Synthesis report.* Brussels, Belgium: Development Researchers' Network.

Mesthrie, U. (2006, May 19–21). The Place of India in South African History. Unpublished paper delivered at the South Africa/India: Re-imagining the Disciplines Colloquium, Johannesburg, South Africa.

Michel, T. (2003). *Fethullah Gülen as educator.* Retrieved October 1, 2007, from http://en.fgulen.com/content/view/1222/14/

Microsoft Corporation. (2003). *Jordan, Microsoft sign deal to enhance its strategies.* Retrieved January 7, 2007, from http://www.jordanembassyus.org/10052003002.htm

Microsoft Corporation. (2005a). *Microsoft's government leaders forum: Arabia* (Conference Report). Dubai, United Arab Emirates: Microsoft Corporation.

Microsoft Corporation. (2005b, February 22). *School technology innovation centre opens in Jordan.* Retrieved May 10, 2007, from http://www.microsoft.com/emea/presscentre/pressreleases/STICTopStory.mspx

Microsoft Corporation. (2007). *School innovation and technology centre programme overview.* Amman, Jordan: Microsoft, Jordan.

Millennium Villages (2007). *About the Villages.* Retrieved December 28, 2007, from http://www.millenniumvillages.org

Ministerio das Relacoes Exteriores, Brazil. (2005, May 26). *Memorando sobre cooperação bilateral nos campos social e educacional entre a República Federativa do Brasil e o Japão.* Retrieved May 5, 2007, from www.japaocentenario.mre.gov.br

Ministry of Education of the Kyrgyz Republic. (2006). *Monitoring learning achievement (4th grade). Nationwide study of the quality of education in primary schools.* Bishkek, Kyrgyz Republic: Ministry of Education.

Ministry of Foreign Affairs, Japan [MOFA]. (2002). *BEGIN: Basic Education for Growth Initiative* (Provisional Translation). Retrieved October 10, 2007, from http://www.mofa.go.jp/region/africa/education3.html

Ministry of Foreign Affairs, Japan [MOFA]. (2005, May 26). *Joint press statement on technical cooperation between Japan and the Federative Republic of Brazil.* Retrieved December 3, 2006, from http://www.mofa.go.jp/region/latin/brazil/pv0505/press-2.html

MOFA. (2005). *Reform of the UN Security Council "Why Japan should become a permanent member?"* (Pamphlet) Retrieved October 10, 2007, from http://www.mofa.go.jp/policy/un/reform/index.html

MOFA. (2006, September 8). *Critical Comments on the Ranking of Developed Countries Made by CGD, a US non-governmental think tank.* Retrieved October 10, 2007, from http://www.mofa.go.jp/policy/oda/other/index0609.html

MOFA. (n.d.[a]). *Japan's official development assistance: Accomplishment and progress of 50 years.* Retrieved October 10, 2007, from http://www.mofa.go.jp/policy/oda/cooperation/anniv50/pamphlet/index.html

MOFA. (n.d.[b]). *BEGIN. Basic Education for Growth Initiative.* Retrieved May 1, 2008, from http://www.mofa.go.jp/region/africa/measure/index.html

Ministry of Public Education of the Republic of Tajikistan. (2002). *Monitoring Learning Achievement in Elementary Schools of Tajikistan and the Problem of School Non-attendance.* Dushanbe, Tajikistan: Ministry of Public Education.

Mittelman, J. (2000). *The globalization syndrome.* Princeton, NJ: Princeton University Press.

Mizuno, K. (2002). *Statement at the mid-term review meeting of UNCTAD.* Retrieved October 10, 2007, from http://www.mofa.go.jp/mofaj/press/enzetsu/14/emi_0403e.html

Morais, M. G. (2005). *South–South cooperation, policy transfer and best-practice reasoning: The transfer of the Solidarity in Literacy Program from Brazil to Mozambique.* ISS Working Paper Series, n. 406. The Hague, Netherlands: Institute of Social Studies.

Moreno Fraginals, M. (2002). *Cuba/España, España/Cuba: Historia común*. Barcelona, Spain: Crítica.

Morrow, R. A., & Torres, C. A. (2003). The state, social movements and educational reform. In R. F. Arnove & C. A. Torres (Eds.), *Comparative education: The dialectic of the global and the local* (pp. 92–114). Lanham, MD: Rowman and Littlefield Publishers.

Mosha, H. J., & Dachi, H. A. (2004). Decentralization of education delivery and provision as a strategy for poverty alleviation in Tanzania. In J. Galabawa & A. Narman (Eds.), *Education, poverty and inequality* (pp. 169–197). Dar es Salaam, Tanzania: KAD Associates.

Muskin, J. A. (1999). Including local priorities to assess school quality: The case of Save the Children community schools in Mali. *Comparative Education Review, 43*(1), 36–43.

Nagao, M. (2004). Could Japan be a good math & science teacher for Africa? *Journal of International Cooperation in Education, 7*(1), 53–70.

Naidoo, V., & Schutte, C. (1999). Virtual institutions on the African continent. In G. Farrel (Ed.), *The development of virtual education: A global perspective* (pp. 89–124). Vancouver: The Commonwealth of Learning.

Naik, C. (1980). An action-research project on universal primary education: Maharashtra State, India. *Assignment Children*, 51–52.

Nalle, S. T. (1989). Literacy and culture in early modern Castile. *Past & Present, 125*, 65–96.

Nath, S. (2002). The transition from non-formal to formal education: The case of BRAC, Bangladesh. *International Review of Education, 48*(6), 517–524.

Naudet, D. (1999). Adapting agency solutions to country "problems": The lessons of twenty years of aid to the Sahel region. In Association for the Development of Education in Africa (Ed.), *Partnerships for Capacity Building and Quality Improvements in Education* (pp. 37–42). Paris: Association for the Development of Education in Africa.

New Partnership for Africa's Development [NEPAD]. (2001a). *The new partnership for Africa's development*. Retrieved July 1, 2007, from http://www.avmedia.at/nepad/indexgb.html

NEPAD. (2001b). *Reversing the brain drain*. Retrieved July 1, 2007, from http://www.nepad.org/2005/files/health.php

NEPAD. (2001c). *Bridging the education gap*. Retrieved July 1, 2007, from http://www.nepad.org/2005/files/health.php

NEPAD. (2001d). *Skills development*. Retrieved July 1, 2007, from http://www.nepad.org/2005/files/health.php

NEPAD. (2001e). *Integrating higher education*. Retrieved July 1, 2007, from http://www.nepad.org/2005/files/health.php

Ntuli, P. (1998). Who's afraid of the African renaissance? *Indicator South Africa*, Winter, 15–18.

Nuevo método para aprender el inglés, fundado en la naturaleza de este idioma y en las reglas de su gramática: y combinado con los principios del sistema de enseñanza mutua, facilitando á los niños desde la edad más tierna, y muy útil para todos. (1834). Cádiz, Spain: Imprenta de D. Domingo Feros.

Nyerere, J. (1980). Unity for a new order. In K. Haq (Ed.), *Dialogue for a new order* (pp. 3–10). New York: Pergamon Press.
Open Society Institute. (2002). *Education development in Kyrgyzstan, Tajikistan, and Uzbekistan: Challenges and ways forward.* Budapest, Hungary: Education Support Program, Open Society Institute. Retrieved October 1, 2007, from http://www.osi-edu.net/esp/events/materials/final.doc
Organization for Economic Co-Operation and Development [OECD] (2007). *2007 Development Co-Operation Report.* Paris: OECD, DAC.
Pérez, J. (2001). L'idéologie de l'état. In C. Hermann (Ed.), *Le premier âge de l'état en Espagne (1450–1700)* (pp. 191–216). Paris: CNRS.
Perraton, H., & Creed, C. (2000). *Applying new technologies and cost effective delivery systems in basic education.* Cambridge, UK: International Research Foundation for Open Learning.
Phillips, D. (2004). Toward a theory of policy attraction in education. In G. Steiner-Khamsi (Ed.), *The global politics of educational borrowing and lending* (pp. 54–67). New York: Teachers College Press.
Pinto, R. (2006, May 19–21). Race and imperial loss: Accounts of East Africa in Goa. Unpublished paper delivered at the South Africa/India: Re-imagining the Disciplines Colloquium, Johannesburg, South Africa.
Plan y reglamento para las escuelas gratuitas de enseñanza mutua de esta ciudad, Pueblo-Nuevo y Ceiba-Mocha. (1835). Matanzas, Spain: Imprenta de la Real Marina.
Prahalad, C. K. (2005). *The fortune at the bottom of the pyramid: Eradicating poverty through profits.* Upper Saddle River, NJ: Wharton School Publishing.
Previti, L. F. (1985). Educazione popolare, scuole di mutuo insegnamento e asili infantili di carità a Pisa. In *Una città tra provincia e mutamento. Società, cultura e instituzioni a Pisa nell'età dellaa Restaurazione* (pp. 153–198). Pisa, Italy: Archivio di Stato.
Psacharopoulos, G. (1990). *Why educational policies can fail: An overview of selected African experiences: World Bank discussion papers.* Washington, DC: World Bank.
Rahman Rahman Huq. (1992). *Cost comparison of BRAC NFP and government primary schools* (Final No. 1). Dhaka, Bangladesh: Academy for Educational Development.
Randel, J., German, T., & Ewing, E. (2000). *The reality of aid 2000: An independent review of poverty reduction and development assistance.* London: Earthscan Publications.
Rappleye, J. (2006). Theorizing educational transfer: Toward a conceptual map of the context of cross-national attraction. *Research in Comparative and International Education, 1*(3), 223–240.
Real Sociedad Económica de Amigos del Pais de la Habana. (1818). *Memorias de la Real Sociedad Económica de la Habana: Coleccion primera que comprehende doce números. Correspondientes a los doce meses del año 1817.* Havana, Cuba: Oficina del Gobierno y de la Real Sociedad Patriótica.
Republic of South Africa, Department of Foreign Affairs. (2005). *Cape Town Ministerial Communiqué, India–Brazil–South Africa (IBSA) Dialogue Forum.* Retrieved February 8, 2007, from http://www.dfa.gov.za/docs/2005/ibsa0311.htm

Revista Bimestre Cubana [author not noted]. (1832). Programa de los premios que ofrece la Real Sociedad Patriótica para el año de 1832, *Revista Bimestre Cubana, 2*(5), 268–269.

La Revue Américaine [author not noted]. (1826). Guatemala, *La Revue Américaine, 1*(3), 353–365.

Ringrose, D. (1996). *Spain, Europe and the Spanish miracle, 1700–1900.* Cambridge, UK: Cambridge University Press.

Ritzer, G. (1992). *Sociological theory.* New York: McGraw-Hill.

Robertson, S. (2006, March 7–11). Regionalism, "Europe/Asia" and higher education. Presentation from *Association of American Geographers [AAG] Annual Conference.* Chicago, IL: Palmer House Hilton.

Robertson, S. (2008). "Producing" Knowledge Economies: The World Bank, the KAM, Education and Development. Forthcoming in M. Simons, M. Olssen, & M. Peters, (Eds.), *Re-reading education policies: Studying the policy agenda of the 21st century.* Rotterdam, Netherlands: Sense Publishers.

Robertson, S., Novelli, M., Dale, R., Tikly, L., Dachi, H., & Alphonce, N. (2007). *Globalisation education and development: Ideas, actors and dynamics.* London: DfID.

Roldán Vera, E., & Schupp, T. (2005). Bridges over the Atlantic: A network analysis of the introduction of the monitorial system of education in early-independent Spanish America. In J. Schriewer & M. Caruso (Eds.), *Nationalerziehung und Universalmethode: Frühe Formen schulorganisatorischer Globalisierung* (pp. 58–93). Leipzig, Germany: Leipziger Universitätsverlag.

Roldán Vera, E., & Trentín, G. (2006). *Cádiz, London and Buenos Aires in the "Atlantic World." The Introduction of the Monitorial System of Education in South America, Rethinking the Iberian Atlantic.* Berlin: Centre for Comparative Education Research, Humboldt University.

Ruggie, J. G. (1997). *Globalization and embedded liberalism compromise: The end of an era?* Retrieved March 19, 2007, from www.ciaonet.org/wps/ruj01

Rugh, A., & Bossert, H. (1998). *Involving communities: Participation in the elivery of education programs.* Washington, DC: Creative Associates International.

Ruiz Carnal, J. (2002). *Algunas raíces de la escuela pública primaria de Sevilla.* Sevilla, Spain: Nodo.

Sack, R., Cross, M., & Moulton, J. (2004). *Evaluation of Finnish education sector development cooperation.* Helsinki, Finland: Ministry of Foreign Affairs of Finland.

Said, E. (1983). *The world, the text and the critic.* Cambridge, MA: Harvard University Press.

Samoff, J. (1993). The reconstruction of schooling in Africa. *Comparative Education Review, 37*(2), 181–222.

Samoff, J. (Ed.). (1994). *Coping with crisis: Austerity, adjustment and human resources.* London: Cassell.

Samoff, J. (1995). How do you get girls educated in the Sahel, except through conditionality? External agencies and education in Africa. Report from *Annual Meeting of the Comparative and International Education Society,* Boston.

Samoff, J. (1996a). Chaos and certainty in development. *World Development, 24,* 611–633.

Samoff, J. (1996b). Which priorities and strategies for education? *International Journal of Educational Development, 16*(3), 249–271.

Samoff, J. (1999a). Education sector analysis in Africa: Limited national control and even less national ownership. *International Journal of Educational Development, 19*(4–5), 249–272.

Samoff, J. (1999b, September). *When research becomes consulting.* Oxford, UK: Oxford International Conference on Education and Development.

Samoff, J. (2003). Institutionalizing international influence. In R. Arnove & C. Torres (Eds.), *Comparative education: The dialectic of the global and the local* (pp. 52–91). Boulder, CO: Rowman & Littlefield.

Samoff, J. (2004). From funding projects to supporting sectors? Observations on the aid relationship in Burkina Faso. *International Journal of Educational Development, 24*(4), 397–427.

Samoff, J., & Carrol, B. (2004a). *From manpower planning to the knowledge era: World Bank policies on higher education in Africa.* Paris: UNESCO Forum on Higher Education, Research and Knowledge.

Samoff, J., & Carrol, B. (2004b). The promise of partnership and continuities of dependence: External support to higher education in Africa. *African Studies Review, 47*(1), 67–199.

Samoff, J., with Assié-Lumumba, N. T. (1996). *Analyses, agendas, and priorities for education in Africa: A review of externally initiated, commissioned and supported studies of education in Africa, 1990–1994.* Paris: UNESCO, for the ADEA Working Group on Education Sector Analysis.

Sánchez de Madrid, J. (1823). *Juegos músicos o método de enseñanza mútua para aprender la ciencia música en la parte teórica dividida en dos partes.* Cádiz, Spain: Imprenta de la Sincera Unión del Ciudadano Maza.

Sander, O. (1993). Turkey and Turkic world. *Central Asian Survey, 13*(1), 37–44.

Sarker, S. (2005). Knowledge transfer and collaboration in distributed U.S.–Thai teams. *Journal of Computer-Mediated Communication, 10*(4), article 15. Retrieved June 15, 2007, from http://jcmc.indiana.edu/vol10/issue4/sarker.html

Sarraillh, J. (1957). *La España ilustrada de la segunda mitad del siglo XVIII.* Mexico & Madrid: FCE.

Saul, J. (2003). Globalization, imperialism, development: False binaries and radical resolutions. In L. Panitch & C. Leys (Eds.), *Socialist register 2004: The new imperial challenge* (pp. 220–244). London: Merlin Press.

Sautman, B. (1994, June). Anti-black racism in post-Mao China. *The China Quarterly, 38*, 413–437.

Sawamura, N. (2002). Local spirit, global knowledge: A Japanese approach to knowledge development in international cooperation. *Compare, 32*(3), 339–348.

Sayed, Y., & Soudien, C. (2003). (Re)Framing education exclusion and inclusion discourses: Limits and possibilities. *IDS Bulletin, 34*(1), 9–19.

Scholte, J. A. (2006). Globalisation: Crucial choices for Africa in ESRC. In *Africa after 2005: From promises to policy forum and report by the ESRC and Development Studies Association.* London: Church House, Westminster.

Schriewer, J. (1990). The method of comparison and the need for externalization: Methodological criteria and sociological concepts. In J. Schriewer, in cooperation with B. Holmes (Ed.), *Theories and methods in comparative education* (pp. 25–83). Frankfurt/Main, Germany: Lang.

Schriewer, J. (1994). *Welt-System und Interrelations-Gefüge: Die Internationalisierung der Pädagogik als Problem vergleichender Erziehungswissenschaft* (Vol. 34). Berlin: Humboldt-Universität zu Berlin.

Schriewer, J. (2004). Multiple internationalities: The emergence of a world-level ideology and the persistence of idiosyncratic world-views. In C. Charle, J. Schriewer, & P. Wagner (Eds.), *Transnational intellectual networks: Forms of academic knowledge and the search for cultural identities* (pp. 473–533). Frankfurt/Main, Germany: Campus.

Schriewer, J., & Caruso, M. (2005). Globale Diffusionsdynamik und kontextspezifische Aneignung. Konzepte und Ansätze historischer Internationalisierungsforschung. In J. Schriewer & M. Caruso (Eds.), *Nationalerziehung und Universalmethode: Frühe Formen schulorganisatorischer Globalisierung* (pp. 7–30). Leipzig, Germany: Leipziger Universitätsverlag.

Schriewer, J., & Martinez, C. (2004). Constructions of internationality in education. In G. Steiner-Khamsi, (Ed.), *The global politics of educational borrowing and lending*, (pp. 29–53). New York: Teachers College Press.

Scott, M. (1986, June 19). Blacks and red faces: Allegations of racism embarrass the Chinese authorities. *Far Eastern Economic Review, 20*.

Selinger, M. (2004). Cultural and pedagogical implications of a global e-learning programme. *Cambridge Journal of Education, 34*(2), 223–239.

Sichone, O. (2006). *Personal communication with Crain Soudien.* Cape Town, South Africa: University of Capetown.

Silova, I., Johnson, M. S., & Heyneman, S. P. (2007). Education and the crisis of social cohesion in Azerbaijan and Central Asia. *Comparative Education Review, 51*(2), 159–180.

Simmel, G. (1950). On the significance of numbers for social life. In K. Wolff (Ed.), *The sociology of Georg Simmel* (pp. 87–104). Glencoe, IL: Free Press.

Simon, D. (2003). Deteriorating human security in Kenya: Domestic, regional and global dimensions. In J. A. Grant & F. Söderbaum (Eds.), *The new regionalism in Africa* (pp. 67–92). Aldershot, UK: Ashgate.

Skocpol, T. (1993). Wallerstein's world capitalist system: A theoretical and historical critique. In M. A. Seligson & J. T. Passé-Smith (Eds.), *Development and underdevelopment. The political economy of inequality* (pp. 231–238). Boulder, CO: Lynne Rienner Publishers.

Snow, P. (1988). *The star raft: China's encounter with Africa.* Bath, UK: The Bath Press.

Soares de Lima, M., & Hirst, M. (2006). Brazil as an intermediate state and regional power: Action, choice and responsibilities. *International Affairs, 82*(1), 21–40.

Sogge, D. (2002). *Dar y Tomar.* Icaria: Barcelona [Translated in English under the title *Give and take: What's the matter with foreign aid?* London: Zed Books, 2002].

Solberg, A. (2005). *The Gülen schools: A perfect compromise or compromising perfectly?* Retrieved October 1, 2007, from http://kotor-network.info/papers/2005/Gulen.Solberg.pdf

Some, D. K., & Khaemba, B. M. (2004). *Internationalisation of higher education: The African experience and perspective.* Eldoret, Kenya: Moi University Press.

Somoza Guevara, H. H. (1959). Apuntes para la historia del método lancasteriano en Guatemala. *Antropología e historia de Guatemala, V*(2), 33–62.
Sosa Abella, G. (2006). *Representación e independencia 1810–1816*. Bogotá, Colombia: Instituto Colombiano de Antropología e Historia.
Soudien, C. (2005). Inside but below: The puzzle of education in the global order. In. J. Zajda (Ed.), *International handbook on globalisation, education and policy research* (pp. 501–516). Dordrecht, Netherlands: Springer.
South African Permanent Mission. (2003, May 27). *Statement by the South African permanent mission to the 13th High Level Committee on the review of technical co-operation among developing countries*. Speech from Thirteenth High Level Committee on the Review of Technical Co-operation Among Developing Countries, United Nations, New York.
Southern African Development Community [SADC]. (1997). *Protocol on education and training*. Retrieved July 1, 2006, from http://www.sadc.int/
State Student Admission Commission. (2004). *Abiturient, 12*. Baku, Azerbaijan: State Student Admission Commission.
Steiner-Khamsi, G. (2002). Re-framing educational borrowing as a policy strategy. In M. Caruso & H. E. Tenorth (Eds.), *Internationalisierung-Internationalisation* (pp. 57–89). Frankfurt/Main, Germany: Lang.
Steiner-Khamsi, G. (2004a). Globalization in education: Real or imagined? In G. Steiner-Khamsi (Ed.), *The global politics of educational borrowing and lending* (pp. 1–6). New York: Teachers College Press.
Steiner-Khamsi, G. (2004b). Blazing a trail for policy theory and practice. In G. Steiner-Khamsi (Ed.), *The global politics of educational borrowing and lending* (pp. 201–220). New York: Teachers College Press.
Steiner-Khamsi, G. (Ed.). (2004c). *The global politics of educational borrowing and lending*. New York: Teachers College Press.
Steiner-Khamsi, G. (2006). The development turn in comparative education. *European Education: Issues and Studies, 38*(3), 19–47.
Steiner-Khamsi, G. (2008). Creating demand in the age of the global market: International knowledge banks and the production of educational crises. Forthcoming in: *State and market in a globalized world: Transatlantic perspectives*. Heidelberg, Germany: Universitätsverlag Winter.
Steiner-Khamsi, G., & Quist, H. (2000). The politics of educational borrowing: Reopening the case of Achimota in British Ghana. *Comparative Education Review, 44*(3), 272–299.
Steiner-Khamsi, G., & Stolpe, I. (2006). *Educational import: Local encounters with global forces in Mongolia*. New York: Palgrave Macmillan.
Stiglitz, J. E. (2000). Scan globally, reinvent locally: Knowledge infrastructure and the localisation of knowledge. In D. Stone, (Ed.), *Banking on knowledge: The genesis of the Global Development Network* (pp. 24–43). London and New York: Routledge.
Stiglitz, J. E. (2006). *Making globalization work*. New York: W. W. Norton.
Stone, D. (Ed.). (2000). *Banking on knowledge: The genesis of the Global Development Network*. London and New York: Routledge.
Stromquist, N., & Monkman, K. (2000). Defining globalization and assessing its

implications on knowledge and education. In N. Stromquist & K. Monkman (Eds.), *Globalization and education: Integration and contestation across cultures*. Lanham, MD: Rowman and Littlefield.

Subrahmanian, R. (2003). Introduction: Exploring processes of marginalisation and inclusion in education. In *IDS Bulletin, 34*(1), 1–8.

Sullivan, M. J. (1994, June). The 1988–1989 Nanjing anti-African protests: Racial nationalism or national racism? *The China Quarterly, 138*, 438–57.

Swainson, N. (1998). *Promoting girls' education in Africa: The design and implementation of policy interventions*. Education Research Paper No. 25. London: DfID.

Sweetser, A. T. (1999). *Lessons from the BRAC Non-Formal Primary Education Program* (USAID-funded). Washington, DC: Academy for Education Development.

Theroux, P. (1993). Going to see the dragon. *Harper's Magazine, October*, 3–56.

Thompson, G. A. (1829). *Narrative of an official visit to Guatemala from Mexico*. London: John Murray.

Tikly, L. (2003a, May 29). GATS, globalisation and skills for development in low-income countries. In R. Carr-Hill, K. Holmes, P. Rose, & T. Henderson (Eds.), *Education and the general agreement on trade in services: What does the future hold? Report of the Fifteenth Conference of Commonwealth Education Ministers preliminary meeting*. London: Commonwealth Secretariat.

Tikly, L. (2003b). The African renaissance, NEPAD and skills formation: Policy tensions and priorities. *International Journal of Educational Development, 23*(5), 543–564.

Tikly, L. (2004). Education and the new imperialism. *Comparative Education, 40*(2), 173–198.

Torres Santomé, J. (1979). *La educación en la Sociedad Económica de Amigos del País de Santiago (S. XVIII-XIX)*. Salamanca: Ediciones de la Universidad de Salamanca.

Tronchot, R. R. (1972). *L'Enseignement mutuel en France de 1815 à 1833, les luttes politiques et religieuses autour de la question scolaire*. Le Mans, France: Archives de la Sarthe.

Turam, B. (2003). National loyalties and international undertakings: The case of the Gülen community in Kazakhstan. In H. Yavuz & J. Esposito (Eds.), *Turkish Islam and the secular state: The Gülen movement* (pp. 184–207). Syracuse, NY: Syracuse University Press.

ul Haq, M. (1980). Beyond the slogan of South–South cooperation. In K. Haq (Ed.), *Dialogue for a new order* (pp. 139–152). New York: Pergamon Press.

Undur-Ulaan school. (2007). *School Master Plan, 2007–2010*. Undur-Ulaan, Arkhangai, Mongolia: unpublished document.

United Nations [UN]. (2004). *South–South cooperation in support of the New Partnership for Africa's Development: Experiences of Africa–Latin America and the Caribbean*. New York: UN.

UN. (2005). *Understanding knowledge societies*. New York: UN.

UN. (2006). Secretary-General, in message for South-South Cooperation Day, urges international community to support stronger ties among developing countries. SG/SM/10808 OBV/604. Retrieved January 8, 2007, from http://www.un.org/News/Press/docs/2006/sgsm10808.doc.htm

United Nations Children's Fund [UNICEF]—Dhaka. (1992). *Assessment of basic competencies of children in Bangladesh: A status report.* Dhaka, Bangladesh: UNICEF.

UNICEF—Regional Office for Central and Eastern Europe and the Commonwealth of Independent States. (2007). *Education for some more than others? A regional study on education in Central and Eastern Europe and the Commonwealth of Independent States (CEE/CIS).* Geneva, Switzerland: UNICEF Regional Office for CEE/CIS.

United Nations Development Programme [UNDP]. (1999). *UNDP/Japan partnership supporting South–South cooperation: Innovative triangular cooperation towards the Millennium Development Goals (1999–2004).* New York: UNDP.

UNDP. (2004). *Forging a global South: United Nations Day for South–South cooperation.* Retrieved September 18, 2006, from http://tcdc1.undp.org/PDF/Forging%20a%20Global%20South.pdf

UNDP Newsroom. (2006, April 27). *Japan steps up contribution to UNDP operations in Africa.* Retrieved October 17, 2007, from http://content.undp.org/go/newsroom/april-2006/japan-africa-20060427.en;jsessionid=axbWzt8vXD9

UNDP SU/SSC. (2003). *UNDP/Japan partnership supporting South–South cooperation: Innovative triangular cooperation towards the Millennium Development Goals (1999–2004).* Retrieved October 20, 2007, from http://tcdc.undp.org/doc/TriangCoop.pdf

UNDP Tokyo. (n.d.). *Japan and UNDP: UNDP–Japan partnership for a better future.* Retrieved October 22, 2007, from http://www.undp.or.jp/english/partnerships.shtml

United Nations Development Programme and the United Nations Population Fund [UNDP & UNFPA], Executive Board. (2004a, June 7). *Report on the implementation of South–South cooperation.* DP/2004/26. Retrieved October 20, 2007, from http://www.un.org/Depts/dhl/events/south/toc/toc6.pdf

UNDP & UNFPA, Executive Board. (2004b, September 2). *Third cooperation framework for South-South cooperation (2005–2007).* Retrieved October 22, 2007, from http://www.undp.org/execbrd/word/DPCFSSC3.doc

United Nations Education, Science and Cultural Organization [UNESCO]. (2002). *Education for All: Is the world on track? Education for All global monitoring report 2002.* Paris: UNESCO.

UNESCO. (2006a). *Education for All global action plan: Improving support to countries in achieving the EFA goals.* Paris: UNESCO.

UNESCO. (2006b). *Education for all: Note on south-south cooperation.* Retrieved December 2, 2006, from http://unesdoc.unesco.org/images/0014/001462/146252e.pdf

UNESCO. (2006c). *2007 EFA global monitoring report. Strong foundations: Early childhood care and education.* Paris: UNESCO.

UNESCO, Executive Board. (2006a, January 23). *Report by the director-general on the financial implications of creating and implementing a South–South cooperation programme in education.* 174 EX/10. Paris: UNESCO.

UNESCO, Executive Board. (2006b, March 27). *Report by the director-general on the financial implications of creating and implementing a South–South cooperation programme in education: Corrigendum.* 174 EX/10 Corr. Paris: UNESCO.

UNESCO, Executive Board. (2006c, June). *Education for All: Note on South–South cooperation.* ED/EFA/2006/ME/7. Paris: UNESCO.
UNESCO, Executive Board. (2006d, August 25). *Report by the director-general on the Global Action Plan to achieve the Education for All (EFA) goals.* 175 EX/8. Paris: UNESCO.
UN General Assembly. (2003, August 25). *State of South–South cooperation: Report of the secretary-general.* A/58/319. New York: UN.
UN General Assembly. (2005, August 16). *The state of South–South cooperation: Report of the secretary-general.* A/60/257. New York: UN.
UN Office for the Coordination of Humanitarian Affairs. (2006). Bangladeshi aid group to continue despite death. *Humanitarian News and Analyses, IRIN Asia,* January 4. Retrieved April 25, 2008, from http://www.irinnews.org?Report.aspx?ReportId=33624
U.S. Central Intelligence Agency. (2007). *The world factbook: Bangladesh.* Retrieved March 19, 2007, from https://www.cia.gov/library/publications/the-world-factbook/geos/bg.html
U.S. Government. (2006). *U.S. overseas loans and grants. Obligations and loan authorizations July 1, 1945–September 30, 2006.* Retrieved December 27, 2007, from http://qesdb.usaid.gov/gbk/
Vale, P., & Maseko, S. (1998). South Africa and the African renaissance. *International Affairs, 74*(2), 271–285.
Vanity Fair. (2007). *Africa. A special issue.* Guest-edited by Bono with 20 historic covers photographed by Annie Leibovitz. New York: Condé.
Varma, A., & Malviya, A. (1996). *Daunting challenge: An alternative strategy for effective delivery of primary education.* New Delhi, India: Oxfam America Inc.
Vavrus, F. (2003). *Desire and decline: Schooling amid crisis in Tanzania.* New York: Peter Lang.
Vavrus, F. (2005). Adjusting inequality: Education and structural adjustment policies in Tanzania. *Harvard Educational Review, 75*(2), 174–201.
Veríssimo, J. N. (2006). O estabelecimento da escola lancasteriana no Funchal. In *Anais do VI Congresso Luso-Brasileiro de história da educaçao* (pp. 2478–2483). Uberlândia, Brazil: Universidade de Uberlândia.
Wai, D. (1982). *Interdependence in a world of unequals: African-Arab-OECD economic cooperation for development.* Boulder, CO: Westview.
Wallerstein, I. (1974). *The modern world system: Capitalist agriculture and the origins of the European world-economy in the sixteenth century.* New York: Academic Press.
Wallerstein, I. (2004). *Die grosse Expansion: Das moderne Weltsystem III. Die Konsolidierung der Weltwirtschaft im langen 18: Jahrhundert.* Vienna: Promedia.
Weiler, H. (1984). The political dilemmas of foreign study. In E. G. Barber, P. G. Altbach, & R. G. Meyers (Eds.), *Bridges to knowledge: Foreign students in comparative perspective* (pp. 184–195). Chicago: The University of Chicago Press.
Whitty, G., Power, S., & Halpin, D. (1998). *Devolution and choice in education: The school, the state and the market.* Buckingham, UK: Open University Press.
Wilks, A., & Lefrançois, F. (2002). *Blinding with science or encouraging debate? How World Bank analysis determines PRSP policies.* Retrieved September 21, 2002, from www.brettonwoodsproject.org/topic/adjustment/blinding/blindful.pdf

Williams, G. (2006). Reforming Africa: Continuities and changes. In I. Frame (Eds.), *Africa South of the Sahara: Europa Regional Surveys of the World* (pp. 3–11). London: Routledge Kegan Paul.

Williams, P. (2007). State failure in Africa: Causes, consequences and responses. In I. Frame (Ed.), *Africa South of the Sahara: Europa regional surveys of the world* (pp. 31–37). London: Routledge Kegan Paul.

Williamson, J. (1993). Development and the "Washington Consensus." *World Development*, *l*(21), 1239–1336.

Williford, M. (1967). The educational reforms of Dr. Mariano Gálvez. *Journal of Inter-American Studies*, *10*(3), 461–473.

World Information Technology and Services Alliance [WITSA]. (2006). *Digital planet 2006*. Austin: WITSA.

Wolf, J., Kane, E., & Strickland, B. (1997). *Planning for community participation in education* (ABEL Technical Paper No. 1). Washington, DC: U.S. Agency for International Development, Bureau for Africa, Office of Sustainable Development.

World Bank. (1995). *Priorities and strategies for education: A World Bank review*. Washington, DC: Author. Retrieved October 8, 2003, from www.worldbank.org/poverty/strategies/sourcons.htm

World Bank. (2002). *PRSP Sourcebook*. Washington, DC: World Bank.

World Bank. (2005, October 12). *Education for All—Fast Track Initiative. Fact sheet: About aid effectiveness*. Washington, DC: World Bank.

World Development Movement [WDM]. (2004, April 29). *Press release*. London: WDM.

World Economic Forum. (2004). *Jordan's education initiative: An initiative of the global institute for partnership and governance*. Geneva, Switzerland: World Economic Forum.

World Economic Forum. (2007a). *Global education initiative*. Geneva, Switzerland: World Economic Forum.

World Economic Forum. (2007b). *World Economic Forum website*. Retrieved March 21, 2007, from http://www.weforum.org

Yanik, L. (2004). The politics of educational exchange: Turkish education in Eurasia. *Europe-Asia Studies*, *56*(2), 293–307.

Yavuz, H. (2003). Islam in the public sphere: The case of the Nur movement. In H. Yavuz and J. Esposito, (Eds.), *Turkish Islam and the secular state: The Gülen movement* (pp. 10–18). Syracuse, NY: Syracuse University Press.

Zhou, Y. (2005). Statement at the eleventh session of the Intergovernmental Follow-up and Coordination Committee on Economic Cooperation among Developing Countries in Havana, 21 March 2005. Retrieved October 10, 2007, from http://www.g77org/ifcc11/undp.htm

About the Editors and the Contributors

Linda Chisholm, Ph.D., director of the Education, Science and Skills Development research program at the Human Sciences Research Council in Pretoria and visiting professor of education at the University of the Witwatersrand, Johannesburg, South Africa. She is editor of the *Southern African Review of Education*, the journal of the Southern African Comparative and Historical Education Society (SACHES). Recent books include *Education, Growth, Aid and Development* (University of Hong Kong, CERC Monograph Series, 2008; with G. Bloch and B. Fleisch) and *Changing Class: Education and Social Change in Post-Apartheid South Africa* (HSRC Press, 2004).

Gita Steiner-Khamsi, Ph.D., professor of comparative and international education at Teachers College, Columbia University in New York, U.S.A., and president of the Comparative and International Education Society (CIES) in 2009. Her last three books include *How NGOs React: Globalization and Education Reform in the Caucasus, Central Asia, and Mongolia* (Kumarian Press, 2008; with I. Silova), *Educational Import: Local Encounter with Global Forces in Mongolia* (Palgrave Macmillan, 2006; with I. Stolpe), and *The Global Politics of Educational Borrowing and Lending* (Teachers College Press, 2004). She is the editor of the series *International Perspectives of Educational Reform*, published by Teachers College Press.

Adriana Abdenur, Ph.D., assistant professor of international affairs at The New School in New York. Trained as an urban sociologist, her research interests focus on international development, urbanization and inequality, and environmental sociology. She is involved in two research projects, both of them cross-regional. The first is a comparative study of how intensifying economic competition has been transforming urban policy in emerging economies. The second is a study of technical cooperation ties among Brazil, South Africa, India, and China. A native of Brazil, she has also lived and worked in Ecuador, China, France, and Mozambique. She is currently a fellow at the India China Institute.

Zahra Bhanji, Ph.D. candidate, education administration and comparative, international and development education, Ontario Institute for Studies in Education (O.I.S.E.), University of Toronto, Canada. Her dissertation is on *Transnational Private Authority in Education Policy: A Case of Microsoft Corporation in Jordan and South Africa*. In 2008, she published an article in *Globalisation, Societies and Education* entitled "Transnational Corporations in Education: Filling the Governance Gap Through New Social Norms and Market Multilaterialism." She has taught in the Business School at Humber College and in the Bachelor of Education Program at O.I.S.E, University of Toronto. She has previously worked on development projects in rural India, in corporate philanthropy with the Aga Khan Foundation Canada, and in the political office of two Ontario Cabinet ministers in Canada.

Marcelo Caruso, Ph.D., adjunct professor, Comparative Education Centre, Humboldt University, Berlin, Germany. He is a comparative historian with a focus on Western Europe und Latin America. His two most recent books include the edited volume *Importing Modernity in Postcolonial State Formation: The Appropriation of Political, Educational, and Cultural Models in Nineteenth-Century Latin America* (Frankfurt: Peter Lang, 2007; with Eugenia Roldán Vera) and a monograph on his dissertation research, translated in Spanish and entitled *La biopolítica en las aulas: Prácticas de conducción en las escuelas elementales del Reino de Baviera, Alemania (1869–1919)* (Buenos Aires: Promoteo, 2006).

Colette Chabbott, Ph.D., adjunct professor, International Education Program, Graduate School of Education and Human Development, George Washington University, Washington, D.C., U.S.A. She is a comparative sociologist, and her book *Constructing Education for Development, International Organizations and Education for All* (RoutledgeFalmer, 2003) is widely used in courses on international development and education. Her article "Carrot Soup, Magic Bullets, and Scientific Research for Education for Development" won the 2007 Article of the Year Award from the *Comparative Education Review*. Since 1990, she has advised various international organizations—including UNICEF, CARE, Save the Children, and BRAC—on expanding primary education in Asia.

Hillary A. Dachi, Ph.D., head, Department of Educational Planning and Administration, Faculty of Education, University of Dar es Salaam, Tanzania. He started his career as a primary school teacher, working in several primary schools in Mbinga and Bagamoyo districts of Tanzania. He completed a B.Ed. and then an M.A. in education at the University of Dar es Salaam. In 2000, he completed his doctoral studies at the University of Bristol with a dissertation on *Household Private Costs and the Resourcing of Public Primary Schooling in Tanzania*. Upon completion of his doctoral studies, he returned to the University of Dar es Salaam to take up an academic position in the Department of Educational Planning and Administration.

Sandra Gillespie, Ph.D., lecturer, International Christian University, Tokyo, Japan. She also holds appointments as adjunct faculty in the Department of Education at Waseda University as well as at the Tokyo-based extension of Teachers College, Columbia University. She established and currently directs the Writing Center at Teachers College in Tokyo and serves as the coeditor of the *Language Research Bulletin*. Her dissertation on South–South transfer from the Ontario Institute for Studies in Education at Toronto University won the Gail Kelly Award for Outstanding Doctoral Dissertation given by the Comparative and International Education Society. Her book *South–South Transfer: A Study of Sino–African Exchanges* was published by Routledge in 2001.

Yoko Mochizuki, Ph.D., Education for Sustainable Development (ESD) specialist, United Nations University—Institute of Advanced Studies (UNU–IAS), Yokohama, Japan. Prior to joining UNU-IAS, she was an adjunct assistant professor at the Department of Human Development, Teachers College, Columbia University. Her current research focuses on the theory and practice of ESD within the context of the UN Decade of ESD (2005–2014) and the sociology of international development. She teaches a course on globalization and education at the Sociology Department of Keio University in Tokyo. She has published articles in the *Journal of Education for Sustainable Development* and in the *International Journal of Environment and Sustainable Development*.

Michelle Morais de Sá e Silva, Ph.D. candidate, comparative and international education, Teachers College, Columbia University, New York. Her background in development studies (M.A., Institute of Social Studies, The Hague, The Netherlands) and international relations (B.A., University of Brasilia, Brazil) combined with her professional experience in international education have guided her research interests toward policy transfer, South–South cooperation in education, and conditional cash transfers. Her study entitled *South–South Cooperation, Policy Transfer and Best-Practice Reasoning: The Transfer of the Solidarity in Literacy Program from Brazil to Mozambique* (The Hague, Netherlands: Institute of Social Studies, 2005) addresses issues of ownership and sustainability in the practice of development cooperation between two countries of the South.

Joel Samoff, Ph.D., professor, Center for African Studies, Stanford University, U.S.A. He is a trained political scientist, and his work focuses on education politics, policy, planning, and administration in the development context. Drawing on both academic research and applied analyses for governments and international agencies, his work has had a significant impact on research and practice of development studies in education. His principal geographic areas of focus are eastern and southern Africa. Among his numerous publications are *Coping with Crisis: Austerity, Adjustment and Human Resources*; *Education and Social Transition in the Third World* (with Martin Carnoy); and *From Manpower Planning to the Knowledge Era: World Bank Policies on Higher Education in Africa* (with Bidemi Carrol). He is the North America editor of *International Journal of Educational Development* and a member of the editorial boards of other journals in education and development. His current work focuses on the political economy of foreign aid.

Iveta Silova, Ph.D., assistant professor of comparative and international education at the College of Education, Lehigh University, Pennsylvania. She holds a Ph.D. in comparative education and political sociology from the Graduate School of Arts and Sciences, Columbia University, New York. She is the coeditor (with Alex Wiseman) of *European Education: Issues and Studies* (a quarterly peer-reviewed journal published by M. E. Sharpe). Her last three books are *How NGOs React: Globalization and Education Reform in the Caucasus, Central Asia, and Mongolia* (Kumarian Press, 2008; with Gita Steiner-Khamsi); *Education in a Hidden Marketplace: Monitoring of Private Tutoring* (Open Society Institute, 2006; with Mark Bray and Virginija Budiene); and *From Sites of Occupation to Symbols of Multiculturalism: Reconceptualizing Minority Education in Post-Soviet Latvia* (Information Age Publishing, 2006).

Crain Soudien, Ph.D., professor of education and former director of the School of Education at the University of Cape Town, South Africa. He is the president of the World Council of Comparative Education Societies (WCCES). He teaches in the fields of sociology and history of education and has published more than 100 articles, reviews, and book chapters in the areas of race, culture, educational policy, comparative education, educational change, public history, and popular culture. He is the coeditor of two books on District Six in Cape Town and another on comparative education, the author of *The Making of Youth Identity in Contemporary South Africa:*

Race, Culture and Schooling, and the coauthor of *Inclusion and Exclusion in South African and Indian Schools.* He was educated at the University of Cape Town and holds a Ph.D. from the State University of New York at Buffalo. In addition to his academic work, he is involved in a number of local, national, and international social and cultural organizations.

Leon Paul Tikly, Ph.D., professor, Graduate School of Education, Bristol, United Kingdom. He is director of a Research Programme Consortium on Implementing Education Quality in Low-Income Countries, funded by the Department for International Development (DfID). The consortium includes partners based in the United Kingdom, Africa, South Asia, and Latin America. His other current research interests include the impact of globalization on education in low-income countries and the achievement of black and minority ethnic learners in the UK. He started his career as a science teacher first in London and then in a school for South African refugees in Tanzania. He completed his postgraduate studies at the University of Glasgow. His Ph.D. thesis is on *Education Policy in South Africa Since 1947.* During the transition period between apartheid and democracy in South Africa, he worked as a policy researcher at the Education Policy Unit of the University of the Witwatersrand in Johannesburg, where he helped formulate education policy for the new provincial and national governments.

Index

Abdenur, Adriana: chapter by, 157–70; references to work by, 7, 11
Abugre, C., 143
Adedeji, A., 106
Afghanistan, 8, 192, 197, 203, 204–6, 208, 209
Africa: Asia's relations with, 5; and BRAC, 9, 196, 197–98, 207; and changes in models, 9; and China, 10, 77, 80, 160, 210–25; and ECDC, 74; "good governance" in, 107, 108, 113; higher education in, 123–56; identities in, 117–18; and implications of South–South cooperation, 11; and India, 77; and internationality, 18; and Japanese ODA, 64, 67–70, 71, 80, 82; and need for South–South cooperation research, 8; neoliberalism in, 115–17; new class of donors for, 244; and phases of South–South cooperation, 43; regionalism in, 6–7, 103–22; treatment of students from, 7, 214–21, 224; and triangular practices, 157, 162, 164, 165, 166; UNDP commitment to, 63, 68, 72. *See also specific region or nation*
African National Congress (ANC), 230
African Union (AU), 103, 105–6, 107, 108, 111, 113, 114, 116
African Virtual University (AVU), 109–10, 111, 112, 116
Aga Khan Foundation, 186, 206
Agai, B., 176
Aggleton, P., 115
Ahmed, J., 204, 205
Ahmed, M., 193, 196
Aid: standardization of, 12, 152–53, 245–47, 251, 252, 257–58. *See also* Foreign aid; Funding; *type of aid*
Ajulu, R., 107

Ake, C., 108
Akhter, S., 194
Akkok, F., 173, 179, 183–84, 185
Aksornkool, N., 52
Al-Husainy, S. M., 196
Alam, M. A., 204, 205
Alphonce, N., 103, 104, 113, 114, 115
Altruism, 10, 165–66, 169
Alzona, E., 33
Amin, S., 43, 51, 228–29
Anderson, S. B., 196
Angola, 43, 44
Annan, Kofi, 49, 69
Appadurai, A., 227
Argentina, 47, 52, 56
Arnove, R. F., 17
Ashton, D., 113
Asia-Africa Business Forum, 77
Asia-Pacific Economic Cooperation (APEC), 104
Asian Development Bank, 186, 246, 252
Assessment, 152–53, 250
Association of African Universities (AAU), 110, 111, 113, 117
Association for the Development of Education in Africa (ADEA), 109, 110, 111, 112, 144–45, 197–98
Association of Southeast Asian Nations (ASEAN), 104, 106
Attrition, school, 127–28, 149–50
Aydin, M., 173
Aypay, A., 177
Azerbaijan, 8, 9, 173–91, 197

Baki Ozəl Türk Litseyi, 179
Balci, A., 173, 179, 183–84, 185
Balci, B., 175, 177, 179, 180, 181, 186–87, 188
Bandung Conference (1955), 42, 241

Bangladesh, and E-9 Initiative, 79
Bangladesh Rural Advancement
 Committee (BRAC): in Afghanistan, 8,
 192, 197, 203, 204–6, 208, 209; and
 Africa, 9, 196, 197–98, 207; assessment
 of, 194; definition of, 192–95; and
 dependency, 208; Education Support
 Program of, 198; and EFA, 192–93, 195,
 196, 207; and elites, 9; expansion of,
 207; funding for, 192, 195, 197, 203–4,
 206–7, 208; NFPE model of, 192–204,
 206–7, 209; and phases of South–South
 cooperation, 52; and sharing by doing
 and mentoring, 204–7; and sharing
 by showing, telling, advising, and
 coaching, 197–204; and teachers, 8, 9,
 193, 200, 201, 202, 205, 206, 208; and
 transfer concept, 8; and UNICEF, 8,
 192, 194, 195–97, 200–204, 205, 207,
 208
Banking model, 134
Barnet, M., 88
Barrett, Craig, 91, 98
Bashkin, O., 18
Basic education, 65, 67–68, 82, 114, 136,
 144, 148, 182
Beckham, E., 230
Begum, K., 194
Bell, Andrew, 19
Bell-Lancaster-System: benefits of, 19;
 characteristics of, 18, 19, 21; global
 spread of, 4, 9, 19–22; and Latin
 American Monitorial Schools, 25, 26,
 27, 29, 30, 31, 32, 34; transformations
 and adaptations of, 9, 20
Bergesen, A., 17
"Best-practices": and changes in South–
 South cooperation, 52, 53; and
 importance of South–South
 cooperation, 256; and meaning of
 South–South cooperation, 40; and
 motivation for South–South
 cooperation, 244; and myths about
 South–South cooperation, 56; and
 phases in South–South cooperation, 46–
 51; and standardization of aid, 245,
 246; and target-setting, 255; and TNCs
 as propellers of transfer, 87, 89, 93, 99,
 100, 101; and transfers among equals,
 2; and what-went-right approach, 247
Bhanji, Zahra: chapter by, 87–102;
 references to work by, 6, 87, 88, 89, 93

Bilateralism, 2, 5, 6, 165, 168, 244. See
 also specific initiative
Binns, H. B., 19
Boas, M., 107, 108
Boler, T., 115
Bolivia, 47, 52, 163
Bolsa Escola program, 48
Bond, P., 106, 107
Borrowing/lending literature, 12, 40, 51
Bossert, H., 196
Boukary, H. D., 198
BRAC. *See* Bangladesh Rural
 Advancement Committee
Brazil: and E-9 Initiative, 79; as "prime
 mover" country, 75; role in South–
 South cooperation of, 2, 44, 47, 48, 51,
 52, 56; triangular cooperation practices
 of, 7, 157–70; and UN, 69. *See also*
 Brazilian Cooperation Agency (ABC);
 India-Brazil-South Africa (IBSA) Forum
Brazilian Cooperation Agency (ABC),
 157, 161–64, 165–66, 167
British and Foreign School Society
 (BFSS), 19, 21, 30
Broadman, Harry G., 77
Bruns, B., 247, 248, 256
Bryant, C., 55
Buenos Aires: and Latin American
 Monitorial Schools, 23, 32, 35; TCDC
 Conference in (1976), 70, 81; Technical
 Cooperation Conference in (1978), 44,
 46
Buffett, Warren, 243
Bull, B., 88
Bullock, A., 115–16
Burgess, H. J., 19
Bustos Rodríguez, M., 24

Cádiz, Spain: bourgeois society in, 22–26;
 centrality of, 22–26, 28, 34, 35;
 constitucion de, 22, 24, 33; impact of
 transfer from, 4, 27–34; and Latin
 American Monitorial Schools, 22–38
Calderón España, M. C., 25, 27, 28, 30, 33
Canada, 197, 206, 248
CARE, 203, 204
Carnoy, M., 113, 227
Cartaya Cotta, P., 31
Cartel of Good Intentions, 257–58
Caruso, Marcelo: chapter by, 17–38;
 references to work by, 4, 5, 6, 9, 10, 19,
 28

Index

Caste. *See* Race/class
Castells, M., 227, 228, 231
Catalytic Fund, 248, 249, 251, 252
Catholic Church, 26, 34
Celebrities, as donors, 243, 244
Center for Higher Education Trust (CHET), 230
Center for South African–Indian Studies, 236
Central Asia: post-Soviet, 188–90; Turkish initatives in, 8, 9, 173–91
Centrality: of Cádiz, 22–26, 28, 34, 35; and implications of South–South cooperation, 13; of lending, 27–28; and South–South transfer as centrality of North–South axis, 2; and spread of Bell-Lancaster-System, 4, 19–22; and world-systems analysis, 5, 17–18
Chabbott, Colette: chapter by, 192–209; references to work by, 8, 10, 192, 193, 196
Chambers, John, 89, 91, 94, 98
Chandler, D. S., 32
Chatterjee, P., 228
Chen, T. H., 219, 222
Cheru, F., 105, 107, 108, 113
Cheung, T. M., 213
Chiejine, I., 201
China: and Africa, 10, 77, 80, 160, 210–25; and Brazil's triangular practices, 158, 168, 197; and changes in models, 9; and changes in South–South cooperation, 53; and Cold War, 39; "color and money" in, 214–24; and E-9 Initiative, 79; and EFA, 79, 80; foreign policy of, 211–14, 223–24; and G-77 natlons, 73, 74, 78, 79; and High-Level Meeting, 75; motivation of, 10; and myths of South–South cooperation, 56; and new world order, 212, 224; and phases of South–South cooperation, 43, 50; as "prime mover" nation, 64, 75, 82; reform in, 212–14; role in South–South cooperation of, 2; and South–South cooperation in UN system, 71, 76, 80, 82; shift to market economy in, 67; and triangular cooperation, 7; and UNDP, 76, 80; worldview of, 212–13
China Guangcai Program, 76
China-Africa Business Council (CABC), 76
Chisholm, Linda: chapter by, 1–13; references to work by, 115, 117, 257
Chowdhury, A.M.R., 204, 205

Cisco Systems, 88, 89, 90, 91, 92, 93–94, 97, 98, 99, 100
Class. *See* Race/class
The Clubhouse, 95
Coaching, and BRAC, 201–4
Cold War, 6, 39–40, 42, 45, 47, 64, 173
Coleman, D., 246
Colombo Plan for Cooperative Economic and Social Development in Asia and Pacific, 64
Colonialism, 10, 226, 233, 239
Columbia University, 244, 256–57
Colvin, R., 87
Commission for Africa (CFA), 103, 105, 106, 107, 108, 109, 110, 112, 113–14, 115, 116, 117
Common Market for East and Southern Africa (COMESA), 105, 106
Community of Portuguese Language Countries, 164, 166
Compañia Lancasteriana, 32
Comprehensive Development Framework (CDF), 142, 143, 144
Computer Associates, 90
Computer Industry Almanac Inc., 91
Conference on Technical Cooperation among Developing Countries, 44
Cordorniú y Ferreras, Manuel, 32
Córdova, Mariano, 29
Corning Cable Systems, 90
Cornwell, R., 108
Corts Giner, M. I., 27, 28, 30, 33
Costa Vaz, A., 167
Counter-penetration notion, 137
Country-led development, 130–32
Cox, A., 90
Creed, C., 91
Crispim, D., 167
Crossley, M., 41, 51
Cuba: and Cold War, 39; independence of, 23, 35; and Latin American Monitorial Schools, 28, 30–31, 33, 34, 35; and phases of South–South cooperation, 43, 44, 47, 50, 51, 52; teacher training in, 33
Cuesta Mendoza, A., 31
Culture: and myths in South–South cooperation, 56–57; and regionalism in Africa, 117–18; and TNCs in education, 101; and triangular practices, 166–67, 169; and Turkish initiatives, 174, 175, 176, 181, 182, 185, 187, 188

Cummings, W. K., 196
Cussó, Roser, 246
Cutler, C., 87

Dachi, Hillary: chapter by, 103–22; references to work by, 6–7, 11, 103, 104, 113, 114, 115
Dadoo, Yusuf, 230
Dakar framework, 114
Dale, R., 103, 104, 113, 114, 115
Dall, F., 196
D'Amico, S., 246
Daniels, C., 35
De la Sagra, R., 31
De Young, A., 185
Debt AIDS Trade Africa (DATA), 69
Del Marmol, M. M., 27, 28
Dell Computer, 90
Demir, C., 173, 179, 183–84, 185
Demirel, Suleyman, 177
Demobilization, 40, 45–46
Democracy, 8, 107, 108, 113, 173, 174, 186, 187, 214
Dependency: and BRAC, 208; and changes in South–South cooperation, 53; and conceptualizing the South, 3; and foreign aid, 126, 129, 130, 132, 153, 154, 155; and implications of South–South cooperation, 11, 12; intellectual, 154; and knowledge transfer, 228; and phases of South–South cooperation, 43; and standardization of aid, 245–47, 251, 252, 257–58; and target-setting, 251–55, 257, 258; way out of, 241–58; and what-went-right approach, 247–51
DeStefano, J., 198
Deutsche Gesellschraft fur Technische Zusammenarbeit (GTZ), 162
Developing countries: and changes in South–South cooperation, 53; and international education agenda, 52; and myths of South–South cooperation, 54, 56–57; and phases of South–South cooperation, 42, 43, 44, 45, 46–47, 48, 50; and triangular practices, 168; and Turkish initiatives, 176. *See also specific nation*
Devraj, R., 163
Dewey, John, 18
Diabre, Z., 63
Digital divide, 115

Dikötter, F., 211–12, 224–25
Dinke textbooks, 202–3
Discovery Schools (Jordan), 90, 95, 96, 99
Doha, Qatar, Second South Summit in, 74, 78, 79
Dolowitz, D., 48
Dominance/subordination, 6, 12, 239–40
Domínguez Ortiz, A., 23
Donors. *See* Funding; *specific donor*
Donors to African Education (DAE), 109, 144. *See also* Association for the Development of Education in Africa
Dropout rates, 252
Dunn, Henry, 30
Durkheim, Emile, 161

E-9 nations, 51–52, 79–80
East, Mark, 95–96
East Africa Community (EAC), 103, 105, 111
East Timor, 157, 162, 163, 164, 165, 166
East–East transfer, 257
Easterly, William, 244, 251
Ebrahim, H., 230
Economic Community of West African States (EWOWAS), 105
Economic Cooperation among Developing Countries (ECDC), 73, 74, 75–76, 77, 78
Economic Forum, 243
Economic and Social Research Council (ESRC), 107
The Economist, 44
Education for All (EFA): and BRAC, 192–93, 195, 196, 207; conferences about, 51, 65, 148, 149, 192–93, 195, 196; and donor concerns, 242; Fast Track Indicative Framework of, 242, 245, 247–56; and foreign aid, 148, 149; and importance of South–South cooperation, 256; as international conference, 51, 65, 148; and international education agenda, 51–52; and Japan, 5, 68; mainstreaming of South–South cooperation into, 78–80; and myths of South–South cooperation, 55; and new class of donors, 244; 1990 agreement about, 247; and phases of South–South cooperation, 50; and regionalism in Africa, 109, 114; and standardization of aid, 245, 247

Education in the Americas, 199
Education Management Information System (EMIS), 245
Education Program Development Fund, 248, 251, 252
Edwards, M., 42, 48
Efficiency, 133–34
Egypt, 79, 98, 99, 101
Elites: and Africa-China exchange, 213; and BRAC, 9; and India–South Africa relations, 233; and knowledge transfer theory, 228, 229; and monitorial school system, 9; and regionalism in Africa, 6, 104, 105, 107, 118; and Turkish initiatives, 174, 179
Equality/inequality, 1, 2, 3, 4, 5, 7, 10, 11–13, 214–21, 224
Ertl, H., 242
Escobar, A., 40, 42, 53, 54
Escuelas Nuevas (EN), 199
Espigado Tocino, G., 26
Ethiopia, 151, 197, 198, 199, 256
Eun-Myo Park, K., 93
European Community (EC), 206
European Social Forum, 47
European Union (EU), 6, 104, 105, 106
Evans, M., 55
Evans, P., 165
Exchanges, 2, 7. *See also specific exchange*
"Export of professionals," 44
"Externalization to world situations" concept, 40, 49, 58

Fatema, K., 195, 200
Feenberg, A., 228
Fernández Bulete, V., 27
Ferrer Benimeli, J. A., 24
Fine, B., 4
Finnemore, M., 88
Fisher, R., 218
Fiske, E., 196
Fontana, J., 21
Food and Agriculture Organization (FAO), 50
Ford Foundation, 145
Foreign aid: critiques of, 124, 142, 153; definition of, 7, 123; and dependency, 126, 129, 130, 132, 153, 154, 155; effectiveness of, 125, 135, 154; as flawed process, 125–26; function of, 123; and globalization, 126–27; and government, 131, 140–41, 155; and higher education as global undertaking, 126–27; and human capital theory, 132, 133; and international conferences, 148–50; language/terminology of, 127–32, 135, 152, 154, 155; and national policy making, 145–47; and neoliberalism, 143; and ownership, 130–32, 155; as partnership, 124, 125, 128–30, 132, 155; as pathway of influence, 135–55; as problematic, 123–26; and research, 147–48, 151; role of, 125; and standardization, 152–53; and structure of aid relationship, 125, 128–32, 135–55; as tool, 125–26, 132–34; as transfer, 123, 125, 153–55. *See also specific nation or project*
"The Foreign Work," 19
Forum for African Women Educationalists (FAWE), 109, 110, 111, 112, 113, 114, 145
Forum on China-Africa Cooperation, 212
France, 20, 33, 34, 36, 197, 243, 248
Freedom House, 187
Freire, Paulo, 18, 39, 43–44, 134
Fundaçao Oswaldo Cruz (FIOCRUZ), 157, 162, 163
Funding: and Africa-China exchange, 221–23; bilateral, 242; for BRAC, 192, 195, 197, 203–4, 206–7, 208; and donor concerns, 242–44; "gap" in, 252; and importance of South–South cooperation, 256; as influencing and promoting South–South cooperation, 1; from new class of donors, 242–44, 251; and regionalism in Africa, 112–13; and size of donation, 243; and standardization of aid, 245–47, 251, 252, 257; and target-setting, 251–55; and Turkish initiatives, 182, 185, 186, 189; and "unruly donors," 12, 243; and what-went-right approach, 247, 248, 251. *See also specific organization or type of funding*
Funnel of causation, 136–37

G-7 nations, 74
G-8 nations, 48, 67, 69–70, 71, 247
G-X nations, 47
G-20 Group, 168
G-77 nations, 42, 43, 46, 51, 73–74, 78, 79
Galabawa, J.C.J., 117
Galagan, P., 100

Gandhi, Mahatma, 226, 230, 236
García Fernández, M. N., 24
Gardner, R., 196
Gates, Bill, 91–92, 98, 243
Gates (Bill and Melinda) Foundation, 206, 243
Gender studies, 237–38
General Agreement of Tariffs and Trade (GATT), 46
General Agreement on Trade in Services (GATS), 116–17
Georgia (Central Asia), 177
Germany, 69, 163, 243, 248
Ghana, 167, 256
Gil Novales, A., 32
Gillespie, Sandra: chapter by, 210–25; references to work by, 9, 10, 160
Global Coalition for Africa (GCA), 68
Global Development Network (GDN), 40, 48
Global Fund, 243
Global Gateway, 251
Global Information Technology Report, 92
Global policy agendas, 113–15, 118
Globalization: and conceptualizations of South–South cooperation, 40; and conceptualizing the South, 3–4; and foreign aid, 126–27; and implications of South–South cooperation, 12; and Japanese ODA, 80–81; and knowledge transfer theory, 227; and myths of South–South cooperation, 55; and phases of South–South cooperation, 46, 47, 49; and reasons for borrowing reforms, 242; and regionalism, 103, 104, 106, 107; and study of transnational policy transfer, 1–2; and TNCs role in education, 87; and "weakness" of South, 6
Goldblatt, D., 107
Goldman, R., 222
"Good governance," 112–13
Governments, 2, 5, 6, 131, 140–41, 155, 175, 186–87, 190
Grant, James, 104, 195–96, 207
Great Lakes Initiative (GLI), 110
"Great Student Exchange Project," 174
Green, F., 113
Grindle, M., 55
Grossberg, L., 237–38
Guatemala, 23, 28, 29–30, 32, 33, 34
Guimaraes, S., 44

Guinea-Bissau, 18, 36, 43, 52
Gül, A., 174
Gülen (Fetullah) movement (Turkey), 8, 9, 175–90
Gupta, P., 230

Haas, E. B., 54
Haas, P., 88, 90–91
Haiti, 52, 164, 167, 169
Halpin, D., 115
Haufler, V., 87
Havana, Cuba, First South Summit in, 73, 74
Hayhoe, R., 213, 224
Heisohn, N., 52
Held, D., 107
Hettne, B., 104
Hevi, Emmanuel John, 210–11, 212, 219, 220, 222
Hewlett Packard, 90, 97, 99
Heyneman, S. P., 182, 185, 246
High-Level Meetings of Pivotal Countries for South–South and Triangular Cooperation, 75, 79, 80
Higher education: and Africa-China exchange, 210–25; and foreign aid in Africa, 123–56; function of, 116; as global undertaking, 126–27; marketization of, 116–17; privatization of, 116; and regionalism in Africa, 109, 110, 114, 116–17; and Turkish initiatives, 174, 177, 184–85
Hirst, M., 167
HIV/AIDS, 47, 48, 49, 55, 75, 110, 114, 115, 162, 163, 165, 169, 243
Hofmeyr, I., 235, 236
Hofstede, G., 227–28
Hogan, D., 19
Hoogvelt, A., 227
Hopman, S., 20
Hoppers, W., 196
Huerta Martínez, A., 30, 31
Human capital theory, 132, 133
Human Sciences Research Council in South Africa, 230
Hutchison, A., 211

IBSA. See India-Brazil-South Africa (IBSA) Forum
Identity, 34–36, 104, 117–18, 174, 175, 180–81, 190, 238–39
Inácio Lula da Silva, Luiz, 157, 167

Index

Inclusion and Exclusion Project, India–South Africa, 231–34, 237
India: and Africa, 77; and BRAC, 197, 199–200, 201; and changes in models, 9; colonialism in, 226, 233; and E-9 Initiative, 79; Japanese loans to, 65; and myths of South–South cooperation, 56; Oxfam-America in, 199–200; and phases of South–South cooperation, 47; as "prime mover" country, 75, 82; role in South–South cooperation of, 2, 10; and spread of Bell-Lancaster-System, 19; and technical assistance among developing countries, 158; and triangular cooperation, 7, 163, 168–69; and UN, 69. *See also* India-Brazil-South Africa (IBSA) Forum; India–South Africa relations
India-Brazil-South Africa (IBSA) Forum, 47, 64, 158, 163, 168, 229–30
India–South Africa Joint Ministerial Commission, 226, 229–30
India–South Africa relations: and colonialism, 10, 226, 233; historic links between, 10, 230; and Inclusion-Exclusion Project, 231–34, 237; and knowledge transfer, 226, 229–40; and multinationals, 229; and North–South relations, 231; questions arising in, 237–40; and race/class issues, 10, 231–34, 237; and Reimaging the Disciplines Colloquium, 231, 234–37; and social development, 229
Indian Council for Social Science Research, 235
Information and communication technologies (ICTs), 2, 6, 227–28
Innovative Teachers Network, 96
INSEAD, 92
Intel Corporation, 88, 89, 90, 91, 93, 94–95, 97, 98, 99
Inter-American Development Bank, 48
Inter-University Council for East Africa (IUCEA), 110, 111, 112
International agencies/organizations (IAs): and changes in South–South cooperation, 53; and international education agenda, 52; and meaning of South–South cooperation, 40, 57–58; and modalities of transfer and cooperation, 6; and myths of South–South cooperation, 54; and new class of donors, 244; and phases of South–South cooperation, 41, 48, 49, 50, 51; and standardization of aid, 246, 257; and technical assistance, 158; and triangular practices, 162, 164; and Turkish initiatives, 187, 188, 189. *See also specific agency*
International conferences, 148–50. *See also specific conference*
International Institute for Educational Planning (IIEP), 110, 145
International Monetary Fund (IMF), 45, 140, 142–43
International NGO Forum on Indonesian Development, 142
International Teacher's Network (ITN), 99
Internationality, meaning of, 18
Iraq, 18, 35–36, 197
Ishikawa, S., 64
Islamic Movement, 175–80, 181, 186–90
Isomorphism, 34–36

Jansen, Jonathan D., 254
Japan: and Africa, 64, 67–70, 71, 80, 82; and basic education, 65, 67–68, 82; and BRAC, 197; domination of science by, 117; as donor, 5; and EFA, 5; "hardware" education aid of, 65–66, 67; influence of, 5, 8; ministries of, 65, 66, 79, 157; modalities of transfer and cooperation, 5; motivations of, 160; ODA of, 64, 67–72, 73, 79, 80–82, 243; role in South–South cooperation of, 2; from TCDC to North–South cooperation of, 64–70; and triangular cooperation, 51, 64, 73, 81, 82, 158–59, 163, 166–67; and UN membership, 69, 70, 81; UN/UNDP collaboration with, 5, 64, 67, 69, 70–72; and UNESCO, 5; and what-went-right approach, 248
Japan International Cooperation Agency (JICA), 50, 66, 68, 70, 71, 82, 163
Japan Overseas Cooperation Volunteers (JOCV) program, 66
Japan-Brazil Partnership Program (JBPP), 157, 166–67
Japanese Human Resources Development Fund (JHRDF), 71, 77
Jawaharlal Nehru University, 230, 238
Jervis, R., 56
Jiménez Gámez, R., 25, 26, 28

Johnson, M. S., 182
Jomo, K. S., 4
Jones, Phillip, 40, 246, 250
Jones Shafer, R., 29, 32
Jordan: role in Middle East of, 101; role in South–South cooperation of, 2; and TNCs in education, 6, 88–102
Jordan Education Initiative (JEI), 6, 88–102
Joshi, A., 193, 196
Junta general, 32
Junta protectora, 21–22, 27, 28

Kaestle, C. F., 19
Kamen, H., 23
Kamibeppu, T., 65, 66, 67, 79
Kane, E., 196
Kappaz, C., 55
KATEV, 185
Kazakhstan, 173, 177, 178, 180, 181, 182, 184–85
Kearney, Juan, 21, 22, 28
Kenya, 110, 151, 254, 256
Khaemba, B. M., 117
Khatib, S., 90
Khor, M., 107
King, K., 251
Kissinger, Henry, 207–9
Kitaev, I., 116
Knowledge banks, 40, 48, 53, 92, 245–46, 250–51, 255–56. See also *specific bank*
Knowledge transfer, 12, 226–40
Koizumi, Jun'ichiro, 69, 157
Krach Family Foundation, 90
Kuroda, K., 65
Kyrgyzstan, 173, 177, 178, 181, 182, 183–84, 251

Labor Resource and Research Institute (LaRRI), 106, 107
Lana, X., 55
Lancaster, Joseph, 19
Language, 118, 127–32, 135, 152, 154, 155, 183–84, 189, 218, 255
Larkin, B. D., 211
Lassibille, G., 116
Latin America, 67, 164, 165, 167. See also *specific nation*
Latin American Monitorial Schools: and Bell-Lancaster-System, 19–22, 25, 26, 27, 29, 30, 31, 32, 34; Cádiz and, 22–38; and conditions of lending, 22–26; and Madrid, 22, 26, 27, 28, 29, 31, 33–34, 36; and peripheries, 17–19, 34–36; and teacher training, 28, 31, 33; transfer of, 17–19, 26, 27–33, 34–36. See also *specific city or nation*
Laugharn, P. A., 198
Lefrançois, F., 142, 143
Lending and borrowing, 22–26, 27–28, 158–60, 161
Leyendecker, R., 115
Lightfoot, C., 31
Lindt, A., 52
Lira González, A., 29
Little, A., 196
Lovell, C., 193, 195, 200
Luhmann, Niklas, 242

McGrew, A., 107
McKinsey Corporation, 90
McNeill, D., 88
Madeley, J., 43, 47
Malaysia, 64, 75, 77
Mali, 198, 208, 256
Malviya, A., 199, 200
Mamedov, N., 187
Manning, R., 82
Mao Tse-Tung, 10, 43, 51, 212, 213, 214
Marinova, B., 173
Marrakech, Morocco, South–South cooperation conference in, 74, 77
Marsh, D., 48
Martinez, C., 40, 49, 242
Maseko, S., 105, 106, 117
Matsuura, Koichiro, 5, 79
Maxwell, K. R., 24
Mayer, M., 106
Mazrui, A., 106, 137
M'Bow, Amadou Mahtar, 224
Mehnert, K., 18
Meneses, M. P., 54
Menhaj Educational Technologies, 96, 99
Mentoring, 204–7
Mesthrie, Uma, 236
Mexico: and definition of South, 3; and E-9 Initiative, 79; independence of, 23, 35; and international education agenda, 52; and internationality, 18; and Latin American Monitorial Schools, 28, 29, 32, 33, 34, 35; and myths of South–South cooperation, 56
Michel, T., 176, 177
Microsoft Corporation, 88, 89, 90, 91–92, 93, 95–97, 98, 99

Index

Middle East: economic development in, 67; Jordan's role in, 101; TNCs as propellers of transfer in, 87–102. *See also specific nation*
Militarization of aid, 244
Millenium Summit (UN, 2000), 229
Millennium Development Goals (MDGs), 68, 74, 110, 114, 228, 229, 242, 244, 246, 247, 252
Millennium Villages Project (Columbia University), 244, 256–57
Mingat, A., 247, 248, 256
MIT Media Laboratory, 94
Mittal Steel, 229
Mittelman, J., 106, 108, 113, 118
Mizuno, K., 81
Mochizuki, Yoko: chapter by, 63–86; references to work by, 5, 6, 7, 10, 11, 50
Models, changes in, 9–10
Mohamad, Mahathir, 77
Mongolia, 3, 12, 251, 252–54, 255
Monitorial system of education. *See* Bell-Lancaster-System; Latin American Monitorial Schools
Monitoring of Learning Achievement (MLA), 183
Monkman, K., 228
Monterrey Consensus (2002), 251
Morais de Sá e Silva, Michelle: chapter by, 39–59; references to work by, 4–5, 6, 10, 11, 48, 55, 241
Moreno Fraginals, M., 30
Morrow, R. A., 47
Mosha, H. J., 113
Mozambique, 44, 52
Multilateralism, 2, 5, 56, 58, 88, 113, 165, 168, 244, 250–51, 256
Museum of Science–Boston, 94
Muskin, J. A., 198

Naidoo, V., 116
Naik, C., 195
Nalle, S. T., 23
Nananaskis Summit (2002), 67
Nanjing Anti-African protests, 214, 218
Nath, S., 194
Nation-state, role in regionalism of, 6
National education policy, and foreign aid, 145–47
"National ownership," 257
National Research Foundation (NRF), 235

National Society for the Education of the Poor in the Principles of the Established Church, 19
Nationalism, 18, 35–36, 175, 183, 188–89, 190
Naudet, D., 153
Nehru, Jawaharlal, 43, 51
Neoliberalism, 106–7, 115–17, 143
NEPAD. *See* New Partnership for African Development
Nepal, 197, 201
Netherlands, 197, 248
Network analysis, 158, 160–61, 170
Networked Readiness Index, 92
Networking, 167–68, 169, 173
Networking Academy Program (Cisco Systems), 93–94, 97
New Delhi Agenda for Cooperation, 158
New Directions strategy, 73, 75
New International Economic Order (NIEO), 43, 45
New Partnership for African Development (NEPAD), 103, 105–14, 115, 229–30, 239
New Zealand, 3, 52
Nigeria, 79, 256
Non-Aligned Movement (NAM), 42, 46, 51, 229, 241
Nongovernmental organizations (NGOs): and BRAC, 198, 206; and definition of South–South cooperation, 39, 257; and international education agenda, 52; and modalities of transfer and cooperation, 5, 9; and phases of South–South cooperation, 51; and promotion of South–South cooperation, 2; and regionalism in Africa, 6, 103, 104, 105, 113; and standardization of aid, 246; and triangular practices, 162; and Turkish initiatives, 174, 182, 188. *See also specific organization*
North: and BRAC, 208; and changes in South–South cooperation, 53; and implications of South–South cooperation, 11; and international education agenda, 52; and myths of South–South cooperation, 54, 55, 56; and phases of South–South cooperation, 43, 44, 47, 51; and regionalism in Africa, 103; and TNCs in education, 102; and transfers, 36, 102; and triangular cooperation, 159, 169

North American Free Trade Agreement (NAFTA), 104, 106
North–South axis, South–South transfer as centrality of, 2
North–South relations, 2, 7, 11, 69, 231
North–South–South transfers, 12, 255–58
Novak, A., 173
Novelli, M., 103, 104, 113, 114, 115
Ntuli, P., 115
Nuevo método para aprender el inglés (1834), 26
Nursi, Said, 175
Nyerere, Julius, 42, 43, 51, 136
Nyoni, Sithembiso, 48

Official Development Assistance (ODA), 243, 245, 246–47, 251, 254, 255, 257–58
Open Society Institute (OSI), 186, 187, 243
Operation Lifeline Sudan, 201–4
Organization for African Unity (OAU), 105, 108, 111
Organization for Economic Co-Operation and Development (OECD), 68–69, 182, 243
Ownership, 7, 130–32, 155, 257
Oxfam-America, 199–200

Pakistan, 79, 197, 199, 206, 208, 209
Pande, R., 193, 196
Partners in Learning (Microsoft Corporation), 95, 96, 97
Partnerships, 7, 124, 125, 128–30, 132, 155
Pérez, J., 23
Periphery/peripheries, 4, 5, 13, 17–26, 34–36, 257
Perraton, H., 91, 107
Peru, 47, 52
Philippines, 33, 35
Phillips, D., 242
Pinto, R., 230
Pio, Carlos, 41
Polat, Nedim, 187
Political strengthening, 40, 41–45, 57
Politics: of lending and borrowing, 159, 160; and triangular cooperation, 170; and Turkish initiatives, 176, 177, 181, 182, 186–88, 189, 190
Porter, T., 87
Poverty, 142–43, 144, 158, 163, 229, 256

Power, S., 115
Pragmatism, 7, 11, 164–65, 169
Prahalad, C. K., 87
Prebish, Raul, 43
"Prime mover" countries, 75, 80. *See also* specific country
Princeton University, 230
Private organizations, 177–78, 182, 189–90. *See also* Transnational corporations
Psacharopolous, G., 151
Puerto Rico, 23, 31–32, 33, 34, 35
Pune model, 199

Race/class: and Africa-China exchange, 10, 211–23, 224; and India–South Africa relations, 10, 231–34, 237; and transfer theory, 239; and Turkish initiatives, 178–79
Rahman, S., 194
Rahman-Ranman Huq, 194
Rakotomalala, R., 247, 248, 256
Ramírez, Alejandro, 32
Rania al-Abdullah (queen of Jordan), 93, 95, 101
Rappleye, J., 40
Recruitment, of African professionals, 150–51
Regionalism: characteristics of new, 110–11; critiques of, 106–7, 108; definition of, 104; donor support for, 112–13; and global policy agendas, 113–15, 118; and globalization, 103, 104, 106, 107; and governance, 107, 108, 112–13; and identity, 104, 117–18; and implications of South–South cooperation, 11; "mediation" in, 7; and neoliberalism, 106–7, 115–17; and North–South relations, 11; phases of, 6; and private education, 116; role of nation-state in, 6; role in South–South cooperation of, 2; and technical assistance among developing countries, 158; "transformative," 108, 113, 118; and triangular practices, 167, 168, 169; waves of, 104–5; and Westphalian state model, 107–8
Reimagining the Disciplines Colloquium, India–South Africa, 231, 234–37
Religion, 19, 179, 180, 190. *See also* Gülen movement
Research: commissioned, 147–48; and foreign aid, 147–48, 151; indigenous,

Index

115, 118; need for triangular cooperation, 170; and regionalism in Africa, 115, 118
Ringrose, D., 23, 24
Rivadavia, Bernardino, 32
Robertson, S., 103, 104, 106, 113, 114, 115, 251
Rockefeller Foundation, 243
Roldán Vera, Eugenia, 29, 32
Rubicon, 94, 99
Ruggie, J. G., 88
Rugh, A., 196
Rumbek (Sudan), 201–3
Russia, 7, 9, 117, 168, 176, 181. *See also* Soviet Union
Rwanda, 256

Sachs, Jeffrey, 244
Said, E., 12
Samoff, Joel: chapter by, 123–56; references to work by, 7, 10, 11, 116, 128, 140, 148, 151, 253
Sánchez de Madrid, J., 26
Sander, O., 173
Sarker, S., 227, 228
Sarraillh, J., 25
Saul, J., 4
Sautman, B., 211, 212, 214, 218
Save the Children, 186, 198, 203, 204
Sayed, Y., 232
Scholarships/tuition, 221–23
Scholte, J. A., 107
School Technology Innovation Centre (STIC), 96, 99–100
Schriewer, Jürgen, 18, 19, 40, 49, 92, 242
Schupp, Thomas, 29
Schutte, C., 116
Scott, M., 220
Second African Union Meeting of Experts in Higher Education, 114
Segregation, and Africa-China exchange, 219–21
Self-reliance, 40, 41–45, 57
Selinger, M., 93
Shanghai Textile University, 213
Sichone, Owen, 238, 239
Sierra Leone, 8, 50, 200–201, 207, 208
Silova, Iveta: chapter by, 173–91; references to work by, 8, 182
Simmel, Georg, 158, 160–61, 163, 168
Simon, D., 106, 107
Skocpol, T., 17

Snow, P., 211
Soares de Lima, M., 167
Sociedad Lancasteriana, 34
Sociedades Económicas, 4, 9, 25–26, 27–33, 35
Söderbaum, F., 104
Sogge, D., 56
Solberg, A., 175, 176
Solidarity in Literacy Program, 48
Some, D. K., 117
Somoza Guevara, H. H., 29, 33
Soros Foundation, 186
Soros, George, 243, 244
Soudien, Crain: chapter by, 226–40; references to work by, 9, 10, 12, 227, 232
South: conceptualizing the, 3–5, 257; meaning of, 3, 17; as periphery, 17; and South–South transfer, 17; "weakness" of, 6. *See also* South–South cooperation/transfer; *specific nation*
South Africa: colonialism in, 226, 233; and India, 10, 226, 229–40; and myths of South–South cooperation, 56; and phases of South–South cooperation, 47; as "prime mover" country, 75; and race/caste issues, 218; and regionalism, 6, 117, 118; role in South–South cooperation of, 2; and technical assistance among developing countries, 158; and triangular cooperation, 7, 163, 168–69. *See also* India-Brazil-South Africa (IBSA) Forum; India–South Africa relations
South African Permanent Mission, 168
South–North–South, 12
South–South Cooperation Trust Fund, 71, 80
South–South cooperation/transfer: advocates of, 52–53; and borrowing/lending literature, 40, 51; calls for increase in, 4; as centrality of North–South axis, 2; and "color and money," 225; conceptualizing, 3–5, 12–13; as consequence of North–South transfer, 2; critiques of, 54; definition/meaning of, 1, 4, 39, 40, 49, 241; and demobilization, 45–46; economics of, 182–86; history/phases of, 4, 6, 39–40, 41–51, 57, 58; importance of understanding, 2, 8, 241–42, 256–58; misconceptions about, 10–11; motivations for, 8, 242–

South–South cooperation/transfer (*continued*) 44; myths about, 53–57, 58; NAM as first signpost of, 241; need for study of, 12; as new slogan, 1; and North, 43, 44, 47, 51, 52, 53, 54, 55, 56, 102; and political strengthening, 40, 41–45, 57; politics of, 186–88; potential of, 11, 58; purposes/functions of, 12, 42–43, 49, 51, 78, 82, 242, 257; rationales for, 41; and reasons for borrowing reforms, 242–44; reconceptualization of, 77, 78; "renaissance" of, 47; and self-reliance, 40, 41–45, 57; special features of, 56; UN conceptualizations of, 63–86; and what has changed, 52–53. *See also specific topic*

Southern African Development Community (SADC), 103, 105, 106, 110, 111, 112, 117

Southern African Development Coordination Conference (SADCC). *See* Southern African Development Community (SADC)

Southern and East African Consortium for Monitoring Education Quality (SACMEQ), 110, 111, 112

Southern Sudan Education Authority, 203

Soviet Union, 9, 46, 67, 173, 179–80, 181, 182, 185, 188. *See also* Russia

Spain: introduction of Bell-Lancaster system in, 19–22. *See also* Cádiz, Spain

Special Unit for Technical Cooperation among Developing Countries (SU/TCDC), 64

Sri Lanka, 206, 208

Standardization: of aid, 12, 152–53, 245–47, 251, 252, 257–58; and implications of South–South cooperation, 12; and regionalism in Africa, 111; worldwide, 97–98

State Student Admission Commission, 184

Statistics, educational, 245–46, 249–50

Steiner-Khamsi, Gita: chapter by, 241–58; references to work by, 12–13, 39, 40, 43, 48, 51, 92, 97, 159, 160, 242, 255

Stiglitz, J. E., 45, 246

Stolpe, I., 51, 242, 255

Stone, D., 246

Strickland, B., 196

Stromquist, N., 228

Subrahmanian, R., 231

Sudan, 8, 197, 201–4, 207, 208
Sullivan, M. J., 213, 214, 216
Sumra, S., 116
Sweden, 205, 243
Sweetser, A. T., 196

Tajikistan, 173, 177, 182, 183, 251
Tan, J., 116
Tanzania, 116, 136, 140, 151, 206, 256
Target-setting, 251–55, 257, 258
Teach to the Future program (Intel Corporation), 95, 97
Teacher training: and BRAC, 193, 205, 206, 208; and monitorial schools, 22, 28, 31, 33; and TNCs in education, 90, 95, 99
Teachers: and Africa-China exchange, 214, 217; and BRAC, 8, 9, 193, 200, 201, 202, 205, 206, 208; challenges facing, 185; and cross-national testing, 153; and monitorial school system, 9; paraprofessional, 193, 200, 201; and Turkish initiatives, 179, 180, 182, 185. *See also* Teacher training
Technical assistance, 124, 174, 186. *See also* Brazil: triangular cooperation practices of; Technical Cooperation among Developing Countries (TCDC)
Technical Cooperation among Developing Countries (TCDC), 46, 50, 63, 64–70, 73, 74, 76, 78, 81, 159, 161–62, 167
Tests, standardized, 152–53
Thailand, 64, 75
Third World, 39, 42, 43, 46, 53, 166, 210, 212, 213, 224
Thomas, H., 115–16
Thomas, J., 55
Three-Worlds Theory, 10, 213
Tikly, Leon: chapter by, 103–22; references to work by, 6–7, 11, 103, 104, 113, 114, 115, 116
Tokyo International Conference on African Development (TICAD), 68
Toptan, Koksal, 174
Torres, C. A., 47
Transfer: and binary understanding of relationships, 238; and changes in models, 9–10; and colonialism, 239; concept of, 7, 8; dominance and subordination in, 239–40; enacting, 27–33, 34–36; foreign aid as, 123, 125, 153–55; historic dynamics of, 17–19; and identity, 238–39; modalities of, 5–

8, 257; and North, 36; and obstacles to aid as transfer and exchange, 153–55; policy, 48–49, 52, 54; and race, 239; South and South–South, 17; TNCs as propellers of Middle East, 87–102; and world-systems analysis, 17–18. *See also* Knowledge transfer; South–South cooperation/transfer; Transnational studies; *specific transfer*

Transnational corporations (TNCs): as epistemic community, 90–91, 92, 100, 102; and India–South Africa relations, 229; and modalities of transfer and cooperation, 5, 6, 257; and promotion of South–South cooperation, 2; as propellers of transfer in Middle East, 6, 87–102; and regionalism in Africa, 107. *See also specific corporation*

Transnational studies, 1–2, 235–36

Transparency International, 246

"Traveling reforms," 1–2, 242, 245

Trentin, G., 32

Triangular cooperation: and bilateralism, 165, 168; Brazil's practices of, 157–70; definition of, 157, 158–59; framework for, 159–61; and implications of South–South cooperation, 11; and Japan, 51, 64, 73, 81, 82, 158–59, 163, 166–67; motivations for, 163–68, 169; and multilateralism, 165, 168; and myths of South–South cooperation, 55–56; need for further research about, 170; as new form of cooperation, 7; and North, 159, 169; and North–South cooperation, 7; and phases of South–South cooperation, 51; and politics, 170; purpose/functions of, 169; and regionalism, 168, 169; role in South–South cooperation of, 2; and UNDP, 63, 77, 158–59

Truman, Harry, 39, 42

Turam, B., 176, 179, 180, 181, 188

Turkey: as Big Brother, 188–90; Gülen movement in, 8, 9, 173–91; initiatives in Central Asia and Azerbaijan by, 8, 9, 173–91; Ministry of Education in, 174–75; role in international arena of, 173, 188; role in South–South cooperation of, 2

Turkish International Cooperation Agency (TIKA), 173–74

Turkish Official Development Assistance (ODA), 174

Turkmenistan, 173, 177, 178, 179, 181, 183–84, 186, 187

Uganda, 151, 206, 256

UK Department for International Development (DfID), 231, 232, 234, 242

Ul Haq, Mahbub, 39, 43, 51, 54, 58

UN Economic and Social Council (ECOSOC), 73

UN International Conference on Financing for Development (Monterrey, 2002), 251

Undur-Ulaan school (Mongolia), 252–54

UNESCO (United Nations Education, Science and Cultural Organization): declining role of, 135; and EFA movement, 78–80; influence of, 144; and international conferences, 149; International Institute of Education Planning of, 145; and Japan, 5; Matsuura appointment as director-general of, 5; and myths of South–South cooperation, 55; and phases of South–South cooperation, 42, 48, 49, 50, 51–52; and politics of South–South cooperation, 186; and private education, 116; and regionalism in Africa, 113, 114, 116; and South–South cooperation in UN system, 2, 64, 78–80, 81; and standardization of aid, 246; and TNCs in education, 99; and what-went-right approach, 250

UNFPA, 64, 74, 75, 77, 78

UNICEF: Accelerated Learning (or Winter) Program of, 205; and BRAC, 8, 192, 194, 195–97, 199, 200–204, 205, 207, 208; and EFA movement, 78; Operation Lifeline Sudan of, 201–4; in Sierra Leone, 200–201; and Turkish initiatives, 183, 186

United Arab Emirates, 92, 99

United Kingdom, 33, 34, 163, 197, 206, 226, 230, 231–34, 243, 248

United Nations: Charter of, 67; conceptualizations of South–South cooperation by, 63–86; and Haitian peacekeeping force, 167, 169; and IBSA agreement, 229; and Japan, 67, 68, 69, 70, 81; reform of, 69; Security Council of, 69, 70, 81, 168, 169. *See also specific organization or program*

United Nations Conference on Trade and Development (UNCTAD), 42, 73
United Nations Development Fund for Women (UNIFEM), 93, 95
United Nations Development Program (UNDP): and Africa, 63–64, 68, 72; and Asia-Africa cooperation, 77; and IBSA Forum, 163; and Japan, 5, 64, 68, 69, 70–72; and mainstreaming South–South cooperation into EFA movement, 78, 79, 80; and new class of donors, 244; and phases of South–South cooperation, 44, 45, 48, 50; role in South–South cooperation of, 2; and South–South cooperation in UN system, 70–78, 79, 80, 81, 82; Special Unit for South–South cooperation of, 63–64, 159; Special Unit for Triangular Cooperation of, 158; and triangular cooperation, 63, 77, 158–59. *See also* Technical Cooperation among Developing Countries
United Nations Population Fund, 165
United States, 197, 243, 248
United States Agency for International Development (USAID), 187
University of Cape Town, 230
University of London, 230
University of Pretoria, 230
University of Sussex, 230, 231–34
University of Witwatersrand (Wits), 230, 234–37
U.S. Agency for International Development (USAID), 90, 196, 203–4, 242, 243
Uzbekistan, 173, 177, 181, 182, 183, 186, 187, 189, 197

Vale, P., 105, 106, 117
Varma, A., 199, 200
Venezuela, 23, 33, 47, 52
Villaurrutia, Jacobo de, 32

Wallerstein, I., 17
Watson, K., 41, 51
Weiler, H., 224
Welsby, P. A., 19
West Africa, 36
West–East–East transfers, 257
Westphalian state model, 107–8
What-went-right approach, 247–51

Whitty, G., 115
Wilks, A., 142, 143
Williams, G., 4
Williams, P., 4
Williamson, J., 45
Williford, M., 30
Wolf, J., 196
Women, 93–94, 109, 114, 140, 182, 200, 205, 206, 229
Working Group on Higher Education (WGHE), 145
World Bank: and ADEA, 109; case studies by, 151–52; commissioned research by, 147–48; and EFA-FTI approach, 78, 247, 248; and foreign aid, 126–53; Globe Development Network of, 40, 246; and importance of South–South cooperation, 256; and Japan, 64, 68; as knowledge banks, 245, 246, 250, 251; pathways of influence of, 135–53; and phases of South–South cooperation, 45, 48; and politics of South–South cooperation, 186; publications of, 77, 139–40, 151–52; recruitment of African professionals by, 150–52; and regionalism in Africa, 109, 113, 114; role in South–South cooperation of, 2; and what-went-right approach, 248
World Conference on Higher Education (WCHE), 114
World Development Movement (WDM), 106
World Economic Forum (WEF), Jordan Education Initiative of, 88–102
World Education Forum (Senegal, 2000), 148, 149
World Health Organization (WHO), 48
World Information Technology and Services Alliance (WITSA), 98
World Social Forum, 47, 51
World Trade Organization (WTO), 46, 47, 48
World-systems theory, 5, 12, 17–18

Yanik, L., 174, 175, 180, 181
Yavuz, H., 175
Yo, Si Puedo (YSP) program, 52
Yokozeki, Y., 65

Zambia, 151
Zhou Yiping, 72, 74